STATISTICS

IN

CRIMINAL JUSTICE TODAY

STATISTICS

IN

CRIMINAL JUSTICE TODAY

Frank Schmalleger,
Patrick Webb, and
Stephen Marson

cognella®
SAN DIEGO

Bassim Hamadeh, CEO and Publisher
Carolyn Meier, Publisher
Amy Smith, Associate Editorial Manager
Jeanine Rees, Production Editor
JoHannah McDonald, Licensing Coordinator
Natalie Piccotti, Director of Marketing
Kassie Graves, Senior Vice President, Editorial
Alia Bales, Director, Project Editorial and Production

Printed in the United States of America.

cognella® | ACADEMIC PUBLISHING
3970 Sorrento Valley Blvd., Ste. 500, San Diego, CA 92121

For Ava Solano.
—Frank Schmalleger

For my wife, Tammy, and our son Patrick.
—Patrick Webb

For Tea and Lea from their favorite brother.
—Stephen Marson

Brief Contents

Detailed Contents

CHAPTER 1

Introduction to Statistics

Statistics is the grammar of science.
—Karl Pearson

Objectives

1. Introduce and discuss the universal need for and use of statistics.
2. Identify the use of statistics in criminal justice and criminology.
3. Define and explain several fundamental terms used in statistics.
4. Discuss the context of statistics, including research methods.

Human Nature and Research

Whether one realizes it or not, all human beings are constantly involved in research of one kind or another; thus, mankind is made up of researchers. More specifically, we all engage in the process of making decisions based on calculated observations and assumptions. For instance, several students (after reviewing a course catalog or receiving academic advisement) might decide to enroll in a statistics course. For the most part, their decision will be influenced by the need to complete a statistics course as a requirement for graduation. In short, the decision to enroll in a statistics course (or any required course) is based on the likelihood of earning a favorable grade with the intent of ultimately graduating with a degree. In fact, some students (who are currently reading this paragraph) have decided to read this entire chapter prior to the first day of class. The basis of their decision might stem from the assumption that the more they are familiar with the information in the text, the more likely they will earn a favorable grade in the course. In essence, from a practical approach, statistics is about making assumptions and decisions based on the assessed likelihood of various kinds of relationships. Outside of academics, individuals often make calculated decisions in terms of who they associate with what activities they engage in, as well as what they decide to wear, eat, and drink. Thus, all of humanity is comprised of researchers.

IMAGE 1.1

The Universal Need for and Use of Statistics

In general, statistics is the collection, analysis, and interpretive use of information (which is often referred to as data). Students who take statistics courses often do so to meet academic requirements. In other words, they must take the course despite not having any actual interest in learning about the subject. On rare occasions, there are students who are either curious about the subject matter or who have some degree of interest in the practical application of statistical techniques. Moreover, it is not uncommon for students enrolled in statistics courses to have faulty assumptions about statistics. Students may either question the practical value of statistics or fail to recognize the necessity and diversity of statistical-based research. Table 1.1 lists several disciplines that use statistics as a guide to test propositions for the purpose of verifying their truthfulness:

TABLE 1.1 **Statistics and Disciplines/Majors**

Discipline/Major	Without statistics, one would not be able to ...
Biology	• Determine whether medicines or other forms of treatments are safe for use by the public
Economics	• Predict the number of products that might be sold in a given time period or measure the effectiveness of a particular marketing program
Engineering	• Understand the type (and amount) of materials needed to construct a structure (i.e., building, bridge, etc.) or determine the length of time with regard to how long structures and materials can be expected to last or hold up under certain conditions
Political Science	• Discover the factors (e.g., voting preferences) associated with certain political parties in geographical areas, predict voting results, or assess the popularity of certain political candidates or topics
Psychology	• Understand the impact of therapy on the lives of individuals or predict the likelihood of certain forms of behavior exhibited among individuals or groups
Sociology	• Determine the extent to which certain social characteristics (i.e., beliefs, customs, etc.) exist within societies or predict the likely direction and acceptance of technological changes

As indicated, statistics play a vital role in several disciplines and academic majors. It is our hope that you will recognize the value of statistics as you become familiar with the subject, regardless of your current or future academic major or discipline.

The Role of Statistics in Criminal Justice and Criminology

The use of statistics in the disciplines of criminal/juvenile justice covers a variety of areas/topics and goals. Consider the information in Table 1.2:

TABLE 1.2 **Statistics and Criminal Justice**

Area/Topic	Use of statistics may include the following activities
Law Enforcement	• To review arrest rates • To deploy officers in certain geographical locations (based upon reported crimes) • To predict criminal behavior based upon characteristics that are consistent with a theory
Courts	• To discover the types of crimes associated with potential charges filed • To determine and review conviction rates • To predict the types of specialized courts needed based on offense convictions in a certain jurisdiction • To identity sentencing patterns
Parole/Probation	• To identify factors associated with successful community reentry for parolees • To identify factors associated with unsuccessful probation completion within a certain jurisdiction
Deviant Behavior	• To predict the likelihood of crime/delinquency in certain settings (i.e., communities, schools, etc.) • To identify successful treatment strategies for juveniles
Intervention and Prevention	• To identify successful programs and policies that decrease criminal/delinquent activities in school settings • To differentiate and rank problematic behaviors in prison populations

Now that we have identified the universal significance of statistics in relation to various topics, areas, and goals within the criminal and juvenile justice systems. Let's explore several specific research studies that highlight the value and necessity of statistics.

Topics of Interest Among Researchers in Criminal Justice and Criminology

Victim Statements and Guilty Pleas

Do victim video statements have any influence on guilty pleas offered by defendants? Previous research points to the value of victim video statements in family court cases. Examples include accuracy of information (both verbal and nonverbal) and a decreased likelihood of victims recanting their statements. Walton et al. (2021) conducted a study designed to determine if victim video statements increase the rate at which defendants offer a guilty plea. By using an experimental design, two groups were compared. This included individuals who provided victim video statements ($n = 168$) compared to those who only provided written statements ($n = 108$). After controlling for certain factors (i.e., seriousness of charges, etc.), a logistic regression analysis revealed that guilty pleas were more likely associated with the use of video victim statements (44%) compared to written statements (30%). This includes a statistically significant increase in the odds of offering a guilty plea at 1.77 ($p > .05\%$). Further research may examine the efficacy of victim video statements among other criminal justice practitioners. This includes police, attorneys, and court personnel.

Police Foot Patrol and Crime

Does police foot patrol reduce violent crime in areas designated as hotspots? Prior research questions the role of foot patrols as a deterrent to crime; however, the use of such patrols may be effective in certain high-crime areas. Ratcliffe et al. (2011) conducted research to determine if police foot patrol reduced violent crime in hotspot areas in Philadelphia. During the summer of 2009, nearly 200 patrol officers were assigned to violent hotspot areas using an experimental design within two areas (target and control). When comparing the target areas of patrol with the control areas, the target areas experienced lower levels of crime. Using a linear regression analysis, an odds ratio revealed a 23% reduction in crime. Additional research may investigate other factors that may have an influence on the reduction of crime. This may include determining whether the amount of patrol bears a direct (or indirect) influence on crime rates in hotspot areas.

Minority Perceptions and Police

Do perceived stereotypical classifications and social identity threat lead to distrust toward police? Social identity threat exists when the positive image of the social group that a person identifies with is threatened by negative stereotypes of that group held by others who do not belong to it. Past studies have examined the influence of social identity threat among minorities, especially when they interact with police. This often results in increased levels of anxiety among minorities who are stopped by police. Subsequently, it is not uncommon for police to interpret these responses as indicators of guilt. Kahn et al. (2017) conducted research to determine if minorities who view themselves as possessing stereotypical characteristics possess low levels of trust toward police. By using an experimental design, the study consisted of non-minorities as the comparison group and minorities as the intervention group. With a total of 1,200 respondents, this required the completion of a series of scales designed to gauge respondent assessment of (1) how they view themselves from a stereotypical standpoint and (2) whether their race-based social identity had a negative impact when interacting with police. Furthermore, respondents were also required to complete measures designed to gauge their level of trust and cooperation with police. Compared to White respondents, the results revealed that minority respondents who reported high scores of perceived stereotypical characteristics as well as race-based identity threat were less likely to trust and cooperate with police. Additional research includes how the use of further social group identities and perceptions may lead to similar outcomes. Examples include those who are classified as minorities in relation to sexual orientation and gender identity.

Online Violence and Aggressive Behavior

Does self-control mediate the relationship between exposure to online violent video games and aggressive behavior? Current and previous research demonstrates a link between violent online video games and aggressive behavior, especially among youth. Examples of such behavior include hostility and poor academic performance, as well as acts of online aggression (e.g., bullying, shame). Zheng et al. (2021) conducted research that investigated the association between exposure to violent video games and online aggression. More specifically, they explored whether self-control has a mediating impact on online aggressive behavior among nearly 600 Chinese college students. By using an online survey, student respondents were required to list their favorite video games, along with corresponding ratings. They were also required to complete a series of additional scales, which measured (1) online aggressive behavior, (2) anger rumination, and (3) self-control. The results of their analysis suggest that high levels of self-control may have a moderating impact on online aggressive behavior. Additional research may examine the influence of factors related to online aggressive behavior that involve different research designs (i.e., longitudinal, experimental).

Streetlights and Crime Rates

Do streetlights have an impact on crime in high-population areas? Within the area of environmental criminology, a means of reducing crime has been the use of streetlights. A number of studies suggest that high visibility is associated with lower probabilities of crime. Xu et al. (2018) examined the impact of streetlights on crime rates in Detroit, Michigan. Through the use of various resources (e.g., GIS, crime, and census data), they examined the impact of nearly 60,000 overhead streetlights within approximately 139 square miles. This included an analysis of over 135,000 crimes between January and December of 2014. By using a series of statistical measures, their analysis revealed that higher levels of street lighting are associated with lower crime rates. Future studies should examine the influence of different research designs, such as population survey data. Additional variables may include the use of certain areas, as well as temperature, in measuring the association between the intensity of streetlighting and crime rates in populated areas.

As a student, you might experience difficulty understanding some of the terms used in these examples. If so, there is no need to be alarmed or discouraged. What is important that you are able to recognize the value of statistics in association with research topics that might be of interest to you and others.

Fundamental Terms Used in Statistics

There are several key terms that serve as the foundation for learning statistics. They include *statistics, theory, hypothesis, population, sample, descriptive/inferential statistics*, and *units of analysis*.

Statistics refers to the collection, analysis, and interpretive use of information or data. Most of the information in this text will center around the process of analyzing data. For instance, suppose one is interested in determining the type of offense that most youth are arrested for in a specific area (e.g., city, state, etc.). To find the offense type, one could use a data source, such as the Uniform Crime Reports (UCR) as provided by the Federal Bureau of Investigation. This option allows individuals to download data on actual reported crimes that have already been collected by law enforcement agencies in the United States. Through the use of specific examples, we will further discuss this option as a data source in the future chapters of this text.

Frequently, statistics are used to test theories and hypotheses. A **theory** is an explanation of a phenomenon based on logic and verifiable evidence. In most cases, a theory includes a series of propositions often referred to as hypotheses (or a hypothesis). To that end, a **hypothesis** is a single proposed explanation of a phenomenon that suggests a relationship between two or more variables. For instance, deterrence theory suggests that when criminal justice authorities respond to certain crimes (e.g., terrorism, homicide) in a severe manner (e.g., death penalty, etc.), their response will likely discourage individuals from committing similar crimes. Several hypotheses of this theory include the notion that the punishment imposed in response to certain crimes must be (1) swift, (2) severe, and (3) certain. From this standpoint, statistics can be used to analyze measures of how long an individual receives punishment and whether the speed at which the punishment was imposed has an impact on their future behavior. In short, one may argue that a hypothesis is simply an assumption of a relationship that stems from a theory. One hypothesis might contain a set of propositions which claim that certain variables (such as age, grades in school, level of family income, or place of residence) appear to be related to delinquent behavior. The use of statistics can help you identify which of these variables are most closely associated with delinquency, thus helping to support or fail to support assertions made by a hypothesis or a theory. Table 1.3 illustrates the relationship between an individual theory and corresponding hypotheses. The use of statistics may include either (1) testing a theory as well as/or (2) testing the hypothesis (es) of such.

TABLE 1.3 **Theory and Hypotheses**

Theory	General Strain Theory—antisocial behavior is the result of multiple sources of strain.
Hypotheses	1. Failure to achieve positive valued goals is associated with antisocial behavior.
	2. Removal of positive stimuli is associated with antisocial behavior.
	3. Presentation of negative stimuli is associated with antisocial behavior (Agnew, 1992)
Theory	Neutralization Theory—techniques or rationalizations that individuals use to justify antisocial behavior.
Hypothesis	1. Denial of responsibility: Individuals claim that they were influenced by external forces and that they are not responsible for their actions.
	2. Denial of injury: The belief that no one was actually harmed as a result of an offense.
	3. Denial of the victim: Those who engage in offenses see themselves as victims of those who have harmed them. This often leads to acts of revenge (Sykes and Matza, 1957).
Theory	Social Bond Theory—antisocial behavior is the result of weak social bonds.
Hypothesis	1. Attachment: The priority (and value) of social relationships results in a socialization process that suppresses antisocial behavior.
	2. Involvement: The need to keep an individual busy in the engagement of conventional activities reduces the likelihood of antisocial behavior.
	3. Belief: The belief that laws have a valuable function in society and should be followed reduces the likelihood of antisocial behavior (Hirschi, 1969).

In statistics, units of analysis serve as the basis of research. A **unit of analysis** is an element that is being analyzed or observed. This may include people, places, things, and ideas. In the area of social sciences, individuals or categories of individuals (i.e., groups) are often selected for various reasons. As indicated in Table 1.4, consider the following units of analysis derived from each previously identified research study:

TABLE 1.4 **Research and Units of Analysis**

Research question/topic	Units of analysis
Does the existence of victim video statements bear influence on guilty pleas offered by defendants?	Victims (video statements) Defendants (guilty pleas)
Does police foot patrol reduce violent crime in areas designated as hotspots?	Police (type of patrol measure) Crime rates
Do perceived stereotypical classifications and social identity threat lead to distrust toward police?	Perceptions (among minorities) Social identity Trust of police
Does self-control mediate the relationship between exposure to online violent video games and aggressive behavior?	Online video game (exposure) Aggressive behavior Self-control
Does the existence of streetlights have an impact on crime in high-population areas?	Streetlights Crime rates

Overall, there are two types of statistics: descriptive and inferential statistics. **Descriptive statistics** are used to describe data. They often include summary information, such as raw numbers, proportions, and averages, which represent the statistics of a sample. For example, suppose the total number of youth crimes committed during a certain period is consistent with the following information in Table 1.5:

TABLE 1.5 **Youth Crime Statistics in 2020**

Year	Number of Youth Crimes
2020	424,300

As indicated, the number 424,300 is summary information, which simply describes the amount of youth crime in 2020 (Puzzanchera et al., 2022). In short, descriptive statistics describe *what exists*. On the other hand, **inferential statistics** are used to infer data from a sample to make assumptions about a larger collection of individuals from which the sample was gathered. For instance, suppose you are interested in determining if the average student test score in a statistics class consisting of 30 students (which is your sample) is greater than the average student test scores of the other 780 students in the school. Let's assume that the average student test score in the class is 75. Even though the statistic of 75 was calculated from the number of students in just one class, the number implies (or infers) that other students in the school can be expected to have a similar score. Compared to descriptive statistics, inferential statistics also identify *what similarities or differences may exist* within a group.

Chapter Learning Assessment Questions

To gauge your understanding of the information provided, complete the following questions:

Objective 1

1. Without statistics, in the area (or topic) of biology, one would not be able to
   a. determine whether medicines or other forms of treatments are safe for use by the public.
   b. discover the factors (e.g., voting preferences) associated with certain political parties in geographical areas.
   c. understand the impact of imprisonment on the lives of individuals.
   d. None of the above

Objective 2

2. Which of the following applications of statistics might be specifically used by local police departments?
   a. To identify factors associated with successful (or unsuccessful) probation completion
   b. To identify sentencing patterns
   c. To deploy officers in certain geographical locations
   d. None of the above

Objective 3

3. Which of the following is an example of a unit of analysis?
   a. The number of health clinics in minority communities
   b. The number of students expelled from school
   c. A category of individuals in a specific setting
   d. All of the above

Answers

1. a
2. c
3. d

Research Methods: The Fundamental Context of Statistics

Before we further explore the basics of statistics, there are several terms and processes that must be introduced as they relate to research methods. In general, research methods serve as an important contextual framework in which statistics exist. This includes three areas of information: (1) experiments, (2) data types and collection measures, and (3) sources of data (Hagan, 1997).

Experiments

Experiments and statistics go hand in hand. At its core, an experiment is an investigative process designed to determine the existence of a relationship. Suppose a researcher is interested in identifying the factors associated with the development of heart disease among police officers. To investigate this relationship, they would likely conduct an experiment. During the course of their experiment, a researcher would likely perform analytical calculations (i.e., statistics). To that end, an experiment provides meaning and purpose with respect to the use of statistics. In general, there are numerous types of experiments in the area of social sciences. In this chapter, we will discuss classic experimental designs and quasi-experimental designs.

Classic Experimental Design

Imagine you are interested in whether youth who are exposed to violence by playing video games are more likely to engage in violent (or aggressive) behavior toward others. By using an experimental approach, often referred to as a classical experimental design, a researcher can manipulate the existence (and the amount) of violent content a young person is exposed to (Hagan, 1997). Those who are exposed to violent content are known as the experimental group, and those who are not exposed to such are referred to as the control group. To ensure fairness, the placement of youth in either the experimental or control group begins with a process of randomization, which is often based on certain characteristics (i.e., age, grade level, etc.). Once groups are determined, data is analyzed (i.e., statistics) and interpreted in order to support (or not support) certain research-based assumptions (e.g., hypothesis, theory).

Policing, Absenteeism, and Mindfulness

In terms of policing and health, suppose one is interested in whether mindfulness is associated with lower levels of health-related absenteeism among police officers. If a researcher believes (or hypothesizes) that the number of incidents of absenteeism will decrease because of the use of meditation exercises by officers, the researcher will have to begin this study by randomly assigning officers to either the experimental or control group. Prior to this process, placement within each group should include officers who share similar characteristics. Examples of such may include gender, experience, or prior health-related status. Actual placement in each group should include a non-biased approach, previously referred to as randomization. Once group placement has been completed, initial observations of absenteeism will take place. The experimental group will engage in mindfulness techniques (i.e., breathing exercises, etc.), and the control group will engage in traditional types of exercises (i.e., weightlifting, running, etc.). After a specific time period, say 6 months or 3 years, members of the experimental group will likely report lower numbers of health-related absenteeism. On the other hand, members of the control group will likely report similar numbers of absenteeism prior to the experiment time frame. From these results, the differences between the two groups are attributed to the exposure to the techniques (often described as intervention measures) experienced by members of the experimental group.

Kansas City Preventive Patrol Experiment

A notable example of the classical experimental design was the Kansas City Preventive Patrol Experiment, which was conducted in Kansas City, Missouri, in 1972. One of the key functions of this research was to examine the impact of visible police presence on citizen's fear of crime (i.e., safety). By using a total of 15 beats (3 groups of 5 beats), this study included 2 experimental groups (for a total of 10 beats) and 1 control group (for a total of 5 beats). The two experimental groups were responsible for engaging in two types of patrol within their respective group of five beats. This included reactive (i.e., responding to calls, etc.) and proactive (i.e., initiating contact, etc.) policing. The control group, which was really a comparison group, did not receive any different types of police responses during the study. Within the patrol groups designated in the proactive policing approach, the number of officers was either doubled or tripled compared to the number of patrol officers prior to the study. At the conclusion of the study in 1973, the results revealed that increased patrol measures did not have an impact on citizens' perceptions of safety or the prevention of crime (Kelling, 1974).

Quasi-Experiment

In general, an experiment is a study in which a researcher manipulates one or more independent variables to observe the effect on a dependent variable. In an experiment, the researcher has control over the assignment of participants to different conditions, and the goal is to determine cause-and-effect relationships. Sometimes, however, the control over aspects of the social setting is beyond the influence of a researcher.

Given the nature of the criminal justice system, the impact associated with manipulating (or depriving) individuals from receiving treatment or intervention is unnecessary, unethical, and, in some cases, illegal. To that end, researchers in criminal justice often employ what is referred to as quasi-experiments (Hagan, 1997).

A quasi-experiment is a study that resembles an experiment but does not have the same level of control over the assignment of participants to conditions. In a quasi-experiment, the researcher does not manipulate the independent variables and cannot make causal inferences with the same degree of confidence as in an experiment. Instead, the goal is usually to establish a correlation between variables. In sum, the main difference between an experiment and a quasi-experiment is the level of control the researcher has over the assignment of participants to conditions and the degree of confidence in making causal inferences (Hagan, 1997).

In comparison to classical experimental studies, it is not uncommon for quasi-experiments to avoid the use of control groups as well as random assignments. Instead, these studies might use only comparison groups. Another way to think about the difference between an experiment and a quasi-experiment is that quasi-experimental designs give researchers control over the "when and to whom" of measurement, even though others decide the "when and to whom" of exposure to the experimental intervention.

Minority Students and Zero-Tolerance Policies

Suppose one was curious as to whether an increase of minority students at a specific public school would have an impact on the number of suspensions based on the use of zero-tolerance policies. This includes identifying two schools that have similarly low numbers of minority students, along with corresponding low numbers of suspensions. Over a period of 3 years, both schools experience increased minority student enrollment of 25%. Upon reviewing the number of suspensions in both schools, one school reported higher minority suspension numbers. Compared to a similar school, the increase in minority student suspensions is attributed to the higher enrollment of minorities.

Impact of Drug Treatment Programs Among Probationers

One quasi-experimental study examined the impact of a drug treatment program among probationers. The experimental group included probationers who completed a substance abuse treatment program. The comparison group consisted of probationers who completed standard probation measures. Their findings revealed that, compared to the comparison group, probationers within the experimental group were less likely to engage in recidivism. Specific categories include a decrease in violent, property, and drug offenses (Hollis et al., 2019).

Experiments and Statistics

As noted within the examples provided, experimental designs are critical for understanding the value of research within the areas of criminal and juvenile justice. Moreover, as indicated in each topic, the results of the research provide key insights with respect to specific assumptions. Despite the necessity of these outcomes, the process of conducting research is less likely to take place without the use of statistics.

Types of Data and Data Collection Measures

In addition to research experiments, statistics play a vital role in research as a result of the types of data selected as well as data collection measures employed. Defined as the process of gathering information, data collection is important, as it reveals a number of key aspects in conducting research. In particular, it helps to identify what (as in what is the nature of a problem), when (as in when the problem occurs), where (as the location of the problem), how (as in how the problem occurs), and who (as in who is likely to experience a problem). Furthermore, data collection can also uncover attitudes related to both processes and solutions. In general, there are two types of data collection processes: quantitative and qualitative. The word *quantitative* refers to the collection of numerical data. Examples include arrest numbers for certain offenses, fine amounts, number of days spent in jail, or years of incarceration. On the other hand, *qualitative* refers to the collection of data that is non-numerical. Examples of such include interviews among individual police chiefs, observing courtroom professionals during a high-profile trial, or engaging in case studies related to the investigation of school shootings.

Quantitative Data Collection Techniques

Our discussion of quantitative data collection techniques will include four types: (1) surveys, (2) mail surveys, (3) telephone, and (4) internet.

Surveys

Types and examples of the most commonly used quantitative collection techniques (e.g., surveys) are listed below. A survey (also known as a questionnaire) is an instrument designed to gather information through the use of questions and responses (Hagan, 1997). For instance, if one desired to identify the opinions of police officers with regard to public protests, one might use a survey. In general, there are two ways in which a survey can be completed. *Official report surveys* involve the collection of information from individuals by representatives of an organization or institution. Instances in which individuals complete the surveys themselves (without the assistance of anyone else) are *self-report surveys*. In the study of crime statistics, the National Crime Victimization Survey (NCVS) is an example of data derived from self-report surveys.

Mail Surveys

The majority of individuals in the United States are familiar with a common type of self-report survey known as a mail survey. Several advantages of mail surveys include the absence of interviewer bias and respondent privacy. To that end, a mail survey might be useful in gathering sensitive information, such as criminal or victimization experiences. The disadvantages of mail surveys may include misinterpretation of questions, slow submission of completed surveys, and high rate of nonresponses. For example, imagine a researcher who is interested in the study of violence among prison inmates based on their prior criminal conviction history of violent behavior. Through the use of a mail survey, a number of questions require that the respondents identify their current and prior involvement in criminal activities. Because of the nature of these questions, as well as the belief that the responses to such might lead to further criminal charges, an inmate might refuse to provide answers to those questions or complete the survey altogether (Hagan, 1997).

Telephone Surveys

Telephone surveys are used in the same manner as face-to-face or mail surveys. The only difference is that this data collection technique involves the use of a phone. The interview process may include an actual person or a recording. The process may include both open and closed questions. The advantage of telephone surveys is that interviewees are not likely to experience influence from the interviewers, which can happen by observing an interviewer's body language or facial expressions. The disadvantage of such, when responding to automated recordings of questions, is that the interviewee is not able to ask for clarification when posed with questions they are unclear about (Hagan, 1997).

Internet Surveys

Given the development and use of technology, internet surveys have become common. In general, there are two types of internet surveys: web-based and email surveys. Other types of internet communication include the use of virtual face-to-face interaction as well as individual and group chat options. The advantages of such include greater efficiency (in relation to time and expenses) in comparison to mail and face-to-face surveys. The disadvantages of internet surveys include (1) high programming and design expenses within certain media platforms, (2) not everyone has access to the internet (which is referred to as potential sampling bias), (3) the potential lack of ethical research measures such as signed consent and the securing of confidential data, and (4) the prospect of unlawful access to data through hacking (Hagan, 1997).

Qualitative Data Collection Techniques

Our discussion of qualitative data collection techniques will include four types: (1) interviews, (2) depth interviews, (3) structured interviews, and (4) unstructured interviews.

Interviews

Defined as a conversation with the purpose of gathering information, interviews are often used in the field of research. Compared to surveys, they provide context in which respondents may find helpful in understanding the meaning of the information provided during the interview as well as the purpose of the interview. There are three types of interviews that are common within research: depth (or in-depth), structured, and unstructured interviews (Hagan, 1997).

Depth Interview

A depth interview is considered an intensive and detailed (data gathering) conversation. In the area of crime investigations, depth interviews are also known as interviews, which (under certain circumstances) may develop into interrogations. In most cases, this interview process is used to test a hypothesis. For instance, suppose a detective believes that a person of interest (or suspect), based on their initial responses (e.g., verbal, physical, etc.) to certain questions, has committed a serious crime. Upon observation of unusual (or questionable) behavior by the suspect, the interviewer (detective) may engage in more specific and detailed interview techniques (Hagan, 1997).

Structured Interview

Unlike the depth interview, the structured interview is not intensive or in-depth. It gathers concise responses, which makes it more efficient compared to the depth interview. This approach is often used for specific responses to specific inquiries. The disadvantage of this technique is that it fails to gain contextual information, which may be helpful in uncovering meaningful insight (Hagan, 1997). An example of this approach is often used when interviewing crime victims by law enforcement staff or administrators. This does not require extensive or in-depth questions and usually takes place in order to assign information for specific personnel (e.g., detectives) who will investigate the alleged criminal activity.

Unstructured Interview

Finally, the unstructured interview, in comparison to the depth or structured interview, offers more freedom to share information on behalf of the interviewee. For the most part, this technique uses questions that call for open-ended responses (Hagan, 1997). An example of such may include the gathering of information by a psychologist or psychotherapist.

Participant Observation

Participant observation refers to the process of conducting a study whereby a researcher engages (or participates) in the activities being studied (Hagan, 1997). Examples may include conversations or behaviors. The basis of this data collection approach stems from the *Verstehen* approach, which states that a researcher is not able to fully understand the dynamics of group behavior unless they are immersed in the lifestyle and culture of the group being studied. For instance, some college students, especially those classified as juniors or seniors, have experienced participant observation through internships. Overall, there are numerous types of participant observation. In this chapter, we will discuss complete participation and complete observation.

Types of Participant Observation

Complete Participation

Complete participation is the process in which a researcher is fully engaged as a participant. This includes identifying with the group (as a member) and potentially influencing decisions (Hagan, 1997). Examples of such include undercover agents posing as drug dealers in order to arrest criminals. This process is similar to what is referred to as disguised observation, in which one only *appears* to fit in without actually *trying* to fit in through certain activities. This approach to data collection is highly subjective, but there are certain steps that can be used to ensure objectivity.

Complete Observation

Complete observation is the process in which a researcher only observes behavior (Hagan, 1997). Unlike complete participation, the researcher is not immersed in the lifestyle or activities of the group. Within the scope of criminal investigations, witnessing the commission of a crime by a detective is an example of complete observation. This process, compared to complete participation, is objective.

Case Studies

The process of gathering data in an in-depth manner is referred to as a case study. It can be centered on a specific person, theme, or situation and often includes an extensive amount of details within a time period. Within the study of organized crime, case studies were used to gather information from current and former members of the mafia.

Secondary Data Analysis

Defined as the use of data collected by someone else, secondary data analysis offers a number of benefits for those who prefer quick access to data. However, users of such are limited to the types of data available. In other words, the type of data secured from someone else might only serve as a benefit to their research agenda compared to your research agenda. This approach is often encouraged among students who may have a limited time frame in which to work with data. An example of such includes the use of data downloaded from a public access website, such as the UCR, as provided by the Federal Bureau of Investigation (FBI).

Evaluation Research

Evaluation research (ER) is a type of applied research designed to inform decision-making and policy development. An example of such includes determining whether an increase in penalties (i.e., fines, sentencing, etc.) associated with the illegal possession of a firearm will lower gun-related crimes in certain areas. An advantage of ER is that it often provides measurable outcomes that may reveal the efficacy of a policy or decision. A possible disadvantage is that ER is a time-consuming and detail-oriented process.

There are numerous types of ER; however, we will introduce only two types: impact and process evaluation. Impact evaluation is designed to examine the relationship between input and output. For example, suppose an law enforcement agency (LEA) decided to increase the number of arrests among those who engaged in drug trafficking near public schools. Would this decision lead to a decrease in drug trafficking near public schools? To answer this question, one may employ the use of impact ER. On the other hand, rather than focusing on the impact of a decision, process evaluation is designed to examine the steps used to meet certain goals. For instance, an LEA decided to increase arrests for the purpose of lowering the likelihood of crime in a certain area. Let's say after 18 months, the crime rate failed to drop. Based on this unexpected outcome, one might examine whether the process of instituting arrests may serve as the basis of the problem. Examples of such may include officers who are not complying with arrest priorities in certain areas, as well as other high-priority initiatives within the LEA. In short, impact studies refer to outcomes, and process studies focus on how measures are implemented.

Types of Data Collection Measures and Statistics

The types of data (and data collection measures) discussed provide a wealth of options in terms of conducting various types of research. Research that combines both numerical and non-numerical data, often referred to as mixed methods, is a data collection approach that includes the best of both worlds. In general, regardless of the types of data and data collection options, the process of conducting sound research often involves the use of statistical testing procedures.

Common Sources of Data in Criminal Justice

Our final aspect of research methods is associated with sources of data. Within criminal justice, there are a number of commonly used and available data. This includes the UCR and the National Incident-Based Reporting System (NIBRS).

UCR

The UCR is a collection of data reported by LEAs, which is made available by the FBI. The UCR consists of Part 1 and Part 2 crimes. Part 1 crimes consist of two indexes: violent crime and property crime. Examples of violent crime include murder, forcible rape, robbery, and aggravated assault. Examples of property crimes include burglary, larceny-theft, motor vehicle theft, and arson. Part 2 crimes are referred to as non-index crimes, which include simple assault, gambling, and drunkenness. From a practical standpoint, if someone is interested in identifying whether the number of burglaries has increased within a certain area and time period, they can gain access to this data through the use of the FBI website. An advantage of the UCR is that the data is freely available to the public. A disadvantage, known as the hierarchy rule, is that the UCR only records the most serious offenses committed during an incident. For instance, if an individual commits armed robbery at a bank, and during their attempt to flee, they shoot and kill a police officer, UCR will only report the nonnegligent manslaughter or murder offense and not the armed robbery offense (Hagan, 1997).

NIBRS

NIBRS is a reporting system that includes information on individual crime incidents and arrests as reported by LEAs. Given the shortcomings of the UCR, NIBRS was developed for the purpose of providing more extensive amounts of detailed data. For instance, UCR provides summary reporting data for 8 offenses; NIBRS provides detailed incident information for at least 22 offenses and

52 data elements, which affords greater specificity of data. Other improvements in the availability of data include new definitions, as well as distinctions between attempted and completed crimes. The efficacy of such improvements is often fully appreciated when certain topics in criminal justice are examined, especially in the area of criminal victimization. Imagine the difficulty of trying to identify the specific characteristics of students (i.e., race, classification, etc.) who were victims of property crimes. If one is interested in creating policies designed to protect those who are likely to experience property crime, how is one able to gain access to such detailed data owing to the limitations of the UCR reporting system? From this standpoint, it appears that access to more detailed data is associated with more opportunities for analysis and possible solutions (Hagan, 1997).

Surveys

Aside from secondary data (UCR, NIBRS), surveys exist as a valuable source of data for criminal justice practitioners. There are numerous options related to the use of surveys. For instance, one can gather information for the purpose of exploration, such as the discovery of new information or the use of previously discovered information within a new group or population. An example of such is gauging the opinions of students who attended unique institutions of higher education (such as historically Black colleges and universities) in which research that reflects the opinions of students with regard to certain topics does not exist. In general, surveys are noted for the identification of interviewer opinions, which may include a variety of topics such as the death penalty or the use of deadly force.

NCVS

Another common source of survey data provided by the Department of Justice and the Bureau of Justice Statistics is the NCVS. The data in this survey (as derived from the U.S. Census Bureau) is composed of individuals who are at least 12 years old from over 30,000 households. The NCVS provides data on crimes, offenders, and victims, along with household and crime characteristics. The use of the NCVS is an idea for those interested in the study of factors associated with crime victimization in the United States.

Sources of Data and Statistics

The numerous sources of data, both public and private, offer a vast number of options for conducting research. In fact, some data sets include variables that can be used in interdisciplinary research. An example of such includes access to data in which statistical testing can be used to measure the influence of gender in relationship to certain juvenile justice dispositional outcomes. This type of research encompasses variables from both sociology and juvenile justice. In general, regardless of the data sources and disciplinary topics, statistics will serve as the basis for measuring all theoretical frameworks, hypotheses, or research questions.

The Structure of This Textbook

This textbook is organized into three main sections: descriptive statistics, probability, and inferential statistics.

Section 1: Descriptive Statistics

Chapters 2–3 discuss the use of variables and levels of measurement, along with measures of central tendency (mean, median, mode). Chapters 4–5 provide insight into dispersion and information related to the use of visual statistics (tables, graphs, charts).

Section 2: Probability

Chapter 6 identifies the use of probability, which includes proportion, the normal curve, and the z-score. Chapter 7 provides information related to the use of hypotheses, type I and type II errors, statistical significance and thesteps used in statistical testing.

Section 3: Inferential Statistics

Chapters 8–9 discuss the use of a one-sample z-test and the use of the independent and dependent sample t-tests. Chapters 10–11 address the use of the analysis of variance test, along with the two-factor ANOVA test. Finally, Chapters 12–14 identify the use of the chi-square, correlation, and linear regression tests.

Chapter Summary

This chapter emphasized the following information:

Objective 1 – The universal need for and use of statistics

- The value of statistics within various disciplines/majors.

Objective 2 – The use of statistics in criminal justice and criminology

- The role of statistics in the criminal and juvenile justice systems.

Objective 3 – Define and explain several fundamental terms used in statistics.

- Statistics is the collection, analysis, and interpretive use of information/data.
- A theory is an explanation of a phenomenon based on logic and verifiable evidence. It usually includes a hypothesis.
- A hypothesis is a set of propositions that offer an explanation of a phenomenon and which often identifies a relationship between two or more variables.
- A unit of analysis represents an element of interest in the use of statistics and research.
- Descriptive statistics are used to describe data.
- Inferential statistics are used to infer data from a sample in order to make assumptions about a population.

Objective 4 – Discuss the context of statistics, including research methods.

- Experiments
- Types of data and data collection techniques
- Sources of data

Discussion

As an expert in criminal justice, you have been invited to offer an explanation for the high number of homicides in certain areas of a city. What type of evidence would you consider using to evaluate a specific theory that claims to explain the increased homicide rate? Would you offer any type of additional information related to the evidence provided? Explain.

Terms

Statistics
Theory
Hypothesis
Units of analysis
Descriptive statistics
Inferential statistics

Bibliography

Agnew, R., & White, H. R. (1992). An empirical test of general strain theory. *Criminology, 30*(4), 475–500.

Hagan, F. E. (1997). *Research methods in criminal justice and criminology* (pp. 347–348). Allyn and Bacon.

Hirschi, T. (1969). Key idea: Hirschi's social bond/social control theory. *Key Ideas in Criminology and Criminal Justice, 1969*, 55–69.

Hollis, M. E., Jennings, W. G., & Hankhouse, S. (2019). An outcome evaluation of a substance abuse program for probationers: Findings from a quasi-experimental design. *American Journal of Criminal Justice, 44*(3), 395–408.

Kahn, K. B., Lee, J. K., Renauer, B., Henning, K. R., & Stewart, G. (2017). The effects of perceived phenotypic racial stereotypicality and social identity threat on racial minorities' attitudes about police. *Journal of Social Psychology, 157*(4), 416–428.

Kelling, G. L., Pate, T., Dieckman, D., & Brown, C. (1974). *The Kansas City preventive patrol experiment: A technical report.* Police Foundation.

Puzzanchera, C., Sladky, A., & Kang, W. (2022). Easy access to juvenile populations: 1990–2021. EZAPOP. www.ojjdp.gov/ojstatbb/ezapop

Ratcliffe, J. H., Taniguchi, T., Groff, E. R., & Wood, J. D. (2011). The Philadelphia foot patrol experiment: A randomized controlled trial of police patrol effectiveness in violent crime hotspots. *Criminology, 49*(3), 795–831.

Sykes, G. M., & Matza, D. (1957). Techniques of neutralization: A theory of delinquency. *American Sociological Review, 22*(6), 664–670.

Walton, D., Brooks, R., & Li, J. (2021). The use of victim video statements in family violence cases increases the rate of early guilty pleas. *Journal of Interpersonal Violence, 36*(13-14), 6098–6116.

Xu, Y., Fu, C., Kennedy, E., Jiang, S., & Owusu-Agyemang, S. (2018). The impact of streetlights on spatial-temporal patterns of crime in Detroit, Michigan. *Cities, 79*, 45–52.

Zheng, X., Chen, H., Wang, Z., Xie, F., & Bao, Z. (2021). Online violent video games and online aggressive behavior among Chinese college students: The role of anger rumination and self-control. *Aggressive Behavior, 47*(5), 514–520.

Credit

CHAPTER 2

Variables and Measurements

One measurement is worth a thousand expert opinions.
—Donald Sutherland (1960)

Objectives

1. Define and explain the different kinds of variables and their use.
2. Discuss the categories of statistical tests and variable properties.
3. Identify and explain levels of measurement and their classification.
4. Determine the appropriate level of measurement.
5. Describe the operationalization of criminal justice concepts to include reliability and validity.
6. Introduce and review statistical notation.

Introduction—Details Make the Difference

Responding to unanticipated situations is common in all aspects of the criminal justice system. Police are required to respond to crimes in progress, prosecutors are expected to bring a variety of criminal charges corresponding to available evidence, and correctional officers must often deescalate specific events while simultaneously maintaining custody and control of inmate populations. One common denominator of responding successfully as a criminal justice professional is a working knowledge of the details of each situation, and accurate information is vital to a successful response. During an active shooter event, for example, it is important that responding officers know the description and location of the shooter (or shooters), as well as the number of shooters involved and weaponry used. In essence, details make the difference. The same is true in the use of statistical tests, many of which will be discussed in upcoming chapters. Before we begin that discussion, however, we must talk about two prerequisite detailed-oriented topics: variables and measurements.

Variables

A key process associated with statistics is the examination of relationships between variables. A **variable** is a characteristic of interest (Schoenfeld and Arcavi, 1988). What is unique about a

variable A characteristic of interest.

dependent variable A characteristic or phenomenon that one wishes to investigate.

independent variable A characteristic or phenomenon that may explain the existence of a dependent variable.

variable is that it can represent almost anything of value in research. For instance, one may be interested in determining whether student-led protests are associated with criminal justice reform. In this example, both *student-led protests* and *criminal justice reform* are considered variables.

Independent and Dependent Variables

Statistics are often used to identify relationships between variables that may be associated with each other. As indicated in Table 2.1, this includes what is referred to as dependent and independent variables. A **dependent variable** is a characteristic or phenomenon that one wishes to investigate. An **independent variable** is a characteristic or phenomenon that may explain the existence of the dependent variable (Leatham, 2012). Unfortunately, not all criminal justice professionals use the same language. Thus, it is important to become aware of the various terminologies used by different professionals who conduct research as a part of the criminal justice community.

As mentioned previously, in determining whether student-led protests are associated with criminal justice reform, *student-led protests* is the *independent variable*, and *criminal justice reform* is the *dependent variable*. Table 2.1 provides a list of research study questions in which corresponding independent and dependent variables are identified.

TABLE 2.1 **Independent and Dependent Variables**

Research Study Questions	Independent Variable	Dependent Variable
Does anonymity lead to crime reporting among minorities?	Anonymity	Crime reporting among minorities
Does prior experience among Black youth affect their willingness to cooperate with police?	Prior experience with police among Black youth	Willingness to cooperate with police
Does the depiction of negative police-minority interactions by the media affect crime reporting in a Black community?	Media depiction of negative police-minority interactions	Crime reporting in a Black community

Based on the information provided in Table 2.1, it is important to understand that both the independent and dependent variables must be measurable, which serves as one of the most important and challenging functions of statistics in research. Consider the following:

Research Study Question:
Does prior experience among Black youth affect their willingness to cooperate with police?

Independent Variable:
Prior experience with police among Black youth

What steps might be used to measure the independent variable? One common measure may include asking an individual, through the use of a survey, to identify the number of encounters they have had with the police. This may include questions that provide the following:

A dichotomous response option:
Have you ever interacted with a police officer?

a. Yes
b. No

A fill-in-the-blank option:
If you have interacted with a police officer, please include the number of experiences ________.

A question may include the following responses in the form of numerical categories, often referred to as a Likert scale option:

Please indicate how many times you have interacted with a police officer.

a. 0–5
b. 6–10
c. 11–15
d. More than 16

Dependent Variable:
Willingness to cooperate with police

What steps may be used to measure the dependent variable? This may include asking an individual to identify the extent to which they are willing to cooperate with police. The question may include the following Likert scale option:

You are likely to share information with the police.

a. Strongly disagree
b. Disagree
c. Undecided
d. Agree
e. Strongly agree

Association and Causation

It is important to note that independent variables do not always cause (or directly influence) dependent variables, especially in relationships where significant associations occur. Independent and dependent variables may be associated with each other, but the association does not always suggest that one variable exclusively causes (or directly influences) the other. For instance, studies suggest that poor academic performance (independent variable) is related to delinquency (dependent variable) among youth. Based on this statement, one may assume that poor academic performance causes delinquency; however, there may be other variables (e.g., peer influence, home life) that may explain delinquency. As noted by the underlined terms, paying attention to the words used in defining relationships is important. Again, association should not necessarily be interpreted as evidence of causation.

Categories of Statistical Tests and Variable Properties

Categories of Statistical Tests

In addition to understanding the types and use of variables in statistics, categories of statistical tests are also important. More specifically, statistical tests are divided into two categories:

- Parametric
- Nonparametric

In short, parametric tests are more powerful than nonparametric tests. Parametric tests have the advantage of using more information about the data. However, parametric tests are less powerful than nonparametric tests when the data violates specified characteristics for the test being calculated. The difference between parametric and nonparametric tests will be clarified after our discussion of levels of measurement. Furthermore, additional details regarding these categorical differences will be covered in subsequent chapters.

Categories of Variable Properties

Another important characteristic of variables is their properties, which may fall into either one or two overall categories. These categories are identified as *exhaustive* and *mutually exclusive*. A category that is considered exhaustive is one in which its properties may contain all possible values.

For example, suppose an inmate who was arrested 11 times is encouraged to complete a survey which includes the following questions:

During my adult experience (18+), I have been arrested a total of ________ times:

a. 0–2
b. 3–5
c. 6–8
d. 9–10

As revealed by the available options, the choice of 11 is not provided. Thus, the question violates the option of exhaustiveness. As a remedy, consider the following set of revised options, which includes an appropriate range of scores.

During my adult experience (18+), I have been arrested a total of ________ times:

a. 0–2
b. 3–5
c. 6–8
d. 9 or more

exhaustive A characteristic of a variable in which its properties may contain all possible values.

mutually exclusiveness A property in which there is no overlap of categories within a variable.

On the other hand, mutually exclusiveness refers to a property in which there is no overlap of categories within a variable.

For instance, consider the following as derived from the previous example:

During my adult experience (18+), I have been arrested a total of ______ times:

a. 0–2
b. 2–5
c. 5–8
d. 8–10

As indicated, notice that each category does not allow for the selection of a single option with certain values. For instance, if an individual was arrested 5 times, they would not be able to select a single category. Selecting both option b and c is not acceptable. In fact, most surveys will provide specific instructions that forbid the option of choosing more than one selection. This question violates the option of mutually exclusiveness.

Now that we have discussed a number of important characteristics of variables (which include both categories and properties), we will discuss the specific levels of measurement commonly used in statistics. This includes nominal-, ordinal-, interval-, and ratio-level data.

Chapter Learning Assessment Questions

To gauge your understanding of the information provided, complete the following questions:

Objective 1

1. Suppose someone is interested in determining if a relationship exists between reading and vocabulary among youth. In this statement, reading is defined as a(n):
   a. Independent variable
   b. Dependent variable
   c. Both A and B
   d. None of the above

Objective 2

2. Suppose a police officer who has 15 years of experience is encouraged to complete a survey that includes the following question:

How many years of experience as a law enforcement officer do you have? Please select only one option from the following:

a. Less than 1 year
b. 2–5 years
c. 6–9 years
d. 10–12 years

The question represents an example of which of the following?

a. A violation of mutually exclusiveness
b. A violation of exhaustiveness
c. Both a and b
d. None of the above

Answers

1. a
2. b

Levels of Measurement

All variables are classified based on their specific type. The classification system was developed through the efforts of Stanley Smith Stevens (1946). Often referred to as *levels of measurement*, there are four types of measurements (or classifications), as identified in Figure 2.1: nominal, ordinal, interval, and ratio. Each of the four types of measurements falls under two general classifications. Nominal and ordinal variables are recognized as categorical-level variables, while interval and ratio variables are considered continuous-level variables.

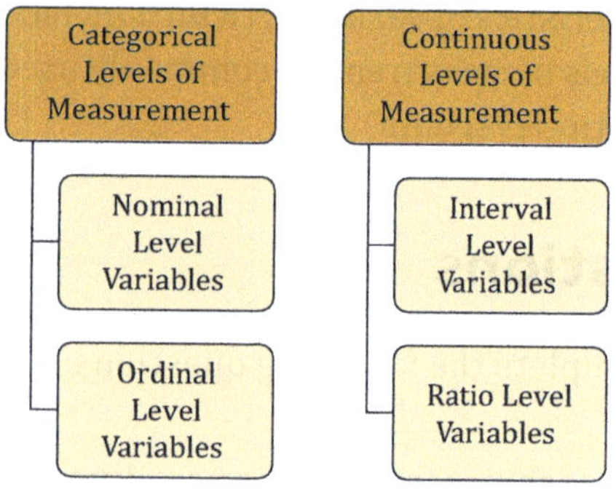

FIGURE 2.1 Levels of Measurement

Question: Why must we learn to categorize data into the four levels of measurement?

Answer: Level of measurement is the prerequisite for determining the type of statistical test that is required when conducting an analysis. We will further discuss the importance of this relationship in subsequent parts of this chapter.

Categorical Level—Nominal Variable

nominal variable A variable that represents an outcome that is identified in a single category.

A **nominal variable** is a variable that represents an outcome that is identified in a single category. In Table 2.2, respondents were asked if they believed anonymity leads to crime reporting among minorities. Given that the possible outcomes (i.e., responses) are either "yes" or "no," the outcome associated with the question is considered a nominal variable.

TABLE 2.2 **Nominal Variables and Responses**

Does anonymity lead to crime reporting among minorities?	Frequency
Yes	67
No	32
Total	99

Categorical Level—Ordinal Variable

An **ordinal variable**, which is similar to a nominal variable in that they are both categorical levels of measurement, is a variable that represents an outcome that is ranked. Examples of ordinal variables may consist of a variety of concepts, such as actual numbers, academic classification, and levels of offenses. For instance, Table 2.3 provides a list of criminal offenses based on classification type.

ordinal variable A variable that represents an outcome that is ranked.

TABLE 2.3 **Ordinal Variables and Offense Classification**

Criminal Offense of Assault by Classification	Frequency
Assault, first-degree misdemeanor	12
Assault, second-degree misdemeanor	23
Assault, third-degree misdemeanor	26
Total	61

Of all the levels of measurement, ordinal is the most complex *and* the most used in criminal justice research. As a result, more so than any other level of measurement, ordinal data has the largest number of statistical tests to select from. Selecting an appropriate statistical test for ordinal data is a complex enterprise. There are literately hundreds of tests for ordinal data while just a handful for nominal, interval, and ratio. For example, Gwent (2014) has published a 428-page book of ordinal formulas that describe the various methods a researcher can employ for the assessment of how well judges agree. This single book addresses the ordinal assessment of consistency of judges' opinion and nothing else. Although all other levels of measurement can assess consistency of judges, none of them would require an entire book to describe the statistical process.

The mathematical characteristic that propels ordinal to be the most complex level of measurement is the concept focusing on the lack of "equality in the distance among consecutive data points." This takes time to understand and is best comprehended by example rather than by a definition.

In 1932, Rensis Likert devised an often-used ordinal scale based on the following options:

- Strongly Agree
- Agree
- Not Sure
- Disagree
- Strongly Disagree

From Likert scale research, two critically important issues were discovered that enable greater control and accuracy for the statistical analysis of ordinal data. First, in collecting data on a questionnaire, it is best *not* to use questions but rather make a statement that makes the research subject react in a prescribed manner. Furthermore, questions within a questionnaire often place the research subject on the defensive. Second, we have the "rule of 5." That is, when creating an ordinal scale, statistical analysis is more manageable with ranks of at least 5 rather than 4 or less.

- Strongly Agree
- Agree

} Is the distance between these two data points equal all others?

- Not Sure
- Disagree

} Is the distance between these two data points equal all others?

- Strongly Disagree

FIGURE 2.2 Distance Between Responses Within an Ordinal Scale

We have laid the groundwork for understanding the complexity of ordinal data. As illustrated in Figure 2.2, we must ask the question, "Is the distance between 'Strongly Agree' and 'Agree,' equal to the distance between 'Not Sure' and 'Disagree'?"

If the question is answered by the response "I don't know," then we can conclude we have ordinal data. Simply stated, the prime characteristic of ordinal data is that we cannot be sure that the distance between *any* two consecutive data points is equal to the distance between any other consecutive data points with a shared measurement. Because ordinal data does not have equal distances between consecutive data points, serious limitations emerge in the type of statistical test that may be employed. As a rule of thumb, parametric statistics should not be used with ordinal data.

With every rule, there seems to be an exception. Here we find the greatest and longest debate among statisticians. Is it ever acceptable to use parametric statistical tests with ordinal data? Cureton (1978) has attempted to resolve this debate by formulating the concept of "quasi-interval" data. Both sides of this debate offer convincing arguments, and after nearly 80 years of heated discourse, there is no final disposition. One method for attempting to ensure accuracy with quasi-interval data is establishing a standard to determine if ordinal data can be treated as interval. A synthesis of the literature suggests that three criteria or characteristics can be used to treat ordinal data as if it is interval data.

These are the following:

- *A large sample size*: A sample must include at least 100 subjects.
- *The rule of 5*: The ordinal measure must have a minimum rank of 5. This helps explain the popularity of Likert scales.
- *Normally distributed*: With a sample size of at least 100, the data can be illustrated in a bar chart. If the overall impression suggests a bell-shaped curve, we have compliance with the quasi-interval standard.

Continuous Level—Interval Variable

The **interval variable** is a variable that represents a numerical outcome in which zero does not have a true point of measurement. In addition, each interval (or numerical value) in a distribution of numbers is equal. For instance, a thermometer has a series of numbers (representing temperature readings) in which zero, like any other number, has the same value in providing a temperature reading. To that end, zero does not indicate the absence of temperature; thus, it does not have a true point of measurement. In addition, each numerical value identified in a thermometer is of equal value. This means that 99 degrees is one degree more than 98 degrees and one degree less than 100 degrees.

interval variable A variable that represents a numerical outcome in which zero does not have a true point of measurement.

Table 2.4 provides the ages of Black youth certified as adults. Certification of juveniles as adults may exist as a result of court proceedings. The ages are numerical; thus, the outcomes are interval. In addition, the values (ages) can be added or subtracted from one another; thus, those who are 13 years of age are two years from those who are 15 years of age. A final example of an interval-level variable is identified in Figure 2.3, in which numerical scores from an occupational prestige model are provided. As noted previously, each score is of equal value in relation to the other. For instance, someone who received a 70 has ten more points than someone who received a score of 60. Since the scores do not have a true point of zero, stating that someone with a score of 70 has twice the score of someone who scored 35 is not reasonable.

TABLE 2.4 **Interval Variables and Age**

Ages of Black Youth Certified as Adults	Frequency
13	18
14	25
15	53
16	61
17	62
Total	219

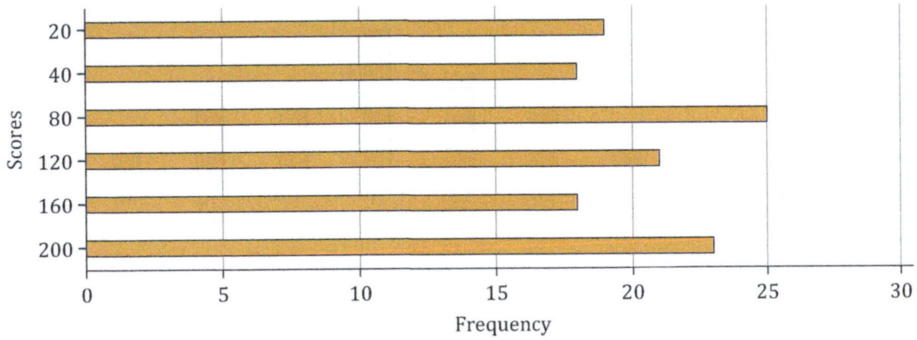

FIGURE 2.3 Occupational Prestige Scores

ratio variable A numerical outcome in which each value in a distribution of numbers is equal to one another, and zero has a true point of measurement.

Continuous Level—Ratio Variable

The final level of measurement is the ratio variable. Similar to the interval variable, the **ratio variable** represents a numerical outcome in which each value in a distribution of numbers is equal to one another. However, unlike the interval variable, zero has a true point of measurement. In other words, zero represents the actual (or true) absence of a characteristic or item.

Table 2.5 identifies the number of states in which police officers were convicted of misconduct in the United States in 2019. One column reflects the number of officers convicted; the other column provides the frequency in which those convictions occurred in each state. As noted, zero is included (a point of measurement) in that it represents the absence of officer convictions in 44 states in 2019. Figure 2.4 provides the length of time a juvenile is questioned by the police. The time of juvenile questioning is reflected in minutes, while frequency represents the number of juveniles who are questioned at a certain time. Are you able to determine which period reflects the greatest number of juveniles who have been questioned by police?

TABLE 2.5 **Continuous Variables and Number of Convictions**

Number of Police Officers Convicted of Misconduct, 2019	Frequency
0	44
1	2
2	1
3	2
4	1
Total	50

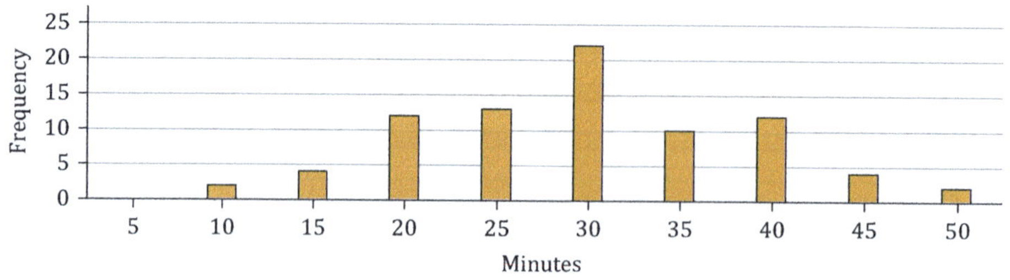

FIGURE 2.4 Time Period and Frequency of Interviews Among Youth

Determining the Appropriate Levels of Measurement

In addition to understanding the various types, levels, and basic characteristics of measurement in relation to data, it is also important to recognize an unfortunate phenomenon in how statistics might be employed. As mentioned previously, without knowledge of the level of measurement with respect to data, it is possible to analyze data in an inappropriate manner. For example, let's assume that someone is interested in determining whether race is associated with the commission of a type of crime, such as property or violent crime. In this example, race is defined as a nominal-level variable. The type of crime (property or violent) is also defined as a nominal-level variable. Since each variable represents a nominal level of measurement, it is important to use a statistical test that corresponds to the use of nominal-level measurements. Using a statistical test that corresponds to the use of ordinal, interval, or ratio data would lead to inappropriate statistics and faulty assumptions. More specifically, failing to recognize the appropriate levels of measurement with respect to data will result in an error in the analysis of the data.

Let's explore this problem further. In relation to our example, what if someone used a statistical test that corresponds to the use of ratio-level variables? As we have already established, both *race* and *crime type* are nominal-level variables. If we treated *race* and *crime type* as ratio-level variables, our statistical tests might reveal the existence of differences between race and crime type which might be inaccurate, resulting in error. From a practical standpoint, this may lead to the development of programs (or policies) designed to address the *assumed relationship* between our variables of interest. Imagine how much time, effort, and expense might be utilized as a result of our assumed relationship—a relationship based on the inappropriate use of a statistical test.

To that end, all inferential statistical tests are linked to the level of measurement—without exceptions. Thus, determining the level of measurement is the prerequisite for deciding on the type of statistical analysis to use.

Continuous and Discrete Data

A second method to assess the level of measurement includes categorizing variables into *continuous* and *discrete.* This style of assessing the level of measurement focuses on examining the mathematical area between two consecutive data points.

With *continuous* data, we examine the substantive nature between two data points in a numbering system or simply ask the question, "Can we systematically measure the content between two consecutive data points?" For example, a judge can impose a sentence of 5 years in prison. Can we measure the substance within the first year of the sentence? Yes, we can. We can divide a year into months, weeks, days, hours, minutes, seconds, and so on.

With *discrete* data, we also examine the substantive nature between two data points but find nothing to measure. For example, sex and race are common variables employed in criminal justice research. What can we measure between male and female or White and Black? We cannot because there is nothing to measure.

As one becomes familiar with statistics identified in research, one may notice that the terms interval and ratio-level variables are used synonymously. This is due to their similarities in terms of characteristics. If one desires to conduct research and is given a choice in terms of which type of data is available, it is highly recommended that one selects a type of data that corresponds to a continuous-level variable. For instance, as indicated in Table 2.6, suppose one is interested in determining if there is a difference between gender and the commission of a certain offense (DWI) in a specific geographical location. In this example, gender would likely represent a nominal variable. On the other hand, the commission of a DWI would represent a ratio variable. When comparing the two variables, notice how the continuous (ratio) variable provides more detailed information. Consider the following:

TABLE 2.6 **Differences Between Categorical and Continuous-Level Data and DWI**

Categorical (Nominal)				
	Mutually exclusive/ exhaustive	Rank Order	Equal Intervals	True Zero
Offenses (DWI)	28 reported incidents out of a total of 236 incidents are female	**NA**	**NA**	**NA**
Continuous (Ratio)				
	Mutually exclusive/ exhaustive	Rank Order	Equal Intervals	True Zero
Offenses (DWI)	28 reported incidents out of a total of 236 incidents are female	**First-degree offense** **Second-degree offense** **Third-degree offense**	**Yes**	**Yes**

Not only does a continuous variable offer more detailed information, but it also can be transformed into a categorical variable. To the contrary, a categorical variable cannot be transformed into a continuous-level variable. From this standpoint, selecting data with the highest level of measurement provides more information, which offers more opportunities in terms of analyses and outcomes.

Chapter Learning Assessment Questions

To gauge your understanding of the information provided, complete the following questions:

Objective 3

1. Suppose someone is interested in determining whether gender is related to occupational choices among college students. Gender is considered a ________ variable:
   a. nominal level
   b. ordinal level
   c. interval level
   d. ratio-level variable

Objective 4

2. An incorrect statistical test may
   a. exist due to a lack of knowledge regarding the levels of measurement
   b. lead to the inappropriate use of statistics
   c. result in an error in the analysis of data
   d. result in the development of programs and policies based on an assumed relationship between variables
   e. all of the above

Answers

1. a
2. e

The Operationalization of Criminal Justice Concepts

Operationalization refers to the idea of making something measurable. How, for example, can we measure something as seemingly as simple as "crime"? It can be difficult to operationalize the concept of crime because there are many different types of crime, including crimes that have victims and those that are sometimes referred to as victimless. Crimes that have victims vary greatly from violent to nonviolent, with many gradations in between. A major obstacle to developing good research in criminal justice lies in adequately operationalizing a concept (like crime) so that it can be measured. In fact, the development of good measurement can be the most difficult part of conducting research. Standards exist for measurements we use in research. These two standards primarily include reliability and validity.

operationalization The process of making something measurable.

reliability Consistency in relation to the use of a measurement tool, as well as the results of a measurement.

Reliability

In the study of measurement, the term **reliability** is best defined as consistency, trustworthiness, and, in a practical sense, getting the same (or similar) answer each time. This includes consistency with respect to both measuring tools and results. Reliability does not suggest accuracy. To that end, it is possible to obtain the wrong answer on a consistent basis. For instance, suppose a marksman is experimenting with a new gun. Normally, the marksman is able to land 98% of their bullets at the "bull's-eye" target area of 6 (see Figure 2.5). With this new gun, his bullets consistently landed at the two o'clock target area. In short, his aim was reliable but nevertheless not accurate.

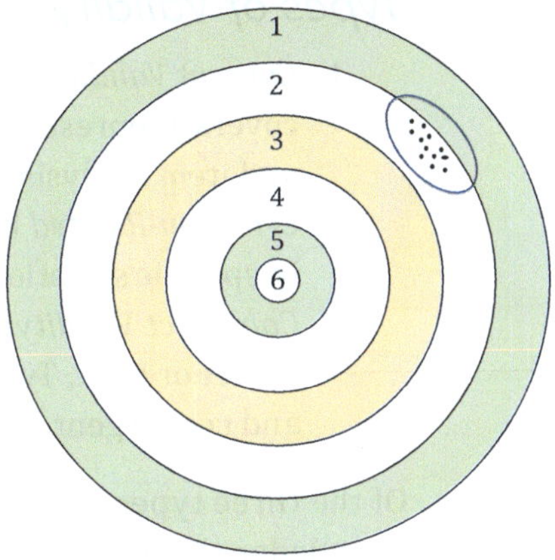

FIGURE 2.5 Reliability

Types of Reliability

There are five types of reliability. They include the following:

- *Test-Retest* – The correlation of scores of a test that has been administered twice to a group of subjects. A group is administered a measure, which is scored; then, the group is given the same test and scored. To have test-retest reliability, the score must be highly similar.
- *Alternate Form* – The correlation between scores of two distributions obtained on the administration of two tests that have been constructed as having identical content.
- *Split-half Reliability* – From a single administration, a test is divided into two equal parts. A correlation is calculated for the two halves.
- *Interitem or Internal Consistency* – Assesses how well the different items measure the same issue of concept. The mean of all possible split-half reliabilities. Difficult to use without a computer. Commonly used today.
- *Scorer Reliability* – The correlation of two scores obtained by independent examiners. For example, if two judges give the same sentence to a defendant, we have reliability.

The above types of reliability are not presented in rank-order priority. Each of these categories is tied to the type of instrument being assessed. Thus, it is the instrument's characteristics that dictate the appropriate type of reliability. One commonality that each type of reliability shares is the threshold of good reliability, which is 0.8. Reliability coefficients below 0.8 are thought to have questionable reliability.

validity Accuracy of measurement in relation to what is intended to be measured.

Validity

In the study of measurement, the term **validity** refers to what a test measures, how well it does so, and that it does not measure something other than the intended measurement target. As with reliability, validity also points to the accuracy of both the measuring tool and the results of such. There are three types of measurement validity, and they are ranked from least complex to most complex.

Types of Validity

1. *Content Validity*—the systematic examination of the test content to determine whether it covers a representative sample of the behavior domain to be measured. Types: face validity and item analysis
2. *Criterion-Related Validity*—the effectiveness of a test in predicting an individual's behavior in specific situations. Types: concurrent, predictive, and synthetic validity
3. *Construct Validity*—the extent to which a test may be said to measure a theoretical construct or trait. Types: correlations with other tests, factor analysis, internal consistency, and convergent and discriminate validation

Of the three types of validity, criterion-related validity and construct validity require advanced knowledge that goes beyond the mission of this text. However, content validity is both important and immediately comprehendible at this point.

Without content validity, any statistical analysis of an independent variable would be suspicious at best and merely random at worst. Let's take an example of a test item within an instrument designed for a convicted rapist currently serving time.

All women are angry.

a. Strongly Agree
b. Agree
c. Not Sure
d. Disagree
e. Strongly Disagree

Normally, the first reaction to this item would be shock in that someone would consider including the item in a questionnaire. The item is patently offensive. An offensive item would likely discourage subjects from completing the survey or to not take the items seriously. Items that are offensive lack content validity and should be excluded from statistical analysis. The next step for content validity is to conduct a field study and generate frequency distribution for each item. On an experimental basis, let us administer the item to 100 convicted rapists and assess how effective the item is in gathering responses. Suppose the following represents our results :

[item stem] All women are angry.		
%	Label	Response
0%	a.	Strongly Agree
0%	b.	Agree
99%	c.	Unsure
0%	d.	Disagree
1%	e.	Strongly Disagree

According to the standard for assessing content validity, this item appears to be of no value. With content validity, we should see a distribution of responses. Except for one inmate, everyone replied with "Unsure." Statistically, this means that the item failed to discriminate or categorize the subject responses. Without the ability to distinguish among the subjects, an item has no value and lacks an acceptable level of content validity.

How to Use Reliability and Validity in Criminal Justice

Reliability is defined as consistency, while validity is defined as accuracy. Both are important in the assessment of instruments. Gaining knowledge regarding the application of statistics with respect to the use of instruments is critically important. For the criminal justice (or social science) professional, the actual process of developing a measure is an experience that will likely take place in one's future the field. This includes reviewing and developing instruments for research as well as policy evaluation within institutional settings.

The first step in gaining familiarity with the instruments available for research in the arena of criminal justice is to review the following publication:

Brodsky, S. L., & Smitherman, H. O. (1983). *Handbook of scales for research in crime and delinquency.* Plenum Press.

Within this text are measurement scales developed by criminal justice professionals for criminal justice professionals. Notice the date of publication. Unlike other types of scholarship, instruments tend to get better with age. Old instruments, particularly revised ones, demonstrate higher levels of reliability and validity than newer instruments. This is because older instruments are commonly subjected to continuing statistical analysis.

Statistical Notation

In statistics, there are a number of calculations that must be completed. This includes a variety of techniques and formulas. Before we introduce these procedures, it is important to understand basic statistical notation.

Scores

Observations for One Variable

In research, scores (or values) represent a host of phenomena (i.e., people, places, etc.). In statistics, scores are often represented by the letter X. For instance, if a student scored a 28 on an exam, you might see the following notation:

$$X = 28$$

Observations for Two Variables

In some instances, we may have a series of scores that represent two variables. For instance, in comparison to the previous example, this includes the additional variable of an IQ score. Consider the following:

$X = 28$ (exam score of a student) and $X = 105$ (IQ score of a student)

Observations for Three Variables

Finally, one may observe evidence of a total of three variables. For instance, this includes a student's exam score, IQ score, and the median income of each student's parents.

$X = 28$ (exam score of a student)

$X = 105$ (IQ score of a student)

$X = 25{,}000$ (median income of student's parents)

Studies often point to the possibility of an association between all variables included in a table. In other words, a student's exam score, IQ score, and the median income of their parents might be associated with each other. By including multiple variables in a table, one is likely to recognize the possibility of a relationship between variables.

In addition to the use of X, the letter N has representational significance in statistics. More specifically, the letter N is used to identify how scores are identified within a set.

Finally, the use of N will likely include a distinction on the basis of either upper or lower case. An uppercase N is used to reflect the number of values within a population. A lowercase n is used to identify the actual number of values in a sample.

Summation Notation

A common practice in statistics is the addition (or summation) of scores within a set. This includes the use of what is referred to as sigma, which is represented by the following Greek letter symbol:

$$\sum$$

In short, $\sum$ is used to reflect the total amount of scores.

There are a number of key details associated with the use of the summation symbol ($\sum$).

1. The summation symbol of $\sum$ always reveals what scores should be added. For example, $\sum X$ refers to finding the sum of all values that represent X. As an example, consider the following distribution values (78, 56, 65, 91, 82, 73, and 68). By placing the summation symbol before X, we are required to add the total amount of X in the table (78 + 56 + 65 + 91 + 82 + 73 + 68), which produces a total of 513. In this case, we would likely see the following:

$$\sum X = 513$$

2. In addition *to the addition of scores*, the summation symbol $\sum$ is also used with other mathematical operations. To determine a correct score, it is critical that certain operations are computed in a specific sequence. Commonly referred to as the **order of operations**, consider the following steps:
   a. Scores that exist within parentheses must be computed first.
   b. Scores that call for squaring must be computed secondly.
   c. From left to right, scores that involve division or multiplication should be done thirdly.
   d. Summation (addition) of scores is computed next.
   e. Finally, other addition and/or subtraction is completed.

To demonstrate the practical functions of the order of operations, consider the following three examples:

Example 1

Suppose we observed a distribution of values that included the following (3, 5, 7, 2, 9, 6, 4). To compute $\sum X$, we will add the scores together:

$$\sum X = 3 + 5 + 7 + 2 + 9 + 6 + 4 = 36$$

We will now compute $\sum X^2$. This involves the process of (1) squaring each score and (2) finding the sum of the scores. This includes the following:

$$\sum X = 9 + 25 + 49 + 4 + 81 + 36 + 16 = 220$$

Finally, we will compute $(\sum X)^2$, which includes parentheses. This requires (1) finding the sum of the scores and (2) squaring the sum.

$$(\sum X)^2 = (36)^2 = 1{,}296$$

Example 2

TABLE 2.7 **Scores Subtracted by 1**

X	$(X - 1)$
3	2
5	4
7	6
2	1
9	8
6	5
4	3

Based on the scores in Table 2.7, we will extend our knowledge by computing $\sum(X - 1)$. By performing the operation within the parenthesis, this includes the scores in the right-hand column, which reflect each score in the left-hand column subtracted by 1. Once completed, we add the scores together to compute the sum.

$$\sum(X - 1) = 2 + 4 + 6 + 1 + 8 + 5 + 3 = 29$$

TABLE 2.8 **Scores Subtracted by 1 and Squared**

X	$(X - 1)$	$(X - 1)^2$
3	2	4
5	4	16
7	6	36
2	1	1
9	8	64
6	5	25
4	3	9

Based on the information in Table 2.8, we will now extend our knowledge by computing $\sum(X-1)^2$. This involves (1) squaring the scores that exist within the parentheses and (2) adding the scores together.

$$\sum(X-1)^2 = 4 + 16 + 36 + 1 + 64 + 25 + 9 = 155$$

Example 3

Under certain circumstances, parentheses, exponents, and multiplication may not always exist. By using the same scores in the previous example, consider the following, which requires the computation of $\sum X - 1$. This includes (1) finding the sum of the scores and (2) subtracting one from the sum.

$$\sum X - 1 = 36 - 1 = 35$$

Example 4

TABLE 2.9 **Scores for Calculation**

X	Y	XY
3	1	3
5	2	10
7	1	7
2	4	8
9	2	18
6	4	24
4	3	12

Based on the information in Table 2.9, we will compute $\sum X$, $\sum Y$, $\sum X \sum Y$, and $\sum XY$. This includes the following steps:

Step 1 – To compute $\sum X$, add the values identified in the first column.

$$\sum X = 3 + 5 + 7 + 2 + 9 + 6 + 4 = 36$$

Step 2 – To compute $\sum Y$, add the values identified in the second column.

$$\sum Y = 1 + 2 + 1 + 4 + 2 + 4 + 3 = 17$$

Step 3 – To compute $\sum X \sum Y$, add the values in the first and second columns. Once completed, multiply the sums together.

$$\sum X \sum Y = 36(17) = 612$$

Step 4 – To compute $\sum XY$, multiply the scores in the first and second columns. Once completed, add the sums to determine the total number.

$$\sum XY = 3 + 10 + 7 + 8 + 18 + 24 + 12 = 82$$

Chapter Learning Assessment Questions

To gauge your understanding of the information provided, complete the following questions:

Objective 5

1. Suppose research reveals that mentoring reduces delinquency among youth in a southern state. If a similar finding occurs in a northern state, this is considered an example of ________:
   a. reliability
   b. validity
   c. both a and b
   d. none of the above

Objective 6

2. Find the $\sum X^2$ of the following scores:

X
3
2
4
1

   a. 30
   b. 10
   c. 14.5
   d. 8

Answers

1. a
2. a

Final Thoughts

Identifying and understanding the levels of measurement among variables is critical in statistics. Aside from gaining insight into the basic characteristics of variables, keep in mind that as the level of measurement increases, the amount of measurement information also increases. As mentioned previously, understanding the levels of measurement for a given variable is key in determining which type of statistical test should be used. For instance, suppose one was interested in determining if the race of an individual is related to whether they are arrested. They might begin by determining what level of measurement race is considered (which is their independent variable), which is nominal (i.e., Black, White, etc.). They would also have to determine what level of measurement constitutes arrest (their dependent variable), which is also nominal (i.e., arrested or not arrested). Since both variables are nominal, a chi-square test may be used as a means of exploring the impact of race on arrest decisions. Furthermore, both validity (accuracy) and reliability (consistency) are equally important in the interpretation of statistical results.

Discussion

You have been questioned by a local news reporting agency that gained access to police promotion data. The data reveals that White applicants are more likely to receive opportunities to serve in administrative positions (i.e., sergeant, lieutenant, etc.) than minorities. The local news representative is convinced that this is a case of racial discrimination and requests your opinion. How would you respond? If you agree, explain. If not, and more data is needed before you can decide, identify what types of data may influence your response.

Research has attempted to demonstrate the value of same-sex mentoring as a means of lowering recidivism among delinquent youth. Imagine a study that analyzed the impact of same-sex mentoring among delinquent youth in two locations. One of the locations offers mentoring; the other location offers mentoring and academic tutoring. Do you think this is an appropriate approach to analyzing the impact of mentoring? Explain.

Chapter Summary

This chapter emphasized the following general information:

Objective 1 – Variables and their use

- The importance of variables in statistics, which includes both dependent and independent variables. A variable is a characteristic of interest (persons, places, etc.).
- A dependent variable is a characteristic or phenomenon that one wishes to investigate. An independent variable is a characteristic or phenomenon that may explain the existence of the dependent variable.
- An association between variables does not always suggest causation.

Objective 2 – Categories of statistical tests and variable properties

- Exhaustive is a characteristic of a variable in which the properties of such may contain all possible values.
- Mutually exclusiveness is a property in which there is no overlap of categories within a variable.

Objective 3 – Levels of measurement

- Nominal and ordinal variables are recognized as categorical-level variables, while interval and ratio variables are considered continuous-level variables.
- A nominal variable represents an outcome that is identified in a single category (male or female).
- An ordinal variable represents an outcome that is ranked (freshman, sophomore, etc.).
- An interval variable represents a numerical outcome in which zero does not have a true point of measurement, and each value is not equal to one another.
- A ratio variable represents a numerical outcome in which zero has a true point of measurement, and each value in a distribution of numbers is equal to one another.

Objective 4 – Determining the appropriate level of measurement

- The level of measurement among variables determines the type of statistical test used.
- If given the choice, always select data that corresponds to the continuous level of measurement.

Objective 5 – Operationalization, reliability, and validity

- Levels of measurement and their corresponding differences and similarities.
- Operationalization refers to the idea of making something measurable.
- Reliability refers to consistency in relation to the use of a measurement tool or the results of a measurement.
- Validity refers to the accuracy of measurement in relation to what is intended to be measured.

Objective 6 – Introduce and review statistical notation

- Scores are represented by the letter X.
- The number of scores in a set are represented by the letter N.
- The sum of scores is represented by $\sum$.

Terms

Variable
Dependent variable
Independent variable
Levels of measurement
Nominal variable
Ordinal variable
Interval variable
Ratio variable
Parametric
Nonparametric
Reliability
Validity

Chapter Review Questions

1. Explain the difference between reliability and validity.
2. A variable is a characteristic of interest, which may include:
    a. People
    b. Places

   c. Things
   d. Ideas
   e. All the above
3. Explain the difference between independent and dependent variables.
4. What is the rule of 5?
5. Which of the following questions best represents the rule of 5?
   a. The use of technology within elementary schools may prepare students to perform well in middle school.
      a. Strongly disagree
      b. Disagree
      c. Not sure
      d. Agree
      e. Strongly agree
   b. The use of technology within elementary schools may prepare students to perform well in middle school.
      a. Strongly disagree
      b. Disagree
      c. Somewhat disagree
      d. Not sure
      e. Somewhat agree
      f. Agree
      g. Strongly agree
   c. The use of technology within elementary schools may prepare students to perform well in middle school.
      a. Disagree
      b. Somewhat disagree
      c. Somewhat sure
      d. Not sure
      e. Somewhat agree
   d. The use of technology within elementary schools may prepare students to perform well in middle school.
      a. Somewhat sure
      b. Not sure
      c. Somewhat agree
      d. Agree
      e. Strongly agree

6. The ______ variable represents an outcome that is identified in a single category.
   a. nominal
   b. ordinal
   c. interval
   d. ratio
7. The ______ variable represents an outcome that is ranked.
   a. ordinal
   b. interval
   c. ratio
   d. nominal
8. The ______ variable represents a numerical outcome in which zero has a true point of measurement.
   a. nominal
   b. ordinal
   c. interval
   d. ratio
9. The ______ variable represents a numerical outcome in which zero does not have a true point of measurement.
   a. nominal
   b. ordinal
   c. interval
   d. ratio
10. Explain the difference between parametric and nonparametric statistics.
11. A statistician desires to test a hypothesis that low levels of education are associated with low levels of crime reporting in a community. The statistician gathers data from a sample of 275 individuals over the age of 18.
    a. What is the independent variable?
    b. What is the dependent variable?
12. A researcher believes that arrests are associated with the deterrence of certain offenses in a neighborhood. He gathers data from a total of 150 arrestees.
    a. What is the independent variable?
    b. What is the dependent variable?
13. Suppose a researcher desires to test a hypothesis in which the construction of inmate spaces (i.e., dayrooms, recreation areas) is associated with the amount of violent crimes in a prison setting. The researcher gathers data from 120 recently constructed prisons in the United States.
    a. What is the independent variable?
    b. What is the dependent variable?

14. A researcher is convinced that the amount of money spent toward education by a school district is associated with lower numbers of (1) status offenses, (2) acts of juvenile delinquency, and (3) long-term school suspensions.
    a. What is the independent variable?
    b. What is the dependent variable?
15. A researcher desires to test a hypothesis that claims that police officers who engage in physical exercise, compared to officers who do not, are more likely to experience lower rates of absenteeism.
    a. What is the independent variable?
    b. What is the dependent variable?
16. Identify the level of measurement for each of the following:
    a. A suspect's race, sex, or national origin.
    b. An officer's rank.
    c. A juvenile's age.
    d. The total amount of time a defendant receives as a result of sentencing by a judge.
    e. The amount of money confiscated by police during an arrest.
    f. The classification of inmates in a prison. This includes low-risk, medium-risk, and high-risk.
    g. A district attorney's decision to file or not file charges.
17. Identify the level of measurement for each of the following:
    a. The amount of years a judge has presided in a municipal court.
    b. The type of attorney (public defender, private) a defendant has retained.
    c. Within a sample of juveniles, whether those juveniles have taken prescribed medicine designed to address aggression and oppositional defiance toward authority.
    d. Among arrestees, the number of days spent in pretrial detention.
    e. The type of degree of felony associated with an offense. An example of such may include first-degree felony robbery, second-degree felony robbery, and third-degree felony robbery.
    f. The use of force by a police officer. This includes (1) physical presence, (2) verbal response, (3) empty hand techniques, (4) nondeadly weaponry, and (5) lethal force.
    g. The number of gun control laws among states with the highest gun-related homicide rates.
18. Parametric tests are more powerful than nonparametric tests because they
    a. use more information about the data.
    b. use nominal-level data.
    c. use ordinal-level data.
    d. use both nominal and ordinal-level data.
19. A research study, which was conducted in South Carolina, reveals that truancy is associated with low self-esteem among youth. For the purpose of determining whether the results of

this study are consistent in other states, you decide to conduct a similar study in North Carolina. This is scenario is an example of:

a. Reliability
b. Validity
c. Test-Retest

20. An applicant who applied for an employment position, recently received a letter that he was not selected for the desired position. In response to such, the applicant contacted a human resources representative and asked why he was not selected for the position. The applicant was told that he received a low score in the area of intelligence. As a result of such, the applicant asked the representative to offer an explanation as to how intelligence was measured or defined. This scenario is an example of:
    a. Reliability
    b. Validity
    c. Test-Retest

Answers

1. Reliability refers to the consistency of a measuring tool and or results. Validity refers to the accuracy of the measuring tool and or results.
2. e
3. Independent variables refer to variables that influence the dependent variable. Dependent variables refer to the variables that are being influenced by the independent variable(s).
4. The use of a Likert scale in which an ordinal measure must have a minimum rank of five responses.
5. a
6. a
7. a
8. d
9. c
10. Parametric statistics use continuous-level data (interval, ratio). Nonparametric statistics use categorical-level data (nominal, ordinal).

11a. Low levels of education
11b. Low levels of crime reporting
12a. Arrests
12b. Deterrence of certain offenses
13a. Construction of inmate spaces
13b. The amount of violent crimes
14a. Amount of money
14b. Lower numbers of (1) status offenses, (2) acts of juvenile delinquency, and (3) long-term school suspensions
15a. Physical exercise
15b. Rates of absenteeism

16a. nominal
16b. ordinal
16c. interval
16d. ratio
16e. ratio
16f. ordinal
16g. nominal
17a. ratio
17b. nominal
17c. nominal
17d. ratio
17e. ordinal
17f. ordinal
17g. ratio
18. a
19. c
20. b

Matching: Place the letter of the definition with its corresponding term:

____1. Variable	a. a characteristic or phenomenon that one wishes to investigate
____2. Dependent variable	b. identifies data on the basis of their characteristics
____3. Independent variable	c. a characteristic of interest that is changeable and concrete
____4. Levels of measurement	d. may explain the existence of the dependent variable
____5. Nominal variable	e. represents an outcome that is ranked
____6. Ordinal variable	f. represents an outcome that is identified in a single category
____7. Interval variable	g. represents a numerical outcome in which zero has a true point of measurement, and each value in a distribution of numbers is equal to one another
____8. Ratio variable	h. represents a numerical outcome in which zero does not have a true point of measurement, and each value is not equal to one another
____9. Parametric	i. less likely to reveal a true difference between variables and is more likely to produce a type II error
____10. Nonparametric	j. more likely to reveal a true difference between variables and is less likely to produce a type II error
____17. Validity	k. consistency of measurement
____18. Reliability	l. accuracy or truthfulness of a measurement

Answers

1. c
2. a
3. d
4. b
5. f
6. e
7. h
8. g
9. j
10. i
17. l
18. k

Bibliography

Brodsky, S. L., & Smitherman, H. O. (1983). *Handbook of scales for research in crime and delinquency.* Plenum Press.

Cureton, E. (1978). Psychometrics. In W. Kruskal & J. Tanur (Eds.), *International encyclopedia of statistics* Free Press.

Gwent, K. (2014). *Handbook of inter-rater reliability.* Advanced Analytics.

Leatham, K. R. (2012). Problems identifying independent and dependent variables. *School Science and Mathematics, 112*(6), 349-358.

Stevens, S.S. (1946). On the theory of scales of measurement. *Science, 103*(2684), 677–680.

Chapter 2 SPSS and Workbook Questions

SPSS and Levels of Measurements

To develop a frequency display associated with the four levels of measurement using SPSS, we will focus only on two types of measurement. This includes the nominal and ordinal levels of measurement in relation to the topic of criminal justice reform.

For the nominal-level measurement, our frequency display is based on the following research question: Do you support criminal justice reform? The response options are "yes" and "no."

For the ordinal-level measurement, our frequency display is based on the following research statement and question: Most individuals believe that the specific area that currently needs the greatest amount of criminal justice reform is policing. What is your opinion regarding this statement? Response to this question includes the selection of ordinal-level options, which range from "strongly disagree" to "strongly agree."

Entry of Data—SPSS

1. Select variable view to include information associated with the variables of interest. With the data related to the nominal level, this includes the term *support*. With the ordinal-level data, this includes the term *priority*.
2. In the first row, with the nominal level data, include the term *support* under the column identified as *name*. With the ordinal-level data, repeat the same procedure by including the term *priority*.
3. In the column identified as *label*, you might choose to include a more specific description of the variable, such as *do you support CJ reform* or *the specific area that currently needs the greatest amount of criminal justice reform is policing.*
4. Select data view to include the corresponding scores in the columns identified as *support* and *priority*. Be sure to include only one score in each cell.
5. Return to variable view and include specific value labels for each variable. For the variable of *support*, this would include 0 = no support and 1 = support. For the variable *priority*, this would include 1 = strongly disagree, 2 = disagree, 3 = somewhat disagree, 4 = somewhat agree, 5 = agree, and 6 = strongly agree.

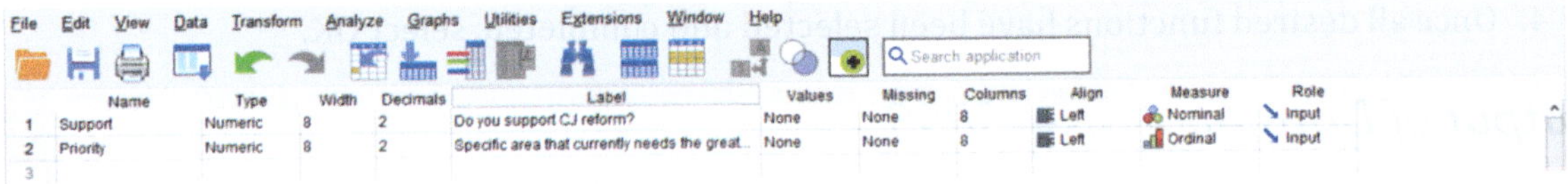

IMAGE 2.1

IMAGE 2.2

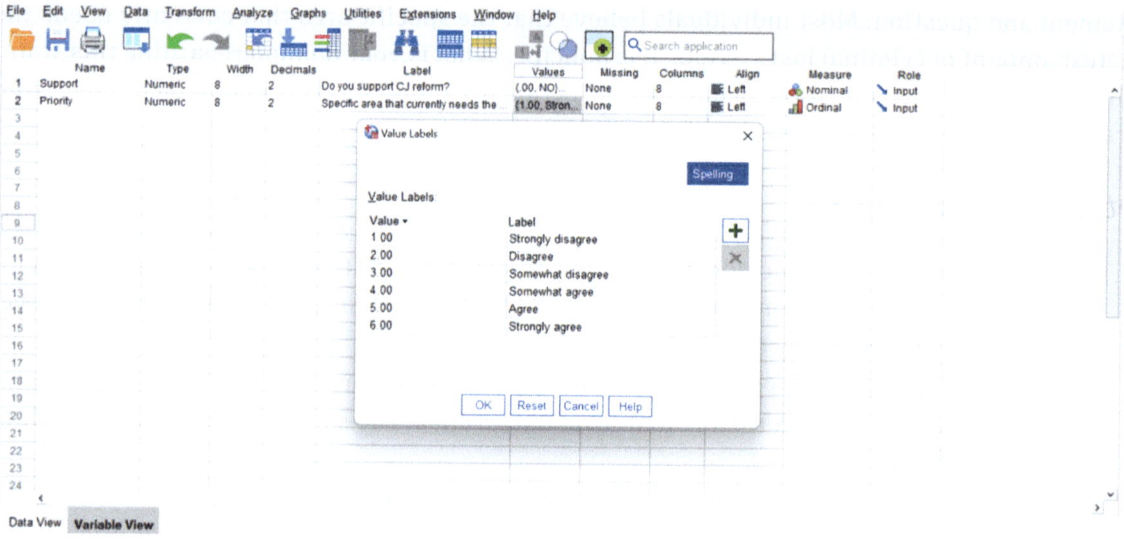

IMAGE 2.3

Analysis of Data—SPSS

1. Select *analyze*, select *descriptive statistics*, and select *frequencies*. At this point, you should see two box-shaped areas in which the variables are identified in the box on the left.
2. Select both variables and move them to the box on the right, which is identified as the variables box.
3. Below the box on the left, select the display frequencies option.
4. Once all desired functions have been selected and completed, select OK.

Output of Data Analysis—SPSS

The output of the data analysis includes a total of three tables. Table 1 includes information that identifies the name and number of each variable. It also includes the number of missing variables. Specific variable details related to the question of whether a person supports CJ reform are included in Table 2. This includes frequencies and corresponding percentages of each response. Table 3 includes the responses to whether policing should serve as the basis of priority with respect to CJ reform. This includes similar information (in comparison to Table 2), such as the frequencies and corresponding percentages of each response.

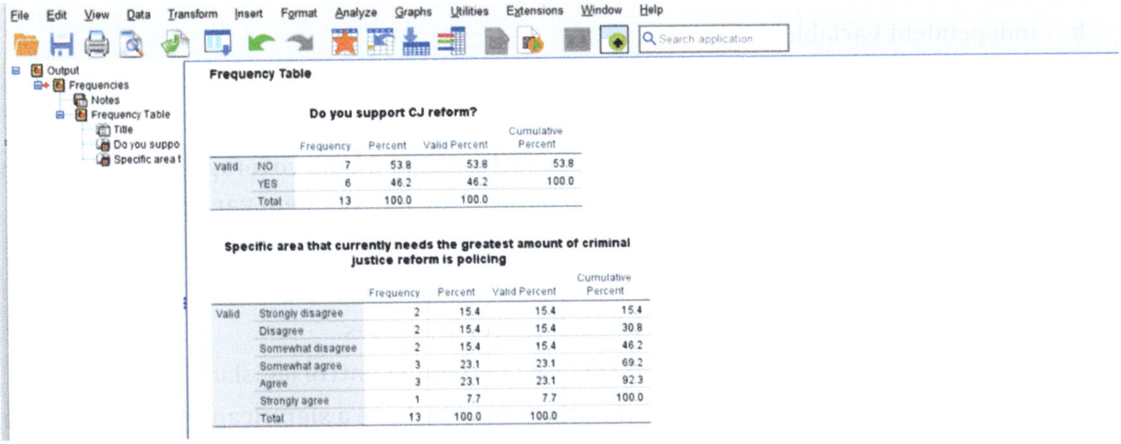

Do you support CJ reform?

		Frequency	Percent	Valid Percent	Cumulative Percent
Valid	NO	7	53.8	53.8	53.8
	YES	6	46.2	46.2	100.0
	Total	13	100.0	100.0	

Specific area that currently needs the greatest amount of criminal justice reform is policing

		Frequency	Percent	Valid Percent	Cumulative Percent
Valid	Strongly disagree	2	15.4	15.4	15.4
	Disagree	2	15.4	15.4	30.8
	Somewhat disagree	2	15.4	15.4	46.2
	Somewhat agree	3	23.1	23.1	69.2
	Agree	3	23.1	23.1	92.3
	Strongly agree	1	7.7	7.7	100.0
	Total	13	100.0	100.0	

IMAGE 2.4

Workbook Questions

Objective 1—Variables and Their Use

- The importance of variables in statistics, which includes both dependent and independent variables. A variable is a characteristic of interest (persons, places, etc.).
- A dependent variable is a characteristic or phenomenon that one wishes to investigate. An independent variable is a characteristic or phenomenon that may explain the existence of the dependent variable.
- An association between variables does not always suggest causation.

Corresponding Questions

1. A(n) ________ is a characteristic or phenomenon that one wishes to investigate.
   a. variable
   b. independent variable
   c. dependent variable
   d. a or b
2. A variable is a characteristic of interest which may include:
   a. people
   b. places
   c. things
   d. ideas
   e. all of the above

3. A(n) ______ is a characteristic or phenomenon that may explain the existence of the dependent variable.
   a. variable
   b. independent variable
   c. dependent variable
   d. a or b
4. Suppose one is interested in determining the influence of media coverage with respect to mass shootings and the development of legislation. The independent variable is
   a. the development of legislation.
   b. media coverage of mass shootings.
   c. the amount of legislation related to gun control measures.
   d. the perceptions of policymakers associated with gun control legislation.
5. Research reveals that parent-child communication may have a significant influence on the academic performance of children (Caro, 2011). The independent variable is:
   a. parent-child communication
   b. academic performance of parents
   c. academic performance of children
   d. type of parent-child communication
6. A well-known theory in criminology suggests that youth who are labeled deviant are likely to engage in delinquent behavior. The dependent variable is:
   a. the well-known theory
   b. youth who are labeled deviant
   c. youth who engage in delinquent behavior
   d. the source of the label (e.g., parent, teacher, etc.)
7. Suppose that two individuals, person A and person B, are both charged with the possession of an illegal weapon. Person A receives probation for 18 months. Person B (who has a criminal record) receives a prison sentence of 24 months. The dependent variable(s) is/are
   a. the charge of possession of an illegal weapon.
   b. the probation sentence of 18 months.
   c. the prison sentence of 24 months.
   d. both b and c

Answers

1. a
2. e
3. b
4. b
5. a
6. c
7. d

Objective 2—Categories of Statistical Tests and Variable Properties

- Exhaustive is a characteristic of a variable in which the properties of such may contain all possible values.
- Mutually exclusiveness is a property in which there is no overlap of categories within a variable.

Corresponding Questions

1. Suppose a student who is a criminal justice major has completed 10 criminal justice courses within the major. During her experience as a student in a research methods course, she is encouraged to complete a survey that includes the following question:
   As a student who desires to obtain a degree in criminal justice, you have completed a total of ______ criminal justice course(s).
   a. 1–2
   b. 3–4
   c. 5–6
   d. 7–9

   The question provided ______________.
   a. is a violation of exhaustiveness
   b. is a violation of mutually exclusiveness
   c. is a reasonable question
   d. none of the above
2. A prison inmate who has been incarcerated for over 50 years is encouraged to complete a survey that includes the following question:

   As an individual sentenced to prison, you have been incarcerated for a total of ______ years.
   a. 0–10
   b. 11–20
   c. 21–30
   d. 31–40
   e. 41–50

   The question provided ______________.
   a. is a violation of exhaustiveness
   b. is a violation of mutually exclusiveness
   c. is a reasonable question
   d. none of the above

Answers

1. a
2. a

Objective 3—Levels of Measurement

- Nominal and ordinal variables are recognized as categorical-level variables, while interval and ratio variables are considered continuous-level variables.
- A nominal variable represents an outcome that is identified in a single category (male or female).
- An ordinal variable represents an outcome that is ranked (freshman, sophomore, etc.).
- An interval variable represents a numerical outcome in which zero does not have a true point of measurement, and each value is not equal to one another.
- A ratio variable represents a numerical outcome in which zero has a true point of measurement, and each value in a distribution of numbers is equal to one another.

Corresponding Questions

1. ________ and ________ variables are recognized as categorical-level variables.
   a. Ordinal/interval
   b. Interval/ratio
   c. Nominal/ratio
   d. Nominal/ordinal
2. ________ and ________ variables are recognized as continuous-level variables.
   a. Ordinal/interval
   b. Interval/ratio
   c. Nominal/ratio
   d. Nominal/ordinal
3. A(n) ________ variable represents an outcome that is identified in a single category.
   a. Nominal
   b. Ordinal
   c. Interval
   d. Ratio
4. A researcher is interested in determining whether the gender of an adolescent plays a role in juvenile court referral decisions. In this example, *gender* is identified at which level of measurement?
   a. Nominal
   b. Ordinal
   c. Interval
   d. Ratio
5. A(n) ________ variable represents an outcome (or variable) that is ranked.
   a. nominal
   b. ordinal
   c. interval
   d. ratio

6. As part of an assignment, a graduate student is required to examine the relationship between rank and employment satisfaction within a law enforcement agency. In this example, *rank* is identified at which level of measurement?
   a. Nominal
   b. Ordinal
   c. Interval
   d. Ratio
7. A(n) ________ variable represents a numerical outcome in which zero does not have a true point of measurement, and each value is not equal to one another.
   a. nominal
   b. ordinal
   c. interval
   d. ratio
8. In selecting a dissertation topic, a doctoral-level student decides to examine the relationship between the number of times a young person interacts with gang members and engages in gang activities. In this example, the number of times a young person interacts with gang members is identified at which level of measurement?
   a. Nominal
   b. Ordinal
   c. Interval
   d. Ratio
9. A(n) ________ variable represents a numerical outcome in which zero does have a true point of measurement, and each value is equal to one another.
   a. nominal
   b. ordinal
   c. interval
   d. ratio
10. Suppose a researcher desires to examine the influence of gender with respect to arrest decisions among police in a certain jurisdiction. In this statement, *gender* best represents which of the following levels of measurement?
    a. Nominal
    b. Ordinal
    c. Interval
    d. Ratio
11. Research suggests that age is associated with the commission of certain offenses (Massoglia and Uggen, 2010). This is commonly associated with the the aging-out theory. A researcher desires to test this theory. During this process, the researcher is unable to gain access to data that identifies the ages of the individuals and decides to use the academic classification

instead. In this statement, *academic classification* best represents which of the following levels of measurement?

a. Nominal
b. Ordinal
c. Interval
d. Ratio

12. To identify the amount of annual income a law enforcement executive earns, which of the following levels of measurement is appropriate?
    a. Nominal
    b. Ordinal
    c. Interval
    d. Ratio

Answers

1. d
2. b
3. a
4. a
5. b
6. b
7. c
8. d
9. d
10. a
11. c
12. d

Objective 4—Determining the Appropriate Level of Measurement

- The level of measurement among variables determines the type of statistical test used.
- If given the choice, always select data that corresponds to the continuous level of measurement.

Corresponding Questions

1. The level of measurement among variables determines ________.
    a. the number of statistical tests used
    b. the type of statistical test used
    c. whether a statistical test will be used
    d. all of the above
2. Imagine a research project where someone is interested in determining whether race is associated with crimes committed in a specific location. The types of race in the research

include Whites and Blacks, and the types of crime are either property or violent crimes. Based on this information, which of the following represents the inappropriate use of a statistical test?

a. If race was identified as a ratio-level variable
b. If crime was identified as a ratio-level variable
c. If both race and crime were identified as ratio-level variables
d. All of the above

3. Suppose one decides to measure the relationship between the type of felony charges and sentencing. The type of felony charges may include first, second, or third degree felony. The type of sentencing may include prison, probation, or community-based treatment. Based on this information, which of the following represents the inappropriate use of a statistical test?
   a. If felony type was identified as a nominal-level variable
   b. If sentence type was identified as an ordinal-level variable
   c. If both felony and sentence type were identified as ratio-level variables
   d. All of the above
4. From a practical standpoint, the inappropriate use of a statistical test may lead to the:
   a. misuse of time
   b. misuse of effort
   c. misuse of resources
   d. all of the above
5. As a result of hearing a lecture about the importance of legislation associated with the rights of victims, four graduate students decided to collaborate for the purpose of conducting research. Their agreed topic is based on the question of whether race (IV) bears influence on the receipt of state-level victim compensation (DV). In their study, race is defined as White, Black, or Hispanic; the receipt of victim compensation is defined as either yes or no. During this process, the students disagreed over which statistical test should be used because of a disagreement based on the variables. As a result of such, select the appropriate answer:
   a. Student a believes that both variables are nominal.
   b. Student b believes that both variables are ordinal.
   c. Student c believes that the IV is nominal and the DV is ordinal.
   d. Student d believes that the IV is nominal and the DV is ratio.
6. After hearing information based on the use of treatment programs in prison settings, a researcher decides to test the effectiveness of therapy (IV) in association with recidivism (DV) among those convicted of serious violent crimes. More specifically, the effectiveness of therapy is based on the use of a Likert scale, and recidivism is based on the number of convictions. Based on the details, which of the following is true?
   a. The IV and DV are nominal variables.
   b. The IV and DV are ordinal variables.
   c. The IV is ordinal the DV is ratio.
   d. The IV is ratio, and the DV is ordinal.

Answers

1. b
2. d
3. d
4. d
5. a
6. c

Objective 5—Operationalization, Reliability, and Validity

- Levels of measurement and their corresponding differences and similarities.
- *Operationalization* refers to the idea of making something measurable.
- *Reliability* refers to consistency in relation to the use of a measurement tool or the results of a measurement.
- *Validity* refers to the accuracy of measurement in relation to what is intended to be measured.

Corresponding Questions

1. ________________ refers to the idea of making something measurable.
   a. Operationalization
   b. Reliability
   c. Validity
   d. None of the above
2. In a study by Alami et al., 2014, that measures the influence of two-parent households and self-esteem among youth, self-esteem is defined and measured by scores within a scale. This is an example of:
   a. operationalization
   b. reliability
   c. validity
   d. none of the above
3. The differential association theory argues that criminal behavior is learned as a result of association with individuals who engage in crime (Sutherland and Cressy, 1960). Within this framework, researchers have conducted studies with respect to how association is defined and measured. Examples of such include (1) how often association occurs and (2) the types of activities that occur during the association. This is an example of:
   a. operationalization
   b. reliability
   c. validity
   d. none of the above

4. _______ refers to consistency in relation to the use of a measurement tool or the results of a measurement.
   a. operationalization
   b. reliability
   c. validity
   d. none of the above
5. During an annual physical exam, an individual steps on a weight scale and discovers that they are 180 lbs. During the next 3 days, as a result of weighing themselves every morning, the individual's weight does not change. This is an example of
   a. operationalization
   b. reliability
   c. validity
   d. none of the above
6. A common approach to addressing juvenile delinquency includes what is referred to as restorative justice. A key component of restorative justice is restitution (Kuehn et al. 2014). If restitution is an effective response to delinquency in a certain area, studies related to such might be conducted in other areas where delinquency rates are increasing. This is an example of
   a. operationalization
   b. reliability
   c. validity
   d. none of the above
7. _______ refers to the accuracy of measurement in relation to what is intended to be measured.
   a. Operationalization
   b. Reliability
   c. Validity
   d. None of the above
8. While reviewing arrest offenses as reported by a law enforcement agency, you notice the offenses of shoplifting and motor vehicle theft. Based on the definition of the selected term in the previous question, the offense of shoplifting best represents the following:
   a. operationalization
   b. reliability
   c. validity
   d. none of the above

Answers

1. a
2. a
3. a
4. b
5. b
6. b
7. c
8. c

Objective 6—Statistical Notation

- Scores are represented by the letter X.
- The number of scores in a set are represented by the letter N.
- The sum of scores is represented by $\sum$.

Corresponding Questions

1. Find the $\sum X$ of the following scores:

X
4
8
3
6

a. 21
b. 20
c. 12
d. none of the above

2. Find the $\sum X^2$ of the following scores:

X
3
6
2
4

a. 60
b. 56
c. 65
d. none of the above

Answers

1. a
2. c

Bibliography

Alami, A., Khosravan, S., Moghadam, L. S., Pakravan, F., & Hosseni, F. (2014). Adolescents' self-esteem in single and two-parent families. *International Journal of Community Based Nursing and Midwifery, 2*(2), 69.

Caro, D. H. (2011). Parent-child communication and academic performance. Associations at the within-and between-country level. *Journal for Educational Research Online, 3*(2), 15–37.

Kuehn, S., Yarnell, J., & Champion, D. R. (2014). Juvenile probationers, restitution payments, and empathy: An evaluation of a restorative justice-based program in Northeastern Pennsylvania. *International Journal of Criminology and Sociology, 3*, 377–387.

Massoglia, M., & Uggen, C. (2010). Settling down and aging out: Toward an interactionist theory of desistance and the transition to adulthood. *American Journal of Sociology, 116*(2), 543–582.

Mircioiu, C., & Atkinson, J. (2017). A Comparison of Parametric and Non-Parametric Methods Applied to a Likert Scale. *Pharmacy (Basel, Switzerland), 5*(2), 26. https://doi.org/10.3390/pharmacy5020026

Schoenfeld, A. H., & Arcavi, A. (1988). On the meaning of variable. *The mathematics teacher, 81*(6), 420-427.

Sutherland, E., & Cressey, D. (1960). Principles of criminology (6th ed.). J. B. Lippincott.

Credits

CHAPTER 3

Measures of Central Tendency

The best way of increasing the [average] intelligence of scientists would be to reduce their number.
—Alexis Carrel

Objectives

1. Define and explain the use of an average and measures of central tendency.
2. Discuss and explain the types of data distribution shapes.
3. Identify and explain the use of each type of measure of central tendency.
4. Explain the relationship between measures of central tendency and levels of measurement.
5. Explain the relationship between mean/median and distribution shape.
6. Describe the use of "special needs" measures of central tendency.

Introduction—Recognition and Representation

Unfortunately, it is not uncommon for businesses to receive counterfeit currency. Once this type of fraud is identified, local law enforcement is often notified, and the investigative work begins. Because of the serious nature of this offense, a law enforcement agent must possess specialized skills useful in distinguishing counterfeit from noncounterfeit currency. Many of the officers who specialize in detecting and investigating counterfeit currency work for the Department of Treasury at the state or federal level. During training, these officers learn the details of U.S. currency. Such details include knowing the weight, texture, and color, as well as the characteristics of each type of currency. Instead of studying what is counterfeit, they focus on recognizing that which is considered noncounterfeit. In other words, they look for the *best representation* of what a noncounterfeit currency should look like. Seen this way, anything that deviates from the noncounterfeit is likely considered counterfeit. This same principled relationship is true in statistics, especially in relation to the study of data. This chapter will discuss a key aspect of data analysis commonly referred to as *determining the average*, which is often considered the best representation of a distribution of scores.

Average and Measures of Central Tendency

Average

When collecting data, it is important to understand a few basic characteristics of the data. This includes determining what single number may adequately represent the data in a distribution. This process is referred to as discovering (or calculating) the average. In short, the **average** is a value that summarizes a group of values. In other words, it is a number *that best represents a series of numbers in a distribution*. Determining the average is useful in many ways. For instance, suppose an instructor is interested in determining the average midterm grade of 200 students in a course. The calculated midterm grade average may inform the instructor of the extent to which students understand the content provided in the course. In this chapter, three types of averages, also referred to as measures of central tendency, will be discussed. **Measures of central tendency** are calculations that produce individual values that best represent the collective values in a distribution. They include the mean, median, and mode. Within a normal or bell-shaped curve, the mean, median, and mode share the same location. The decision on which type of measure of central tendency to employ is based on the characteristics of the distribution. It is also associated with the level of measurement of the data, which was introduced in the previous chapter.

average A value that summarizes a group of values, a number that best represents a series of numbers in a distribution.

measures of central tendency Calculations that produce individual values that best represent the collective values in a distribution.

Types of Data Distribution Shapes

Before we examine the various types and practical functions of central tendency, it is important to provide a visual illustration of data distribution shapes. This includes normal (or symmetric) distribution, along with positively and negatively skewed distributions.

A **normal distribution** is a set of scores in which the majority cluster in the middle and the remaining scores decrease toward the ends.

normal distribution A set of scores in which the majority cluster in the middle and the remaining scores decrease toward the ends.

For example, the following information illustrates the association between age and willingness to contact the police during the past 3 years (Figure 3.1). By observing the data, notice how the majority of scores are located in the middle of the area, and the remaining scores taper off toward the ends of the number line on both sides. Based on this information, we can assume that individuals near the age of 40 are more likely to have contacted the police in the past 6 months.

Not all distributions are normal distributions. Some distributions are skewed. This includes both positive and negative skewed distributions.

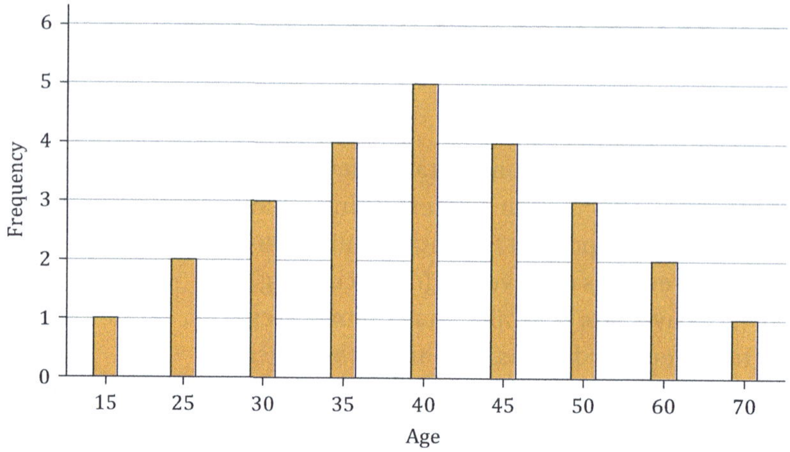

FIGURE. 3.1 Age and Frequency of Contacting the Police, 36 Months

positive skewed distribution A set of scores in which a cluster of scores appears on the left-hand side of a distribution.

negative skewed distribution A set of scores in which a cluster of scores appears on the right-hand side of the distribution.

A **positive skewed distribution is a set of** scores in which a cluster of scores appears on the left-hand side of a distribution.

For instance, Figure 3.2 shows the relationship between age and offensive behavior within a 6-month period. The overall shape of the distribution provides a trend in which scores are clustered to the left. The remaining scores taper off towards the right of the distribution of scores. Based on this information, one can assume that misdemeanor behavior within the past 6 months is most likely to occur among individuals near the age of 15.

A **negative skewed distribution:** A set of scores in which a cluster of scores appears on the right-hand side of the distribution.

Figure 3.3 shows the relationship between age among those individuals who contacted the police for noise disturbances within a certain time frame. By examining the distribution of data, we can see that the cluster of scores is located to the far right. From this, we can infer that individuals who are nearly 70 years of age are most likely to report instances of noise disturbances to the police in the past 18 months.

By recognizing various types of data distributions, one is able to understand the value of visual content. Instead of relying upon written information, identifying the shapes of distribution offers a clear and concise snap-shot. With this type of information, one is able to determine patterns which not only shape perceptions but also drive decisions. We will discuss additional information regarding the power and practicality of visual content in chapter.

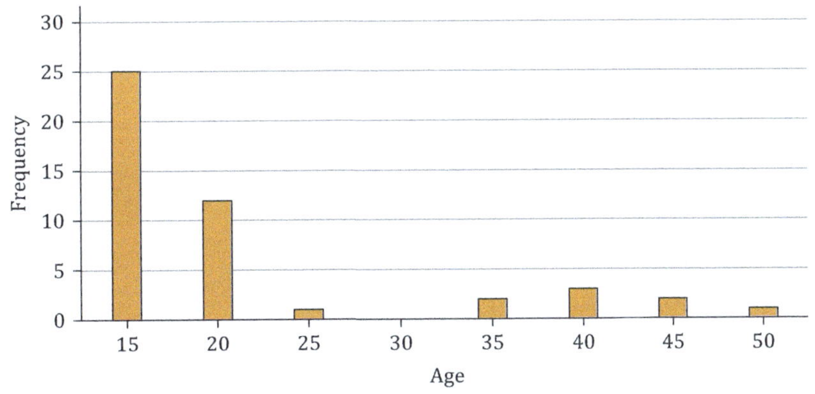

FIGURE. 3.2 Age and Frequency of Misdemeanor Assaults

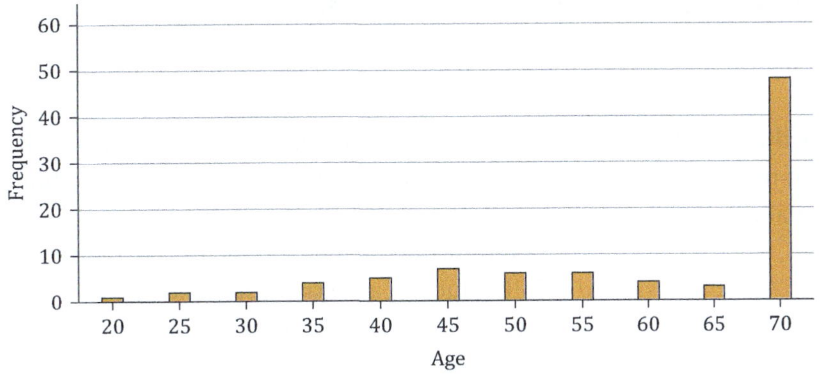

FIGURE 3.3 Age and Frequency of Contacting the Police, 18 Months

Chapter Learning Assessment Questions

To gauge your understanding of the information provided, complete the following questions:

Objective 1

1. If a college professor is interested in determining how well his students performed on their first exam during the semester, the professor may likely decide to perform a calculation that is referred to as a(n) ________.
   a. average
   b. normal distribution
   c. a positive skewed distribution
   d. a negative skewed distribution

Objective 2

2. Which of the following represents the type of distribution in which the cluster of scores appears on the right-hand side of a distribution scale:
   a. normal distribution
   b. positive skewed distribution
   c. negative skewed distribution
   d. none of the above

Answers

1. a
2. c

Types of Measures of Central Tendency

Mean

The **mean** is a value that represents the average of all values in a distribution. It cannot be used with any level of measurement (like the mode) or ordinal data (like the median). It can only be used with interval or ratio data.

mean A value that represents the average of all values in a distribution.

Computing the mean involves two steps: (1) finding the sum of all values in a distribution and (2) dividing the sum by the number of values in a distribution.

$$\bar{x} = \frac{\Sigma x}{n},$$

where

$\bar{x}$ = the sample mean
Σ = the summation (addition) of values
x = value (in a distribution)
n = size of the sample

Identified in Table 3.1 is the police response time (in minutes) to 911 calls in five citywide areas.

TABLE 3.1 **Police Response Times to 911 Calls**

Location of 911 Calls	Response Time (Minutes)
North	12
South	7
East	7.5
West	10
Southwest	15

To compute the mean police response time, perform the following steps:
Formula for computing the mean:

$$\bar{x} = \frac{\Sigma x}{n}$$

Include the individual values (i.e., response times) and sample size (number of values)

$$\bar{x} = \frac{12 + 7 + 7.5 + 10 + 15}{5}$$

By finding the sum of the values, divide the sum by the sample size

$$\bar{x} = \frac{51.5}{5}$$

The computed mean

$$\bar{x} = 10.3$$

Based on the response times of five areas in the city, the mean police response time is 10.3 minutes.

In our final example, the number of youth who were exonerated, along with the amount of time served in prison, are provided below.

To compute the mean years of youth incarceration, calculate the following:

$$\bar{x} = \frac{\Sigma x}{n} = \frac{3 + 2.5 + 2 + 4 + 6 + 6 + 5}{7} = \frac{28.5}{7} = 4.07$$

Based on the data provided, the mean years of incarceration among youth exonerees is 4.07 years.

In general, most distributions are bell-shaped or normally distributed, and using the mean as a measure of central tendency is appropriate. However, if the distribution *is not* normally distributed, the mean is not appropriate *and* can easily distort the generalizations and inferences that will be made regarding the subjects within the sample.

The Various Functions of the Mean

Compared to the median and the mode, the mean offers a variety of functions and characteristics in statistics. For this reason, we will discuss a few significant tasks related to the mean one may likely experience. This includes (1) identifying the mean as a division of the total amount of scores in an equal manner and (2) the use and significance of the weighted mean.

Dividing the Total Amount of Scores in an Equal Manner

There are numerous ways to develop an understanding of the mean. For instance, one may think of the mean as the amount each individual score receives after the total amount is divided equally among individuals.

- For instance, suppose a group of five children ($n = 5$) are provided a box of stickers. As the children open the box, they discover that the box includes a total of 60 stickers ($\Sigma x = 60$).

- If the children divide the number of stickers among themselves in an equal manner, each child should receive a total of 12 stickers. This process is reflective of the following:
- $\Sigma x = 60/5 = 12$.

Based on the following example, a researcher is able to determine the answer to a problem in which only limited details are provided.

- For example, suppose the children decide to sell their stickers to other children in school. If they earn an average of $2 per child, what is the total amount of money earned by the group?
- Even though we are not aware of the exact amount each child has earned, we are aware that if each child pooled their money together and distributed the amount equally, the average amount each child would get would be $2.
- For each child to receive $2, the total must be 5 ($2) = $10. To check this answer, we are able to use the following formula:
- $\Sigma x = 10/5 = 2$.

By thinking of the mean as the total amount of scores being divided equally among each score in a distribution, one is capable of computing various aspects of the mean (i.e., sample size, total amount of items, etc.) that might be missing. This ability is beneficial when verifying the accuracy of statistics when various types of data averages are reported.

Weighted Mean

There may be instances where computing the overall mean involves more than one sample. For instance, as indicated in Table 3.2, suppose we have two samples of data which include the following:

TABLE 3.2 **Data of Two Different Samples**

Sample 1	Sample 2
$n_1 = 4$	$n_2 = 6$
$M = 8$	$M = 5$

To compute the overall mean, we must

1. compute the overall sum of the scores from both samples (Σx),
2. find the total number of scores from each sample (n), and
3. divide the overall sum of the scores by the total number of the scores.

The formula is based on the following:

$$M = \frac{\Sigma x}{n} = \frac{\Sigma x_1 + \Sigma x_2}{n_1 + n_2}$$

Based on the data identified in Table 3.3, consider the following steps:

Finding the overall number of scores involves adding the number of scores in the first sample with the scores in the second sample. This includes 4 + 6 = 10. In a similar manner, finding the overall sum of the scores involves adding the sum of scores from the first sample to the sum of scores from the second sample. This requires 32 + 30 = 62. The final step includes dividing the overall sum of scores (62) by the total number of scores (10), which produces the overall mean score of 6.2.

TABLE 3.3 **Data of Two Different Samples With Combined Data**

Sample 1	Sample 2	Combined Sample
$n_1 = 4$	$n_2 = 6$	$n = 10$
$\Sigma x = 32$	$\Sigma x = 30$	$\Sigma x = 62$
$M_1 = 8$	$M_2 = 5$	$M = 6.2$

Notice that computing the overall mean did not involve simply adding the means of each sample and dividing the sum by 2. This is because each sample has a different number of scores. In essence, this distinction is referred to as the process of computing the weighted mean.

Median

The **median** is a value that represents a midpoint of the values in a distribution. Unlike the mode, which can be used with any level of measurement, the median can only be used with ordinal, interval, or ratio data. The median is used with data that is ranked. When referring to a midpoint of measurement, the median reflects the value that falls 50% below it and 50% above it. In other words, think of the median as having an equal number of values on either side. Computing the median involves two steps: (1) listing the values in a distribution from lowest to highest (or highest to lowest) and (2) locating the value that falls in the middle of the distribution.

median A value that represents a midpoint of the values in a distribution.

Consider the following example:

Suppose the following reflects the property crime rate per 100,000 residents in 5 states.

Listed below are the distribution of values in a rank-ordered fashion:

From least to greatest				
1.2	1.8	2.3	3.1	4.5
		or		
From greatest to least				
4.5	3.1	2.3	1.8	1.2

As indicated above, 2.3 is the value that is in the middle of both distributions; thus, 2.3 represents the median. Notice that the total number of values in the distribution is an odd number. Under these conditions, identifying the median involves merely counting the number of values on either side of a specific value. However, what steps should be used in finding the median with a distribution that has an *even* number of values?

Table 3.4 provides the property crime rate per 100,000 residents in 6 states.

TABLE 3.4 **Property Crime Rates of Six States**

State	Property Crimes per 100,000 Residents
Alabama	1.8
Mississippi	1.2
Louisiana	2.3
Georgia	3.1
Florida	3.3
Texas	4.5

Listed below are the distribution of values in a rank-ordered fashion:

From least to greatest					
1.2	1.8	2.3	3.1	3.3	4.5
		or			
From greatest to least					
4.5	3.3	3.1	2.3	1.8	1.2

With a total of six values (an even number), there are two values that are identified as "middle" scores (2.3 and 3.1). Computing the median involves finding the sum of the two values and dividing the sum by 2.

$$2.3 + 3.1 = 5.4$$
$$5.4 / 2 = 2.7$$

Among the 6 states, the median property crime rate is 2.7 per 100,000 residents.

Value of the Median

When attempting to find the average, some may prefer to use the median as opposed to the mean. The reason for this preference is that the median is not sensitive to (or influenced by) extreme scores, which are commonly referred to as **outliers**. Consider the following example identified in Table 3.5.

Notice the values in Table 3.5 and how five of the values tend to be in the same general area or range (between 120 and 130). There is also a value (45.34) that seems to be out of place in comparison to the other five values.

TABLE 3.5 **DWI Arrests in Six Texas Cities**

Cities in Texas	DWI Arrests per 10,000 Residents
Austin	125.10
Dallas	128.34
Houston	130.10
San Antonio	122.66
Fort Worth	127.56
El Paso	45.34

To demonstrate the difference between computing the median and the mean, let's begin by computing the median, which includes the rank-ordered values:

45.34	122.66	125.10	127.56	128.34	130.10

By adding the two values in the middle (125.10 + 127.56 = 252.66) and dividing the sum by 2 (252.66 / 2 = 126.33), the median DWI arrest per 10,000 residents is 126.33.

Now, let's compute the mean.

This includes adding the values (45.34 + 122.66 + 125.10 + 127.56 + 128.34 + 130.10 = 679.10) and dividing the sum by the number of values in the distribution (679.10 / 6 = 113.18). The mean DWI arrest per 10,000 residents is 113.18.

Notice the differences between the median and the mean (126.33 and 113.18), a difference of 13.15. Which of the two values best represents the total number of values in Table 3.3? The value derived from the median (126.33) is more representative in that it lies more closely in relation to the other values in the table. On the other hand, the value of 113.18, derived from computing the mean, is a value that does not lie closely to the other values. It represents a value that is sensitive to the influence of the extreme score (outlier) of 45.34. In this example, the median is preferred in that its value is not influenced by the outlier in comparison to the mean.

Mode

The **mode** is a value (or category) that occurs most frequently in a distribution. There are circumstances in which two categories have the highest frequencies. Table 3.6 identifies five categories of delinquency in which more than one category has the highest frequency (e.g., individual and other). This is referred to as a bimodal as opposed to a single mode. Finally, the mode is also identified using continuous data (e.g., interval or ratio level).

mode A value (or category) that occurs most frequently in a distribution.

TABLE 3.6 **Frequency of Delinquency Factors**

Explanations of Delinquency	Frequency
Community Factors	15
Family Factors	18
Peer Association Factors	25
Individual Factors	26
Other	26

The Relationship Between Measures of Central Tendency and Levels of Measurement

As identified in Chapter 2, understanding the characteristics of data includes knowledge of their respective levels of measurement. To that end, we are able to recognize how the levels of measurement are associated with the type of average that corresponds to it. More specifically, consider the following:

- The mode is used with nominal data.
- The median is used with ordinal, interval, and ratio-level data.
- The mean is used with interval and ratio-level data.

For a practical understanding of the relationship between measures of central tendency and levels of measurement, consider the following data set in which all three types of measures of central tendency will be used to determine the average.

X
4
3
6
5
9
2
3

The mode:

X
4
3
6
5
9
2
3

In order to locate the mode, we determine *which score appears the most* in the distribution. Since 3 is listed twice, the value of 3 is considered the mode.

The median:

X	X (Least to Greatest)	X (Greatest to Least)
4	2	9
3	3	6

X	X (Least to Greatest)	X (Greatest to Least)
6	3	5
5	**4**	**4**
9	5	3
2	6	3
3	9	2

To calculate the median, we must first place the values in numerical order. This may include from least to greatest or from greatest to least. Once this is complete, we identify which score has the same number of values on either side. When observing both columns, we are able to recognize that the individual value that has the same number of values above and below (which includes a total of 3 values) is 4. Thus, the median for the distribution is 4.

The mean:

X
4
3
6
5
9
2
3

Finally, to compute the mean, we find the sum of all the values in the distribution. This includes a sum of 32. Once the sum has been computed, we divide the sum by the number of scores (7) in the distribution. This gives us a mean of 4.57. By finding the average of the same distribution by using each of the three types of averages, we are now able to recognize the different results. This includes 3 (mode), 4 (median), and 4.57 (mean).

Chapter Learning Assessment Questions

To gauge your understanding of the information provided, complete the following questions:

Objective 3

1. If a distribution of scores has an outlier, which of the following measures of central tendency should be used?
   a. The mean
   b. The median
   c. The mode
   d. None of the above

Objective 4

2. Which of the following is used with ranked data?
   a. The mean
   b. The median
   c. The mode
   d. None of the above

Answers

1. b
2. b

The Relationship Between Mean/Median and Distribution Shape

In general, the mode offers more options in relation to levels of measurement compared to the mean. This includes four different types of measurement. However, both the median (which uses three different types of measurement) and mean (which uses two types of measurement) offer more advanced-level differences through the use and analysis of variables. As mentioned previously, there are a number of significant aspects that distinguish the mean and the median. For instance, in comparison to the median, the mean is sensitive to extreme scores, which may lead to misleading results. Furthermore, both the mean and median can be used to determine if data distributions are normal or skewed. To that end, it is customary to include both types of data characteristics when reporting averages in association with data.

Finally, as alluded to earlier, a normal distribution reflects a visual illustration where the median and mean are located in the same position. If the mean is located to the right of the median, we have a positively skewed distribution. However, if the mean is located to the left of the median, we have a negatively skewed distribution.

Special Needs Measures of Central Tendency

Let's say that the kitchen sink faucet is loose. It must be tightened. There are two options. The first is to hire a plumber at $250 to do a 3-minute job or buy the highly specialized "basin wrench" for approximately $20 and tighten the nut yourself. In the world of tools, the only tool that can successfully tighten a nut under a kitchen sink is the basin wrench. Once you buy a basin wrench, it is highly likely that you will never use it again. Like the basin wrench, there are measures of central tendency that are the best and can only be employed with a particular data set. Like the basin wrench, you may only use the calculations once in a lifetime. The following is an introduction to the "basin wrench" measures of central tendency.

When attempting to identify the measure of central tendency with a small sample, there are two commonly used options. They are the "trimmed mean" and the "winsor mean." Both measures of central tendencies were developed for interval data within small samples that include an outlier. Prior to calculating the trimmed or winsor mean, it is necessary to closely inspect the outlier with the question, "Is the outlier the result of a typographical error?" These errors must be addressed prior to pursuing any calculations. Although there are complex mathematical theories that support their use (Weisberg, 1992), we will reduce both techniques to their simplest form. Within criminal justice, they are likely to be useful tools for those incarcerated in prisons and jails.

Trimmed Mean

The most popular use of the trimmed mean is at the Olympic gymnastics games. To ensure the reduction of bias by a judge to support their country winning a medal and to eliminate the problem of outliers, the highest and lowest data points are removed from the distribution prior to calculating the mean. This is a two-step process:

1. Arrange the data points horizontally from lowest to highest.
2. Identify the two data points that are located at the beginning and the end and remove them.
3. Calculate the mean.

The following are frequencies of violent action by inmates at a specified cell block. Notice that this data has been ranked on a horizontal axis from lowest to highest, and we have formatted the two values at the ends of the sequence in bold:

0 3 4 5 5 5 5 6 8 8 **21**

Once the values at the opposite ends have been removed, we calculate the mean of data:

$$\frac{3\ 4\ 5\ 5\ 5\ 5\ 6\ 8\ 8}{9} = 5.4$$

When comparing the averages of one cell block to another, all cell blocks would be required to use the identical trimmed mean process.

trimmed mean Requires the removal of outliers within a small distribution.

Winsor Mean

The winsor mean was first designed by Charles P. Winsor circa 1946. Winsor was distressed when he realized that many scientists who find an outlier (and not the result of a typographical error) reject the outlier from the data analysis. Winsor conjected that removing the outlier was mathematically problematic. Thus, he proposed the following steps:

1. Arrange the data points horizontally, from lowest to highest.
2. Identify the outlier, replace it with the next number, and add 1.
3. Calculate the mean.

Employ the same cell block data from above; here is an illustration. We set the outlier in bold and replaced it with the number to the left plus 1:

0 3 4 5 5 5 5 6 8 8 **21**

We take the 8 because it is housed next to the outlier and add 1 (or $8 + 1 = 9$), then we calculate the mean.

$$\frac{0\ 3\ 4\ 5\ 5\ 5\ 5\ 6\ 8\ 8\ 9}{11} = 5.3$$

winsor mean Requires replacing an outlier with the next number within a small distribution and adding 1 to that number.

Both the trimmed mean and the winsor mean produce very close answers.

The last and final two "basin wretch" measures of central tendency are the geometric mean and the harmonic mean. Unlike the trimmed and winsor means, the geometric and harmonic mean were designed for large data sets and not small ones.

Geometric Mean

Like the trimmed and winsor means, the geometric mean is highly specialized. The geometric mean is limited to calculating the central tendency for rates.

Within the banking industry and in accounting, the geometric mean is used daily. In fact, there are statutory mandates to use the geometric mean when calculating the average interest rate. Consider the formula:

$$\sqrt[n]{x_1 \times x_2 \times x_3 \ldots \times x_n}$$

We take all the data points and multiply them. That will be a large number, and with large samples, it will not be possible to calculate using a handheld calculator.

For making a prediction for a future *rate*, use the arithmetic mean—that is, the sum of all the rates—and then divide by the n (the total number of rates). Here the arithmetic mean offers the best estimate of a future rate. When dealing with interest rates, that change in value because of the natural order of compounding interest rates, use the geometric mean. How often do we calculate the geometric mean for criminal justice data? Perhaps once in a lifetime. From a practical standpoint, the geometric mean might be used to investigate claims of financial fraud, often considered a type of white-collar crime.

geometric mean Used to calculate the central tendency for rates.

Harmonic Mean

The harmonic mean dovetails on the trimmed or winsor mean. Using the harmonic mean is most appropriate when the set of numbers contains outliers that might skew the result. The trimmed or winsor mean is used for small samples, whereas the harmonic mean is used for large samples. The harmonic mean is a powerful measure of central tendency with a large distribution with a larger number of outliers.

harmonic mean Used for large distributions.

Two caveats:

1. With a small number of outliers, its measure of central tendency will be grossly distorted. Thus, only use the harmonic mean with a large sample with a large number of outliers.
2. The harmonic mean cannot be used on a data set consisting of negative numbers or zeros.

It is unlikely that the harmonic mean will be used with criminal justice data. However, if you have a large sample with a large number of outliers, the harmonic mean is the best measure of central tendency. Following is the formula:

$$n \,/\, \left[\left(1 / x^1\right) + \left(1 / x^2\right) + \left(1 / x^3\right) + \ldots + \left(1 / xn\right)\right]$$

Chapter Learning Assessment Questions

To gauge your understanding of the information provided, complete the following questions:

Objective 5

1. In a distribution of data, if the mean is located to the right of the median, this is referred to as which of the following?
   a. Normal distribution
   b. Positive skewed distribution
   c. Negative skewed distribution
   d. None of the above

Objective 6

2. Utilizing the trimmed mean approach, the mean of the following data set is ______.
   a. 4.6
   b. 5.1
   c. 4.4
   d. 5.11

X
2
12
3
4
3
7
5

Answers

1. b
2. c

Final Thoughts

Identifying the best representative characteristics (i.e., average) of a distribution of values is an essential foundation for understanding and using statistics. As identified in this chapter, the one-size-fits-all approach does not exist. Selecting the appropriate measure (e.g., mean, median, mode) is based on the level of measurement associated with the value of interest.

Discussion

During the final stage of the interview process with a local law enforcement agency, you have been given the option of discussing your potential salary. In the discussion, the human resources manager offers you a choice of receiving only one of two documents that identify your potential salary. Document (A) provides the median salary amount, and document (B) provides the mean salary amount with respect to your position. Which document would you select? Explain.

Chapter Summary

This chapter emphasized the following general information:

Objective 1 – The use of an average and measures of central tendency

- An average is a value that summarizes or best represents a group of values.
- Measures of central tendency are calculations that produce individual values that best represent the collective values in a distribution.

Objective 2 – Types of data distribution shapes

- A normal distribution is a set of scores in which the majority clusters in the middle, and the remaining scores decrease toward the ends.
- A positive skewed distribution is a set of scores in which the cluster of such appears on the left-hand side of a distribution.
- A negative skewed distribution is a set of scores in which the cluster of such appears on the right-hand side of a distribution.

Objective 3 – The use of each type of measure of central tendency

- The mean is a value that represents the arithmetic average of all values in a distribution.
- The median is a value that represents a midpoint of all values in a distribution.
- An outlier is an extreme value (or values) in a distribution.
- The mode is a value (or category) that occurs most frequently in a distribution.

Objective 4 – The relationship between measures of central tendency and levels of measurement

- The mode is used with nominal data.
- The median is used with ordinal, interval, and ratio-level data.
- The mean is used with interval and ratio-level data.

Objective 5 – The relationship between mean/median and distribution shape

- A normal distribution includes a visual illustration where the mean and median are located in the same position.
- A positively skewed distribution includes a visual illustration where the mean is located to the right of the median.
- A negatively skewed distribution includes a visual illustration where the mean is located to the left of the median.

Objective 6 – The use of "special needs" measures of central tendency

- The trimmed mean requires the removal of outliers within a small distribution.
- The winsor mean requires replacing an outlier with the next number within a small distribution and adding 1 to that number.
- The geometric mean is used to calculate the central tendency for rates.
- The harmonic mean is similar to the mean/winsor mean but is used for large distributions.

Terms

Average
Measures of central tendency
Mean
Median
Mode
Outlier
Trimmed mean
Harmonic mean
Winsor mean
Geometric mean

Chapter Review Questions

1. This measure of central tendency represents the arithmetic average of all values in a distribution:
    a. Outlier
    b. Mode
    c. Median
    d. Mean
2. This measure of central tendency represents a midpoint of all values in a distribution:
    a. Outlier
    b. Mode
    c. Median
    d. Mean
3. This measure of central tendency represents a value (or category) that occurs most frequently in a distribution:
    a. Outlier
    b. Mode
    c. Median
    d. Mean
4. This term represents an extreme value (or values) in a distribution:
    a. Outlier
    b. Mode
    c. Median
    d. Mean
5. This type of mean, which is used in a small distribution, includes the removal of outliers:
    a. Trimmed Mean
    b. Winsor Mean
    c. Geometric Mean
    d. Harmonic Mean
6. This type of mean, which is used in a small distribution, requires replacing an outlier with the next number within a small distribution and adding 1 to that number:
    a. Trimmed Mean
    b. Winsor Mean
    c. Geometric Mean
    d. Harmonic Mean
7. This type of mean is used to calculate rates:
    a. Trimmed Mean
    b. Winsor Mean

c. Geometric Mean
d. Harmonic Mean

8. This type of mean, similar to the trimmed/winsor means, is used with large distributions:
   a. Trimmed Mean
   b. Winsor Mean
   c. Geometric Mean
   d. Harmonic Mean
9. When the mean is marked less than the median, this is referred to as a
   a. positively skewed distribution.
   b. negatively skewed distribution.
   c. normal distribution.
10. When the mean is marked greater than the median, this is referred to as a
    a. positively skewed distribution.
    b. negatively skewed distribution.
    c. normal distribution.
11. When the mean and the median are equal, this is referred to as a
    a. positively skewed distribution.
    b. negatively skewed distribution.
    c. normal distribution.
12. Compute the mean, median, and mode for the following five sets of values, which represent the number of self-reported property crimes among youth:

Student 1	Student 2	Student 3	Student 4	Student 5
3	4	2	4	5
5	3	3	5	3
2	6	6	1	1
1	4	2	3	7
0	3	5	7	3

13. Compute the mean, median, and mode for each of the following three sets of values. These values represent the number of inmates in 10 detention facilities in 3 counties:

County 1	County 2	County 3
78	42	45
74	44	55
57	67	76
55	80	73
67	76	47
55	59	53
45	65	65
68	61	69
72	44	57
70	54	48

14. Listed below are the types and number of legal defenses used in court by attorneys between 2017 and 2020. Compute the mean for each type of defense.

Legal Defense	2017	2018	2019	2020
Insanity	3	1	0	1
Duress	2	5	7	8
Mistake	5	4	10	9
Diminished responsibility	3	6	5	8
Intoxication	2	8	9	6
Immaturity	4	4	2	1
Entrapment	1	5	4	1

15. Compute the mean and median for the following salaries and explain their differences:

$125,000
$78,500
$69,250
$74,500
$72,340
$75,540
$77,500

16. Among students enrolled in evening classes, a criminologist conducted a study to gauge student perceptions of lighting at a college campus. Through the use of a survey, 10 students provided numerical feedback by indicating the number of additional lights needed. Compute the mean, median, and mode of the responses provided below:

Student 1	3
Student 2	4
Student 3	4
Student 4	5
Student 5	3
Student 6	5
Student 7	3
Student 8	4
Student 9	5
Student 10	3

17. Four college students enrolled in an advanced-level criminology course were required to view 10 political debates among 2 candidates during the semester. Each candidate stated their opinions regarding the factors associated with crime, as well as possible solutions (Hameleers, 2022). As a result of this process, each student was required to provide feedback, which consisted of identifying each moment the candidate shared an inaccurate crime statistic. Compute the mean, median, and mode of their responses provided below:

Student 1	Student 2	Student 3	Student 4
2	5	3	4
3	3	5	5
4	4	5	5
3	4	5	3
4	5	2	4
5	3	5	5
2	6	3	4
3	3	5	6
5	2	2	4
3	3	3	3

18. The following represents a total of seven prisons in a regional area.

Prison	Security Level	Number of Programs
Glendale	Medium	3
Foster	Maximum	2
Arial Bay	Medium	4
Hempstead	Minimum	4
Aboriginie	Minimum	5
Hilsom	Medium	5
Bural Hills	Minimum	4
Parkland	Minimum	4
Hightower	Maximum	2
Flosom	Maximum	3

Based on the information provided, compute the following:

- Identify the median security level. (Hint – to find the average, one is encouraged to code the categories prior calculation. Examples of such include Minimum = 1, Medium = 2, etc.)
- Identify the mean number of programs.

19. The following represents a total of 10 youths who were taken into custody because of the commission of status offenses (based on their prior number of offenses) and might be eligible for participation in a diversion program.

Offense	Sex	Offense History (Number)	Eligibility for Diversion
Curfew violation	M	3	No
Underage use of alcohol	M	2	Yes
Truancy	F	1	Yes
Running away from home	F	1	Yes
Truancy	M	4	No
Underage use of alcohol	F	2	No
Running away from home	F	1	Yes

Offense	Sex	Offense History (Number)	Eligibility for Diversion
Running away from home	F	1	Yes
Curfew violation	M	1	Yes
Curfew violation	M	3	No

Based on the information provided, compute the mean number of

- males and females (Hint – to find the average, one is encouraged to code the categories prior calculation. Examples of such include Female = 1, Male = 2)
- eligibility for diversion.

20. The following represents data reported by a law enforcement agency in a southern state. Data includes offense type, sex, race, detention decision, and days spent in detention.

Offense	Sex	Race	Detained	Number of Days Detained
Shoplifting	F	B	Y	4
Theft	M	W	N	0
Auto-Theft	M	B	Y	4
Battery	M	B	Y	2
Assault	F	H	Y	3
Vandalism	M	W	N	0
Trespassing	F	B	Y	4
Assault	M	W	N	0
Assault	F	B	N	0
Theft	F	H	Y	5

Based on the information provided, compute the mean number of

- males and females,
- race (for each category), and
- detention status (for each category).

21. The following represents information provided by a nonprofit youth advocacy group. The group is convinced that Black youth are more likely to experience a higher number of hours of detention compared to White and Hispanic youth (Shook and Goodkind, 2009). Data includes the name of the youth, race, offense type, and number of hours spent in detention.

Name	Race	Offense Type	Number of Hours
J. Fox	B	Status	12
L. Williams	W	Delinquency	4
S. McDade	B	Delinquency	3
L. Holcombe	H	Delinquency	4
J. Flemming	W	Status	2
J. Juarez	H	Delinquency	3

Name	Race	Offense Type	Number of Hours
J. Flores	H	Status	4
B. Gibson	B	Delinquency	3
N. Bridgeway	W	Status	3

Based on the information provided, compute the mean based on the following:

- Race

Compute the mean and median based on the hours detained.

Explain why the median is preferred in comparison to the mean.

22. The following represents the amount of annual expenses for housing inmates in a minimum-security prison in a southern state. This includes data for 10 years.

Year	Amount
2001	$36,045
2002	$34,079
2003	$35,508
2004	$36,005
2005	$37,508
2006	$36,871
2007	$33,892
2008	$43,124
2009	$35,712
2010	$34,391

Based on the information provided,

- determine which level of measurement is reflected (nominal, ordinal, interval, ratio), and
- determine the measure of central tendency you would use to determine the average based on your previous response.

23. The following data reflects the annual violent victimization rate among individuals on the basis of age.

Age	Rate per 1000
12–18	19.3
19–21	18.7
22–25	18.2
26–31	16.8
32–40	14.1
41–50	8.3
51–60	5.8
61–70	4.1
71+	2.8

Based on the information provided,

- use the median to determine the victimization rate, and
- use the mean to determine the victimization rate.

Answers

1. d
2. c
3. b
4. a
5. a
6. b
7. c
8. d
9. b
10. a
11. c
12.

	Student 1	Student 2	Student 3	Student 4	Student 5
Mean	2.2	4	3.6	4	3.8
Median	2	4	3	4	3
Mode	NA	4	2	NA	3

13.

	County 1	County 2	County 3
Mean	64.1	59.2	58.8
Median	67.5	60	56
Mode	55	44	NA

14.

Legal Defense	2017	2018	2019	2020	Mean
Insanity	3	1	0	1	1.25
Duress	2	5	7	8	5.5
Mistake	5	4	10	9	7
Diminished responsibility	3	6	5	8	5.5
Intoxication	2	8	9	6	6.25
Immaturity	4	4	2	1	2.75
Entrapment	1	5	4	1	2.75

15.

125,000	125,000
78,500	78,500
69,250	69,250
74,500	74,500
72,340	72,340
75,540	75,540
77,500	77,500
75,540	75,540
81,021.25 (Mean)	75,540 (Median)

The difference between the mean and median is based on the influence of the outlier (125,000). Compared to the mean, the median provides a more accurate average of the salaries provided.

16.

Student	Number of Additional Lights Needed
Student 1	3
Student 2	4
Student 3	4
Student 4	5
Student 5	3
Student 6	5
Student 7	3
Student 8	4
Student 9	5
Student 10	3
	3.9 (Mean)
	4 (Median)
	3 (Mode)

17.

Student 1	Student 2	Student 3	Student 4
2	5	3	4
3	3	5	5
4	4	5	5
3	4	5	3
4	5	2	4
5	3	5	5
2	6	3	4
3	3	5	6

Student 1	Student 2	Student 3	Student 4
5	2	2	4
3	3	3	3
3.4 (Mean)	3.8 (Mean)	3.8 (Mean)	4.3 (Mean)
3 (Median)	3.5 (Median)	4 (Median)	4 (Median)
3 (Mode)	3 (Mode)	5 (Mode)	4 (Mode)

18.

Prison	Security Level	Number of Programs
Glendale	Medium	3
Foster	Maximum	2
Arial Bay	Medium	4
Hempstead	Minimum	4
Aboriginie	Minimum	5
Hilsom	Medium	5
Bural Hills	Minimum	4
Parkland	Minimum	4
Hightower	Maximum	2
Flosom	Maximum	3
	Median (2)	Mean (3.6)

19.

Offense	Sex	Offense History (Number)	Eligibility for Diversion
Curfew violation	M	3	No
Underage use of alcohol	M	2	Yes
Truancy	F	1	Yes
Running away from home	F	1	Yes
Truancy	M	4	No
Underage use of alcohol	F	2	No
Running away from home	F	1	Yes
Running away from home	F	1	Yes
Curfew violation	M	1	Yes
Curfew violation	M	3	No
Mean	M (2), F (2)	NA	No (2.5), Yes (1.6)

20.

Offense	Sex	Race	Detained	Number of Days Detained
Shoplifting	F	B	Y	4
Theft	M	W	N	0
Auto-Theft	M	B	Y	4

Battery	M	B	Y	2
Assault	F	H	Y	3
Vandalism	M	W	N	0
Trespassing	F	B	Y	4
Assault	M	W	N	0
Assault	F	B	N	0
Theft	F	H	Y	5
Mean	M (2), F (2)	B (2), H (5), W (3.3)	Y (1.6), N (2.5)	NA

21.

Name	Race	Offense Type	Number of Hours
J. Fox	B	Status	12
L. Williams	W	Delinquency	4
S. McDade	B	Delinquency	3
L. Holcombe	H	Delinquency	4
J. Flemming	W	Status	2
J. Juarez	H	Delinquency	3
J. Flores	H	Status	4
B. Gibson	B	Delinquency	3
N. Bridgeway	W	Status	3
Mean	B (3), H (3), W (3)	NA	4.22
Median			3.5

In comparison to the mean, the median is preferred because of the accuracy of the value provided. The median is not influenced by extreme scores in a distribution.

22. The level of measurement reflected in the table is ratio. The corresponding measure of central tendency that can be used with a ratio-level variable is the mean.

23.

Age	Rate per 1,000
12–18	19.3
19–21	18.7
22–25	18.2
26–31	16.8
32–40	14.1
41–50	8.3
51–60	5.8
61–70	4.1
71+	2.8
Median	14.1
Mean	12.01

Matching: Place the letter of the definition with its corresponding term:

___1. Average	a. an extreme value (or values) in a distribution
___2. Measures of Central Tendency	b. the arithmetic average of all values in a distribution
___3. Mean	c. calculations that produce individual values that best represent the collective values in a distribution
___4. Median	d. a value that summarizes or best represents a group of values
___5. Mode	e. a value that represents a midpoint of all values in a distribution
___6. Outlier	f. a value (or category) that occurs most frequently in a distribution

Answers

1. d
2. c
3. b
4. e
5. f
6. a

Biblography

Chia, T. H., & Levene, M. J. (2009). Detection of counterfeit US paper money using intrinsic fluorescence lifetime. *Optics Express, 17*(24), 22054–22061.

Hameleers, M. (2022). Separating truth from lies: Comparing the effects of news media literacy interventions and fact-checkers in response to political misinformation in the US and Netherlands. *Information, Communication & Society, 25*(1), 110–126.

Shook, J. J., & Goodkind, S. A. (2009). Racial disproportionality in juvenile justice: The interaction of race and geography in pretrial detention for violent and serious offenses. *Race and Social Problems, 1*(4), 257–266.

Weisberg, H. F. (1992). *Central tendency and variability.* SAGE Publications.

Winsor, C. P. (1946). Which Regression? *Biometrics Bulletin, 2*(6), 101–109. https://doi.org/10.2307/3002018

Chapter 3 SPSS and Workbook Questions

SPSS and Measures of Central Tendency

Suppose a professor provided information to students associated with the benefits of using restorative justice practices. To gauge student understanding of the content, the professor requires the student to complete an unannounced quiz. Shown below are the grades of each student's quiz.

Student	Grade
1	89
2	94
3	86
4	78
5	79
6	85
7	82
8	79
9	93
10	90
11	92
12	97
13	68

Based on the information in the chapter, compute the mean, median, and mode using SPSS.

Entry of Data—SPSS

1. Select variable view to include information that identifies the variables of interest.
2. In the first row, include the term *exam* under the column identified as name.
3. Under the column identified as type, select the option numeric. For the column identified as decimals, select 0 if you prefer to include single-digit numbers. For the column identified as measure, select the scale option.
4. In the column identified as label, you might choose to include a more specific description of the variable.
5. Select data view and include the corresponding scores in the column.

IMAGE 3.1

IMAGE 3.2

Analysis of Data—SPSS

1. Select analyze, select descriptive statistics, and choose frequencies.
2. Select the exam variable, which is located in the box on the left, and move it to the variable(s) box that is located on the right.
3. Select the statistics option and choose the measures of central tendency. Select the mean, median, and mode options.
4. Below the box on the left, select the display frequency table option.
5. Once all desired functions have been selected and completed, select OK.

Output of Data Analysis—SPSS

The output of the data analysis, as provided below, includes two tables. Table 1 includes information from the sample, which identifies the mean, median, and mode. Finally, Table 2 includes details associated with each individual score in the sample. This includes the frequency, as well as three different levels of corresponding percentages.

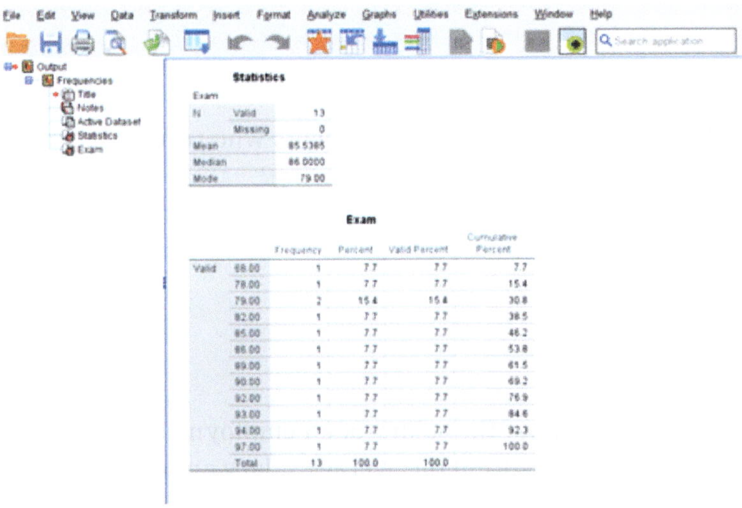

Statistics

Exam

N	Valid	13
	Missing	0
Mean		85.5385
Median		86.0000
Mode		79.00

Exam

		Frequency	Percent	Valid Percent	Cumulative Percent
Valid	68.00	1	7.7	7.7	7.7
	78.00	1	7.7	7.7	15.4
	79.00	2	15.4	15.4	30.8
	82.00	1	7.7	7.7	38.5
	85.00	1	7.7	7.7	46.2
	86.00	1	7.7	7.7	53.8
	89.00	1	7.7	7.7	61.5
	90.00	1	7.7	7.7	69.2
	92.00	1	7.7	7.7	76.9
	93.00	1	7.7	7.7	84.6
	94.00	1	7.7	7.7	92.3
	97.00	1	7.7	7.7	100.0
	Total	13	100.0	100.0	

IMAGE 3.3

Workbook Questions

Objective 1—The Use of an Average and Measures of Central Tendency

- An average is a value that summarizes or best represents a group of values.
- Measures of central tendency are calculations that produce individual values that best represent the collective values in a distribution.

Corresponding Questions

1. A(n) ______ is a value that best represents a group of values in a distribution.
   a. mode
   b. median
   c. mean
   d. average
   e. none the above
2. Calculations that produce individual values that best represent the collective values in a distribution are known as:
   a. measures of central tendency
   b. the mode or median
   c. the mean or median

d. the mean of the median

e. none the above

3. Measures of central tendency include ___ types of averages.

a. 2

b. 3

c. 4

d. 5

e. none the above

4. If a professor desires to calculate the class average of students who recently completed a final exam, that professor is likely to use which of the following?

a. Mode

b. Median

c. Mean

d. Either b or c

e. None the above

5. If a potential job applicant is curious about the salary of an employment position and is concerned about the influence of outliers within the average salary amount, the applicant may select which of the following?

a. Mode

b. Median

c. Mean

d. Either b or c

e. None the above

6. If one is interested in how many types of specific crimes, such as motor vehicle theft, are reported to a law enforcement agency, one may select which of the following?

a. Mode

b. Median

c. Mean

d. Either b or c

e. None the above

Answers

1. d
2. a
3. b
4. c
5. b
6. a

Objective 2—The Use of Each Type of Measure of Central Tendency

- The mean is a value that represents the arithmetic average of all values in a distribution.
- The median is a value that represents a midpoint of all values in a distribution.
- An outlier is an extreme value (or values) in a distribution.
- The mode is a value (or category) that occurs most frequently in a distribution.

Corresponding Questions

1. Based on the following, compute the mean number of the youth from different areas of a city who were diverted from the juvenile court.

Area of City	Number of Youth
Northwest	6
Northeast	4
Southeast	8
Southwest	10
West	6
East	9

2. Identify the mean number of the following property crimes.

Type	Number Reported
Shoplifting	16
Larceny	10
Burglary	23
Theft	25
Arson	1
Vandalism	6

3. Based on the following, compute the total median annual salary, which represents the income of nine police chiefs in a county. If the lowest salary amount was removed, what impact would this have? Would the total median annual salary increase or decrease? Identify the actual amount of increase or decrease.

Location	Salary
Area 1	85,000
Area 2	75,000
Area 3	78,500
Area 4	82,500
Area 5	81,520
Area 6	77,500
Area 7	64,500
Area 8	72,450
Area 9	48,500

4. Based on the following, compute the total median crime rates (serious violent crimes) as reported in 10 small metropolitan cities. If the highest amount was removed, what impact would this have on the total median amount? Would the total median amount increase or decrease? Identify the actual difference.

Year	Violent Crimes (per 10,000)
City 1	34.3
City 2	23.6
City 3	7.86
City 4	19.32
City 5	9.7
City 6	16.89
City 7	22.10
City 8	27.54
City 9	15.68
City 10	14.25

5. Based on the following, identify the mode based on the selection of criminal justice professions among students at a historically Black college or university.

Profession	Number
Law enforcement officer	8
Law enforcement officer (state)	6
Law enforcement officer (federal)	12
Attorney – prosecutor	3
Attorney – defense	2
Probation officer	6
Probation officer (state)	8
Probation officer (federal)	10
Parole officer	0
Parole officer (state)	2
Criminal profiler	7
Forensics expert	5

Answers

1. 7.16
2. 13.5
3. 77,500; 78,000 (median amount would increase)
4. 18.10; 16.89 (median amount would decrease)
5. Law enforcement officer (federal) (12)

Objective 3—The Use of "Special Needs" Measures of Central Tendency

- The trimmed mean requires the removal of outliers within a small distribution.
- The winsor mean requires replacing an outlier with the next number within a small distribution and adding 1 to that number.
- The geometric mean is used to calculate the central tendency for rates.
- The harmonic mean is similar to the mean/winsor mean but is used for large distributions.

Corresponding Questions

1. The __________ mean requires the removal of outliers within a small distribution.
   a. geometric
   b. harmonic
   c. winsor
   d. trimmed
   e. none of the above
2. The ________________ mean is similar to the mean/winsor mean but is used for large distributions.
   a. geometric
   b. harmonic
   c. winsor
   d. trimmed
   e. none of the above
3. The __________ mean requires replacing an outlier with the next number within a small distribution and adding 2 to that number.
   a. geometric
   b. harmonic
   c. winsor
   d. trimmed
   e. none of the above
4. Which of the following is used with small distributions?
   a. Geometric
   b. Harmonic
   c. Winsor
   d. Trimmed
   e. Both c and d

Answers

1. d
2. b
3. e
4. e

Credits

CHAPTER 4

Dispersion

If you torture the data long enough, it will confess.
—Ronald Coase

Objectives

1. Define and explain the use of dispersion.
2. Define, explain the use of, and compute the types of dispersion.
3. Define and explain the use of dispersion for ordinal and nominal data.

Introduction—Variability and Gender

Question: Do you think there is more variation (difference) in the physical height of boys or girls between the ages of 6 and 12? If you said girls, you are correct. In fact, even if two groups consisting of boys and girls were of the same age, say 13, there would be more variation in height among the girls than the boys. This is because, within certain age ranges, girls mature faster than boys. This example points to the significance of dispersion in statistics.

Dispersion

Dispersion, also referred to as variability, is the amount of distance between values in a distribution.

For instance, consider the two groups of values in Table 4.1:

dispersion The amount of distance between values in a distribution.

TABLE 4.1 **Dispersion**

Group 1	Group 2
1	3
(a distance of 5)	(a distance of 1)
6	2
(a distance of 2)	(a distance of 0)

4	2
(a distance of 8)	(a distance of 0)
12	4
(a distance of 4)	(a distance of 1)
8	3

As noted, the distances between values in Group 1 are 5, 2, 8, and 4. In Group 2, the distances (or dispersion) between values are 1, 0, 0, and 1. Thus, the values in Group 1 possess greater levels of distance in comparison to the values in Group 2.

Consider the information in Table 4.2:

TABLE 4.2 **Dispersion, Total, and Mean**

Group 1	Group 2
20	3
(a distance of 5)	(a distance of 14)
15	17
(a distance of 4)	(a distance of 3)
19	20
(a distance of 7)	(a distance of 0)
26	20
(a distance of 6)	(a distance of 20)
20	40
Total = 100	Total = 100
$\bar{x} = 20$	$\bar{x} = 20$

Notice that both groups have the same total amount of values (100) and the same mean (20). However, the dispersion between the values in each group is dissimilar. By simply observing the total and mean scores among the groups, one might assume that the characteristics of the group values are also similar. This explains why dispersion is important. It also explains its relationship with measures of central tendency. In statistics, the dispersion among values is measured in comparison to the mean of the distribution. In other words, we desire to discover how far the scores from the mean are. In short, dispersion and mean work together in describing the fundamental characteristics of values within distributions. In this chapter, we will discuss four types of dispersion: range, variation, standard deviation, and kurtosis.

Types of Dispersion

range A type of dispersion that represents the difference between the highest and the lowest value in a distribution.

Range

The **range** is a type of dispersion that represents the difference between the highest and the lowest value in a distribution. Used with interval- and ratio-level variables, calculating the range involves subtracting the lowest value from the highest value.

The formula for computing the range is identified as follows:

$$r = x_{greatest} - x_{lowest,}$$

where

r = range

$x_{greatest}$ = highest value in a distribution

x_{lowest} = lowest value in a distribution

Consider the information in Table 4.3:

TABLE 4.3 **Number of Arrests by County**

Counties in the State	Arrests
County 1	238
County 2	220
County 3	168
County 4	144
County 5	97
County 6	50
County 7	67

In Table 4.3, the number of arrests is listed by county in a state. This includes the total number of arrests for disorderly conduct among adult females. The highest value is represented by County 1 at 238, and the lowest value is represented by County 6 at 50. The difference between the two values (subtraction of lowest from highest value) is 188.

$$r = 238 - 50$$
$$r = 188$$

Despite the simplicity of computing the range, this type of dispersion offers no information in relation to the other values in a distribution. For this reason, as well as many others, the range is often not considered a preferred source of dispersion among values.

Variance

The **variance** is a type of dispersion that represents the average of the squared differences from the mean. Unlike the range, computing the variance involves the use of more than two values in a distribution.

Used with interval- and ratio-level variables (continuous data), calculating the variance involves the following formula:

$$s^2 = \frac{\Sigma(x_1 - \bar{x})^2}{N - 1},$$

variance A type of dispersion that represents the average of the squared differences from the mean.

where

x_1 = each value (in a distribution)
$\bar{x}$ = the sample mean
Σ = the summation (addition) of values
N-1= number of values in the distribution minus 1

Before we observe a number of examples associated with computing the variance, it is important to discuss the significance of computing deviation scores. In short, deviation scores highlight the value of the mean in relation to each value in a distribution.

Deviation Scores

When computing the variance, the mean is often used to determine what is referred to as the deviation score. A **deviation score** is a number that identifies the distance between the mean of a distribution and an individual score.

The formula for using the deviation score is based on the following:

$$d_1 = x_1 - \bar{x}_1,$$

where

d_1 = the deviation score for a data point
x_1 = the given (or identified) data point
$\bar{x}_1$ = the sample mean

Deviation scores provide two important characteristics of data in relation to the mean:

They provide information in terms of how far a score is from the mean. This is referred to as the absolute value. For instance, data points that are equal to the mean will have deviation scores of 0; on the other hand, deviation scores with larger absolute values are farther away from the mean, while deviation scores with smaller absolute values are closer to the mean. Furthermore, they also provide information in terms of whether the score is greater than or less than the mean. This is referred to as the relative value of each score. The sign of a deviation score will determine whether the relative value is greater than or less than the mean. For instance, positive deviation scores represent raw scores that are greater than the mean, and negative deviation scores represent raw scores that are less than the mean. In summary, by computing the deviation score, one is able to determine the (1) distance and (2) whether a score is above or below the mean.

For instance, suppose the mean (of a distribution of scores) is 5, and you are presented with a score of 3. Your deviation score is 3 - 5 = -2

$$x_1 - \bar{x}_1 = 3 - 5 = -2$$

Notice that the score has a negative sign. This lets us know that the score (-2) is below the mean (5).

If the mean is 8, and you are presented with a score of 17, your deviation score is 17 - 8 = 9

$$x_1 - \bar{x}_1 = 17 - 8 = 9$$

Notice that the score does not have a negative sign. This indicates that the score (9) is above the mean (8).

When computing the deviation score, you will be required to find the deviation score using a distribution of scores. For example, consider the following:

As revealed, the seven scores provided include a sum of 35 ($\Sigma x = 35$) and a mean of 5 ($\bar{x} = 5$). With these statistics, you might be tempted to compute the average of the deviation scores as a measure of variability. Let's see what happens when this mistake is made.

To begin this process, as mentioned previously, the mean is subtracted from each score:

Once the mean is subtracted from each score, find the sum of the squared deviations. The sum of the deviations should equal 0.

Are you able to understand why the sum of the scores equal 0? It is due to the fact that you are adding positive scores with negative scores, which ultimately cancels each score, resulting in the sum of 0. From this standpoint, 0 cannot exist as a measure of variability. As a remedy, the positive and negative signs must be removed. This requires squaring the squared deviation scores. Consider the following:

x	$x - \bar{x}$	$(x - \bar{x})$	$(x - \bar{x})^2$
4	4 − 5	−1	1
3	3 − 5	−2	4
6	6 − 5	1	1
5	5 − 5	0	0
9	9 − 5	4	16
5	5 − 5	0	0
3	3 − 5	−2	4
			$\Sigma (x - \bar{x})^2 = 26$

In the final column, the deviation scores are squared and added together (also referred to as the sum of squares), which results in the sum of 26.

Now that we have described the rationale and steps of computing the deviation score, let's consider the following computation exercises:

TABLE 4.4 **Number of State-Imprisoned Youth in 2015**

State Prisons	**Number**	$x_1 - \bar{x}$	$(x_1 - \bar{x})^2$
Institution 1	28	28 − 20 = 8	$(8)^2 = 64$
Institution 2	31	31 − 20 = 11	$(11)^2 = 121$
Institution 3	16	16 − 20 = −4	$(-4)^2 = 16$
Institution 4	14	14 − 20 = −6	$(-6)^2 = 36$
Institution 5	11	11 − 20 = −9	(−9)2 = 81
	$\bar{x} = \frac{\Sigma x}{n} = \frac{100}{5} = 20$	$\Sigma(x_1 - \bar{x}) = 0$	$\Sigma(x_1 - \bar{x})^2 = 318$

For clarification, computing the variance involves two parts. Part 1 provides insight related to the first part of the formula, while Part 2 addresses the second part of the formula.

Part 1

$$s^2 = \frac{\Sigma(x_1 - \bar{x})^2}{N - 1}$$

In Table 4.4, the number of state-imprisoned youth gang-affiliated inmates in 2015 is identified by institution. As indicated, the numbers of each inmate in each institution are added for a total of 100. This also includes the value of the mean (20). Furthermore, an additional column records the difference between the number of inmates from the mean. Given that the differences include negative values (−4, −6, and −9), the sum is 0. The final column, as revealed in Table 4.4, records the difference between the number of inmates from the mean in which the values are squared and added together for a total of 318.

Part 2

$$s^2 = \frac{\Sigma(x_1 - \bar{x})^2}{N - 1}$$

The final step in computing the variance involves dividing the total by the number of values in the distribution (sample) subtracted by 1.

$$s^2 = \frac{318}{5 - 1} = \frac{318}{4} = 79.5$$

Based on the calculation, the variance of youth gang members imprisoned in 2015 is 79.5.

TABLE 4.5 **Number of Victim Impact Statements Used in Courts by District**

District	**Number**	$x_1 - \bar{x}$	$(x_1 - \bar{x})^2$
District 1	12	12 − 12 = 0	$(0)^2 = 0$
District 2	11	11 − 12 = −1	$(-1)^2 = 1$
District 3	16	16 − 12 = 4	$(4)^2 = 16$
District 4	4	4 − 12 = −8	$(-8)^2 = 64$
District 5	17	17 − 12 = 5	(5)2 = 25
	$\bar{x} = \frac{\Sigma x}{n} = \frac{60}{5} = 12$	$\Sigma(x_1 - \bar{x}) = 0$	$\Sigma(x_1 - \bar{x})^2 = 106$

Table 4.5 provides the number of victim impact statements used in courts by jurisdiction (district). This includes the total number of statements for the districts identified (60) and the mean (12). The final column reflects the difference between the number of statements from the mean in which

the values are 1) squared and 2) added together for a total of 106. The final step involves dividing the total (106) by the number of values in the distribution (5) subtracted by 1.

$$s^2 = \frac{106}{5-1} = \frac{106}{4} = 26.5$$

The variance of victim impact statements used in districts 1 – 5 is 26.5.

TABLE 4.6 **Number of Human Trafficking Convictions in County Courts**

Area	Number	$x_1 - \bar{x}$	$(x_1 - \bar{x})^2$
County 1	16	16 − 7 = 9	$(9)^2 = 81$
County 2	12	12 − 7 = 5	$(5)^2 = 25$
County 3	8	8 − 7 = 1	$(1)^2 = 1$
County 4	4	4 − 7 = −3	$(-3)^2 = 9$
County 5	9	9 − 7 = 2	(2)2 = 4
County 6	0	0 − 7 = −7	$(-7)^2 = 49$
County 7	0	0 − 7 = −7	$(-7)^2 = 49$
	$\bar{x} = \frac{\Sigma x}{n} = \frac{49}{7} = 7$	$\Sigma(x_1 - \bar{x}) = 0$	$\Sigma(x_1 - \bar{x})^2 = 218$

The number of human trafficking cases is identified in Table 4.6. This is based on local level prosecution within seven different county court locations. Overall, a total of 49 criminal convictions were determined as a result of the charges filed by prosecutors. As revealed in the final column, which reflects the sum of squared deviation scores (or the sum of squares), the total is 218. This value is divided by the total number of values subtracted by 1.

$$s^2 = \frac{218}{7-1} = \frac{218}{6} = 36.3$$

The variance of human trafficking convictions in county courts 1 – 7 is 36.3.

N – *1* or *N*

When computing the variance, you may notice that the sum of squared deviations is either divided by *N* – 1 or *N*. The difference between these two options is based on the following:

N = This option is used when the goal of the process is to identify the variability of scores within a distribution. In essence, we are interested in how much the data spreads (based on the scores) in the *sample*.

N – 1 = This option is selected when the goal is to generalize our findings beyond the scores within a distribution. In other words, we are interested in estimating how much the data spreads in the *population*.

Another explanation that explains the two options is based on the formula used to compute the variance. The formula, which simply divides the squared deviations by *N*, produces an estimate of the population variance that is too small, which results in a biased estimate. This stems from the reality that samples are smaller than populations; thus, they contain less variability. As a remedy, we subtract 1 from the sample size, which slightly increases the variance. As scientists who are guided by ethical principles, if we are going to take risks with regard to producing an error, we will engage in such by overestimating the standard deviation of the population. For instance, if we have a sample size of 20, we divide the sum of squared deviations by 19. If we have a sample size of 150, we will divide by 149.

Another key aspect of $N - 1$, is that the use of such does not reveal a significant difference with large samples in comparison to small samples. Consider the example provided in Table 4.7:

TABLE 4.7 **Difference Between Large and Small Samples and n – 1**

Sample Size	Value of Numerator in Standard Deviation Formula	Biased Estimate of the Population Standard Deviation	Unbiased Estimate of the Population Standard Deviation	Difference Between Biased and Unbiased Estimates
20	350	4.18	4.29	0.11
200	350	1.32	1.33	0.01
2,000	350	0.4183	0.4184	0.0001
20,000	350	0.13228	0.13229	0.00001

Notice how the differences between the biased and unbiased estimates diminish as the sample size increases.

At this point, we have discussed the importance of several key aspects of variance; however, one might not understand the practical value of such. This leads us to our final step in discovering the amount of distance between values in a distribution, which is commonly referred to as standard deviation.

Standard Deviation

The **standard deviation** is a type of dispersion that represents the square root of the average of the squared differences from the mean. In short, it reflects the mean amount of dispersion in a distribution.

standard deviation A type of dispersion that represents the square root of the average of the squared differences from the mean.

Standard deviation involves the same calculation process as the variance with one additional step. Can you guess what that additional step is by observing the following formula?

Computing the standard deviation involves the following:

$$s = \sqrt{\frac{\Sigma(x_1 - \bar{x})^2}{n-1}},$$

where

x_1 = each value (in a distribution)
$\bar{x}$ = the sample mean
Σ = the summation (addition) of values
n–1 = number of values in the distribution (sample) minus 1
$\sqrt{\ }$ = the square root of a value (variance)

Compared to the formula for variance, the formula for standard deviation includes the additional step of calculating the square root of the variance.

TABLE 4.8 **Number of Female Officers in Administrative Positions**

Agency	Number	$x_1 - \bar{x}$	$(x_1 - \bar{x})^2$
Department 1	7	7 − 7.12 = −0.12	$(-0.12)^2 = 0.01$
Department 2	4	4 − 7.12 = −3.12	$(-3.12)^2 = 9.73$
Department 3	10	10 − 7.12 = 2.88	$(2.88)^2 = 8.29$
Department 4	6	6 − 7.12 = −1.12	$(-1.12)^2 = 1.25$
Department 5	8	8 − 7.12 = 0.88	(0.88)2 = 0.77
Department 6	10	10 − 7.12 = 2.88	$(2.88)^2 = 8.29$
Department 7	5	5 − 7.12 = −2.12	$(-2.12)^2 = 4.49$
Department 8	7	7 − 7.12 = −0.12	$(-0.12)^2 = 0.01$
	$\bar{x} = \frac{\Sigma x}{n} = \frac{57}{8} = 7.12$	$\Sigma(x_1 - \bar{x}) = 0$	$\Sigma(x_1 - \bar{x})^2 = 32.84$

Table 4.8 provides the number of female police officers who serve in administrative positions in eight law enforcement agencies (departments).

This includes

a. the sum (57) of the total number of officers and the mean (7.12),
b. the sum of the squared differences between the mean and the values (32.84), and
c. dividing the total (32.84) by the number of values in the distribution (8) subtracted by 1 (which gives us the variance).

$$s^2 = \frac{32.84}{8-1} = \frac{32.84}{7} = 4.69$$

a. Finding the square root of the variance

$$\sqrt{4.69} = 2.16.$$

The standard deviation of female police officers who serve in administrative positions in the 8 law enforcement agencies is 2.16.

As mentioned previously, the standard deviation reflects the distance of each value from the mean. As a rule of thumb, the *greater the variability of scores* in relation to the mean of a distribution, the *greater the standard deviation*. We'll discuss more about this process in the forthcoming chapters.

Range and Standard Deviation

Interestingly, certain measures of dispersion possess unique relationships with each other. An example of such includes the range and standard deviation. Identified through what is commonly referred to as the range rule of thumb, the range can be used to estimate the approximate standard deviation of a distribution of scores.

This includes the following formula:

$$s = \text{range}/4,$$

where

S = standard deviation (estimate)

range/4 = difference between the highest and lowest value in a distribution divided by 4

For instance, suppose one is interested in discovering an estimate of the standard deviation of the following scores: 6, 4, 8, 10, 7, 9.

The range (10 – 2) is 8. Dividing the range (8) by 4 equals 2. Thus, our estimated standard deviation for the scores provided is 2. In comparison, the actual standard deviation is 2.61, which reveals a 0.61 difference between the estimated and actual standard deviation scores. In most cases, using this process will underestimate the actual standard deviation score; however, the score provided is in the general area of the actual score.

In addition, the range rule of thumb can also be used to provide estimates of the largest and smallest scores in a distribution. The lowest score will be approximately 2 standard deviations below the mean. The highest score will be approximately 2 standard deviations above the mean. Consider the following, which includes the mean of our distribution ($\bar{x} = 6.57$), and *s* represents our standard deviation value ($s = 2.61$):

$$\text{Lowest score} = \bar{x} - 2S = 6.57 - 2(2.61) = 1.35$$
$$\text{Highest score} = \bar{x} + 2S = 6.57 + 2(2.61) = 11.79$$

In comparison to our distribution data, consider the following differences between the scores:

TABLE 4.9 **Differences Between Distribution Data and Range Rule of Thumb Data**

Distribution Data	**Range Rule of Thumb Data**
Lowest score = 2	Lowest score = 1.39
Highest score = 10	Highest score = 11.79

As revealed, the range rule of thumb data are estimates and not the actual scores. In short, this example demonstrates the relationships between the use of measures of dispersion. As identified earlier, this approach might be beneficial when one is required to provide approximate values within a limited amount of time.

Functions of Variance and Standard Deviation Scores

At this point, one might be unclear as to understanding the overall practical functions of measures of dispersion, especially the most commonly used, which is the variance and standard deviation. To that end, information derived from the use of variances and standard deviations is commonly used as follows:

1. Determine the consistency of a variable.
2. Determine the amount of spread of data within a distribution. Specifically, if variance and standard deviation scores are large, this points to a great amount of spread of data within a distribution. On the contrary, if the variation and standard deviation scores are small, we can assume that there is a small amount of spread of data within a series of scores.
3. Determine whether data points exist within a specific range in a distribution of scores.

The Combined Value of Measures of Dispersions and Measures Central Tendency

Data that only provides measures of central tendency may produce misleading information. This is especially true when the mean is used to describe or compare distributions of data. For instance, suppose we have records of sentencing among two district court judges. This includes sentencing defendants who were convicted of aggravated assault within the past four years. In general, both judges have a mean of 48 months in terms of sentencing defendants to prison. From this standpoint, it appears that both judges possess similar philosophies of punishment.

However, additional details of the sentencing data may provide a different perspective. This includes the use of variance and standard deviation as indicated in the use of distribution curves.

For instance, the explanation of sentencing for Judge 1 is based on her belief that those convicted of aggravated assault should receive 48 months, with no exceptions. Not surprisingly, she is viewed as being consistent as a judge. On the other hand, the sentencing decisions of Judge 2, despite the similar mean in terms of sentencing, demonstrate a variation in sentencing. Unlike Judge 1, she considers several factors when sentencing defendants. In particular, Judge 2 considers a defendant's criminal history, as well as the location of the aggravated assault.

When looking at dispersion data, as evident in Figure 4.1, Judge 2 renders prison sentencing decisions anywhere between 3 months to 4.5 years. In comparison to Judge 1, Judge 2 is viewed as inconsistent in terms of sentencing. Notice the differences: Despite the same mean score with respect to sentencing, the variability of sentencing reveals a significant difference between the sentencing decisions of the judges.

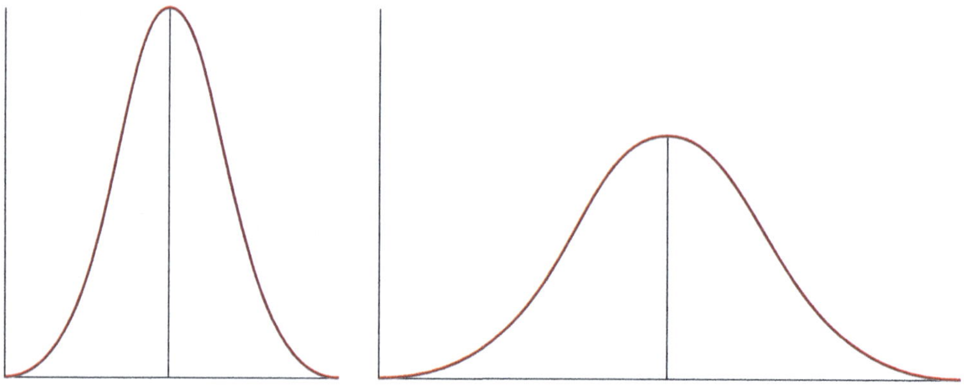

FIGURE 4.1 Differences Between Judges by Mean

Let's consider another example that highlights the value of including both measures of central tendency along measures of dispersion. In this example, we will compare the sentencing between two judges in which additional information is provided. This includes the mean, along with both the variance and the standard deviation of two sets of distributions.

In Table 4.10, we see the sentences of two judges among defendants who were convicted of drug possession.

To begin with, notice the mean differences between the two distributions of sentencing. Compared to Judge 2, Judge 1 has a higher mean number of months in terms of sentencing. With respect to variance, the differences between both sentencing outcomes produce very little practical knowledge. However, the standard deviation provides a significant amount of practical knowledge about sentencing patterns. This is based on the reality that the standard deviation scores are identified as measures of actual months.

When comparing the sentencing differences between the two judges, with the additional details provided, we are able to make several distinctions. Judge 1 has a higher mean in comparison to Judge 2. This might be interpreted that Judge 1 is harsher in sentencing relative to Judge 2. In addition, Judge 1 has a standard deviation that is lower than Judge 2. This means that even though Judge 1 is considered harsher than Judge 2, Judge 1 is more consistent in sentencing than Judge 2. Overall, it appears that we have judges who are either harsh and consistent or lenient and inconsistent.

One critical factor that explains the sentencing differences is the evidence that is used when making such decisions among judges. For instance, Judge 2 considers the age of the victim(s) and the number of offenders involved in the offense. Judge 1, on the other hand, considers the defendant's role in the offense(s) and the employment status of the offender during his decision-making process. This information may be helpful for an attorney who desires to offer beneficial advice for their client, especially if their client possesses any of the factors that explain the differences in sentencing between the judges. Suppose an attorney only reveals to his client the mean amount of sentencing among the judges. The client is likely to prefer that their case be heard by Judge 2 ($\bar{x} = 30.0$) instead of Judge 1 ($\bar{x} = 4.3$). However, by not sharing information about the standard deviation, the client is not aware of the inconsistency of Judge 2, which may result in a longer than expected time of incarceration (Fox, Levine, and Forde, 2012).

TABLE 4.10 **Sentences in Months for Drug Possession by Two Judges**

Sentences in Months for Drug Possession by Two Judges	
Judge 1	Judge 2
34.0	27.0
31.0	44.0
38.0	22.0
33.0	38.0
36.0	18.0
34.0	31.0
$\bar{X} = 34.3$	$\bar{X} = 30.0$
$s^2 = 5.9$	$s^2 = 95.6$
$s = 2.2$	$s = 8.9$

Chapter Learning Assessment Questions

To gauge your understanding of the information provided, complete the following questions:

Objective 1

1. The amount of distance between two values is referred to as:
   a. the mean
   b. the range
   c. measures of central tendency
   d. dispersion

Objective 2

2. To compute a deviation score, one must
   a. subtract the mean from each individual score in a distribution.
   b. subtract each individual score in a distribution from the mean.
   c. subtract the mean from the lowest individual score in a distribution.
   d. None of the above

Answers

1. d
2. a

Kurtosis

Like the other forms of dispersion presented in this chapter, kurtosis is a descriptive statistic. **Kurtosis** is, in fact, a Greek word that translates into English as "peakedness." Thus, kurtosis assesses the appearance of the top (or the head) of a normal distribution.

kurtosis A type of visual that assesses the appearance of the head of a normal distribution.

leptokurtic A visual distribution of data that reveals a high peak or narrow shape.

mesokurtic A visual distribution of data that is considered normal; it is often considered a standard bell curve.

platykurtic A visual distribution of data that indicates a flat shape.

The key to understanding a kurtosis is to focus on the shoulders of a distribution as illustrated:

If we shift the quantities in the shoulder to both the tails and the head of the distribution, the mean and standard deviation will remain unchanged; however, the appearance of the distribution will be quite different. For example, in the following overlayed distributions, we see two distributions that share the same mean and standard deviation, which appear significantly different from a visual standpoint.

In general, kurtosis is a measure of the relationship of the head and the tails of a distribution. Although the shape of the head is more noticeable, the kurtosis focuses more on what is commonly referred to as the fat or flat tails. Statisticians often use these terms to describe the distance between the horizontal axis. Thus, the greater the space between the tails of the distributions and the horizontal axis, the "fatter" the tails are. The following are the basic terms and definitions used to describe kurtosis: mesokurtic, leptokurtic, and platykurtic.

1. **Leptokurtic** – a visual distribution of data that reveals a high peak or narrow shape.
2. **Mesokurtic** – a visual distribution of data that is considered normal; it is often considered a standard bell curve.
3. **Platykurtic** – a visual distribution of data that indicates a fat (or flat) shape.

In the following diagram, notice that the platykurtic has the "fattest tails." The fattiness of the tails is a critically important part of our analysis of a distribution. Essentially, the fatter the tails the more likely that *an unlikely event* will occur.

The formula for kurtosis that is employed in Excel is:

$$\frac{n(n+1)}{(n-1)(n-2)(n-3)}\left(\frac{\Sigma(x-\bar{x})^4}{s^4}\right)-\frac{3(n-1)^2}{(n-2)(n-3)}$$

Two Standard Deviation Approach

We have addressed a variety of methods to assess the configuration of the distribution for interval data. These include the range, variance, standard deviation, and kurtosis. In addition to such, it is important to understand the core purpose and value of analyzing data to determine the extent to which statistically significant relationships exist. This often requires the process of examining the relationship between values in a distribution in relation to the mean, which is often referred to as the two standard deviation criteria or the **two standard deviation approach**. If a value is *outside* of the two standard deviations from the mean, the data suggests that any change is unlikely to be the result of random chance. We will discuss this process in more detail in subsequent chapters.

Final Thoughts

Along with understanding measures of central tendency, understanding the value of dispersion is key with respect to values in a distribution. This includes recognizing the deficiencies of the range and variance in relation to standard deviation. Overall, being able to identify the shortcomings of various approaches is the pathway to developing the most crucial characteristics to reaching one's potential in life—critical thinking and imagination.

Discussion

After observing youth arrest data as reported by a law enforcement agency, you noticed that two samples (of youth arrests) have the same total number of subjects ($n = 78$). They also have the same means of arrest ($\bar{x} = 12.5$) Based on the aforementioned, explain how a person might be likely to assume that every characteristic of each youth (in both groups) is similar.

Chapter Summary

This chapter emphasized the following information:

Objective 1 – Define and explain the use of dispersion

- Dispersion is the amount of distance between values in a distribution.

Objective 2 – Define, explain the use of, and compute the types of dispersion

- Range is a type of dispersion that represents the difference between the highest and the lowest value in a distribution.
- Variance is a type of dispersion that represents the average of the squared differences from the mean.
- Standard deviation is a type of dispersion that represents the square root of the average of the squared differences from the mean.
- Kurtosis is a descriptive statistic that reveals the shape of data in a distribution.

Objective 3 – Define and explain the use of dispersion for ordinal and nominal data

- Interquartile range is a range of scores that include the middle 50% of a distribution.
- Interquartile variation is the measurement of dispersion among nominal-level variables.
- The two standard deviation approach is a criterion in which the amount of data falls within 95% of the mean. This indicates that differences that exist occur beyond the scope of chance.
- Autocorrelation is an assessment of self-prediction in a series of data points occurring over time.

Terms

Dispersion
Range
Variance
Standard deviation
Kurtosis
Two standard deviation approach

Chapter Review Questions

1. The amount of distance between values (or scores) in a distribution includes the
   a. range
   b. variance
   c. standard deviation
   d. all of the above
2. The range is used with which of the following levels of measurement?
   a. Nominal
   b. Ordinal
   c. Interval
   d. Ratio
   e. c and/or d
3. The variance is used with which of the following levels of measurement?
   a. Nominal
   b. Ordinal
   c. Interval
   d. Ratio
   e. c and/or d
4. The standard deviation is used with which of the following levels of measurement?
   a. Nominal
   b. Ordinal
   c. Interval
   d. Ratio
   e. c and/or d
5. The greater the variability of scores in relation to the mean of a distribution, the greater the ___________.
   a. range
   b. variance
   c. standard deviation
   d. interquartile range

6. The two standard deviation approach requires that
   a. the amount of data falls within 95% of the mean.
   b. the amount of data falls within 85% of the mean.
   c. the amount of data falls within 99% of the mean.
   d. the amount of data falls within 68% of the mean.
7. The distribution of data that is narrow is identified as
   a. leptokurtic
   b. normal
   c. platykurtic
8. The distribution of data that is flat is identified as
   a. leptokurtic
   b. normal
   c. platykurtic
9. Compute the range, mean, variance, and standard deviation for the following, which represents the number of self-reported property crimes in youth facilities.

Location	Number
Facility 1	4
Facility 2	3
Facility 3	6
Facility 4	4
Facility 5	3

10. Compute the range, mean, variance, and standard deviation for the following, which represents the number of assaults in each county.

Location	Number
County 1	112
County 2	131
County 3	118
County 4	161
County 5	97
County 6	79
County 7	141
County 8	133
County 9	127
County 10	116

11. Compute the range, mean, variance, and standard deviation for the following, which represents the number of jails in a state by region.

Location	Number
Region 1	20
Region 2	17
Region 3	23
Region 4	14

12. Compute the range, mean, variance, and standard deviation for the following, which represents the types of offenses charged by a local prosecutor within a 1-month period.

Offense	Number
Assault	24
Robbery	19
Theft	16

13. Compute the range, mean, variance, and standard deviation for the following, which represents the number of youth housed in various prisons in a state.

Location	Number
Prison 1	13
Prison 2	9
Prison 3	16
Prison 4	19
Prison 5	15
Prison 6	19
Prison 7	21
Prison 8	16
Prison 9	18
Prison 10	15

14. Compute the range, mean, variance, and standard deviation for the following, which represents the number of jails that include separate holding areas for youth in a region.

Location	Number
Jail 1	4
Jail 2	6
Jail 3	6
Jail 4	7
Jail 5	4
Jail 6	5

15. Compute the range, mean, variance, and standard deviation for the following, which represents the rate of human trafficking victimization within 10 states.

Location	Rates per 100,000
State 1	6.54
State 2	4.87
State 3	3.61
State 4	4.29
State 5	2.34
State 6	2.83
State 7	1.23
State 8	2.71
State 9	3.51
State 10	2.3

Answers

1. d
2. e
3. e
4. e
5. c
6. a
7. a
8. c
9.

Range	3
Mean	4
Variance	1.2
Standard Deviation	1.09

10.

Range	82
Mean	121.5
Variance	473.25
Standard Deviation	21.75

11.

Range	9
Mean	18.5
Variance	11.25
Standard Deviation	3.35

12.

Range	8
Mean	19.66
Variance	10.88
Standard Deviation	3.29

13.

Range	12
Mean	16.1
Variance	10.69
Standard Deviation	3.26

14.

Range	3
Mean	5.33
Variance	1.22
Standard Deviation	1.10

15.

Range	5.31
Mean	3.42
Variance	2.07
Standard Deviation	1.43

Matching: Place the letter of the term with its corresponding definition:

___1. Dispersion

___2. Range

___3. Variance

___4. Standard deviation

___5. Mesokurtic

___6. Leptokurtic

___7. Platykurtic

a. the amount of distance between values in a distribution

b. when the amount of data falls within 95% of the mean, indicating differences that exist outside of chance

c. a visual distribution of data that indicates a skinny (or thin) shape

d. a visual distribution of data that is considered normal; it is often considered a standard bell curve

e. a type of dispersion that represents the square root of the average of the squared differences from the mean

f. a type of dispersion which represents the difference between the highest and the lowest value in a distribution

g. a visual distribution of data that indicates a fat (or flat) shape

___8. Two standard deviation approach

h. a type of dispersion which represents the average of the squared differences from the mean

Answers

1. a
2. f
3. h
4. e
5. d
6. c
7. g
8. b

Bibliography

Fox, J., Levin, J. & Forde, D. (2012). *Elementary statistics in criminal justice research, 4th Ed.,* Pearson Publishing.

Chapter 4 SPSS and Workbook Questions

SPSS and Dispersion

Suppose a staff member of a law school admissions department is interested in discovering information related to a sample of law school applicants. More specifically, this includes the annual income of 40 law school applicants. The information provided may be used by the law school in order to apply for federal funding. Identified below is the annual income amount for each law school applicant.

Student	Income	Student	Income	Student	Income	Student	Income
1	36,500	11	27,600	21	29,800	31	67,436
2	37,900	12	35,967	22	29,564	32	65,327
3	43,500	13	48,546	23	31,329	33	52,631
4	52,342	14	50,327	24	38,436	34	51,252
5	58,654	15	55,821	25	42,438	35	51,298
6	31,300	16	69,881	26	47,326	36	67,903
7	45,321	17	43,531	27	51,287	37	58,216
8	68,445	18	54,328	28	53,269	38	54,298
9	66,234	19	57,438	29	54,281	39	52,428
10	28,550	20	62,432	30	55,545	40	51,274

Based on the information above, compute the range, variance, and standard deviation using SPSS.

Entry of Data—SPSS

1. Select variable view to include information that identifies the variables of interest.
2. In the first row, include the term *income* under the column identified as name.
3. Under the column identified as type, select the option numeric. For the column identified as decimals, select 0 if you prefer to include single-digit numbers. For the column identified as measure, select the scale option.
4. In the column identified as label, you might choose to include a more specific description of the variable.
5. Select data view and include the corresponding scores in the column.

IMAGE 4.1

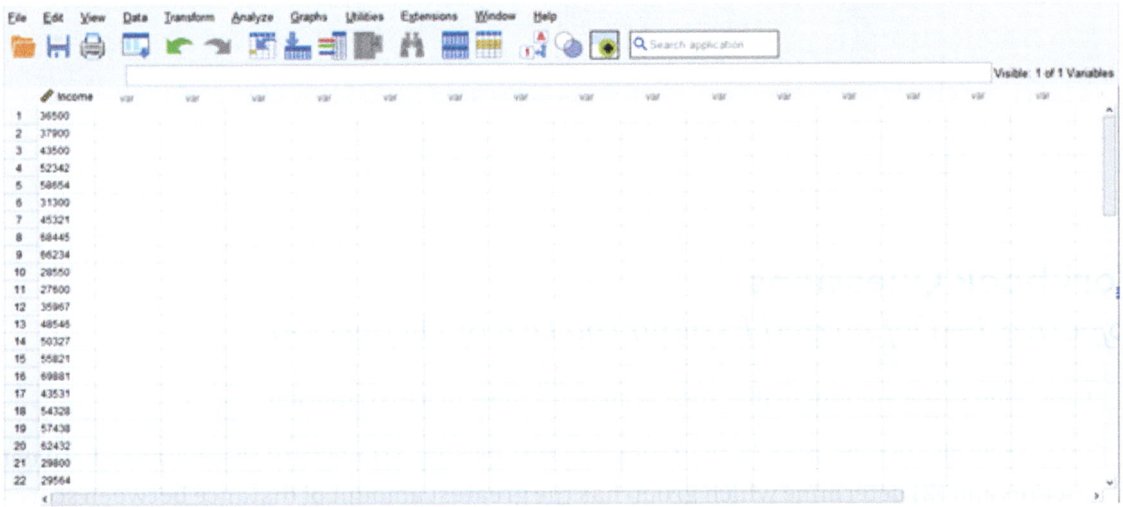

IMAGE 4.2

Analysis of Data—SPSS

1. Select analyze, select descriptive statistics, and choose frequencies.
2. Select the income variable, which is located in the box on the left, and move it to the variable(s) box that is located on the right.
3. Select the statistics option and choose the measures of central tendency. Select the standard deviation, variance, and mean.
4. Below the box on the left, select the display frequency table option.
5. Once all desired functions have been selected and completed, select OK.

Output of Data Analysis—SPSS

As provided below, two tables are included in the output of the data analysis. Table 1 includes information which identifies the standard deviation, variance, and the range. Table 2 includes details associated with each individual income in the sample. This includes each frequency, as well as three different levels of corresponding percentages.

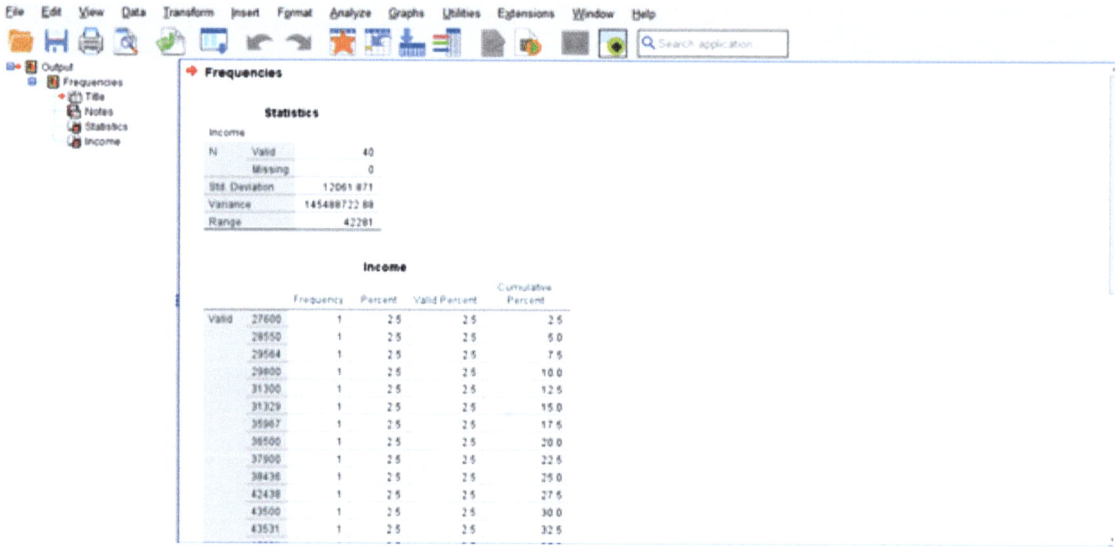

IMAGE 4.3

Workbook Questions

Objective 1—Define and Explain the Use of Dispersion

- Dispersion is the amount of distance between values in a distribution.

1. Based on the information in the following two groups, (1) identify the distance between scores and (2) determine which group has the greatest amount of distance between scores.

Group 1	Group 2
2	1
4	5
3	4
5	2
3	1
2	2.5
4	1
2	7
5	2.5
4	8
$\bar{X} = 3.4$	$\bar{X} = 3.4$

Answers

1.

Group 1	Group 2
2	1
2	**4**
4	5
1	**1**
3	4
2	**2**
5	2
2	**1**
3	1
1	**1.5**
2	2.5
2	**1.5**
4	1
2	**6**
2	7
3	**4.5**
5	2.5
1	**5.5**
4	8
$\bar{X} = 3.4$	$\bar{X} = 3.4$

The scores in Group 2 have the greatest amount of distance between each score.

Objective 2—Define and Explain the Use of Range, Variance, and Standard Deviation

- A range is a type of dispersion that represents the difference between the highest and the lowest value in a distribution.
- A variance is a type of dispersion that represents the average of the squared differences from the mean.
- A standard deviation is a type of dispersion that represents the square root of the average of the squared differences from the mean. In short, it reflects the mean amount of dispersion in a distribution.

Corresponding Questions

1. A variance is a type of dispersion that represents the ______ of the squared differences from the mean.
   a. sum
   b. average
   c. square root
   d. median
2. A ______________ is a type of dispersion that represents the square root of the average of the squared differences from the mean.
   a. range
   b. variance
   c. standard deviation
   d. either b or c

Answers

1. b
2. c

Objective 3—Example Problem(s) and Measures of Dispersion (Range, Variance, Standard Deviation)

See the corresponding pages in the chapter.

- Corresponding Questions

1. Identified below are the number of restorative justice programs identified within university settings. Based on the data provided, compute the range.

Location of Universities in the United States	Number of Restorative Justice Programs
Region 1 (Northeast)	12
Region 2 (Southeast)	6
Region 3 (Northwest)	8
Region 4 (Southwest)	4
Total	30

2. The salaries of police chiefs within each location are identified below. Based on the data provided, compute the range.

Location of Police Department	Salary of Police Chief
Foothills	45,000
Mountain Creek	34,500
Woodville	43,500
Withering	56,500
Little York	31,500
Rockford	46,345
Brickshaw	48,400
Amenity	52,300
Hempfield	49,540
Broward	68,500
Point Lake	42,500

3. The following information represents the number of students who expressed an interest in learning about the use of restorative justice as potential graduate school students. Based on the data provided, compute the range, variance, and standard deviation.

Year	Number of Students
2010	22
2011	17
2012	28
2013	31
2014	16
2015	14
2016	11
2017	13
2018	18
2019	26

4. The following information represents the number of years decided between two judges in response to individuals who were convicted of drug trafficking. Based on the data provided, compute the range, mean, variance, and standard deviation for each county. Which judge, or rather their decision, has the greatest variability?

	Number of Cases									
Judge	**1**	**2**	**3**	**4**	**5**	**6**	**7**	**8**	**9**	**10**
County 1	2	4	3	7	4	8	6	5	7	9
County 2	1	6	8	9	6	3	9	11	8	12

5. A researcher collects data from students that identifies their support for certain measures in response to individuals accused of low-level crimes. This includes the use of restorative justice practices within the criminal justice system in the United States. The following information represents the survey results of students, which is based on the use of a 7-point scale. Based on the data provided, compute the variance and standard deviation.

Perception of Restorative Justice in Response to Low-Level Offenses	Number
1	21
2	26
3	34
4	42
5	38
6	19
7	14

Answers

1. 8
2. 37,000
3. Range = 20; Variance = 46.48; Standard Deviation = 6.81
4. County 1 = Range = 8; Mean = 4.83; Variance = 6.69; Standard Deviation = 2.58
   County 2 = Range = 11; Mean = 6.91; Variance = 10.44; Standard Deviation = 3.23
   The decisions of the judge in County 2 have the greatest amount of variability.
5. Variance = 110.24; Standard Deviation = 10.49

Credits

CHAPTER 5

Visual Information

Graphical excellence is that which gives to the viewer the greatest number of ideas in the shortest time with the least ink in the smallest space.
—Edward R. Tufte

Objectives

1. Discuss the use of a frequency distribution table.
2. Develop a frequency distribution table from a group of scores.
3. Examine the use of a frequency distribution table with categorical data.
4. Demonstrate the relationship between levels of measurement and types of visual content.
5. Explore the use of univariate and bivariate visual content.

Introduction—From Visual to Victory

Imagine receiving an opportunity to engage in a legal case that relates to social justice. In 2017, one of the authors of this text received a phone call from an attorney who specializes in providing legal representation in the pursuit of fair housing in the United States. The case involved minority tenants who were denied adequate housing resources (e.g., running water, heat) who complained to management at an apartment complex. When their complaints were ignored, the tenants shared their concerns with the local news, which resulted in media coverage of their claims. In response, the management team of the apartment complex retaliated against the tenants by imposing an unlawful policy, referred to as the 99-year rule. In this case, the 99-year rule stated that anyone with a felony or misdemeanor conviction within the past 99 years would be evicted from the apartment complex. This led to a number of tenants, who were primarily mothers with children, experiencing an unlawful eviction. In response, the tenants filed a lawsuit in federal court against the apartment complex. Given that the local law enforcement agency facilitated the unlawful eviction, the attorney's strategy involved producing statistical evidence pointing to racial discrimination in arrests. The evidence provided in court, which included the use of visual content (e.g., frequency distribution tables, graphs), ultimately led to a favorable decision on behalf of the tenants.

The Use of a Frequency Distribution Table

As mentioned in the previous example, the visual display of data is critical in providing an understanding of important information.

Frequency Distribution Table

A common type of visual display is what is referred to as a frequency distribution table. A **frequency distribution table** is the presentation of numerical data that reflects the existence of a phenomenon or attribute. This includes the number of times a specific count is identified in a data set. Consider the following:

Suppose a frequency distribution table of information illustrates the treatment of youth in 2019.

Number of Youth Referred to Juvenile Court, 2019	
	f
Males	3,832
Females	1,977
Total	$N = 5{,}809$

frequency distribution table The presentation of numerical data that reflects the existence of a phenomenon or attribute.

Based on data from the National Center for Juvenile Justice (2021), we are able to recognize the variable of gender, which includes male and female youth. The frequency (as indicated with the letter f) provides the actual total count that represents the number of each youth based on their gender. This includes 3,832 males and 1,977 females. The total amount, as reflected by the letter N, provides the complete number of youth referred to juvenile court for alleged drug offenses, which is 5,809.

Proportions

Despite the benefits of displaying the total amount of data, its use may not provide additional important information. For this reason, frequency distributions often include what is referred to as a proportion.

A **proportion** is a number that provides a standardized method of interpreting data for each value relative to the total amount in a distribution. It uses a value that exists between 0.00 and 1.00.

proportion A number that provides a standardized method of interpreting data for each value relative to the total amount in a distribution. It uses a value that exists between 0.00 and 1.00.

Here's a brief example that points to the benefit of standardizing values:

Suppose a student is told by a professor that the student missed only one question on her first-semester exam in a course. The student, who is under the impression that the exam included a total of 10 questions (which results in a score of

90% using a scale of a total of 100%), begins to celebrate and share the good news with her family, friends, etc. Once the student has completed her celebration, the professor reminds the student that the exam only included a total of three questions. Unfortunately, the student's actual exam score is 66.6%. In this example, the scale of 100% serves as a type of standardization that allows one to measure the value of numbers in relation to the total amount in a distribution. The moral of this illustration is that one should consider gaining as much information as possible before making a decision, especially in relation to celebrating a test score.

The formula for computing a proportion is based on the following:

$$p = \frac{f}{N},$$

where

P = proportion
F = frequency
N = total sample amount (size)

As mentioned previously, the standardization scale for proportions is between 0.00 and 1.00. Based on our previous table, consider the application of the formula by reviewing the following questions:

What is the proportion of males?

$$p = \frac{3{,}832}{5{,}809} = 0.66$$

What is the proportion of females?

$$p = \frac{1{,}977}{5{,}809} = 0.34$$

As identified in the previous section, the aforementioned information extends beyond the frequency distribution details. This includes the existence of proportions, which is reflected by the letter *p*. Notice that the proportions exist for both males and females. Given that the range of proportions exists between 0.00 and 1.00, the proportion for males ($N = 3{,}832$) is 0.66, and for females ($N = 1{,}977$), it is 0.34.

Percentages

Along with proportions, percentages also provide a standardization of values that are commonly identified in a frequency distribution. Like the proportion, a **percentage** is a number that provides a standardized method of interpreting data for each value relative to the total amount in a distribution. However, unlike the proportion, the percentage uses the values that exist between 0.00 and 100.00 instead of between 0.00 and 1.00.

percentage A number that provides a standardized method of interpreting data for each value relative to the total amount in a distribution. It uses a value that exists between 0.00 and 100.00

Consider the following formula:

$$p = \frac{f}{N}(100)$$

where
P = percentage
F = frequency
N = total sample amount (size)
(100) = multiply by 100

Both proportion and percentage consist of the same computation of process with one exception, determining the percentage involves the additional step of multiplying the proportion outcome by 100. For instance,

What are the percentages of males?

$$p = \frac{3{,}832}{5{,}809} = 0.66(100) = 66$$

What are the percentages of females?

$$p = \frac{1{,}977}{5{,}809} = 0.34(100) = 34$$

As revealed above, the inclusion of percentage information is provided. As denoted by the abbreviation of pct, the symbol of % is often presented. As indicated, percentages are included for both males and females, along with the total. More specifically, males constitute 66% ($N = 3{,}832$) and females 34% ($N = 1{,}977$) of the total population 100% ($N = 5{,}809$).

Cumulative Frequencies

cumulative frequencies A number that increases in amount because of the addition of numbers that are located behind that number; this number may exist as a frequency, proportion, or percentage.

Another important characteristic of a frequency distribution table is the existence of information that reveals the increasing amount of each score. This is often referred to as the **cumulative frequencies** of the data. More specifically, cumulative frequencies exist when a specific number increases in amount because of the addition of numbers that are located behind that number. In addition, this number may exist as a frequency, proportion, or percentage.

TABLE 5.1 **Amount of Cash Reward for Reporting Information Related to the Crime**

Dollar amount	*f*	*cf*	*p*	*cp*	*%*	*c%*
100	12	12	0.4	0.4	40	40
200	9	21	0.3	0.7	30	70
500	6	27	0.2	0.9	20	90
1,000	2	29	0.06	0.96	6	96
1,500	1	30	0.03	0.99	3	99
	N = 30		$\Sigma = 0.99$		$\Sigma = 99$	

Table 5.1 includes the number of individuals who received a cash reward for providing information that led to the arrest and conviction of individuals found guilty of serious criminal behavior. There are a total of seven columns, in which Columns 3, 5, and 7 include cumulative frequency data. Each cumulative frequency column is an extension of information of the column located to the left. For instance, Column 5 includes the cumulative proportion of the proportion data in Column 4. To understand how cumulative frequencies are developed, let's focus our attention on Column 3. The first number identified under the designation of cumulative frequency (cf) is 12. When 12 is added to the value below 12 in the column to the left, which is 9, the cumulative frequency value is 21. This process is repeated with each additional column and corresponding cumulative.

Rates

Our final characteristic of a frequency distribution table includes rates. A **rate**, like the proportion and percentage, is a type of standardization. More specifically, a rate is a proportion that compares the amount of reported cases with amount of potential cases. This often requires the division of certain values of interest by the population from which those values were derived. For example, if someone stated that 876,321 assaults were committed by youth in 2018, how would you respond? You might respond by asking the question 876,321 out of what? In essence, your response seeks to understand the context in which the number of assaults exists. Does 876,321 assaults represent an amount based on the population of a state, region, county, or metropolitan area? In short, rates can provide valuable insight by including context.

rate A proportion that compares the number of reported cases with the number of potential cases. This often requires the division of certain numbers of interest by the population from which those values were derived.

To compute the rate, consider the following formula:

$$\text{rate} = \frac{\text{f}}{\text{population}},$$

where

F = frequency

Population = total population amount

What was the property crime rate in the United States in 2019?

$$\text{rate} = \frac{6{,}925{,}677}{334{,}319{,}671} = 0.024$$

If someone shared with you that the number of property crimes in the United States was 6,925,677, the information provided may not have any significant value. However, by dividing that number by the United States population, we find a property crime rate of 0.024. To provide a meaningful and practical understanding, it is suggested that the rate is multiplied by 10,000, which gives us the number of crimes per 10,000 individuals. In short, if 10,000 individuals were randomly selected in 2019, we would estimate that 207 individuals experienced a property crime. Consider the following rates of property crimes in the United States between 2015 and 2019 (Uniform Crime Report, 2020).

TABLE 5.2 **Number of Property Crimes in the United States, UCR 2015-2019**

Year	*f*	Population	Rate	Rate per 10,000
2015	8,024,115	324,607,776	0.024	247.19
2016	7,928,530	327,210,198	0.024	242.30
2017	7,682,988	329,791,231	0.023	232.96
2018	7,219,084	332,140,037	0.021	217.35
2019	6,925,677	334,319,671	0.020	207.15

Chapter Learning Assessment Questions

1. A ratio that compares the number of reported cases with the number of potential cases is referred to as a ______.
   a. proportion
   b. percentage
   c. rate
   d. frequency
2. A __________ uses a value that exists between 0.00 and 1.00.
   a. proportion
   b. percentage
   c. rate
   d. frequency

Answers

1. c
2. a

Development of a Frequency Distribution Table From a Group of Scores

At its core, the purpose of a frequency distribution table is to provide data in a clear and organized format. Unfortunately, you might observe a group of scores that are not identified in a particular order. For example, consider the following scores in Table 5.3.

TABLE 5.3 **Multiple Similar Individual Scores**

6	7	7	6
8	9	2	4
3	8	3	6
2	9	1	3
6	5	6	8
7	7	3	2
3	3	9	9
9	2	6	5
1	3	8	7
3	5	9	3

TABLE 5.4 **Grouped Frequency Distribution Table of Scores**

Scale of Measurement	*Corresponding Frequency of Scores*
x	f
9	6
8	4
7	5
6	6
5	3
4	1
3	9
2	4
1	2

As indicated in Table 5.3, notice that the scores identified are not listed in any specific order. Because of the apparent disorder of the scores, it is difficult to observe any trends or draw any conclusions from the data. Furthermore, in Table 5.3, notice how a number of similar individual scores are represented in multiple instances. For instance, the number 7 is identified for a total of 5 times.

As a remedy, for Table 5.3, we will develop what is referred to as an **ungrouped frequency distribution table**. For Table 5.3, which has multiple identical numbers, we will develop a **grouped frequency distribution table**.

As revealed in Table 5.4, the scores in Table 5.3 are now displayed in an orderly manner. The data is readable, and one is able to efficiently recognize trends and potential patterns of development.

Grouped Frequency Distribution Table

As introduced previously, consider the following steps (which were used for the development of Table 5.3):

1. Create two columns.
2. Column 1 will include the highest and lowest score in the distribution, this is referred to as the scale of measurement. In Table 5.3, our highest score is 9, and the lowest score is 1.
3. Column 2 will consist of the actual frequency that corresponds to each score represented in the scale of measurement. For instance, in Table 5.4, notice that the number 6 is located to the right of the number 9. This indicates that a score of 9 is observed a total of 6 times in the distribution of scores.

Overall, Table 5.4 includes the same information listed in Table 5.3 but includes an organization of the scores in the form of a grouped frequency distribution table, which provides an idea of what the scores represent. In many cases, a frequency distribution table may provide additional information, such as proportions and percentages.

In Table 5.5, in order to include the proportions and percentages of each frequency, we must determine the actual frequency values. This includes adding each cumulative *f* to the next *x* in the distribution, which produces a sum of 213. When this step is complete, we are able to include the corresponding proportions and percentages for each score.

TABLE 5.5 **Grouped Frequency Distribution Table With Cumulative Frequencies, Proportions, and Percentages**

fx	Cum*f*	Proportions	CumP	%	Cum%
54	54	0.25	0.25	25	25
32	86	0.15	0.40	15	40
35	121	0.16	0.56	16	56
36	157	0.17	0.73	17	73
15	172	0.07	0.80	7	80
4	176	0.02	0.82	2	82
27	203	0.13	0.95	13	95
8	211	0.04	0.99	4	99
2	213	0.01	0.100	1	100
$\Sigma = 213$					

In Table 5.5, we are able to recognize a group frequency distribution table that includes a wealth of detailed information. This includes (1) frequencies and cumulative frequencies, (2) proportions and cumulative proportions, and (3) percentages and cumulative percentages. Remember, the basis of providing visual information is not to confuse or impress the reader but to aid in their understanding of the phenomenon examined.

Chapter Learning Assessment Question

1. To gauge your understanding of the information provided, complete the following question:The difference between an ungrouped frequency distribution table and a grouped frequency distribution table is:
   a. the number of rows in the distribution tables
   b. the number of columns in the distribution tables
   c. all of the above
   d. none of the above

Answers

1. b

The Use of Frequency Distribution Tables With Categorical Data

For the most part, the visual display of data is based on the use of the interval or ratio level (continuous data). However, it is possible to display data that is nominal or ordinal (categorical data).

Frequency Distribution Display and Nominal Data

A unique difference between continuous, as well as ordinal data is that nominal data does not have to be presented in a particular order.

Consider the following example in Table 5.6, which provides visual evidence of preferred types of law enforcement career options among criminal justice students at two different institutions of higher education. Based on the data provided, we are able to identify the amount of support for three types of law enforcement levels. This includes a total student population of 50 students. Notice how the types of law enforcement agencies are not arranged in any particular order. For instance, within institution 1, the highest number reported preference for a career is with a local agency. This trend of including the highest reported preference is consistent with the other institutions. Thus, the only area of consistency is the greatest amount of reported support ($f = 20$, and $f = 20$) within each institution.

TABLE 5.6 **Preferred Types of Law Enforcement Careers Among Criminal Justice Students**

Institution 1		Institution 2	
Preferred Type	*f*	Preferred Type	*f*
Local agency	**20**	State agency	**20**
State agency	15	Local agency	20
Federal agency	15	Federal agency	10
	N = 50		*N* = 50

TABLE 5.7 **Preferred Types of Training Activities Among Correctional Officers**

Institution 1		Institution 2	
Preferred Type	*f*	**Preferred Type**	*f*
Communication	18	**Communication**	15
Conflict resolution	8	**Conflict resolution**	9
CPR	5	**CPR**	3
Field training	21	**Field training**	11
Recruitment	17	**Recruitment**	21
Report writing	6	**Report writing**	4
Use of force	5	**Use of force**	2
Verbal tactics	3	**Verbal tactics**	4
	N = 83		*N* = 69

In Table 5.7, data related to the responses of correctional officers from two institutions are identified. This includes the preferred types of training that officers can participate in during the year. As revealed, officers at both institutions completed the same questionnaire, which produced different individual numbers of responses associated with each type of training option.

In comparison with the nominal data displayed in Table 5.6, notice the order in which the types of preferred training activities are listed. The preferences are displayed in alphabetical order. In short, whether one chooses the highest frequency of responses or the alphabetical order of the terms that reflect the data responses in a table, the display of nominal data offers a variety of options.

Frequency Distribution Display and Ordinal Data

In comparison to nominal-level data, ordinal-level data requires the arrangement of data to be displayed in an orderly manner. This may include data displayed from lowest to highest or highest to lowest. Regardless of the display preference selected, it is important to visually illustrate orderly data. Remember, the purpose of presenting visual data is to enhance understanding by providing information in a clear and concise manner. Failing to develop visual data will likely result in confusion among readers. For instance, consider the examples in Tables 5.8 and 5.9, which demonstrate the support for house arrest opinions among juvenile probation officers. Which of the two formats of information presented is considered less difficult to understand?

TABLE 5.8 **Opinions Toward the Use of House Arrest Among Juvenile Probation Officers**

Opinions Toward House Arrest	*f*
Strongly unfavorable	12
Unfavorable	8
Somewhat unfavorable	2
Somewhat favorable	6
Favorable	15
Strongly favorable	5
	$N = 48$

TABLE 5.9 **Opinions Toward the Use of House Arrest Among Juvenile Probation Officers**

Opinions Toward House Arrest	*f*
Unfavorable	8
Strongly favorable	5
Favorable	15
Strongly unfavorable	12
Strongly favorable	5
Somewhat unfavorable	2
	$N = 48$

As identified in both Tables 5.8 and 5.9, the opinions of nearly 50 probation officers are displayed. More specifically, this includes their support for the use of house arrest among juvenile youth. Based on a questionnaire, the responses in each table include a total of six options. In Table 5.8, notice how the response options are listed in a specific order: (1) strongly unfavorable, (2) unfavorable, (3) somewhat unfavorable, (4) somewhat favorable, (5) favorable, and (6) strongly favorable. In contrast, are you able to see how the responses are displayed in Table 5.9? The responses are displayed in a manner that is difficult to follow. This example points to the necessity of displaying order and consistency in relation to data results in a table.

Chapter Learning Assessment Questions

1. Which of the following types of data does not require the visual presentation of data in a particular order?
   a. Nominal data
   b. Ordinal data
   c. Interval data
   d. Ratio data

2. When ordinal-level data is provided in a frequency distribution table, it is important to remember that the data ___________.
   a. must be presented from least to greatest
   b. must be presented from greatest to least
   c. must be presented in an orderly manner
   d. either a or b

Answers

1. a
2. c

The Relationship Between Levels of Measurement and Visual Evidence

When individuals think of visual information, they might often think of charts, graphs, and tables. However, as a student of statistics (who has mastered the content in Chapter 2), you know that the development of visual representations is often based on data related to levels of measurement. This may involve different types of content that are listed under either categorical or continuous-level data.

For example, consider the following:

TABLE 5.10 **Levels of Measurement and Types of Visual Content**

Categorical Data	Continuous Data
Pie Graph	Histogram
Bar Chart	Frequency Polygon
	Line Chart
	Scatterplot

Categorical-Level Data

Pie Graphs

pie graph A type of visual information used to emphasize one category in comparison with other categories. It often displays categorical data of no more than four to five categories.

The primary use of a **pie graph** is to emphasize one category in comparison with other categories. For instance, suppose a theory points to the likelihood of males experiencing incarceration at a higher rate than females. The results of the study may utilize a pie graph that displays the differences between the gender categories. Among academic disciplines, pie graphs are often used in economics and accounting. For example, budgets are commonly displayed with pie graphs in order to show differences between categories. The potential problem with pie graphs is that too many categories will likely lead to difficulty in understanding the information provided. For this reason, the use of pie graphs may be limited to data that includes no more than four to five categories.

Consider the following examples of pie graphs:

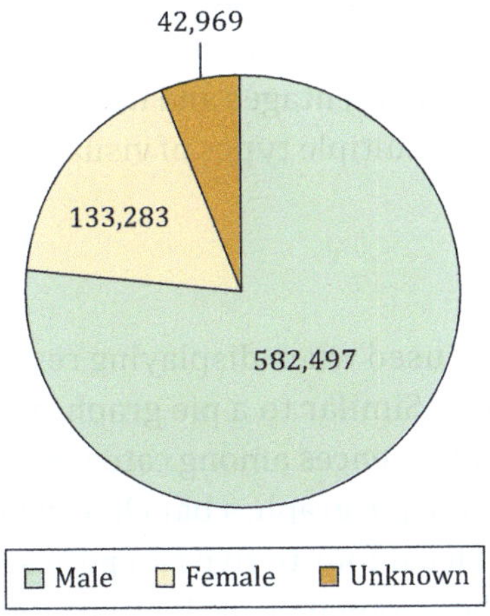

FIGURE 5.1 Violent Crimes by Gender, Offenders (2021)

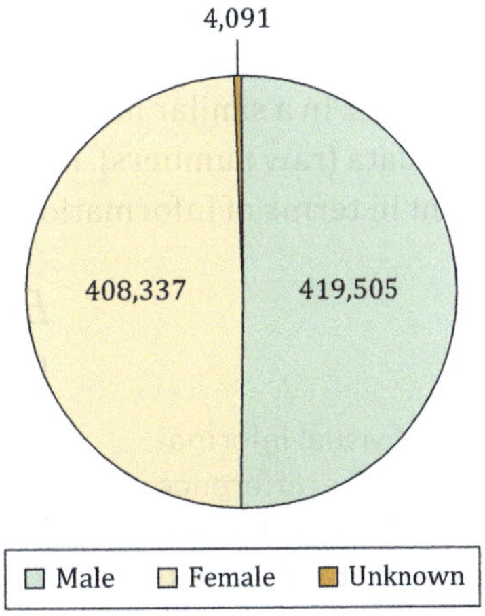

FIGURE 5.2 Violent Crimes by Gender, Victims (2021)

Figures 5.1 and 5.2 display information associated with crime victimization in the United States. This includes reported incidents, as provided by the FBI in 2021, based on gender with regard to alleged offenders and victims. As mentioned previously, the purpose of providing visual information is to assist the reader in gaining an understanding of information. To reach this goal, it may be helpful to consider the (1) placement of data (either inside or outside of the shape), as well as (2) the colors used (light or dark) when attempting to clarify certain group distinctions (e.g., male or female).

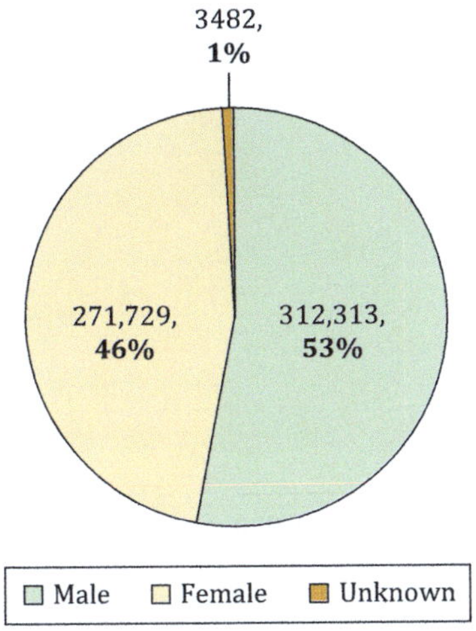

FIGURE 5.3 Aggravated Assault in the United States, Victims by Gender (2021)

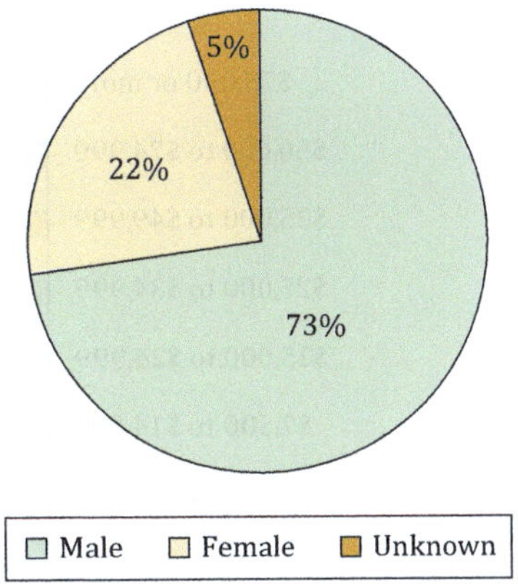

FIGURE 5.4 Aggravated Assault in the United States, Offenders by Gender (2021)

Incidents of aggravated assault, as provided by the FBI in 2021, are included in Figures 5.3 and 5.4. This includes information for both the alleged offender and victim in association with gender. When displaying visual content, it may be beneficial to provide frequency distribution information tables. This may help the reader recognize certain distinctions between variables and certain overall trends. When engaging in this process, it is important to include similar details in both types of data display for the purpose of minimizing confusion on behalf of the reader. For instance, in comparison to data provided in the frequency distribution section, Figure 5.3 includes data percentages. In a similar manner, Figure 5.4 includes data percentages and fails to include the actual count data (raw numbers). In short, it is suggested that multiple types of visual data should be consistent in terms of information presented.

Bar Charts

bar chart A type of visual information used to illustrate the difference among categories through the use of categorical-level data. It is usually designated for information that includes at least four to five categories.

Bar charts are commonly used when displaying research data within the social sciences. Similar to a pie graph, a **bar chart** is used to illustrate the differences among categories by using categorical data. Unlike the pie graph, a bar chart usually provides information for at least four to five categories.

Based on data from the National Crime Victimization Survey in 2020, Figure 5.5 displays data related to victims of property crimes who reported their experiences to the police. In addition, the household incomes of these victims were also reported. In terms of categorical order, the lowest household income is presented first. Observing the data, it appears that the amount of one's household income is associated with the decision to report an incident of victimization to the police. This is an interesting observation in that it is also supported by similar research. In short, this figure points to the value of recognizing research-based relationships between independent and dependent variables as derived from data, which may not be an obvious distinction without the use of a bar graph.

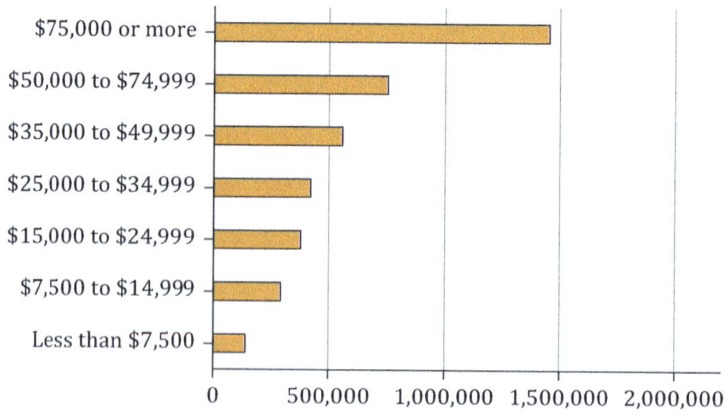

FIGURE 5.5 Property Victimization and Reporting to Police by Household Income (2020)

Continuous-Level Data

Histograms

A **histogram**, which is similar to a pie graph and bar chart, is used to present visual information designed to compare categories. Unlike the pie graph and pie chart, the histogram displays continuous-level (interval/ratio) data. In essence, a histogram illustrates how data is spread within a specific range. Compared to the pie graph and bar chart, the bars in a histogram are displayed without any space between them, which represents the continuous nature of the data identified.

histogram A type of visual information designed to compare categories that uses continuous data. It is often used to display the amount of spread of data within a specific range.

Two types of data exist for use in the development of a histogram. Histograms can be used to present a distribution of (1) raw data, (2) proportions, and/or (3) percentages. Raw data is used for histograms for smaller samples, while proportions and/or percentages are used for large samples and populations. For example, in presenting the distribution of crimes committed by age groups in global countries, proportions and/or percentages would be preferred.

Consider the following examples of histograms:

Names	*Ages*
Javier	26
Janis	38
Robert	33
Henry	41
Jessie	27
Carl	35
Lacey	34
Josey	36
Neal	42
Hank	27
Mary	24
Lisa	32
Candice	42
Kamryn	38
Donald	42
Thomas	40
Paula	36
Tammy	32
Isaiah	36

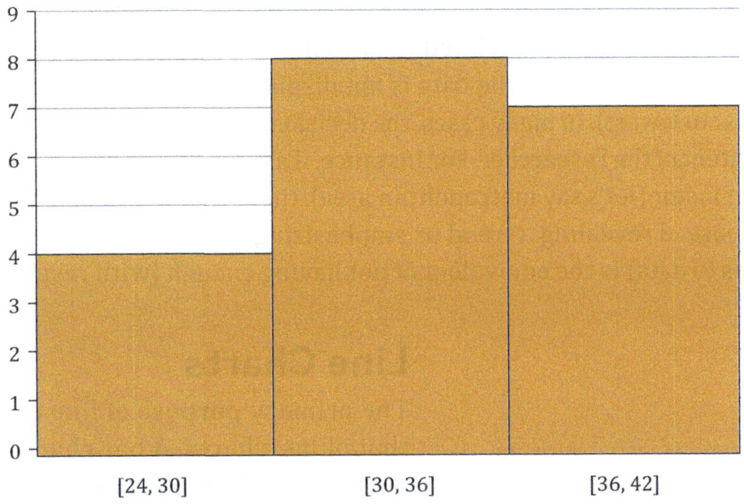

FIGURE 5.6 Exam Grades

Figure 5.6 is an example of a histogram. This includes the names of and ages of graduate students who were recently enrolled in a graduate school program for criminal justice majors. Notice how the ages are listed along the horizonal line at the bottom of the graph. Specifically, there is a 6-point range between the ages within each of the 3 sections, which represents 100% of the population. To the left of the graph, the number of ages (e.g., frequency) for each section are identified.

frequency polygon A type of visual display of information that uses dots to represent the location and spread of continuous-level data.

Frequency polygons are a type of visual content that uses dots when designating the display of continuous-level data. Similar to the histogram, a frequency polygon reveals the amount of spread of data.

Identified in Figure 5.7 are examples of frequency polygons:

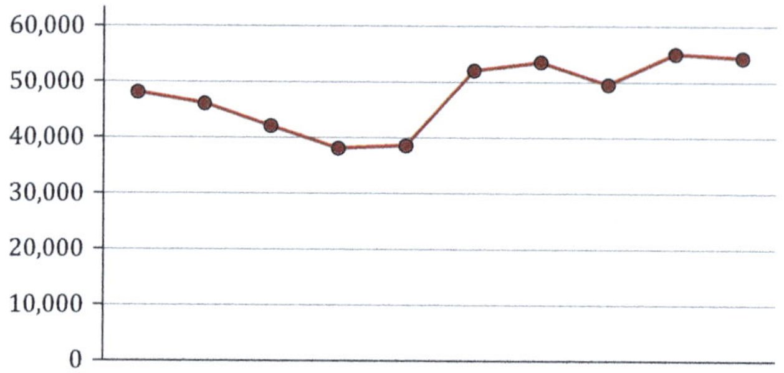

FIGURE 5.7 Salaries of Police Officers

Figure 5.7 displays data related to law enforcement personnel. This includes the salaries of 10 police officers. Notice that the data is not displayed in any particular order (e.g., lowest to highest or highest to lowest). In many cases, the decision to choose the order of display might be determined by the intent of the researcher. For instance, if a researcher believes that salary amount is based on a certain factor (let's say metropolitan area), they will likely display the data in a specific order for the purpose of revealing a trend or emphasizing a point. Overall, in some instances, having more (in terms of data) is the equivalent of not having enough (with respect to understanding).

Line Charts

line chart A type of visual information that uses continuous data to reveal change over time.

The primary purpose of line charts is often confused with that of bar charts. A bar chart is used to show differences between and among categories. On the other hand, a line chart is used to show change over time. Like the histogram and frequency polygon, line charts employed the use of continuous-level data.

Data, as reported by the FBI, is included in Figure 5.8. This includes information that demonstrates the rate of homicide and robbery in the United States. This characteristic of a line chart serves as a powerful benefit, especially as a source of reference when proposing a potential solution or simply raising awareness. Do you have an explanation (theory) that might explain the increase in homicide? Data provided in Figure 5.8 also presents a trend. This includes a downward trajectory of robbery rates. What are some of the factors that may explain this positive trend? Are the data results an indication of effective policies and programs or a reflection of individuals who choose not to report certain offenses? Regardless of explanations, line charts are a valuable source of visual data, especially in relation to research that extends beyond certain time frames (i.e., longitudinal studies).

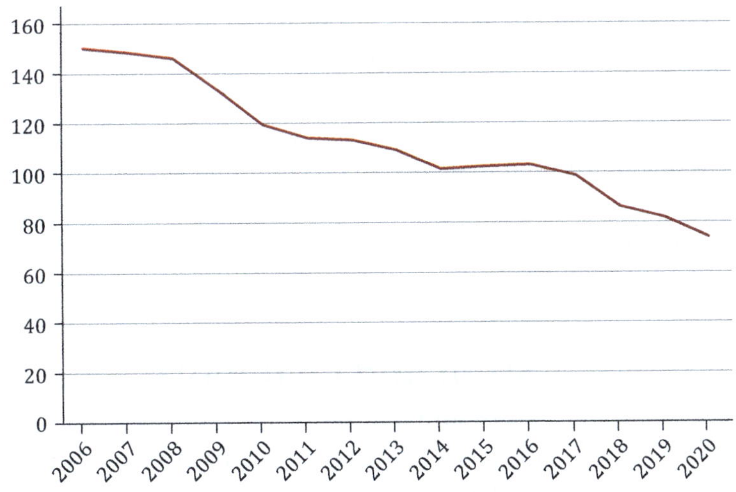

FIGURE 5.8 Robbery Rate, United States, 2006-2020

Scatterplots

A scatterplot is a type of line chart. Unlike most line charts, scatterplots are not specifically developed or used to determine change over a period of time. More specifically, scatterplots determine the association of one variable to another. Scatterplots ask the question: "Do two variables share a pattern of change?" "Do the variables correlate?" That is, as one variable increases in value, does the other variable increase or decrease in a *predictable* manner? Scatterplots are the first of several criteria for establishing cause.

scatterplots A type of line chart that is used to assess the association of one variable to another.

Listed in Figure 5.9 are examples of a scatterplot:

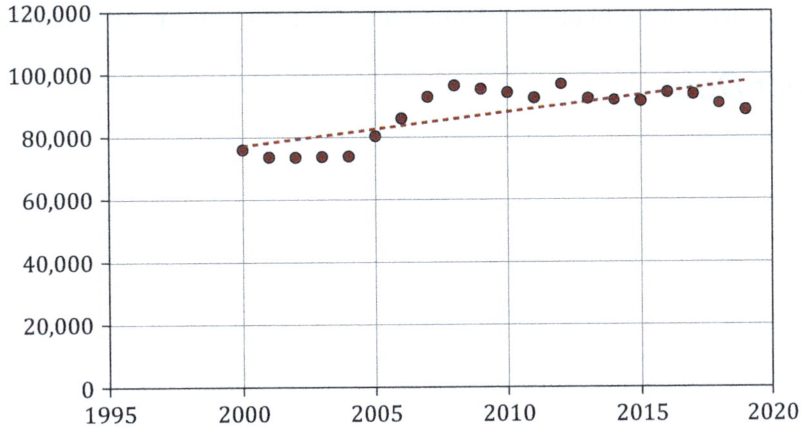

FIGURE 5.9 Private Prisons, State Level (1999-2019)

Data provided by National Prisoner Statistics are included in Figure 5.9. This includes the use of a scatterplot in association with prison data in the United States. More specifically, Figure 5.9 includes prison data in association with the use of private prison facilities. From 2000 to 2019, the trend line points to the increase of private prisons being used by state-level correctional authorities. By examining these longitudinal (data-based) trends, one is able to recognize the value of the scatterplot. For this reason, the scatterplot is often used when attempting to reveal patterns of development that either point to the need for a resource or demonstrate the effectiveness of a program, policy, or measure.

Stem and Leaf Plots

Stem and leaf plots A process of organizing data in which a score is identified in two parts. The stem represents the first digit, and the leaf represents the final digit of a score.

Stem and leaf plots, also referred to as a stem and leaf display, is a process of organizing data. It requires that a score is identified in two parts: the stem and the leaf. Specifically, the stem represents the first digit, and the leaf represents the final digit of a score.

For instance, as identified in Table 5.11, the scores of 12, 28, and 74 are represented in the following stem/leaf format:

TABLE 5.11 **Stem/Leaf Format**

Score	Stem	Leaf
12	1	2
28	2	8
74	7	4

For example, the following are two data sets for incarcerated men. The first data set includes the number of violent acts committed by incarcerated men who have been imprisoned for nonviolent felonies for 24 months. The second data set includes the number of violent acts committed by incarcerated men who have been imprisoned for violent felonies for the same 24 months.

Step 1: Collect Data

Nonviolent Felonies

0 11 6 4 8 7 10 3 6 1 5 0 5 3 6 21 10 2 12 8 8 11 20

Violent Felonies

16 14 30 29 8 54 14 30 25 32 11 23 17 24 42 9 24 31 22 21 14 16 10

Step 2: Arrange Data (Ascending Order)

Nonviolent Felonies

0 0 1 2 3 3 4 5 5 6 6 6 7 8 8 8 10 10 11 11 12 20 21

Violent Felonies

8 9 10 11 14 14 14 16 16 17 21 22 23 24 24 25 29 30 30 31 32 42 54

Step 3: Create Stem

To create a stem, refer to the distribution values in each inmate category. Notice, in Table 5.12, that the lowest value includes a score that begins with a 0, and the highest value begins with a 5. Once the first digit scores are identified (stem data), the last digit scores (leaf data) are included.

Consider the following:

TABLE 5.12 **Sequence of Stem Data**

Sequence	Order of Number Category
0	How many values begin with a "0"
1	How many values begin with a "1"
2	How many values begin with a "2"
3	How many values begin with a "3"
4	How many values begin with a "4"
5	How many values begin with a "5"

Based on the data sequence, consider the following (as identified in Figure 5.10):

Non-Violent Offenders (Mdn = 6)		Violent Offenders (Mdn = 22)
8 8 8 7 6 6 6 5 5 4 3 3 2 1 0 0	**0**	8 9
2 1 1 0 0	**1**	0 1 4 4 4 6 6 7
1 0	**2**	1 2 3 4 4 5 9
	3	0 0 1 2
	4	2
	5	4

FIGURE 5.10 Stem/Leaf of Nonviolent and Violent Offenders

To help understand the stem and leaf plot, notice the numbers that are blocked. These numbers, as indicated in steps 1 and 2, represent violent felons who had 30, 30, 31, and 32 violent acts while incarcerated. The rest of the graph can be interpreted in the same manner. Notice that the leaves on both sides of the stem are skewed. This suggests using the median to assess the difference between the two groups. The two medians, 6 and 22, are far apart. In fact, when we conduct an inferential statistic, we learn that $p < 0.025$. This may suggest that having violent and nonviolent offenders share a cell (or housing area) will increase prison violence. Like most graphics, here is another case in which a critically important observation is made that requires additional research. In any case, offenders incarcerated for violent felonies have a much greater propensity for violence than nonviolent offenders. Should nonviolent felons be protected from violent offenders?

The Misuse of Visual Data

Unfortunately, it is possible to use visual content in a manner that is interpreted as misleading. This often occurs by failing to adhere to the fundamental requirements related to the development of graphic content. For instance, consider the following example:

In a large state-level district area, an opening for the position of state senator has surfaced. Not surprisingly, a number of candidates with prior political experience decided to run for the vacant seat. During their campaigns, two candidates begin to stand out from the others. As expected, both candidates begin to cast dispersion toward each other's track record in relation to addressing crime within certain metropolitan areas in the state. Interestingly, both candidates decide to use graphs to influence voters and gain support for their campaigns. Consider the following data in Table 5.13:

TABLE 5.13 **Number of Homicides 2019–2021**

Year	Number of Homicides
2019	118
2020	125
2021	127

More specifically, as identified in Figures 5.11 and 5.12, candidate (a) used visual information to demonstrate how candidate (b) has failed to provide effective measures designed to address violent crime. On close examination of the tables, the same data is provided; however, the first table conveys the impression that crime has increased considerably. The basis of this distinction is the data provided on the y-axis. Notice how the number lines employed in both graphs have different levels of minimum and maximum ranges. For this reason, identifying the actual number of homicides each year (as in a pie chart) might be more appropriate.

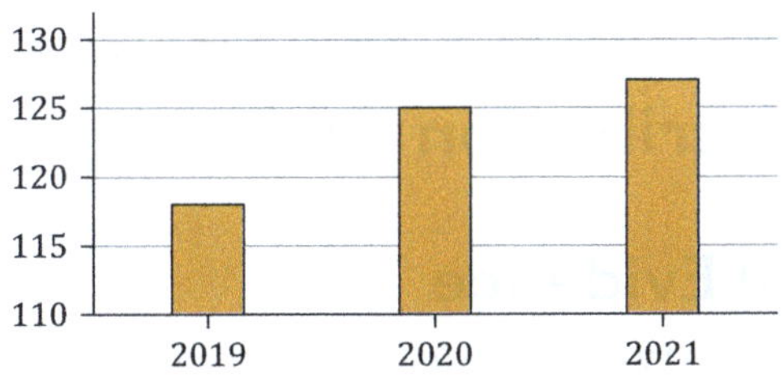

FIGURE 5.11 Number of Homicides 2019-2021

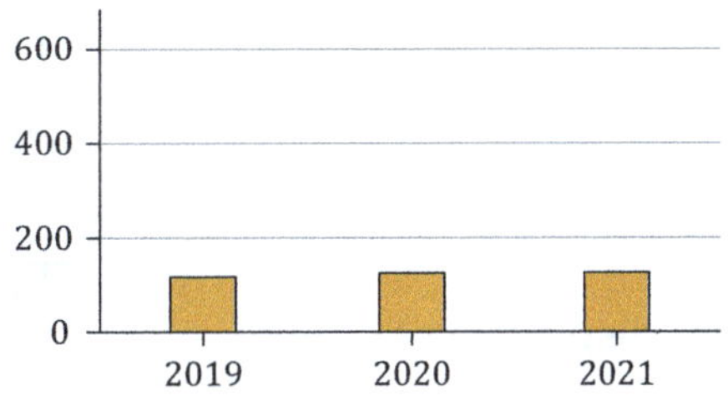

FIGURE 5.12 Number of Homicides 2019-2021

The display of deceptive data may result from deliberate as well as unintended reasons. This includes shaping perceptions, securing funding, or arousing sentiment. Specific tactics include the use of data based on (1) certain time periods, (2) using percentages (with small counts of raw numbers), (3) unfair comparisons (e.g., agencies use different criteria when collecting and defining variables), and (4) dated information.

Chapter Learning Assessment Questions

1. Which of the following types of visual content is not used with continuous-level data?
   a. Stem and leaf display
   b. Frequency polygons
   c. Line charts
   d. Pie charts
2. Which of the following is used to determine whether an independent variable may influence a dependent variable?
   a. Frequency polygons
   b. Pie charts
   c. Histograms
   d. None of the above

Answers

1. d
2. d

univariate display The presentation of information in which one variable is identified.

bivariate display The presentation of information in which two variables are identified.

The Use of Univariate and Bivariate Frequency Distribution Tables

Types of Visual Evidence

When observing numerous types of visual evidence, one might notice a difference between the amount of variables that are included. In most cases, data is either presented as a univariate display or a bivariate display. A univariate display is the display of data that represents only one variable of interest. On the other hand, a bivariate display of data exists when two variables of interest are identified.

TABLE 5.14 **Types of Victim-Offender Relationships in U.S. Domestic Violence, Univariate Table**

Relationship	*f*	%
Acquaintance	6,785	54
Family	1,121	9
Intimate	1,215	10
Stranger	3,367	27
	N = 12,488	100

Table 5.14 is an example of what is considered a univariate display of data. This includes the numbers of each type of victim-offender relationship in association with domestic violence in the United States. More specifically, the table only includes data that reports the frequency of domestic violence experiences on the basis of victim-offender relationships. There is no display of data in relation to any specific factors associated with the victims of domestic violence. Examples include gender, race, or socioeconomic status.

TABLE 5.15 **Types of Victim-Offender Relationship in U.S. Domestic Violence, Bivariate Table**

	Sex of Victim		
Relationship	**Male**	**Female**	*f*
Acquaintance	6,200 60%	585 26%	6,785 54%
Family	648 6%	473 21%	1,121 9%
Intimate	427 4%	788 36%	1,215 10%
Stranger	3,003 29%	364 16%	3,367 27%
	10,278 82%	2210 18%	N = 12,488 100%

Table 5.15 is an example of a bivariate display of data. It includes information in which data from two variables are identified. This includes the type of offender-victim relationship and the gender of the victim.

Are you able to recognize differences on the basis of each victim based on their reported sex? This includes both row and column totals. Observing row totals and percentages involves viewing the data from left to right (a horizontal approach). For instance, among those who reported victimization as a result of intimate relationships, the row total and percentage for males is n = 427 (4%) and females is n = 788 (36%). When viewing the corresponding details in the final column (within the same row), we observe the total row amount *but not the total percentage of the category.* This observation reveals an important distinction between computing and identifying differences between row and column totals and percentages. In our example, row totals are identified by observing data from left to right (horizontal). On the other hand, column percentages are observed from the top to bottom (vertical). For instance, the total row and column percentages, between the sex of the victims, are males (n = 10,278, 82%) and females (n = 2,210, 18%).

Chapter Learning Assessment Questions

1. The presentation of data in which one variable is displayed is known as a(n) ________.
   a. univariate display
   b. bivariate display
   c. categorical display
   d. multinomial display
2. The presentation of data in which two variables are displayed is known as a(n) ________.
   a. univariate display
   b. bivariate display
   c. categorical display
   d. multinomial display

Answers

1. a
2. b

Final Thoughts

Have you ever visited a restaurant (for the first time) and upon receiving a menu (which includes food that you have never tried) discovered there were no photographs of the food offered? For some, this experience is a bit frustrating. The menu example points to the efficacy of providing visual information. A key factor in the provision of such information is clarity and consistency, which is likely to serve as the basis for making informed decisions. This principle holds true in relation to statistics and the use of visual information. As mentioned repeatedly throughout the chapter, visual information serves as a powerful resource within the areas of decision-making as well as areas for further research.

Discussion

As an expert in a legal proceeding, you have been given the responsibility of sharing statistical information in a trial proceeding. In particular, the information provided will likely demonstrate a trend of racial bias in the arrest of youth by a local law enforcement agency. What types of information will you need to meet your objective? Identify what types of visual formats are suggested, along with an explanation for each type.

Chapter Summary

This chapter emphasized the following information:

Objective 1 – The use of a frequency distribution table

- A frequency distribution provides a basic presentation of numerical information reflecting the existence of a phenomenon or attribute.
- A proportion is a number that provides a standardized method of interpreting data for each value relative to the total amount in a distribution. It uses a value that exists between 0.00 and 1.00.
- A percentage is a number that provides a standardized method of interpreting data for each value relative to the total amount in a distribution. It uses a value that exists between 0.00 and 100.00.
- A cumulative frequency is a number that increases in amount because of the addition of numbers that are located behind that number; this number may exist as a frequency, proportion, or percentage.
- A rate is a proportion that compares the number of reported cases with the number of potential cases. This often requires the division of certain numbers of interest by the population from which those values were derived.

Objective 2 – Development of a frequency distribution table from a group of scores

Objective 3 – The use of frequency distribution tables with categorical data

- Nominal-level data does not require the arrangement of data in a specific order.
- Ordinal-level data requires that the arrangement of data is displayed in an orderly manner.

Objective 4 – The relationship between levels of measurement and visual evidence

- A pie graph presents information for categorical variables of no more than four or five categories.
- A bar chart presents information for categorical variables that include at least four or five categories.
- A histogram presents information for individual continuous-level variables.

- A frequency polygon presents information for individual continuous-level variables. This includes the use of dots for the location of data.
- A line chart uses time-related information for the display of trends.
- A scatterplot is a type of line chart that is used to assess the association of one variable to another.
- A stem and leaf plot is a process of organizing data in which a score is identified in two parts. The stem represents the first digit, and the leaf represents the final digit of a score.
- The display of data can be used in a deceptive manner. Specifically, how data is presented within the x- and y-axis may provide a misleading impression.

Objective 5 – Univariate and bivariate displays

- A univariate display provides information in which one variable is identified.
- A bivariate display provides information in which two variables are identified.

Terms

Frequency distribution
Bar chart
Line chart
Pie chart
Histograms
Univariate display
Bivariate display

Chapter Review Questions

1. A __________ uses a value that exists between 0.00 and 100.
   a. proportion
   b. percentage
   c. rate
   d. frequency
2. In comparison to a proportion, computing a percentage involves which of the following?
   a. Dividing a score by 100
   b. Subtracting a score by 100
   c. Multiplying a score by 100
   d. Either a or b
3. A cumulative frequency may exist as a
   a. frequency
   b. proportion
   c. percentage
   d. all of the above

4. Before determining the proportions of data within a grouped frequency distribution, which of the following must be computed?
   a. The scale of measurement numbers must be multiplied by the frequency numbers.
   b. The frequency numbers must be divided by the scale of measurement numbers.
   c. The frequency numbers must be subtracted from the scale of measurement numbers.
   d. The scale of measurement numbers must be divided by the frequency numbers.
5. Based on the following, organize the scores in an ungrouped or group frequency distribution table. For each row, include the following:
   a. proportions and cumulative proportions
   b. percentages and cumulative percentages

1	3	4
2	2	5
1	4	3
3	3	6
2	2	4
3	5	1
1	1	4

6. Based on the data below, construct a frequency table composed of columns for the following grades. Include five range intervals (<59, 60–69, 70–79, 80–89, 90–100). In addition, construct a chart based on the data.

46	57	52	44	58
66	77	72	64	78
76	87	82	74	88
98	109	104	96	110
68	79	74	66	80
46	57	52	44	58
88	99	94	86	100
84	95	90	82	96
44	55	50	42	56
56	67	62	54	68
52	63	58	50	64
48	59	54	46	60
92	103	98	90	104

Grades	Frequency
90–100	11
80–89	8
70–79	7

Grades	Frequency
60–69	10
59>	24
Total	60

7. Based on the data below, construct a frequency table composed of columns for arrests, which includes a cumulative total and percentages. Construct a chart based on the percentages and frequencies. Finally, provide an explanation as to why a specific type of chart was used.

Race	Arrests
Black	132
Latinx	103
White	97

Race	Arrests	%
Black	132	44
Latinx	103	34
White	97	32
Total	332	100%

8. Based on the traffic violation data identified below, construct a frequency table composed of seven intervals (i.e., age ranges) composed of columns that include cumulative totals and percentages. Construct a chart based on the listed frequencies. Finally, provide an explanation as to why a specific type of chart was used.

Age	F	Age	F	Age	F
18	10	29	8	24	9
23	15	34	3	29	8
16	21	27	3	22	12
17	20	28	5	23	11
43	4	54	2	49	1
25	11	36	1	31	4
21	9	32	9	27	6
36	4	47	1	42	1
30	5	41	2	36	2
29	2	40	1	35	3
33	4	44	1	39	1
48	1	59	1	54	2
92	1	103	1	98	1

Age	Freq
16–31	17
32–45	13
46–58	5
59–71	1
72–85	0
86–98	1
99–110	1
Total	38

9. Provide stem and leaf values based on the following data:

	Data			Stem	Leaf	
76	31	23				
81	46	36				
96	50	63				
45	72	77				
52	98	85				
62	66	33				
38	75	21				

10. If one is interested in displaying statistical differences between two institutions (located in the south) and one institution (located in the north), one should consider using which of the following?
    a. Histograms
    b. Bar charts
    c. Pie charts
    d. Line charts
11. If one is interested in displaying visual evidence that reveals the actual ages of youth who were arrested in 2021, one should consider using which of the following?
    a. Scatterplot
    b. Frequency polygons
    c. Bar charts
    d. Line charts
12. A frequency distribution, which compares the number of youth who are released to their parents in comparison to those who are detained prior to adjudication, would best be depicted using a:
    a. pie chart
    b. bar chart
    c. line chart
    d. histogram

13. To present changes in the victimization rate among females within a 10-year period, one is likely to use a __________.
    a. pie chart
    b. bar chart
    c. line chart
    d. histogram
14. A frequency distribution, which compares the number of youth who are released to their parents in comparison to those who are detained prior to adjudication, would best be depicted using a:
    a. pie chart
    b. bar chart
    c. line chart
    d. histogram
15. Construct a bar chart based on the following:

Type of Prison Classification	Frequency
Low-Risk	1,793
Medium-Risk	638
High-Risk	117
Unknown	48
Total	2,596

16. Construct a line chart based on the following:

Number of Youth Tried as Adults	Frequency
2011	7
2012	13
2013	8
2014	7
2015	10
2016	9
2017	6
2018	5
2019	9
2020	11
2021	9
Total	94

17. Construct a histogram based on the following:

Location Within County	Salaries of Police Chiefs
Area 1	75,000
Area 2	58,000
Area 3	63,000
Area 4	67,000
Area 5	69,000
Area 6	74,500
Area 7	83,500
Area 8	81,400
Area 9	63,600
Area 10	48,500
Area 11	55,600
Area 12	58,500
Total	797,600

18. Create a bivariate display for the following information. For each table, include the additional categories of male and female.

Embezzlement, Offender, Race			
	M	F	T
White	11,481	1,004	12,485
Black or African American	6,472	1,464	7,936
Asian	169	127	296
American Indian or Alaska Native	224	45	269
Unknown			1979

Answers

1. b
2. c
3. d
4. a
5.

x	*f*	*fx*	*Proportion*	*Cum. pr*	*%*	*Cum. %*
6	1	6	0.10	0.10	10	10
5	2	10	0.17	0.27	17	27
4	4	16	0.27	0.54	27	54
3	5	15	0.25	0.79	25	79
2	4	8	0.13	0.92	13	92
1	5	5	0.08	0.10	8	100
		$\Sigma = 60$				

6.

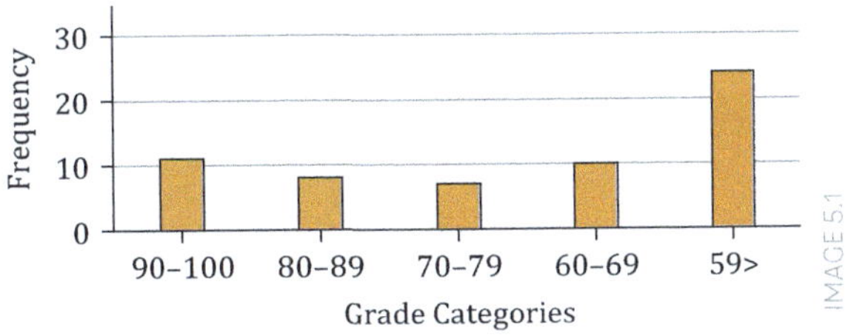

A bar chart was used because of the number of groups.

7.

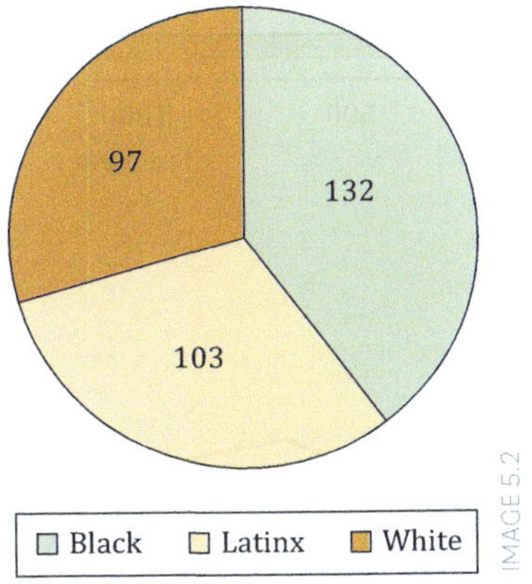

A pie chart was used because of the number of groups.

8.

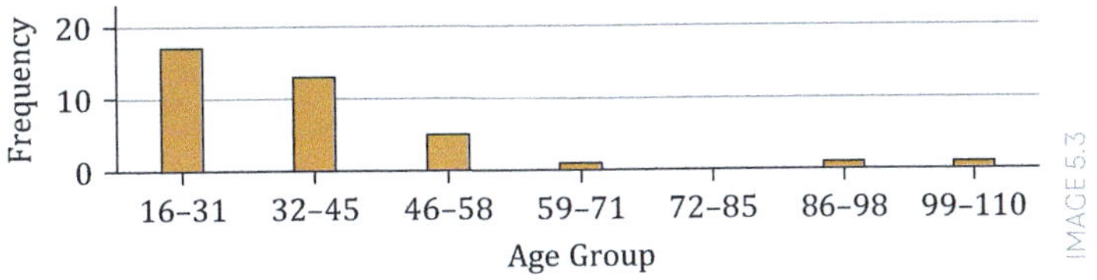

A bar chart was used because of the number of groups.

9.

	Data			Stem	Leaf	
76	31	23		3	1,368	
81	46	36		4	56	
96	50	63		5	02	
45	72	77		6	236	
52	98	85		7	2,567	
62	66	33		8	15	
38	75	21		9	8	

10. c
11. b
12. a
13. c
14. a
15.

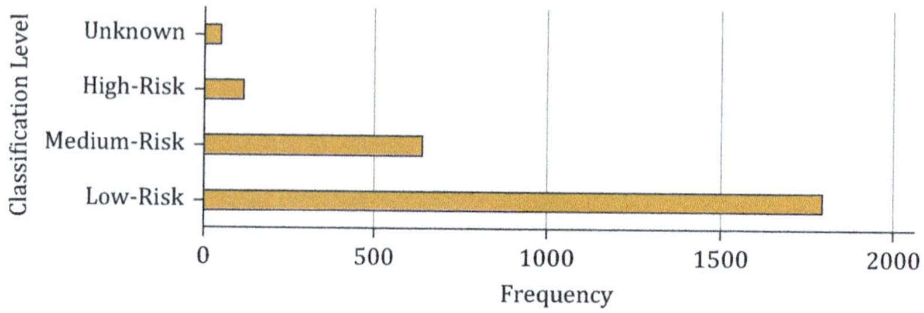

IMAGE 5.4

16.

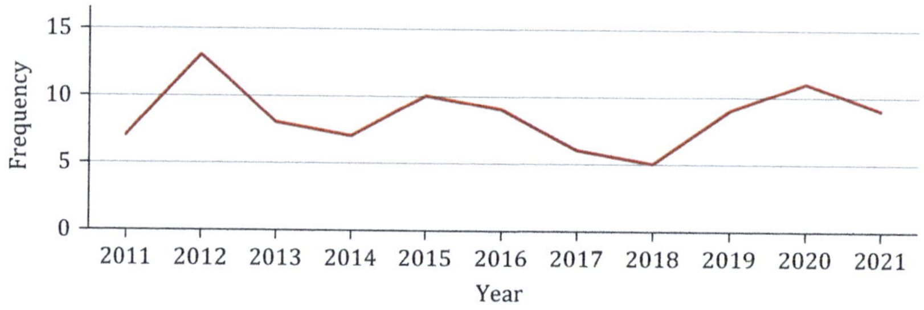

IMAGE 5.5

17.

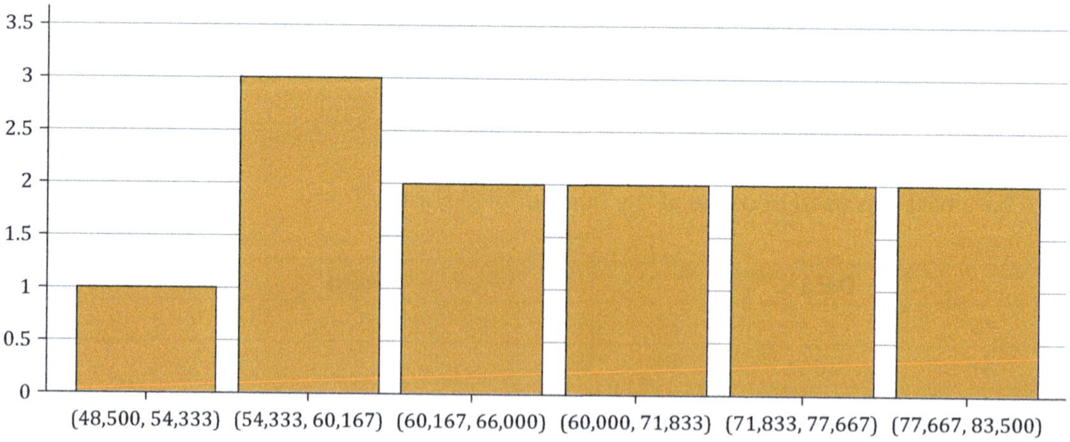

IMAGE 5.6

18.

	M	%	F	%	T	%
White	11,481	63%	1,004	38%	12,485	54%
Black or African American	6,472	35%	1,464	55%	7,936	35%
Asian	169	1%	127	5%	296	1%
American Indian or Alaska Native	224	1%	45	2%	269	1%
Unknown					1,979	9%
	18,346	100%	2,640	100%	22,965	100%

Matching: Place the definition of the term with its corresponding term:

____1. Frequency distribution
____2. Bar chart
____3. Line chart
____4. Scatterplots
____5. Pie chart
____6. Histograms
____7. Stem and leaf plot
____8. Univariate display
____9. Bivariate display

a. categorical variables of at least four or five groups
b. reflecting the existence of a phenomenon or attribute
c. time-related information for the display of trends
d. line chart that examines the association of one variable
e. to another
f. information for individual continuous-level variables
g. categorical variables of no more than four or five groups
h. organizing data in which a score is identified in two parts
i. presentation of data in which two variables are identified
j. presentation of data in which one variable is identified

Answers

1. b
2. a
3. c
4. d
5. f
6. e
7. g
8. i
9. h

Bibliography

National Center for Juvenile Justice. (2021). *National juvenile court data archive: Juvenile court case records 1985–2019.* NCJJ.

Sickmund, M., Sladky, A., & Kang, W. (2021). *Easy access to juvenile court statistics: 1985–2019.* EZAJCS. https://www.ojjdp.gov/ojstatbb/ezajcs/

Uniform Crime Report. (2020). *Crime in the United States, 2019.* U.S. Department of Justice, Federal Bureau of Investigations. https://ucr.fbi.gov/crime-in-the-u.s/2019/crime-in-the-u.s.-2019/topic-pages/property-crime

Uniform Crime Report. (2020). *Crime in the United States, 2015-2019.* US Department of Justice, Federal Bureau of Investigations. https://ucr.fbi.gov/crime-in-the-u.s/2019/crime-in-the-u.s.-2019/topic-pages/property-crime#:~:text=In%202019%2C%20the%20rate%20of,less%20than%20the%202010%20estimate.

Uniform Crime Report. (2022). *Crime in the United States, 2021.* US Department of Justice, Federal Bureau of Investigations. https://cde.ucr.cjis.gov/LATEST/webapp/#/pages/home

National Crime Victimization Survey. (2021). *Property Victimization and Reporting to Police by Household, 2020.* https://ncvs.bjs.ojp.gov/Home

Uniform Crime Report. (2021). *Crime in the United States, 2006-2020.* US Department of Justice, Federal Bureau of Investigations.

Bureau of Justice Statistics, Corrections Statistical Analysis Tools – Prisoners https://csat.bjs.ojp.gov/

Chapter 5 SPSS and Workbook Questions

SPSS and Visual Content

To produce an illustration of a visual using SPSS, consider the following information:

Listed below are the number of days in which property was returned to victims of crime. This includes the time span between the number of days in which the offense was initially reported and when the victim was notified that their item was recovered. A researcher is convinced that the value of the item stolen is associated with the amount of time in which a victim is notified. Develop a graph (or chart) that illustrates if the variables provided below reveal an interesting trend.

Value of Stolen Item	Number of Days
70	10
85	11
100	12
105	12
129	13
131	13
140	13
140	14
175	14
200	15
225	15
220	15
330	16
320	16
330	16
500	18
550	19
600	19
800	20
850	21

Entry of Data—SPSS

1. Select variable view to include information associated with the variables of interest. In our example, this would include both recovery and value.
2. In the first row, include the term *recovery* under the column identified as name.
3. In the column identified as label, you might choose to include a more specific description of the variable. Under the measure column, be sure to select the scale option.
4. For the second group, *value*, follow the same procedure as noted above.
5. Select data view to include the corresponding scores (which are identified in the sample) in each corresponding column.

IMAGE 5.7

IMAGE 5.8

Analysis of Data—SPSS

1. Select graphs and select chart builder. At this point, you will likely see information that encourages you to define your variables based on their appropriate levels of measurement. Once completed, select OK.
2. At the bottom of the screen, select the type of graph or chart, which is based on the levels of measurement of your variables.
3. Since recovery and value are both continuous-level variables, select the scatter-dot option and drag the selection to the designated area. Once completed, select and place the variables in their location. Based on the assumption of the researcher, this would include placing *value* in the area designated for the x value and *recovery* in the area designated for the y value.
4. Once all desired functions have been selected and completed, select OK.

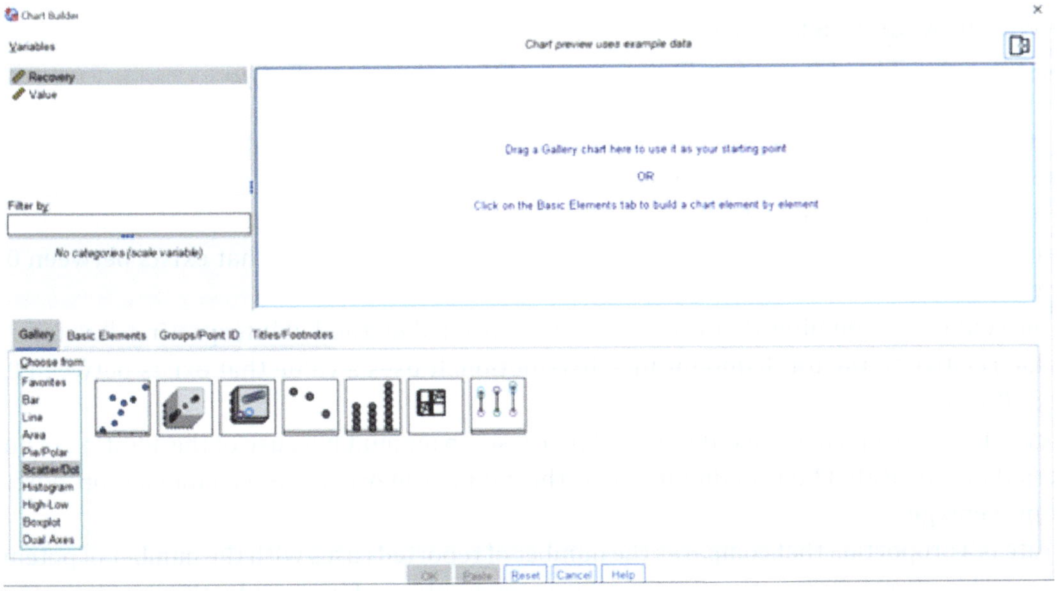

IMAGE 5.9

Output of Data Analysis—SPSS

As provided below, the output of the data analysis includes a scatterplot. The x value (independent variable) identified as *value*, is located on the x-axis. This is located at the bottom of the graph. On the other hand, the y value (dependent variable), identified as recovery, is located on the y-axis, which is located on the left side of the graph. Based on the trend identified between the two variables, are you able to see the association? It appears that as the value of the stolen increases, the time in which the recovery of the item also increases.

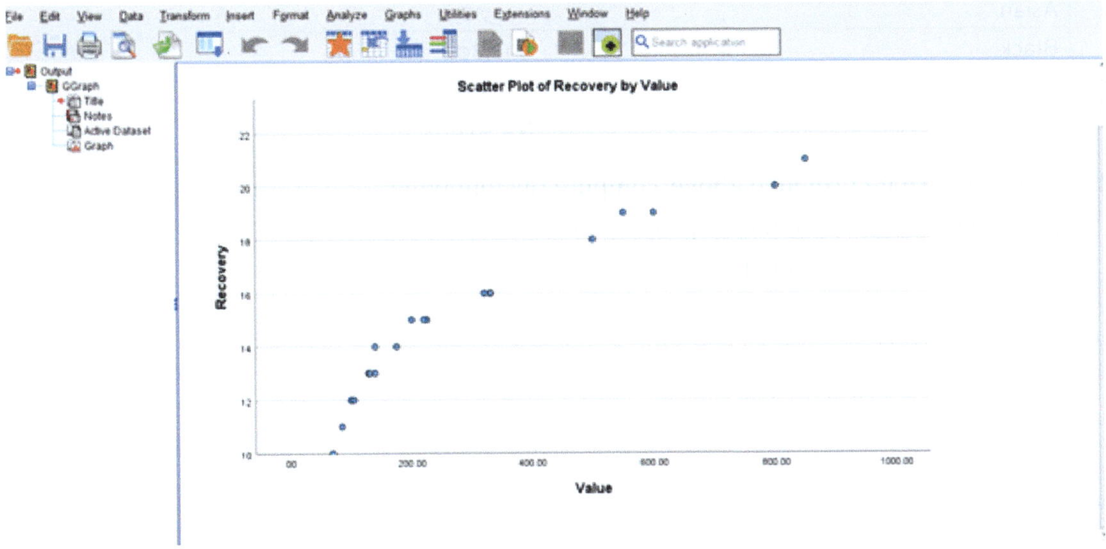

IMAGE 5.10

Workbook Questions

Objective 1—The Use of a Frequency Distribution Table

- A frequency distribution provides a basic presentation of numerical information reflecting the existence of a phenomenon or attribute.
- A proportion is a number that provides a standardized method of interpreting data for each value relative to the total amount in a distribution. It uses a value that exists between 0.00 and 1.00.
- A percentage is a number that provides a standardized method of interpreting data for each value relative to the total amount in a distribution. It uses a value that exists between 0.00 and 100.00.
- A cumulative frequency is a number that increases in amount because of the addition of numbers that are located behind that number; this number may exist as a frequency, proportion, or percentage.
- A rate is a proportion that compares the number of reported cases with the number of potential cases. This often requires the division of certain numbers of interest by the population from which those values were derived.

Corresponding Questions

1. Based on the data below, construct a frequency distribution table composed of columns for the following grades. Include range intervals (80–89, 90–100, etc.). In addition, construct a chart based on the data.

Race of Youth (15 Years) by Referral Offense (Person) in 2019

Race	*f*
Asian	512
Black	18,807
White	19,484
	$N = 38{,}803$

2. Based on the data provided above, compute the following:
   a. Proportion and cumulative proportion
   b. Percentage and cumulative percentage

Answers

2 a.

Race of Youth (15 Years) by Referral Offense (Person) in 2019

Race	*f*	*p*	*cp*
Asian	512	0.01	0.01
Black	18,807	0.49	0.50
White	19,484	0.50	0.100
	N = 38,803		

2 b.

Race of Youth (15 Years) by Referral Offense (Person) in 2019

Race	*F*	*%*	*c%*
Asian	512	1	1
Black	18,807	49	50
White	19,484	50	100
	N = 38,803		

Objective 2—Development of a Frequency Distribution Table From a Group of Scores

Corresponding Questions

1. Based on the following, organize the scores in an ungrouped or grouped frequency distribution table. For each row, include the following:
   a. cumulative frequencies
   b. proportions and cumulative proportions
   c. percentages and cumulative percentages

16	3
12	7
8	18
6	11
9	5
21	4
14	1

Answers

1.

x	Cum$x$	Proportion	Cum. pr	%	Cum. %
16	16	0.12	0.12	12	12
12	28	0.09	0.21	9	21
8	36	0.06	0.27	6	27
6	42	0.04	0.31	4	31
9	51	0.07	0.38	7	38
21	72	0.16	0.54	16	54
14	86	0.10	0.64	10	64
3	89	0.02	0.66	2	66
7	96	0.05	0.71	5	71
18	114	0.13	0.84	13	84
11	125	0.08	0.92	8	92
5	130	0.04	0.96	4	96
4	134	0.03	0.99	3	99
1	135	0.01	0.1	1	100
$\Sigma = 135$					

Objective 3—The Use of Frequency Distribution Tables With Categorical Data

- Nominal-level data does not require the arrangement of data in a specific order.
- Ordinal-level data requires the arrangement of data to be displayed in an orderly manner.

Objective 4—The Relationship Between Levels of Measurement and Visual Evidence

- A pie graph presents information for categorical variables of no more than four or five categories.
- A bar chart presents information for categorical variables that include at least four or five categories.
- A histogram presents information for individual continuous-level variables.
- A frequency polygon presents information for individual continuous-level variables. This includes the use of dots for the location of data.
- A line chart uses time-related information for the display of trends.
- A scatterplot is a type of line chart that is used to assess the association of one variable to another.
- The display of data can be used in a deceptive manner. Specifically, how data is presented within the x- and y-axis may provide a misleading impression.

Corresponding Questions

1. Based on the data below, construct a frequency table composed of columns for arrests that include a cumulative total and percentages. Construct a chart based on the percentages and frequencies. Finally, provide an explanation as to why a specific type of chart was used.

Gender	Arrests
Male	122
Female	47
Other	5

Answers

1.

Gender	Arrests		%
Male	122		70%
Female	47		27%
Other	5		3%
Total	174		100%

Objective 5—Univariate and Bivariate Displays

- A univariate display provides information in which one variable is identified.
- A bivariate display provides information in which two variables are identified.

Corresponding Questions

1. Which of the following is an example of a univariate display?

   a.

Number of Inmates on Death Row by Race

Race	Frequency
Blacks	18
Hispanic	16
Other	3
Whites	8
Total	45

b.

Number of Inmates on Death Row by Race and Gender

Race	Males	Females	Total
Blacks	18	5	23
Hispanic	16	4	20
Other	3	0	3
Whites	8	1	9
Total	45	10	55

c.

Number of Inmates on Death Row by Gender

Males	20
Females	6
Other	2
Total	28

d. both a and c

2. Create bivariate tables that include the variables of male and female for the following tables of information.

Identity Theft—Age

	M	F	T
50 to 59	27,392	23,509	50,901
40 to 49	24,926	22,778	47,704
30 to 39	19,329	17,861	37,190
60 to 69	19,430	17,013	36,443
20 to 29	19,294	3,865	23,159
70 to 79	14,923	1,834	16,757
80 to 89	3,789	735	4,524
10 to 19	1,812	1,197	3,009
90 to Older	613	144	757
0 to 9	231	218	449

Hate Crime Offense Type

	M	F	T
Intimidation	2,148	525	2,673
Simple Assault	2,097	44	2,141
Destruction/Damage/Vandalism of Property	1,643	117	1,760
Aggravated Assault	978	101	1,079
All Other Larceny	243	35	278
Drug/Narcotic Violations	132	15	147
	7,241	837	8,078

Answers

1. d
2.

M	%	F	%	T	%
27,392	21%	23,509	26%	50,901	23%
24,926	19%	22,778	26%	47,704	22%
19,329	15%	17,861	20%	37,190	17%
19,430	15%	17,013	19%	36,443	16%
19,294	15%	3,865	4%	23,159	10%
14,923	11%	1,834	2%	16,757	8%
3,789	3%	735	1%	4,524	2%
1,812	1%	1,197	1%	3,009	1%
613	0%	144	0%	757	0%
231	0%	218	0%	449	0%
131,739	100%	89,154	100%	220,893	100%

	M	%	F	%	T	%
Intimidation	2,148	30%	525	63%	2673	33%
Simple Assault	2,097	29%	44	5%	2141	27%
Destruction/Damage/ Vandalism of Property	1,643	23%	117	14%	1760	22%
Aggravated Assault	978	14%	101	12%	1079	13%
All Other Larceny	243	3%	35	4%	278	3%
Drug/Narcotic Violations	132	2%	15	2%	147	2%
	7,241	100%	837	100%	8,078	100%

Credits

CHAPTER 6

Probability

If nature has taught us anything it is that the impossible is probable.
—Ilyas Kassam

Objectives

1. Identify the significance and types of probability in statistics.
2. Define and explain the significance of a normal curve.
3. Discuss the purpose and use of a z-score.
4. Demonstrate the relationship between a z-score and other data distribution characteristics.
5. Demonstrate the use of a z-table and determine the area of a z-score.

Introduction—Crime Solving and Probability

Imagine conducting an investigation where a string of armed robberies occurred in a certain part of a city. On review of the complaints and reports, you notice a number of similarities. For instance, the robberies occurred between 6 and 7 pm on every second and fourth Friday of the month. In addition, the crimes targeted individuals who were walking from a location where they work and were required to walk to a bus stop to travel home. Based on these details, you decide to work undercover, posing as a "walking worker." As expected, the offender (on the second Friday of the month) attempts to rob someone in your presence, which leads to his arrest. By reviewing the details and noticing consistent patterns of behavior, you were able to predict the likelihood of an occurrence taking place. This illustration points to the use and value of probability in statistics.

Probability plays a significant role in statistics, especially in relation to the use of statistics in research, where it is commonly referred to as hypothesis testing. That topic will be covered in the next chapter. First, it is important to discuss several foundational aspects of probability. This includes the definition of probability, types (or principles) of probability, and the distinctions between probability and frequency distributions.

Probability

Probability refers to the likelihood of an occurrence or outcome. It is usually identified as a statistic.

For example, suppose a jury pool includes a total of nine Blacks and three Whites.

probability The likelihood of an occurrence or outcome, usually expressed as a statistic.

TABLE 6.1 **Jury Members, Criminal Court Trial by Race**

Jury Members of Criminal Court Trial by Race	
Race	***N***
Blacks	9
Whites	3
Total	12

Let's assume that a court clerk selects a jury foreperson by randomly selecting their names using a computer program. In this instance, $P(\text{B})$ refers to the probability of selecting a juror who is Black.

For example:

$$\begin{aligned} P(\text{B}) &= \text{number of Black jurors/total number of jurors} \\ &= 9/12 \\ &= 0.75 \end{aligned}$$

The probability of selecting a Black juror as the jury foreperson is 0.75 (or 75%).

Types of Probability

Another type of probability is referred to as the **converse principle.** Converse probability refers to the probability of an outcome not taking place. It is computed by subtracting 1 from the actual probability of a potential outcome.

Converse probability Refers to the probability of an outcome not taking place. It is computed by subtracting 1 from the actual probability of a potential outcome.

Based on our previous example (Table 6.1), $P(\bar{\text{B}})$ refers to the probability of not selecting a juror who is Black.

$$\begin{aligned} P(\bar{\text{B}}) &= 1 - P(\text{B}) \\ &= 1 - 0.75 \\ &= 0.25 \end{aligned}$$

The probability of not selecting a Black juror as the jury foreperson is 0.25 (or 25%).

In relation to law enforcement arrests and investigations, let's assume that a local police department reported a 51% clearance of property crimes in 2020. This reveals a probability of solving a property crime at 0.51. For any single incident of reported property crime, let's assume it was the last one reported in 2020; the probability of that criminal incident not being cleared is 0.49.

$$P(\bar{\text{C}}) = 1 - P(\text{C})$$

$$= 1 - 0.51$$
$$= 0.49$$

addition principle The probability of obtaining a variety of outcomes equals the sum of their individual probabilities. For instance, the probability of A or B is based on:

$$P(\text{A or B}) = P(\text{A}) + P(\text{B})$$

Another type of probability is the **addition principle**. This principle says that the probability of obtaining a variety of outcomes equals the sum of their individual probabilities.

As an example, suppose a criminal defendant who committed a serious violent crime has a:

0.71 probability of receiving a prison sentence
0.20 probability of being placed on probation
0.09 probability of being found not guilty

The probability of the defendant receiving a prison sentence or being placed on probation is $0.71 + 0.20 = 0.91$. Furthermore, the addition principles assume that all possible outcomes are mutually exclusive. This means, based on our example, that the defendant can only receive either a prison sentence, probation, or acquittal. To that end, finding the sum of all three possibilities includes the following:

$$= P(\text{Prison}) + P(\text{Probation}) + P(\text{Acquittal})$$
$$= 0.71 + 0.20 + 0.09$$
$$= 1$$

The final answer (1) indicates that an outcome must occur. This includes either prison, probation, or acquittal.

multiplication principle States that the probability of receiving a combination of mutually exclusive outcomes equals the product of their separate probabilities.

$$P(\text{A and B}) = P(\text{A}) \times P(\text{B})$$

Our final principle of probability is the **multiplication principle**. The multiplication principle states that the probability of receiving a combination of mutually exclusive outcomes equals the product of their separate probabilities.

Unlike the addition principle, the multiplication principle assumes that both potential outcomes will occur. Furthermore, the calculation of numerous probabilities may occur. Let's assume that a prosecutor has two criminal cases in which one defendant was charged with aggravated assault, and another was charged with first-degree manslaughter. Based on his prior experience, he is convinced that he has a 0.75 chance of securing a conviction for the aggravated assault charge. With the first-degree manslaughter charge, he believes he has a 0.85 chance of securing a conviction. To that end, the probability that he will receive convictions for both cases is provided below:

$$P(\text{A and B}) = P(\text{A}) \times P(\text{B})$$
$$= P(0.75) \times P(0.85)$$
$$= 0.63$$

For both charges, the conviction probability is over 60%.

Difference Between Probability and Frequency Distributions

It is important to draw a distinction between frequency distributions and probability distributions. For instance, consider the following number of property crimes that were solved by a local police department.

TABLE 6.2 **Reported Property Offenses by Type**

Frequency Distribution of Reported Property Offenses by Type		
Type	***N***	***Prop.***
Theft	48	0.34
Motor Vehicle Theft	63	0.45
Larceny	21	0.15
Theft from Motor Vehicle	08	0.06
Total	140	

Table 6.2 includes the number of offenses reported to the local police department. This includes six types of property offenses. Along with the frequencies for each type, included are the proportions, which provide an indication of the offense that is most likely to occur (motor vehicle theft). Based on this data, the police department creates a task force designed to solve motor vehicle theft offenses in the area. After 1 week of operation, the task force reports a clearance probability $P(\text{C})$ of 0.7 and a non-clearance probability $P(\text{N})$ of 0.3 based on three reported incidents of motor vehicle theft. To demonstrate the effectiveness of the newly formed task force, the police chief presents a probability distribution table to city government officials containing the following information:

TABLE 6.3 **Probability of Solving Motor Vehicle Theft Cases**

Outcomes	**Probability Computation**		
CCC	P(CCC)	(0.7)(0.7)(0.7)	0.343
NNN	P(NNN)	(0.3)(0.3)(0.3)	0.027
CNN	P(CNN)	(0.7)(0.3)(0.3)	0.063
NCN	P(NCN)	(0.3)(0.7)(0.3)	0.063
NNC	P(NNC)	(0.3)(0.3)(0.7)	0.063
NCC	P(NCC)	(0.3)(0.7)(0.7)	0.147
CNC	P(CNC)	(0.7)(0.3)(0.7)	0.147
CCN	P(CCN)	(0.7)(0.7)(0.3)	0.147
			Total = 1

TABLE 6.4 **Probability of Motor Vehicle Clearance**

Probability Distribution of Motor Vehicle Theft Clearances for Three Incidents	
X	*P(X)*
0	0.027
1	0.063
2	0.147
3	0.343
	Total = 1

Because of the probabilities listed in Table 6.3, Table 6.4 includes an actual theoretical probability format. Column X reveals the number of motor vehicle theft cases solved within a group of three reported incidents. This includes a total of four options (0 = none cleared, 1 = one cleared, 2 = two cleared, or 3 = three cleared). By adding similar combinations, we can place those totals below, and the sum will equal to 1.

Chapter Learning Assessment Questions

To determine your level of understanding, complete the following questions:

Objective 1

1. The difference between a probability and frequency distribution is that
   a. a frequency distribution is a display of data based on what exists.
   b. a probability distribution is a display of data based on what will likely occur in the future.
   c. a frequency distribution is a display of data based on what will likely occur in the future.
   d. both a and b
2. The ____________ principle refers to the probability of an outcome not taking place.
   a. converse
   b. addition
   c. multiplication
   d. none of the above

1. d
2. a

The Significance of a Normal Curve

Understanding probability provides a strong foundation for understanding the significance of the normal curve. A **normal curve** is a visual distribution of values that is symmetric. For clarification, symmetric refers to an equal amount of distance or space between two sections.

In the following illustration (Figure 6.1), one is able to identify how the information within the normal curve reflects the use and location of data. This includes the mean, as well as confidence intervals and corresponding percentages.

normal curve A visual distribution of values that is symmetric.

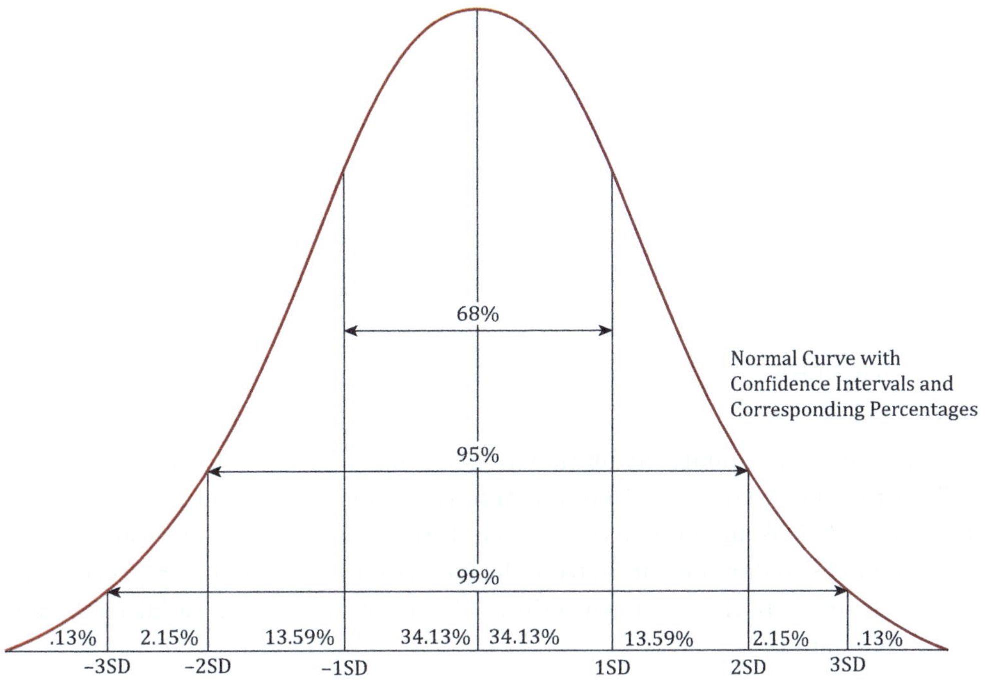

FIGURE 6.1 Normal Curve With Percentages

Figure 6.1 includes a normal distribution curve. As identified, both sides (or areas) of the curve are of equal distance and size (symmetric). In addition, the sections identified (using percentages) represent areas under the curve.

Consider the following example:

From a practical standpoint, as identified in Table 6.5, are the number of youth who experienced arrest on the basis of race. This includes a total of five categories, along with sum and corresponding proportions (probabilities). The mean of the data provided is 64.2.

TABLE 6.5 **Youth Arrests by Race**

Race	*f*	*p*
Asian	7	0.02
Black	146	0.45
Latinx	56	0.18
Other	16	0.05
Whites	96	0.30
	$\sum = 321$	$\sum = 1.00$

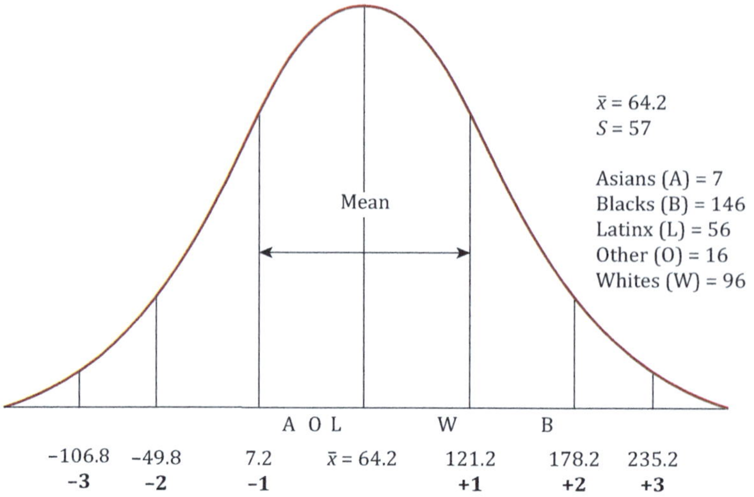

FIGURE 6.2 Normal Curve, Standard Deviation

Figure 6.2 includes additional information. In general, we believe that all of the races (except Blacks) fall within the mean area. To determine the values that exist beyond the mean, the standard deviation (57) is added to and subtracted from the mean (64.2), resulting in 121.2 and 7.2: 121.2 represents 1 standard deviation from the mean to the right, and 7.2 represents 1 standard deviation from the mean to the left. Each additional value represents the addition or subtraction of the standard deviation.

Right side of the curve →

Mean	SD	SD1	SD	SD2	SD	SD3
64.2	+57	121.2	+57	178.2	+57	235.2

← Left side of the curve

SD3	SD	SD2	SD	SD1	SD	Mean
−106.8	−57	−49.8	−57	7.2	−57	64.2

Notice that the value of Blacks (146) falls outside of the mean area. One hundred forty-six lies between 121.2 (1 standard deviation from the mean) and 178.2 (2 standard deviations from the mean). Thus, the probability of Blacks experiencing arrest is greater compared to members of the other racial categories.

By understanding the importance of the use of the standard deviation, one is able to recognize the relative value of scores in a distribution. In short, this process is designed to emphasize the value of context. To further appreciate this distinction, we will now turn our attention to what is referred to as a z-score.

Chapter Learning Assessment Questions

To determine your level of understanding, complete the following questions:

Objective 2

1. To determine one standard deviation from the mean, one must __________.
   a. add the standard deviation to the mean
   b. subtract the standard deviation from the mean
   c. divide the standard deviation from the mean
   d. either a or b
2. If the mean of a distribution is 14 and the standard deviation is 5, the score that is 2 standard deviations from the mean is __________.
   a. 24
   b. 19
   c. 9
   d. none of the above

Answers

1. d
2. a

The Purpose and Use of a z-Score

Imagine a student earns a 48 on an exam. She assumes that her score is among the lowest in comparison to other scores earned by fellow classmates. On discussing her score with her professor, she discovers the mean (class average) is 40. Thus, she realizes that other students did not do as well as she thought they did. With a score of 48 and a class average of 40, she realizes that her score is 8 points above the class average. Despite this awareness, her knowledge of the class average does not reveal how well (or how poorly) she did in relation to the other students. More specifically, is 48 the highest score, second highest score, etc.? If the standard deviation of the distribution exam scores is 5, her score is 1 standard deviation above the mean. If the standard deviation of the exam scores is 10, her score is within 1 standard deviation of the mean. Regardless of whether her score is above or below 1 standard deviation from the mean, she still does not know how well she did in relation to the scores of her classmates.

This example shows the need for additional information. Information about a distribution of scores, such as a single score, the mean, and standard deviation, does not provide significant details of the relative value of a score. As a remedy, values of scores should be transformed into a system (or criteria) that will reveal the actual location of scores in a distribution. This process

z-score A value that reflects the amount of distance between a value and the mean of scores within a distribution.

serves as the basis of what is referred to as z-scores. In short, z-scores provide a standard by which scores can be adequately measured against each other.

A **z-score** is a value that reflects the amount of distance between a value and the mean of scores within a distribution. It also identifies whether the value is greater or less than the mean.

The formula for computing a z-score is based on

$$z = \frac{x - \bar{x}}{s},$$

where

x = each value (in a distribution)
$\bar{x}$ = the sample mean
s = the standard deviation of the distribution

As identified in the definition, a z-score identifies the amount of distance between a value and the mean of scores in a distribution. In other words, the z-score identifies the specific location of a score in comparison to both the mean and other scores. Furthermore, the sign and value (number) of a z-score reveal a significant amount of vital information. For instance, a positive or negative sign indicates whether a z-score is above or below the mean. The value (or actual number) of a z-score reveals the distance between the mean and the score with respect to standard deviations.

For instance, suppose a distribution of a score has a mean ($\bar{x}$) = 40 and a standard deviation (s) = 15.8, and a score (x) = 20.

$$z = \frac{x - \bar{x}}{s}$$

$$z = \frac{20 - 40}{15.8} = \frac{-20}{15.8} = -1.26$$

In terms of the z-score transformation, z = −1.26. The negative sign of the z-score indicates that the score is below the mean. The number also reflects that the score is slightly 1 standard deviation from the mean in the distribution. In order to determine the relative value of the score, consider the following z-scores for the additional scores in the distribution. Are you able to recognize the trend in terms of the values of the z-scores and their location from the mean? Notice that the values of 60 and 20, which are both 20 points away from the mean, are also both positive and negative values.

TABLE 6.6 **Display of Values and z-Scores**

x	z-score	$\bar{x}$	s
60	1.26	40	15.81
50	0.63		
40	0.00		
30	−0.63		
20	−1.26		

Chapter Learning Assessment Questions

To measure your level of understanding, complete the following questions:

Objective 3

1. A z-score reflects the amount of distance between a value and the ______ in a distribution.
   a. median
   b. standard deviation
   c. mean
   d. none of the above
2. By observing a z-score, a negative sign means that the score is ______.
   a. near the mean
   b. far from the mean
   c. one standard deviation from the mean
   d. below the mean
3. When computing a z-score, the first step is to ______.
   a. subtract the mean from a score
   b. subtract a score from the mean
   c. divide the difference between the mean and a score by the standard deviation
   d. none of the above

Answers

1. c
2. d
3. a

The Relationship Between a z-Score and Other Data Distribution Characteristics

A z-score has several unique relationships with other data distribution characteristics that we have previously discussed. This includes the standard deviation, mean, and the value of x. Provided below are steps that will enable one to compute each type of characteristic.

Computing the Standard Deviation Score

Based on the information provided, determine the standard deviation score from the mean (46), z-score (–3.00), and x (30).

With a z-score of −3.00, which reflects a score that is 3 standard deviations from the mean, subtract the mean (46) from the value of x (30), which is −16. The value is then divided by 3 (which represents the distance from the mean), which is 5.33. Thus, the standard deviation is 5.33.

Another option is the employ the following steps, in which we use the z-score formula:

$$z = \frac{x - \bar{x}}{s}$$

Our values are applied to the formula.

$$-3.00 = \frac{30 - 46}{s}$$

By subtracting 46 from 30, we have −16.

$$-3.00 = \frac{-16}{s}$$

To avoid computing with a fraction, we will multiply each value with *s*. This will isolate the value of −16.

$$-3.00(s) = -16(s)$$

$$-3.00(s) = -16$$

Now we will divide both values by −3.00, which will give us our *s*.

$$\frac{-3.00(s)}{-3.00} = \frac{-16}{-3.00}$$

$$s = 5.33$$

Computing the Mean

Determine the mean from a standard deviation score (9), a z-score (+1.00), and x (21). Compute the mean score based on the following:

The z-score includes (+1.00), which reveals that the distance between the score and the mean is 1 standard deviation. We then multiply this score with the standard deviation score $1(9) = 9$. Since the z-score is above the mean, we subtract the score (9) from *X* (21), which is 12. The mean is 12.

Determine the mean based on the following: *X* (12), standard deviation (5), and z-score (−1.15).

With a z-score that is 1.15 standard deviations below the mean, the score is multiplied by the standard deviation score of 5, which gives us $1.15(5) = 5.75$. Given that the score is below the mean, we add the score to X (12), which is $(5.75 + 12) = 17.75$. The mean is 17.75.

Computing the *X* Score

There are instances in which one can determine the value of *X* from a z-score.

Determine the value of *X* based on the following: mean (70), standard deviation (10), and z-score (-1.25).

Notice the placement of the z-score (based on the sign). This indicates that the score is below the mean. It also reveals that the distance between the mean and the score is 1.25 standard deviations. Multiply the standard deviation (10) with the value of the distance from the mean (1.25).

$$1.25\ (10) = 12.5$$

In the formula for computing the z-score, the value of the mean was subtracted from *X*. In this process, we subtract 12.5 from the mean (mean = 70) to determine the value of *X*.

$$70 - 12.5 = 57.5$$
$$X = 57.5$$

Determine the value of *X* based on the following mean (50), standard deviation (8), and z-score +2.15.

The score (+2.15) is above the mean by a distance of 2.15 standard deviations. The standard deviation (8) is multiplied by 2.15 = 17.2. The mean (50) is subtracted from 17.2, which equals −32.8. Thus, $X = -32.8$.

Let's assume that the z-score is now +1.75, the mean is 35, and the standard deviation is 6.5. What is the value of *X*?

Since the distance of the z-score is (1.75), it is multiplied by a standard deviation score of 8 = 14. The mean (35) is subtracted from 14, in which $X = -21$.

Chapter Learning Assessment Questions

To demonstrate your level of understanding, complete the following questions:

Objective 4

1. The value of *X*, based on the following mean (60), standard deviation (9.5), and z-score (0.50) is:

    a. 64.75
    b. 4.75
    c. 0.5
    d. none of the above

2. When determining the value of X, one should ______.
   a. multiply the distance of a z-score (from the mean) by the standard deviation
   b. divide the standard deviation from the mean
   c. subtract the standard deviation from the mean
   d. none of the above
3. Find the value of the z-score based on the following mean (4), standard deviation (7.9), and X (16).
   a. 1.35
   b. 12
   c. 1.51
   d. none of the above

Answers

1. a
2. a
3. c

The Use of a z-Table and the Area of a z-Score

When computing and determining a z-score, visual illustrations may be used to undergird an understanding of the relationship of scores in a distribution—more specifically, scores that define the relationship between standard deviations and the mean. When deciding to use a visual illustration with z-scores, along with a normal distribution course, one common approach is to use a **z-table**, which can be used to display the area under the curve. This may include areas that exist to the right and left of a specific z-score.

z-Table

A **z-table** is a chart that uses numerical information to identify the distance between the mean and a value. The table is located near the end of this textbook.

z-table A chart that uses numerical information to identify the distance between the mean and a value.

Within the table there are columns that provide important information in relation to determining the area under the curve. Column 1 identifies the actual computed z-score. Columns 2–10 identify the area under the curve that corresponds to the actual z-score. Identified in Table 6.7 is a section of a z-table:

TABLE 6.7 **z-Table (Section)**

z	0.00	0.01	0.02	0.03	0.04	0.05	0.06	0.07	0.08	0.09
0.0	0.0000	0.0040	0.0080	0.0120	0.0160	0.0199	0.0239	0.0279	0.0319	0.0359
0.1	0.0398	0.0438	0.0478	0.0517	0.0557	0.0596	0.0636	0.0675	0.0714	0.0753
0.2	0.0793	0.0832	0.0871	0.0910	0.0948	0.0987	0.1026	0.1064	0.1103	0.1141
0.3	0.1179	0.1217	0.1255	0.1293	0.1331	0.1368	0.1406	0.1443	0.1480	0.1517
0.4	0.1554	0.1591	0.1628	0.1664	0.1700	0.1736	0.1772	0.1808	0.1844	0.1879
0.5	0.1915	0.1950	0.1985	0.2019	0.2054	0.2088	0.2123	0.2157	0.2190	0.2224

As an example, suppose one is interested in finding the z-score associated with the race of youth who are likely to experience arrest. Remember the following information:

TABLE 6.8 **Youth Arrests by Race**

Race	*f*	*p*
Asian	7	0.02
Black	146	0.45
Latinx	56	0.18
Other	16	0.05
Whites	96	0.30
	$n = 321$	$\sum = 1.00$

Based on the data provided, this distribution of scores has a mean $(\bar{x}) = 64.2$ and a standard deviation $(s) = 57$, and a score (based on the number of youth with the highest amount of reported arrests) $(x) = 146$.

$$z = \frac{x - \bar{x}}{s}$$

$$z = \frac{146 - 64.2}{57} = \frac{81.8}{57} = 1.43$$

Our z-score of youth who are likely to experience arrest is 1.43. To determine the area under the curve that corresponds to this z-score, we engage in the following steps:

Step 1 – In column 1, locate the number 1.40 under the z-score label.

Step 2 – In column 5, locate the number 0.03, which represents the area between the mean and the z-score.

Step 3 – Identify the actual number in which both values meet at the same location, which is 0.4236.

Step 4 – It is important to understand that the normal distribution represents a total of 1.0 or 100%. Thus, we must account for the remaining area to the left of the mean, which is 0.50. This includes adding 0.4236 to 0.5000 (0.4236 + 0.5000 = 0.9236), which gives us 92.36%.

Consider the following z-table information:

TABLE 6.9 **z-Table (Section)**

z	0.00	0.01	0.02	0.03	0.04	0.05	0.06	0.07	0.08	0.09
0.0	0.0000	0.0040	0.0080	0.0120	0.0160	0.0199	0.0239	0.0279	0.0319	0.0359
0.1	0.0398	0.0438	0.0478	0.0517	0.0557	0.0596	0.0636	0.0675	0.0714	0.0753
0.2	0.0793	0.0832	0.0871	0.0910	0.0948	0.0987	0.1026	0.1064	0.1103	0.1141
0.3	0.1179	0.1217	0.1255	0.1293	0.1331	0.1368	0.1406	0.1443	0.1480	0.1517
0.4	0.1554	0.1591	0.1628	0.1664	0.1700	0.1736	0.1772	0.1808	0.1844	0.1879
0.5	0.1915	0.1950	0.1985	0.2019	0.2054	0.2088	0.2123	0.2157	0.2190	0.2224
0.6	0.2257	0.2291	0.2324	0.2357	0.2389	0.2422	0.2454	0.2486	0.2517	0.2549
0.7	0.2580	0.2611	0.2642	0.2673	0.2704	0.2734	0.2764	0.2794	0.2823	0.2852
0.8	0.2881	0.2910	0.2939	0.2967	0.2995	0.3023	0.3051	0.3078	0.3106	0.3133
0.9	0.3159	0.3186	0.3212	0.3238	0.3264	0.3289	0.3315	0.3340	0.3365	0.3389
1.0	0.3413	0.3438	0.3461	0.3485	0.3508	0.3531	0.3554	0.3577	0.3599	0.3621
1.1	0.3643	0.3665	0.3686	0.3708	0.3729	0.3749	0.3770	0.3790	0.3810	0.3830
1.2	0.3849	0.3869	0.3888	0.3907	0.3925	0.3944	0.3962	0.3980	0.3997	0.4015
1.3	0.4032	0.4049	0.4066	0.4082	0.4099	0.4115	0.4131	0.4147	0.4162	0.4177
1.4	0.4192	0.4207	0.4222	**0.4236**	0.4251	0.4265	0.4279	0.4292	0.4306	0.4319

Consider the location of 92.36 within a normal distribution table (see Figure 6.3).

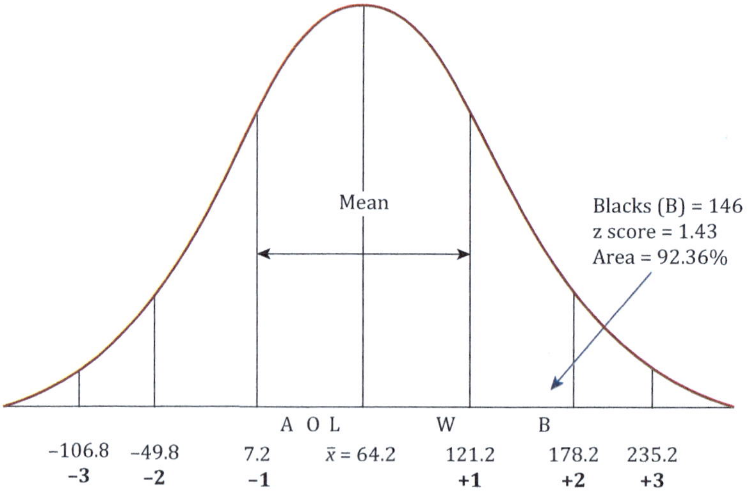

FIGURE. 6.3 Normal Curve and 1 Standard Deviation From the Mean

As revealed, there are two commonly used options when providing visual content with respect to z-scores: z-tables and normal distribution curves.

Let's consider two more examples that call for the use of a z-table. Example 1 provides steps when determining the area to the right of a score. Example 2 discusses the same objective when determining the area to the left of a score.

Example 1

Suppose a researcher is interested in the birth weight of newborn babies in a specific population. Let's assume that the population consists of incarcerated females who recently gave birth. Within the area of the prison, the mean weight of newborn babies is 7.5 pounds, with a standard deviation of 0.9 pounds. What percentage of newborns weigh less than 8 pounds?

To solve, we will (1) compute the z-score and (2) determine the area to the right of the score.

$$z = \frac{8 - 7.5}{0.9} = \frac{0.5}{0.9} = 0.55$$

With a z-score of 0.55, we will use a z-score table. To determine the area to the right of the score, the previously mentioned two-step process is suggested:

1. We must identify the location of 0.55 from the table. This requires observing the first column to the far left and locating the score 0.5. To locate 0.05, find the number by observing the top row of the table. The actual location of 0.55 is where the corresponding values meet, which is 0.2088.

TABLE 6.10 **z-Table (Section)**

z	0.00	0.01	0.02	0.03	0.04	0.05	0.06	0.07
0.0	0.0000	0.0040	0.0080	0.0120	0.0160	0.0199	0.0239	0.0279
0.1	0.0398	0.0438	0.0478	0.0517	0.0557	0.0596	0.0636	0.0675
0.2	0.0793	0.0832	0.0871	0.0910	0.0948	0.0987	0.1026	0.1064
0.3	0.1179	0.1217	0.1255	0.1293	0.1331	0.1368	0.1406	0.1443
0.4	0.1554	0.1591	0.1628	0.1664	0.1700	0.1736	0.1772	0.1808
0.5	0.1915	0.1950	0.1985	0.2019	0.2054	**0.2088**	0.2123	0.2157

2. The area to the left of 0.55 is 0.2088.
3. Based on the question, the percentage of newborns that weigh less than 8 pounds is approximately 20.88%.

Example 2

In a statistics course, the mean final exam score is 73, with a standard deviation of 6.5. What percentage of students earned an exam score of less than 75?

$$z = \frac{75 - 73}{6.5} = \frac{2}{6.5} = 0.307$$

As in the previous example, the locations of each value must be identified in the z-table.

1. The value 0.3 is located at the bottom of the column to the far left. The value 0.07 is located on the top row to the right of column 0.06. Both values, based on the score of 0.307, correspond to 0.1443.

TABLE 6.11 **z-Table (Section)**

z	0.00	0.01	0.02	0.03	0.04	0.05	0.06	0.07
0.0	0.0000	0.0040	0.0080	0.0120	0.0160	0.0199	0.0239	0.0279
0.1	0.0398	0.0438	0.0478	0.0517	0.0557	0.0596	0.0636	0.0675
0.2	0.0793	0.0832	0.0871	0.0910	0.0948	0.0987	0.1026	0.1064
0.3	0.1179	0.1217	0.1255	0.1293	0.1331	0.1368	0.1406	**0.1443**

2. The area to the left of the score (0.307) is 0.1443.
3. In response to the question, approximately 14.43% of students earned a score of less than 75 on their final exam.

Chapter Learning Assessment Questions

To measure your level of understanding, complete the following questions:

Objective 5

1. Suppose a researcher is interested in determining the area under the curve with a z-score of 1.28. By observing a z-table, the value of 1 is located in ______.
   a. column 1
   b. column 2
   c. either a or b
   d. none of the above
2. When converting the area under the curve to a percentage, one must:
   a. multiply the value by 100
   b. divide the value by 100
   c. subtract the value by 100
   d. none of the above

Answers

1. a
2. a

Practical Application of z-Scores

Within criminal justice, learning about z-scores can be rewarding as a result of recognizing the practical application of such standardization. The key component for employing z-scores in criminal justice is the uncanny ability to compare the incomparable. In short, z-scores help us see things that others may not be aware of.

Juvenile Delinquent Facility

A larger-than-average 13-year-old boy was constantly starting fights with other students. On one occasion, he nearly beat another student to death and was sentenced to a state juvenile facility. Initially, his behavior was extremely problematic.

An experienced correctional officer started to examine the inmate's activities and found that his behavior at the learning center was also out of the ordinary. At first, his behavior was problematic, but as he experienced success at learning new words, a sense of calm enveloped him. Figure 6.4 includes a chart that reveals a progression of learning new words:

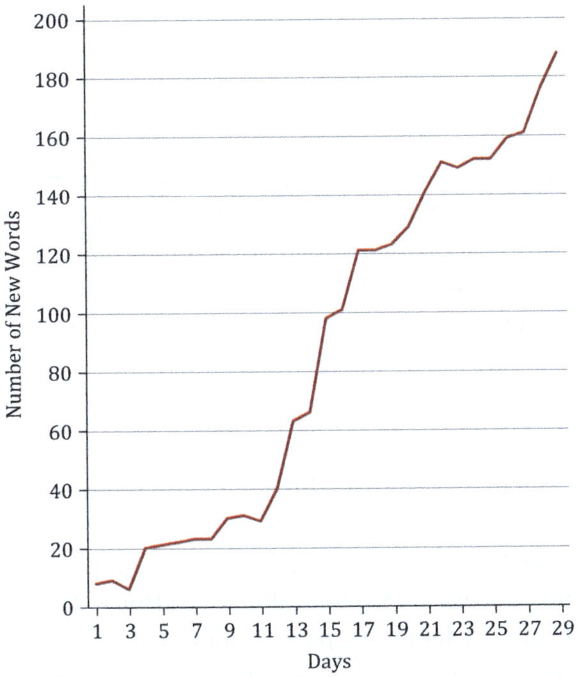

FIGURE. 6.4 Learning and Development

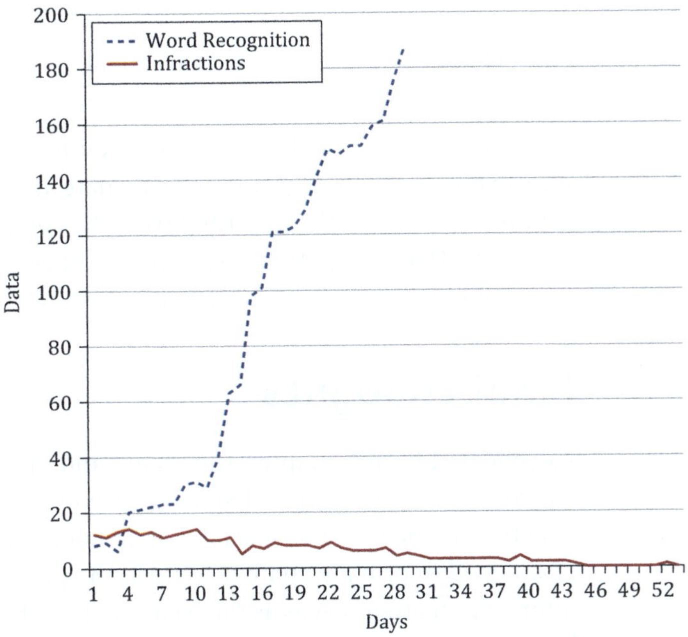

FIGURE. 6.5 Learning and Infractions

As revealed in Figure 6.5, there seems to be a relationship between the increase in learning new words and the decrease in infractions (Marson and Dovyak, 2020). However, as illustrated, merging the two charts offers no clarity:

When we convert the raw data to z-scores, the unseen relationship emerges. See the information in Figure 6.6:

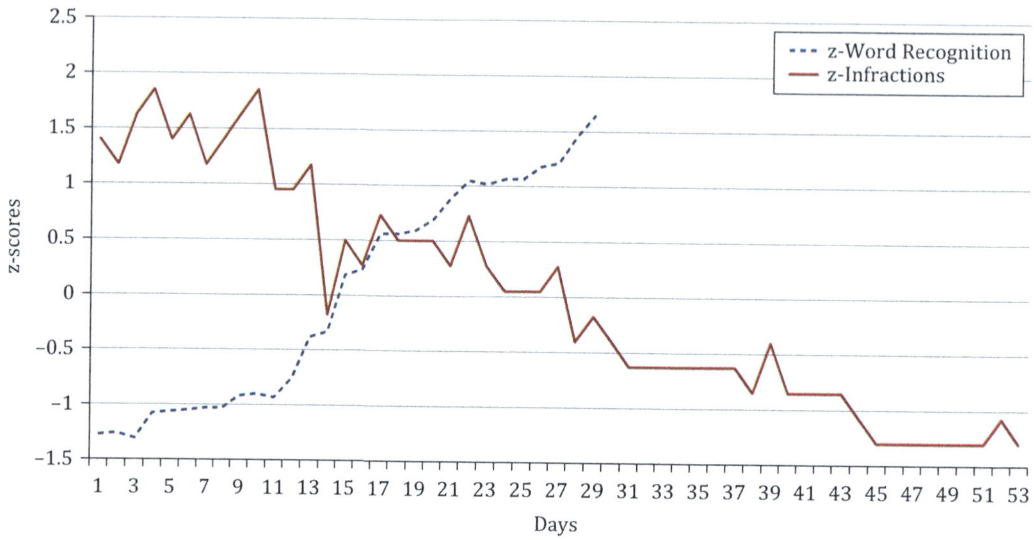

FIGURE. 6.6 Learning and Infractions

The figure makes it clear that success in learning is linked to a decrease in problematic behavior. We can take an additional step and calculate an r with a coefficient of −0.86. Although this coefficient is impressive by statistical standards, the comparative z-scores offer information that is equally insightful. Does this pattern exist among other incarcerated children? Advanced statistical analysis can provide the information. Nevertheless, the question emerged from our ability to use z-scores.

Final Thoughts

As revealed in this chapter, the terms and practical use of probability, the normal distribution curve, and z-scores were discussed. By understanding these basic statistical concepts, one is able to provide key information which explains relationships. More importantly, these tools are often used to provide context. Within the practice and processes of criminal justice efforts, this information often serves as the basis of a) predicting crime, b) deploying patrol units, c) allocating legal cases among attorneys, as well as d) developing and managing risk assessment scales among those convicted of a crime.

Discussion

After observing a report related to the pretrial detention of youth, you discover that the mean time period a male youth is detained is 45 days ($s = 15$). Female youth who experience pretrial detention indicate a mean time period of 23 days ($s = 10$). By randomly selecting a male youth who had experienced 50 days of detention, how would you respond? Does the number reflect the mean, or does it deviate from the mean? Explain.

Chapter Summary

This chapter emphasized the following general information:

Objective 1 – Identify the significance and types of probability in statistics.

- Probability refers to the likelihood of an outcome.
- The converse principle refers to the probability of an outcome not taking place.
- The addition principle is the probability of obtaining a variety of outcomes, which equals the sum of their individual probabilities.
- The multiplication principle is the probability of receiving a combination of mutually exclusive outcomes equals the product of their separate probabilities.

Objective 2 – Define and explain the significance of a normal curve.

- A normal curve is a visual distribution of values that is symmetric in shape.

Objective 3 – Discuss the purpose and use of a z-score.

- A z-score is a value that reflects the amount of distance between a value and the mean.

Objective 4 – Demonstrate the relationship between a z-score and other data distribution characteristics.

Objective 5 – Demonstrate the use of a z-table and determine the area of a z-score.

- A z-table is a chart that uses numerical information to identify the distance between the mean and a value.

Terms

Probability
Normal curve
z-table
z-score

Chapter Review Questions

1. The following is an example of which type of probability principle?

   $-0.57 = 0.43$

   a. Addition
   b. Converse
   c. Multiplication
   d. Either a or c

2. Based on the information in the previous question, the actual second highest probability of experiencing a homicide is ______.
   a. 0.28
   b. 0.51
   c. 0.43
   d. 0.37
3. The following includes information related to the number of days youth were detained in a local detention center. The mean is 18, with a standard deviation of 4.6. Based on the data below, identify which values are above or below the mean.

x	$x - \bar{x}$	z
14	−4	−0.9
21	3	0.7
26	8	1.7
17	−1	−0.2
18	0	0.0
22	4	0.9
10	−8	−1.7
13	−5	−1.1
16	−2	−0.4
15	−3	−0.7
19	1	0.2
23	5	1.1

4. The class mean is 81, and the standard deviation is 4.8. As a student who desires to earn a score in the top 5% of their class, with a current average that is consistent with the class mean, what score does the student need to earn?
5. A sample population has a standard deviation score of 10. Identify the z-scores for the following areas in the distribution:
   a. Below the mean by 5 points
   b. Above the mean by 10 points
   c. Below the mean by 15 points
   d. Above the mean by 25 points
6. If a population has a mean of 50 and a standard deviation of 8, identify the z-scores for the following values:
   a. $x = 75$
   b. $x = 56$
   c. $x = 48$
   d. $x = 36$
   e. $x = 29$

f. $x = 65$

g. $x = 70$

7. A sample population has a standard deviation score of 7. Identify the z-scores for the following areas in the distribution:
   a. Below the mean by 7 points
   b. Above the mean by 14 points
   c. Below the mean by 21 points
   d. Above the mean by 21 points
8. If a population has a mean of 62 and a standard deviation of 5, identify the z-scores for the following values:
   a. $x = 65$
   b. $x = 46$
   c. $x = 38$
   d. $x = 26$
   e. $x = 19$
   f. $x = 55$
   g. $x = 60$
9. As a police cadet, you scored 90 on 4 exams during the academy. Listed below are the mean and standard deviation for each of the four exams. Find the z-score for each exam. In addition, explain how you performed in relation to other cadets.
   a. Exam 1: $\bar{x} = 60$ and $s = 5$
   b. Exam 2: $\bar{x} = 80$ and $s = 12$
   c. Exam 3: $\bar{x} = 70$ and $s = 10$
   d. Exam 4: $\bar{x} = 95$ and $s = 15$

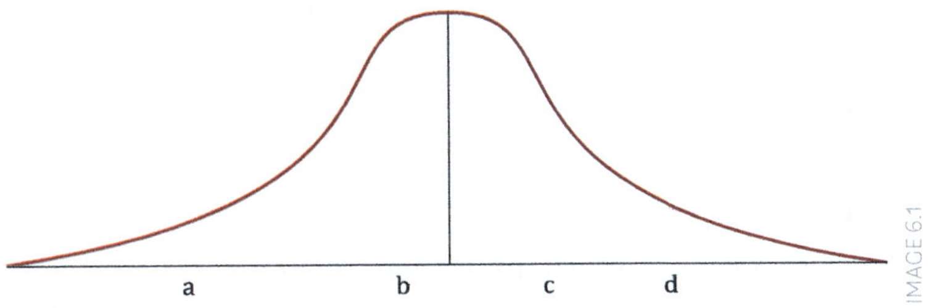

10. Based on the distribution curve provided above, which letter represents the following z-scores:
    a. $z = -0.49$
    b. $z = -2.00$
    c. $z = +2.00$
    d. $z = 0.88$

11. A recent crime report revealed that the probability of recovering a victim's stolen possession is 1.25%. Your response to this statement is
    a. it must be false based on the fact that probability varies between 0 and 10.
    b. it might be true based on the fact that probability varies between −5 and 5.
    c. it must be false based on the fact that probability varies between 0 and 1.
    d. there is not enough information provided to offer a valid response.
12. Within a normal distribution curve, what percentage (%) of the total area is located
    a. between the mean and the value, which is located 1 standard deviation below the mean?
    b. between the mean and the value, which is located 3 standard deviations above the mean?
    c. between the mean and the value, which is located 2 standard deviations below the mean?
    d. between the mean and the value, which is located 2 standard deviations above the mean?
13. Police officers who use lethal force are rare phenomena in policing. Within three major metropolitan areas in a southern state, the mean amount of lethal force incidents in 2015 was 12, with a standard deviation of 4. What is the z-score of lethal force incidents within a law enforcement agency that reported a total of 16 incidents in 2015? Does the z-score fall within the mean or outside of the mean?
14. With a value of 120 ($x = 120$), find the z-score for each of the following:
    a. $\bar{x} = 95, s = 10$
    b. $\bar{x} = 95, s = 5$
    c. $\bar{x} = 75, s = 15$
    d. $\bar{x} = 75, s = 5$
15. With a value of 90 ($x = 90$), find the z-score for each of the following:
    a. $\bar{x} = 80, s = 12$
    b. $\bar{x} = 70, s = 12$
    c. $\bar{x} = 60, s = 15$
    d. $\bar{x} = 50, s = 15$
16. A researcher has just received information about the impact of a tutorial program for students who experience difficulty during their first year in college. At the beginning of the semester, 75 first-year students completed a required standardized test with a mean of 90 and a standard deviation of 15. A first-year student who participated in the tutorial program earned a score of 100 on the standardized test. In light of this information, should the researcher assume that the student's test score is statistically significant from the scores of other students who completed the standardized test?

Answers

1. b
2. d
3.

x	$x - \bar{x}$	z
14	−4	−0.9
21	3	0.7
26	8	1.7
17	−1	−0.2
18	0	0.0
22	4	0.9
10	−8	−1.7
13	−5	−1.1
16	−2	−0.4
15	−3	−0.7
19	1	0.2
23	5	1.1

4. 91
5.
   a. $z = -0.50$
   b. $z = +1.00$
   c. $z = -1.50$
   d. $z = +2.50$
6.
   a. $z = 3.12$
   b. $z = 0.75$
   c. $z = -0.25$
   d. $z = -1.75$
   e. $z = -2.625$
   f. $z = 1.875$
   g. $z = 2.5$
7.
   a. $z = -1.00$
   b. $z = +2.00$
   c. $z = -3.00$
   d. $z = +3.00$
8.
   a. $z = 0.6$
   b. $z = -3.2$
   c. $z = -4.8$
   d. $z = -7.2$

- e. $z = -8.6$
- f. $z = -1.4$
- g. $z = -0.4$

9.
- a. $z = +6.00$
- b. $z = 0.83$
- c. $z = +2.00$
- d. $z = -0.33$

10.
- a. b
- b. a
- c. d
- d. c

11. c

12.
- a. 31.13%
- b. 49.87%
- c. –95.44%
- d. 95.44%

13. z = 1.00
The score falls outside of the mean; 1 standard deviation from the mean.

14.
- a. $z = 2.5$
- b. $z = 5$
- c. $z = 3$
- d. $z = 9$

15.
- a. $z = 0.83$
- b. $z = 1.66$
- c. $z = 2.00$
- d. $z = 2.66$

16. No, the score of 100 (compared to) 90 + 15 = 105 (which is 1 standard deviation from the mean) is not statistically significant from the mean scores.

Matching: Place the letter of the following definitions with its corresponding term.

___1. Probability	a. a visual distribution of values that is symmetric
___2. Normal curve	b. the likelihood of an occurrence or outcome
___3. z-table	c. a value that reflects the amount of distance between a value and the mean
___4. z-score	d. a chart that uses numerical information to identify the distance between the mean and a value

Answers

1. b
2. a
3. d
4. c

Bibliography

Marson, S. M., & Dovyak, P. (2020). The value of z-scores in social work supervision and practice. *Journal of Social Work Education & Practice*, *5*(5), 34–45.

Chapter 6 SPSS and Workbook Questions

SPSS and z-Score

Listed below are the salaries of 20 juvenile detention directors in a regional area. Through the use of a z-score, determine how many salaries are above (or below) the mean.

Director	Salary
1	45
2	56
3	47
4	48
5	55
6	57
7	61
8	62
9	54
10	43
11	63
12	58
13	41
14	46
15	50
16	52
17	53
18	60
19	44
20	64

In order to compute a z-score using SPSS, perform the following steps:

Entry of Data—SPSS

1. Select variable view to include information associated with the variable of interest. In our example, this would include only one variable: salary.
2. In the first row, include the term "salary" under the column identified as name.
3. In the column identified as label, you might choose to include a more specific description of the variable.
4. Finally, in the column identified as measure, select the scale option.
5. Select data view to include the scores in the corresponding column.

IMAGE 6.2

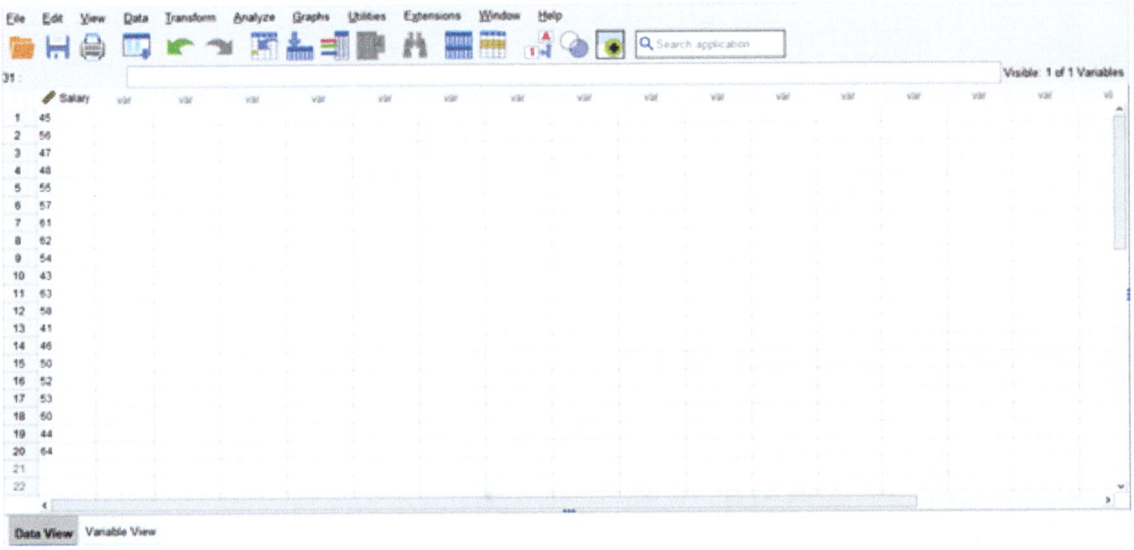

IMAGE 6.3

Analysis of Data—SPSS

1. Select analyze and then select descriptive statistics.
2. At this point, you will see a box (located on the left) that includes the variable salary. Select this variable and move it to the box located to the right, which is identified as variable(s).
3. Once completed, be sure to select the option identified as save standardized values as variables.
4. In the options section, you can select a variety of details associated with the variable of interest. This includes measures of central tendency, etc.
5. Once all desired functions have been selected and completed, select OK.

Output of Data Analysis—SPSS

Shown below are two illustrations. The first reveals the output of the data analysis, which is the descriptive statistics of the variable. This includes information that identifies the sample, the minimum and maximum value, and the mean and standard deviation.

The final illustration provides additional information, which was included in the data editor. This includes the standardized scores that correspond to the values that were initially included. For instance, consider the seventh value in the column: 61. To the left of 61, we now observe the value of 1.12. This relative value of 61 (1.12) is 1 standard deviation from the mean.

In response to the number of salaries that are either above or below the mean, there are a total of 8 salaries.

IMAGE 6.4

IMAGE 6.5

Workbook Questions

Objective 1—Identify the Significance and Types of Probability in Statistics

- Probability is the likelihood of an occurrence or outcome.
- The converse principle refers to the probability of an outcome not taking place.
- The addition principle is the probability of obtaining a variety of outcomes, which equals the sum of their individual probabilities.
- The multiplication principle is the probability of receiving a combination of mutually exclusive outcomes equals the product of their separate probabilities.

Corresponding Questions

1. Based on the information in the following five groups, (1) compute the proportions for each group and (2) determine which group has the greatest probability of experiencing an arrest.

Race/Ethnicity	Frequency	Proportion
Asians	15	
Blacks	48	
Hispanics	51	
Other	7	
Whites	31	

2. Listed below are the number of students, shown by their academic major, who graduated with an undergraduate degree at a local university. In addition, these same students also applied as potential law school students within 1 year of their graduation date. Based on the information provided, (1) compute the proportions for each academic major and (2) determine which academic major experienced the greatest probability of law school acceptance after one year of graduation.

Academic Major of Graduate	Frequency	Proportion
English	12	
Political Science	13	
Criminal Justice	9	
Sociology	8	
Economics	7	
Engineering	4	
Business	9	
Biology	5	
Health	3	
Psychology	7	
Communications	8	

3. A defense attorney believes that she can obtain reduced charges for two of her clients. Client A is facing a charge of aggravated robbery, and Client B is charged with drug trafficking. Based on her record, she has a history of reducing charges based on the following types of offenses:

   0.70 probability (aggravated robbery)
   0.90 probability (drug trafficking)

   Based on the information provided, what is the probability that the defense attorney will secure a reduction in charges in both cases?

   a. 0.63
   b. 0.160
   c. 1.60
   d. None of the above

Answers

1. The proportion for each category includes Asians (0.09), Blacks (0.31), Hispanics (0.33), Other (0.04), and Whites (0.20). Hispanics, at 0.33, have the greatest proportion of experiencing arrest.
2. The proportion for each category includes English (0.14), political science (0.15), criminal justice (0.10), sociology (0.09), economics (0.08), engineering (0.04), business (0.10), biology (0.05), health (0.03), psychology (0.08), and communications (0.09). Compared to all of the academic majors listed, the academic major of political science, at 0.15, experienced the greatest proportion of law school acceptance.
3. a

Objective 2—Define and Explain the Significance of a Normal Curve

- A normal curve is a visual distribution of values that is symmetric; symmetric refers to an equal distance between two sections.

Corresponding Questions

1. The area under a normal distribution curve represents a total of ______.
   a. 68%
   b. 95%
   c. 99%
   d. 100%
2. The mean area of the curve represents ______.
   a. 68%
   b. 95%
   c. 99%
   d. 100%

3. The total area of the mean represents ______________ from the mean.
    a. 1 standard deviation
    b. 2 standard deviations
    c. 3 standard deviations
    d. either b or c
4. _______ from the mean represents 95% of the area under the curve in a normal distribution.
    a. One standard deviation
    b. Two standard deviations
    c. Three standard deviations
    d. either b or c
5. _______ from the mean represents 99% of the area under the curve in a normal distribution.
    a. One standard deviation
    b. Two standard deviations
    c. Three standard deviations
    d. either b or c
6. _______ from the mean represents 68% of the area under the curve in a normal distribution.
    a. One standard deviation
    b. Two standard deviations
    c. Three standard deviations
    d. either b or c

Answers

1. d
2. a
3. a
4. b
5. c
6. a

Objective 3—Discuss the Purpose and Use of a Z-Score.

- The z-score is a value that reflects the amount of distance between a value and the mean. It also identifies whether the value is greater or less than the mean.

Corresponding Questions

1. A z-score of –3.00 indicates that a score is:
    a. 3 points below the mean
    b. 3 points above the mean

c. 3 standard deviations below the mean
d. 3 standard deviations above the mean

2. The *s* in the following formula for the z-score represents:

$$z = \frac{X - \bar{X}}{s}$$

a. sum of squares
b. standard deviation
c. sum of scores in the distribution
d. none of the above

3. When computing a z-score, the first step is to:
a. subtract the population (or sample mean) from a score
b. subtract a score from the population (or sample mean)
c. either a or b
d. none of the above

4. With a mean of 6 and standard deviation of 2.16, compute the z-scores for each of the following scores: 3, 6, 9, 5, 4, 8, 7.
5. Which score(s) in Question 4 is above the mean by 1 standard deviation?
a. 3
b. 9
c. 8
d. 7

6. Convert the following to z-scores: 8, 3, 5, 7, 2, 9, 4.
7. The following information shows the number of young adults who were arrested near a federal housing unit in an urban area. The mean is 12, with a standard deviation of 3.7. Based on the data below, compute the z-scores for each value of x.

x	$x - \bar{x}$	z
11	−1	−0.3
18	6	
22	10	2.7
14	2	
14	2	0.5
19	7	1.9
7	−5	
10	−2	
13	1	0.3
9	−3	
11	−1	−0.3
19	7	

8. Identify the missing values provided below. The mean is 8, with a standard deviation of 11.5. How many scores are above (or below) the mean?

x	x - $\bar{x}$	z
21	13	1.1
18	10	
35	27	
24	16	
31	23	2.0
30	22	
16	8	
13	5	
28	20	
19	11	
17	9	0.8
34	26	

9. A population has a standard deviation score of 5. Identify the z-scores for the following areas in the distribution:
   a. Below the mean by 5 points
   b. Above the mean by 10 points
   c. Below the mean by 15 points
   d. Above the mean by 15 points
10. If a population has a mean of 12 and a standard deviation of 8.2, identify the z-scores for the following values:
   a. $X = 17$
   b. $X = 13$
   c. $X = 29$
   d. $X = 19$
   e. $X = 25$
   f. $X = 25$
   g. $X = 11$
   h. $X = 8$
   i. $X = 21$
   j. $X = 14$
   k. $X = 16$
   l. $X = 29$
11. Research points to the level of stress among criminal justice practitioners. As a measure of stress, provided below are the diastolic blood pressure scores for police officers, attorneys,

and jailers (detention officers). The mean diastolic blood pressure, which measures blood pressure when someone is resting (e.g., seated, relaxed), is 80.

Police	x	z-score	$\bar{x}$	σ
	86		85.60	7.44
	98			
	84			
	81			
	79			
Attorneys	x	**z-score**	$\bar{x}$	s
	105		110.83	12.30
	99			
	97			
	116			
	121			
	127			
Jailers	x	**z-score**	$\bar{x}$	s
	74		81.80	6.69
	85			
	82			
	77			
	91			

Based on the information in the table:

1. For each of the professionals identified, compute their z-score.
2. For each of the groups listed, determine how many scores are above and below the mean.

Answers

1. c
2. b
3. a
4. –1.39, 0.00, 1.39, –0.46, –0.93, 0.93, 0.46
5. b
6. 0.98, –0.92, –0.16, 0.60, –1.30, 1.35, –054
7. 1.6, 0.5, –1.4, –0.5, –0.8, 1.9
8. 0.9, 2.3, 1.4, 1.9, 0.7, 0.4, 1.7, 1.0, 2.3; a total of 8 scores are above the mean

9.
   a. $z = -1.00$
   b. $z = +2.00$
   c. $z = -3.00$
   d. $z = +3.00$

10.
   a. $z = 0.6$
   b. $z = 0.1$
   c. $z = 2.1$
   d. $z = 0.9$
   e. $z = 1.6$
   f. $z = 1.6$
   g. $z = -0.1$
   h. $z = -0.5$
   i. $z = 1.1$
   j. $z = 0.2$
   k. $z = 0.5$
   l. $z = 2.1$

11.

Police	*x*	**z-score**	$\bar{x}$	σ
	86	0.05	85.60	7.44
	98	1.67		
	84	−0.22		
	81	−0.62		
	79	−0.89		
Attorneys	*x*	**z-score**	$\bar{x}$	σ
	105	−0.47	110.83	12.30
	99	−0.96		
	97	−1.12		
	116	0.42		
	121	0.83		
	127	1.31		
Jailers	*x*	**z-score**	$\bar{x}$	σ
	74	−1.17	81.80	6.69
	85	0.48		
	82	0.03		
	77	−0.72		
	91	1.38		

Police – Three scores are below the mean, and two scores are above the mean.
Attorneys – Three scores are below the mean, and three scores are above the mean.
Jailers – Three scores are above the mean, and two scores are below the mean.

Objective 4—Demonstrate the Relationship Between a Z-Score and Other Data Distribution Characteristics

Corresponding Questions

1. The standard deviation score, based on the following, x (23), mean (25), and z-score (1.00), is:
   a. –1
   b. –2
   c. 0.50
   d. 0.75
2. The z-score, based on the following x(16), mean (12), and standard deviation (12.5), is:
   a. 2.24
   b. –4
   c. 4
   d. 0.32

Answers

1. b
2. d

Objective 5—Demonstrate the Use of a z-table and Determine the Area of a z-Score

- A z-table is a chart that uses numerical information to identify the distance between the mean and a value.

1. Suppose a researcher is interested in determining the area under the curve with a z-score of 2.15. By observing a z-table, the value of 2 is located in ______.
   a. column 1
   b. column 2
   c. either a or b
   d. none of the above

z	0.00	0.01	0.02	0.03	0.04	0.05	0.06	0.07	0.08	0.09
0.0	0.5000	0.5040	0.5080	0.5120	0.5160	0.5199	0.5239	0.5279	0.5319	0.5359
0.1	0.5398	0.5438	0.5478	0.5517	0.5557	0.5596	0.5636	0.5675	0.5714	0.5753
0.2	0.5793	0.5832	0.5871	0.5910	0.5948	0.5987	0.6026	0.6064	0.6103	0.6141
0.3	0.6179	0.6217	0.6255	0.6293	0.6331	0.6368	0.6406	0.6443	0.6480	0.6517
0.4	0.6554	0.6591	0.6628	0.6664	0.6700	0.6736	0.6772	0.6808	0.6844	0.6879
0.5	0.6915	0.6950	0.6985	0.7019	0.7054	0.7088	0.7123	0.7157	0.7190	0.7224

0.6	0.7257	0.7291	0.7324	0.7357	0.7389	0.7422	0.7454	0.7486	0.7517	0.7549
0.7	0.7580	0.7611	0.7642	0.7673	0.7704	0.7734	0.7764	0.7794	0.7823	0.7852
0.8	0.7881	0.7910	0.7939	0.7967	0.7995	0.8023	0.8051	0.8078	0.8106	0.8133
0.9	0.8159	0.8186	0.8212	0.8238	0.8264	0.8289	0.8315	0.8340	0.8365	0.8389
1.0	0.8413	0.8438	0.8461	0.8485	0.8508	0.8531	0.8554	0.8577	0.8599	0.8621
1.1	0.8643	0.8665	0.8686	0.8708	0.8729	0.8749	0.8770	0.8790	0.8810	0.8830
1.2	0.8849	0.8869	0.8888	0.8907	0.8925	0.8944	0.8962	0.8980	0.8997	0.9015
1.3	0.9032	0.9049	0.9066	0.9082	0.9099	0.9115	0.9131	0.9147	0.9162	0.9177
1.4	0.9192	0.9207	0.9222	0.9236	0.9251	0.9265	0.9279	0.9292	0.9306	0.9319
1.5	0.9332	0.9345	0.9357	0.9370	0.9382	0.9394	0.9406	0.9418	0.9429	0.9441
1.6	0.9452	0.9463	0.9474	0.9484	0.9495	0.9505	0.9515	0.9525	0.9535	0.9545
1.7	0.9554	0.9564	0.9573	0.9582	0.9591	0.9599	0.9608	0.9616	0.9625	0.9633
1.8	0.9641	0.9649	0.9656	0.9664	0.9671	0.9678	0.9686	0.9693	0.9699	0.9706
1.9	0.9713	0.9719	0.9726	0.9732	0.9738	0.9744	0.9750	0.9756	0.9761	0.9767
2.0	0.9772	0.9778	0.9783	0.9788	0.9793	0.9798	0.9803	0.9808	0.9812	0.9817

2. Based on the table above, find the area to the left of the following z-scores:
   a. z-score = 0.45
   b. z-score = 0.17
   c. z-score = 0.33
   d. z-score = 1.48

Answers

1. a
2.
   a. 67.36%
   b. 56.75%
   c. 62.93%
   d. 93.06%

Credits

CHAPTER 7

Hypothesis Testing

The null hypothesis is never proved or established, but is possibly disproved, in the course of experimentation. Every experiment may be said to exist only to give the facts a chance of disproving the null hypothesis.
—R. A. Fisher

Objectives

1. Explain the use of sample and population.
2. Discuss the difference between sampling error and true differences.
3. Describe the role and steps of hypothesis testing.
4. Define and explain the critical aspects of a hypothesis.
5. Explain the level of risk and how to select an appropriate test.
6. Engage in calculating a hypothesis test, determining statistical significance, and making a decision regarding the null hypothesis.
7. Discuss the role of confidence intervals and confidence levels.
8. Explore additional aspects of significance.

Introduction—From Intervention to Academic Interest

Imagine a professor who has been teaching statistics for quite some time, and has a record of all the overall class grades of each statistics course she has taught for the past 25 years. With a total of 7,500 students, this includes a mean of 72 with a standard deviation of 5. In this example, the 7,500 students represent the population. In light of such, the typical grade that the students have earned is a C.

After reviewing the grades of her most recent class of students, which includes a total of 18 individuals, she noticed a mean score of 68. As a remedy, she decided to expose nine students (50% of the class) to a guest speaker who discussed the practical aspects of statistics. The information provided included a considerable amount of insight that the students found interesting. This included potential earning amounts as researchers as well as the use of statistics in an effort to meet the practical needs of others.

As a result of this intervention, the professor noticed a slight improvement in test scores among the students. This includes a mean of 78, an improvement of 10 points. Based on the information provided at this point, the professor is curious as to whether the sample score is consistent with the population score (72). In other words, do the test scores from the sample (9 students) reflect what one may find among the population (7,500 students)? The basis for these questions stems from the reality that sample data may not serve as an accurate representation of what exists in a population. To address this uncertainty, we engage in what is referred to as hypothesis testing.

Before we discuss the details of hypothesis testing, there are a few foundational terms that we will address. They include *samples* and *populations*, as well as *sampling error* and *true differences*.

The Use of a Sample and a Population

To investigate the relationship between the sample and population mean test scores, one would use probability to determine the outcome. In other words, one would determine if the expected outcome (the belief that exposing students to an intervention is associated with higher test grades) is consistent with the actual outcome (i.e., data that confirms the belief that student exposure to an intervention is associated with higher test grades). Given the number of students who comprise the population ($N = 7{,}500$), our investigation would not involve using the actual total student population; rather, it would only involve a sample. A **sample** is a subset of a population that consists of actual individuals. In the example provided earlier, the sample included the test scores of ($n = 18$) students. If you recall, we are attempting to determine if the sample mean ($\bar{x} = 78$) is consistent (or not consistent) with the population mean ($\mu = 72$). A **population** is defined as the group of reference that the sample represents. As revealed in Figure 7.1, this distinction between sample and population illustrates the basis of inferential statistics. In short, inferential statistics uses probability for the purpose of estimating what may exist in a population using data derived from a sample (Henkel, 1976).

population A group of reference that the sample data (or statistic) represents.
sample A subset of a population composed of the actual group (or number) of research participants.

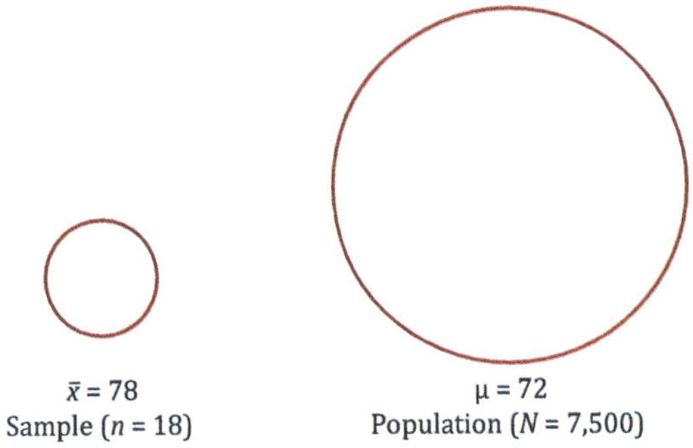

FIGURE 7.1 Difference Between Sample and Population Means

As you might have noticed, in Figure 7.1, there are different symbols for certain statistical terms. This is especially the case when discussing differences between samples and populations. For instance, consider the following distinctions:

TABLE 7.1 **Differences Between Symbols for Samples and Populations**

	Sample	Population
Number of values	n	N
Mean	$\bar{x}$	μ
Standard deviation	s	σ

Given that the subsequent chapters of this text will discuss types of statistical techniques that are used for hypothesis testing, these distinctions will be important in understanding the differences between samples and populations.

Chapter Learning Assessment Questions

To gauge your learning, provide answers to the following questions:

1. A sample statistic is an estimate of a ________.
   a. sample
   b. population
   c. category
   d. none of the above
2. A ________ is composed of the actual number of research participants.
   a. sample
   b. population
   c. category
   d. none of the above
3. When engaging in hypothesis testing, an explanation that describes why a sample is preferred in comparison to a population is:
   a. compared to individuals in a population, those within a sample are more likely to participate in research
   b. compared to individuals in a sample, there may be too many individuals in a population to gather information
   c. compared to individuals in a population, those within a sample are more likely to participate in research if they interact with someone face-to-face
   d. none of the above
4. As a result of hypothesis testing, a researcher discovers that the mean birth weight of newborns in a geographical location (e.g., county) is not consistent with the mean birth weight of newborns in a state.

   Consider the following:

	County 1	State
Birth weight (lbs)	5.10	6.41

Based on the table, the value of 5.10 was computed from the ____________.

a. population
b. sample
c. both a and b
d. none of the above

To determine if the mean birth weight in the county is consistent with the state's mean birth weight, one should employ a ____________.

a. hypothesis test
b. one sample *t*-test
c. two sample *t*-test
d. chi-square test

5. After a year of completing graduate-level courses, a criminology student has developed an assumption associated with the use of a practical crime prevention measure. More specifically, the student believes that individuals who use social media accounts and who indiscriminately accept friend requests are more likely to experience incidents of cyberstalking. To test his assumption, the student engaged in hypothesis testing with a faculty mentor at a college that included 16,800 students. After conducting an initial study, which included 221 students, the results confirmed the student's assumption. Through the use of a survey, this included 85% of the respondents indicated that indiscriminately accepting friend requests increases the probability of experiencing cyberstalking.

   In this scenario, the 221 students consist of the:

   a. sample
   b. population
   c. statistical group
   d. none of the above

   In this scenario, the 85% represents the views of the:

   a. sample
   b. population
   c. statistical group
   d. none of the above

Answers

1. b
2. a
3. b
4. b, a
5. a, b

Now that we have discussed the roles and differences related to a sample and population, we will focus our attention on two other foundational terms related to hypothesis testing. This includes *sampling error* and *true differences.*

Sampling Error and True Differences

TABLE 7.2 **Sampling Error and True Differences**

Number of Times a Coin Was Flipped (n = 5)	Outcome = Heads	
1	**Yes**	**2**/5 = 0.40 (40%)
2	No	
3	**Yes**	
4	No	
5	No	
Number of Times a Coin was Flipped (n = 10)	**Outcome = Heads**	
1	No	**9**/10 = 0.90 (90%)
2	**Yes**	
3	**Yes**	
4	**Yes**	
5	**Yes**	
6	**Yes**	
7	**Yes**	
8	**Yes**	
9	**Yes**	
10	**Yes**	

As indicated in Table 7.2, imagine flipping a coin five times, and the coin lands on heads 40% of the time (2/5 = 0.40). As a result of this outcome, you would probably not suspect anything unusual. However, imagine flipping a coin 10 times, and the coin lands on heads 90% of the time (9/10 = 0.90). This would likely cause you to suspect that something unusual is occurring. Maybe the coin is weighted, or the person who observes and counts the "flips" might have difficulty counting accurately. The second instance of the coin landing on heads at 0.90 (90%) represents an example of sampling error. A **sampling error** is an error that may occur due to chance. On the other hand, the first incident of observing the coin, which lands on heads 2 out of 5 times (0.40 or 40%), represents a true difference. A **true difference** is an occurrence that is not due to chance. In statistics, it is important to identify the basis of differences (sampling error vs true differences) that exist. Overall, hypothesis testing is a process

sampling error A value that represents an occurrence due to chance.

true difference A value that does not represent an occurrence due to chance.

that is used to determine the aforementioned types of differences through the use of statistical calculations (Henkel, 1976).

As previously mentioned, those who engage in hypothesis testing often attempt to obtain a sample that is representative of the population of interest. An inherent characteristic of hypothesis testing (or any type of inferential statistic) is that *a difference will always exist* between a sample and a population (Henkel, 1976). For instance, a sample mean *will never be exactly the same* in comparison to a population mean. An example of a sampling error can often be seen in the results of election polls. For instance, if an individual is running for a local elected position, such as sheriff or district attorney, a local organization may conduct a pre-election poll to determine which candidate is likely to win the election. Suppose an individual is predicted to become the next district attorney as a result of securing 53% of the vote in the poll. In addition to the percentage, the organization will often include a margin of error. Thus, the candidate is likely to become the next local official with a ±5% margin of error. This is translated as a type of confidence in securing the vote between 48% (53% −5%) to 58% (53% − 5%). Including a margin of error speaks to the reality that a sample and population statistic will never be the same.

Chapter Learning Assessment Questions

To gauge your learning, provide answers to the following questions:

1. An error that may occur due to chance is a ________________.
   a. sampling error
   b. margin of error
   c. mean error
   d. none of the above
2. On three separate occasions, during a required shooting exercise, a police officer earns a score of 100%. This is based on the officer's ability to hit the center mass area of a target 20 times out of 20 opportunities. This example is consistent with which of the following terms?
   a. sampling error
   b. mean error
   c. population error
   d. none of the above
3. A margin of error is a type of ________________.
   a. sampling error
   b. population error
   c. mean error
   d. none of the above

Answers

1. a
2. a
3. a

At this point, we have covered information that establishes a foundational understanding of certain statistical terms, which will underscore the purpose (and value) of the function of a hypothesis test.

The Role and Steps of Hypothesis Testing

Do you recall the example of the professor who employed an intervention as a result of observing the grades of her students? The steps outlined in that example are identified below:

1. The professor makes an observation. If you remember, she observed that the exam grades of her students were low.
2. This observation led to the discovery of a problem.
3. The professor developed a strategy in which she used a cost-effective and practical solution designed to motivate active student learning. More specifically, the professor believed that if students were exposed to someone other than herself who had practical experience, that person might motivate students to demonstrate an interest in learning about statistics. In essence, the professor developed what some may refer to as a claim or a hypothesis.
4. Despite the solid logic of her idea, as well as her experience as a professor, she needed to determine whether her hypothesis was supported through the use of statistical testing.
5. Once she is able to see the results of statistical testing, she will either find evidence that supports or fails to support her hypothesis.

As identified in the example, the professor decided to respond to what she observed (a problem) by testing a hypothesis. A **hypothesis** is an idea (or a claim) about a phenomenon that is often verified through testing. By exposing her students to the influence and passion of a guest speaker, she believed that the experience alone would result in a different outcome for her students (positive exam scores). To measure (or test) her idea (or claim), she engaged in a formal process often known as hypothesis testing. **Hypothesis testing** is a process that uses a series of steps designed to produce evidence that either supports (or fails to support) a hypothesis (or a claim). More specifically, hypothesis testing has more to do with computing and discovering evidence that either supports (or fails to support) the null hypothesis (Henkel, 1976).

hypothesis An idea (or claim) about a phenomenon that is often verified through testing.

hypothesis testing A process that uses a series of steps designed to produce evidence that either supports (or fails to support) a hypothesis (or a claim).

Steps of Hypothesis Testing

When conducting a hypothesis test, you should take the following steps:

1. Identify the null and alternative hypotheses. This includes statements that identify the independent variable (IV) and dependent variable (DV) in a study.

   As an example of each step, consider the following:

   H_0 – There is no difference between (IV) youth who have a positive attitude toward school compared to those who do not have a positive attitude toward school and (DV) their involvement in delinquent incidents within an academic year.

   H_1 – There is a difference between (IV) youth who have a positive attitude toward school compared to those who do not have a positive attitude toward school and (DV) their involvement in delinquent incidents within an academic year.
2. Identify the level of risk (or significance). This is determined by the researcher who identifies the extent to which they are willing to be incorrect. This is called making a type I error. In this example, the level of risk indicates that the researcher is 95% confident that there is a difference among youth who have a positive attitude toward school compared to those who do not have a positive attitude toward school and their involvement in delinquent incidents within an academic year.

   Level of risk = 0.05 (5%)
3. Choose the appropriate test. This is based on the level of measurements associated with the independent and dependent variables in the study of interest. Based on the information in Step 1, the IV is **categorical** (that is, it can be either a positive or a negative attitude, thereby fitting into one or the other category), and the DV is continuous (number of delinquent incidents). These levels of measurement require the use of a *t*-test.
4. Compute and identify the statistical test value (STV). STV is a term that identifies a value derived from the calculation of a statistical test. The STV is commonly referred to as the obtained value. We will not actually compute the STV at this time, but let's assume that our STV is 3.15.
5. Identify and compare the critical decision value (CDV) to the STV. This requires the use of a table (located near the end of the text) that identifies the values needed for rejecting the null hypothesis. Since our STV is 3.15, we compare this value with the CDV, which (based on the information identified in the table) is ±2.92.
6. If the STV > CDV, reject the null hypothesis. Given that the STV (3.15) is greater than the CDV (±2.92), we reject the null hypothesis. This does not mean that the alternative hypothesis is true; it simply means that the results of the test do not support the claim identified in the null hypothesis. In other words, the results reveal that there is no evidence that supports the claim that there is no difference between youth who have a positive attitude toward school (compared to those who do not have a positive attitude toward school) and their involvement in delinquent incidents within an academic year. Consider the

categorical Belonging to one group, or category, or another. Racial categories, for example, are often used to classify respondents in certain statistical studies.

following illustration of the results. Notice how the STV (3.15) falls outside of the CDV (±2.92). This demonstrates that the difference between the two groups is statistically significant. For further details, see Figure 7.2.

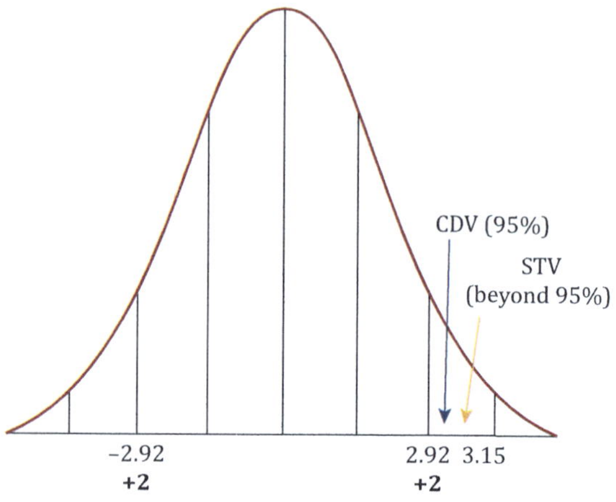

FIGURE 7.2 Normal Distribution Curve

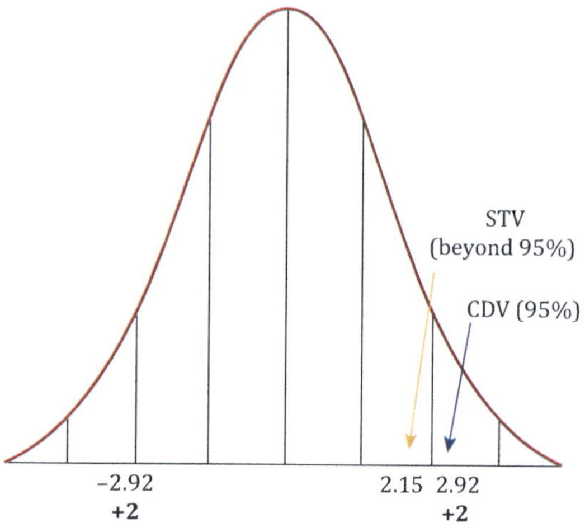

FIGURE 7.3 Normal Distribution Curve

7. If the STV < CDV, fail to reject the null hypothesis. Let's assume that our STV is (2.15), which is less than the CDV (±2.92), and we fail to reject the null hypothesis. To that end, we now have evidence that supports the null hypothesis, which states that there is no difference among youth who have a positive attitude toward school compared to those who do not and the number of delinquent incidents among students. Consider the following illustration and notice how the STV (2.15) does not fall outside of the CDV (±2.92). This demonstrates that the difference between the two groups is not statistically significant. Additional details are provided in Figure 7.3.

Now that we have provided an overview of the steps of hypothesis testing, we will turn our attention to the following questions:

Chapter Learning Assessment Questions

To gauge your learning, provide answers to the following questions:

1. In Step 1 of the hypothesis testing process, the null hypothesis
   a. is consistent with the alternative hypothesis.
   b. is the opposite of the alternative hypothesis.
   c. can be used to replace the alternative hypothesis.
   d. all of the above

2. When conducting a hypothesis test, the level of measurement associated with the independent and dependent variables will determine the ______________ that should be used.
   a. level of risk
   b. level of significance
   c. type of statistical test
   d. type of critical value
3. Which of the following determines whether the null hypothesis should be rejected?
   a. When the STV is greater than the CDV
   b. When the STV is less than the CDV
   c. When the STV is equal to the CDV
   d. Either a or b

Answers

1. b
2. c
3. a

For further information related to hypothesis testing, we will now examine each of the various types and functions of the first step, the hypotheses. This includes the null and alternative hypotheses, directional and nondirectional hypotheses, and type I and type II errors.

Define and Explain Critical Aspects of Hypotheses

Socialization of Children and Adult Development

Research reveals that what an individual is exposed to during their childhood has a bearing on their development and behavior as adults. For instance, those who were exposed to individuals and settings where affection and support were consistently provided are likely to reveal those same characteristics in relationships with others in later years. This often leads to fulfilling and influential lives. On the other hand, youth who were not consistently exposed to these positive experiences often find difficulty in developing meaningful relationships with others as adults. Thus, they are less likely to find fulfillment and purpose in their lives. Settings in which unfavorable experiences may exist among youth are foster homes.

As a type of hypothesis testing, suppose one is interested in determining whether youth who were reared in foster homes (compared to those who were not raised in such settings) are less likely to develop meaningful relationships as adults.

In the previous example, there are two statements of interest that identify the null and alternative hypotheses. Both statements, regardless of the research topic, serve as the basis for the remaining steps of the hypothesis-testing process.

null hypothesis A statement that proposes a lack of difference (or relationship) between variables.

alternative hypothesis A statement that proposes a difference (or relationship) between variables.

Null and Alternative Hypothesis

A null hypothesis is a statement of no relationship between the independent variable and the dependent variable. On the other hand, an alternative hypothesis is a statement of a relationship between the independent variable and the dependent variable (Henkel, 1976).

To illustrate the differences, consider the following:

Suppose one believed that youth who were reared in foster homes (compared to those who were not raised in such environments) *are less likely* to develop meaningful relationships as adults.

The null and alternative research hypothesis could be stated as follows:

H_0 = There is no difference between individuals who were reared in foster homes and those who were not in terms of developing meaningful relationships as adults.

H_1 = There is a difference between individuals who were reared in foster homes and those who were not in terms of developing meaningful relationships as adults.

The formula, which defines these relationships, is identified below:

$$H_0 : \mu_1 = \mu_2$$
$$H_1 : \mu_1 \neq \mu_2$$

where

H_0 = Null hypothesis
H_1 = Alternative hypothesis
μ_1 = population mean of individuals raised in foster homes
μ_2 = population mean of individuals not raised in foster homes

The following are examples of the null and alternative hypotheses in association with various research topics.

1.a. There is no difference between the mean number of arrests among Black youth and White youth (null hypothesis).
1.b. There is a difference between the mean number of arrests among Black youth and White youth (alternative hypothesis).
2.a. There is no relationship between educational attainment and promotion among police officers (null hypothesis).
2.b. There is a relationship between educational attainment and promotion among police officers (alternative hypothesis).
3.a. There is no difference between the mean number of charges filed against Whites and non-Whites arrested for the same offense (null hypothesis).
3.b. There is a difference between the mean number of charges filed against Whites and non-Whites arrested for the same offense (alternative hypothesis).
4.a. There is no relationship between mentoring and recidivism among juveniles (null hypothesis).
4.b. There is a relationship between mentoring and recidivism among juveniles (alternative hypothesis).

TABLE 7.3 **Null and Alternative Hypothesis Statements**

Null Hypotheses	Alternative Hypotheses
There is no difference between the mean number of arrests among Black youth and White youth.	There is a difference between the mean number of arrests among Black youth and White youth.
There is no relationship between educational attainment and promotion among police officers.	There is a relationship between educational attainment and promotion among police officers.
There is no difference between the mean number of charges filed against Whites and non-Whites arrested for the same offense.	There is a difference between the mean number of charges filed against Whites and non-Whites arrested for the same offense.
There is no relationship between mentoring and recidivism among juveniles.	There is a relationship between mentoring and recidivism among juveniles.

Directional and Nondirectional Alternative Hypothesis

In hypothesis testing, it is not uncommon to experience uncertainty in relation to the direction of the differences. For instance, as identified in Table 7.3, the alternative research hypothesis states that there is a difference between the mean number of arrests among Black youth and White youth. Despite this claim, the direction of the difference is not stated. To that end, the difference could reflect an increase or decrease (><). This is referred to as a nondirectional alternative hypothesis.

nondirectional alternative hypothesis A statement that proposes a difference (or relationship) in a nonspecific direction.

directional alternative hypothesis A statement that proposes a difference (or relationship) in a specific direction.

$$H_1: \bar{x}_b \neq \bar{x}_w,$$

where

H_1 = alternative hypothesis
$\bar{x}_b$ = the mean number of arrests among Black youth
$\neq$ = represents "not equal to" or nondirectional difference
$\bar{x}_w$ = the mean number of arrests among White youth

A directional alternative hypothesis involves a claim in which both a difference and a specific direction are identified. From our previous statement, let's assume that the alternative research hypothesis states that the mean number of young Blacks who experience arrest is greater than the mean number of young Whites who experience arrest. As indicated, the claim identifies the following:

$$H_1: \bar{x}_b > \bar{x}_w,$$

where

H_1 = alternative hypothesis
$\bar{x}_b$ = the mean number of arrests among Black youth
$><$ = represents a specific directional difference
$\bar{x}_w$ = the mean number of arrests among White youth

The following are examples of the differences between nondirectional and directional hypotheses:

1.a. There is a difference between the mean number of arrests among Black youth and White youth (nondirectional alternative hypothesis).
1.b. The difference between the mean number of arrests among Black youth is greater than the mean number of arrests among White youth (directional alternative hypothesis).
2. a. There is a relationship between educational attainment and promotion among police officers (nondirectional alternative hypothesis).
2. b. Police officers with higher education are more likely to experience promotional opportunities compared to police officers who do not possess higher education (directional alternative hypothesis).
3. a. There is a difference between the mean number of charges filed against Whites and non-Whites arrested for the same offense (nondirectional alternative hypothesis).
3. b. The difference between the mean number of charges filed against Whites is greater than the mean number of charges filed against non-Whites arrested for the same offense (directional alternative hypothesis).
4. a. There is a relationship between mentoring and recidivism among juveniles (nondirectional alternative hypothesis).
4. b. Juveniles who fail to experience mentoring are more likely to engage in recidivism compared to juveniles who experience mentoring (directional alternative hypothesis).

Type I and Type II Error

Finally, it is important to understand that the null hypothesis plays a significant role in hypothesis testing. Essentially, it serves as a standard to be measured against when engaging in inferential statistics. Thus, the purpose of conducting research is to determine whether the null hypothesis should be rejected. If a relationship (or difference) does exist, one should reject the null hypothesis. If a relationship (or difference) does not exist, one should fail to reject the null hypothesis.

Unfortunately, there are occurrences where mistakes are made in terms of rejecting or failing to reject the null hypothesis. A type I error (α) refers to the mistake of rejecting a true null hypothesis. A type II error (β) refers to the mistake of accepting a false null hypothesis (Henkel, 1976). In short, a type I error is equivalent to convicting an innocent person, while a type II error is akin to acquitting a guilty person (Feinberg, 1971).

type I error The mistake of rejecting a true null hypothesis.

type II error The mistake of failing to reject a false null hypothesis.

TABLE 7.4 **Type I and Type II Errors**

	Fail to Reject the Null Hypothesis	Reject the Null Hypothesis
The null hypothesis is actually true.	Correct response – the null hypothesis is accepted, indicating there is no difference	Incorrect – a type I error (a true null hypothesis was rejected)
The null hypothesis is actually false.	Incorrect – a type II error (a false null hypothesis was accepted)	Correct response – the null hypothesis is rejected, indicating there is a difference

Let's assume that differences exist in the number of complaints among police officers who received de-escalation training compared to officers who did not receive such training. At the start of our analysis, however, we do not know whether such training actually "works." If the null hypothesis (which states there is no difference in the number of complaints) is true and we fail to reject the null hypothesis, we have made the correct response. This would support the idea that *differences do not* exist with respect to the number of complaints among officers who received de-escalation training compared to officers who did not receive such training. However, if we reject the null hypothesis, we have made an incorrect response (type I error). If the null hypothesis is actually false (as it is in this case), and we fail to reject the null hypothesis, then we have reached an incorrect conclusion (type II error). Our rejection of the null hypothesis would erroneously support the notion that *differences do not* exist with respect to the number of complaints among officers who received de-escalation training compared to officers who did not receive such training. On the other hand, if we reject the null hypothesis, we have made the correct response.

Chapter Learning Assessment Questions

To gauge your learning, provide answers to the following questions:

1. Which of the following is an example of an alternative hypothesis?
   a. There is a relationship between poverty and frustration.
   b. There may be a relationship between depression and suicide.
   c. There is no relationship between race and IQ.
   d. None of the above
2. In hypothesis testing, the null hypothesis ______________.
   a. is a statement of no relationship between an independent and dependent variable
   b. is a standard to be measured against when engaging in inferential statistics
   c. should be rejected if a relationship between an independent and dependent variable exists
   d. all of the above
3. Which of the following is not an example of a nondirectional alternative hypothesis?
   a. When measuring fear of crime, there is a difference between males and females.
   b. During criminal sentencing, there is a difference in the types of punishment (e.g., prison, probation) between those with a prior criminal record and those who do not have a prior criminal record.
   c. Upon observing arrest numbers, there is no difference between males and females between the ages of 18–22.
   d. None of the above
4. Which of the following is an example of a type I error?
   a. Failing to reject the null hypothesis when results of a statistical test reveal that a relationship between gender and fear of crime does not exist.

b. Rejecting the null hypothesis when results of a statistical test reveal that a relationship between gender and fear of crime does not exist.

c. Failing to reject the alternative hypothesis when results of a statistical test reveal that a relationship between gender and fear of crime does not exist.

d. Failing to reject the alternative hypothesis when results of a statistical test reveal that a relationship between gender and fear of crime does not exist.

Answers

1. a
2. d
3. c
4. b

Now that we have examined the different aspects of the null and alternative hypotheses, we will discuss the second step of hypothesis testing. This includes the process of establishing the level of risk and selecting the appropriate statistical test.

Level of Risk and Selecting the Appropriate Test

Measuring Recidivism Rates

Imagine you are part of an advisory board that is responsible for making important decisions. As a board member, one of your responsibilities involves making recommendations for budget reduction measures in the department of juvenile justice and delinquency prevention. In particular, you (along with your fellow board members) must choose which programs will receive funding for the next fiscal year. To determine which programs will receive funding, you must provide evidence of program effectiveness. To that end, because of your belief (hypothesis) that restorative justice programs are more effective than traditional programs, you decide to conduct a hypothesis test for the purpose of determining the effectiveness of restorative justice measures. In your hypothesis test, you selected two youth programs that include the following details:

Program A, which utilizes a legalistic approach, produces youth recidivism 25/50 (50%) within a 3-year period. On the other hand, Program B, which employs the use of restorative justice, results in youth recidivism 16/50 (32%) within a similar time period.

As indicated earlier, the independent variable is the type of approach the program has adopted in addressing delinquency among youth. This includes a legalistic approach and a restorative justice approach. The dependent variable for both programs is recidivism. Your hypothesis is that a considerable difference exists in recidivism among youth who participated in restorative justice programs in comparison to youth who did not experience restorative justice. Once the hypothesis test is completed, you share the results with your fellow board members.

While presenting the results, a board member poses a question related to how you determined whether the differences between the two groups of youth are significant. In response to such, you discussed a process associated with what is referred to as **statistical significance**. **Statistical significance** refers to any differences between variables (or groups) that are not based on chance (Henkel, 1976).

statistical significance Any difference between variables (or groups) that is not based on chance.

As indicated in the previous example, a primary goal of hypothesis testing is to conduct statistical testing to determine the existence of evidence that supports (or fails to support) an idea. In alignment with the steps identified in hypothesis testing, this includes the process of predicting an inaccurate outcome that the researcher is willing to accept. This is based on the use of certain probability standards.

Level of Risk

When explaining (or determining) statistically significant differences between variables, statisticians often use what is referred to as **level of risk** (or level of significance) in estimating the extent to which they are willing to be incorrect. The most common levels of risk are 0.05 (5%), 0.01 (1%), and 0.001 (0.1%). In other words, these levels represent the degree to which a statistician is willing to reject a true null hypothesis (a type I error). In most research articles, levels of risk are identified as $p < 0.05$, $p < 0.01$, or even $p < 0.001$, whereas p represents probability or p-value (Henkel, 1976). Based on our example, if a researcher (board member) chooses a level of risk of 0.05, they are stating that they are willing to be incorrect 5 times out of 100 times, which is 5%. This would suggest that the researcher is reasonably confident in the idea that restorative justice will likely lower the probability of recidivism.

level of risk The probability to which a statistician is willing to be incorrect (i.e., reject a true null hypothesis).

Side Bar

Within the natural and social sciences, $p < 0.05$ has been set as the minimum standard to establish statistical significance. Any p-value greater than 0.05 is not accepted as significant.

As indicated in Table 7.5, we are able to recognize the various levels of risk associated with common probability values in statistical testing.

TABLE 7.5 **Levels of Risk**

p	Level of risk	Interpretation
< x.x	X%	One who is willing . . .

Establishing and Interpreting P-Values

The interpretation of p-values is complex. It turns out that the process of learning the steps to interpret p-values offers a framework for comprehending their meaning. Here are a number of important steps:

1. Look at any p-value, for example:

$$p < 0.05$$

2. Drop the "p <" and count the number of spaces after the decimal point. Here we have **two** spaces after the decimal.

$$0.05$$

3. Using the number of spaces after the decimal point, write zeros (0) for each space and place a **1** in front of the **0**'s. Consider the following:

100

4. Return to the original p-value. In this case, we use $p < 0.05$. Drop the p <, all the zeros (0) immediately after the decimal, and then treat the remaining numbers as a whole number. In this case, we have the number:

5

Using the 100 and the 5, we can interpret $p < 0.05$ as follows:

> If we ran this research 100 times, we would commit a type 1 error five times.

If we had a $p < 0.0025$, the interpretation would be as follows:

> If we ran this research 10,000 times, we would commit a type 1 error 25 times.

Without a foundation for understanding hypothesis testing, it is highly unlikely that one can understand (or appreciate) the meaning of p-values. For every inferential statistic (parametric or nonparametric), a p-value exists.

Types of Tests Used in Determining Statistical Significance

When engaging in hypothesis (or any type of inferential) testing, it is important to understand that test selection is based on the type of data that exists. The following serves as a brief overview and does not represent all the tests that are recommended based on various data (or variable) characteristics (Henkel, 1976).

TABLE 7.6 **Levels of Measurement and Test Selection**

Independent Variable	**Dependent Variable**	
	Categorial (Nominal, Ordinal)	Continuous (Interval, Ratio)
Categorial (Nominal, Ordinal)	Chi-Square	*T*-Test, ANOVA
Continuous (Interval, Ratio)	N/A	Correlation

To begin, one must first determine the level of measurement for the independent and dependent variables in their desired study.

If the independent variable (IV) and dependent variable (DV) are categorical, it may include the use of a chi-square test. The purpose of the chi-square test is to determine whether an association exists between two categorical variables. For instance, as revealed in Table 7.7, if you are interested in determining whether classification status among inmates (e.g., high risk, low risk) is associated with inmate placement (e.g., individual cells, dormitory area) within a prison, you would conduct a chi-square test.

TABLE 7.7 **Level of Risk and Prison Housing**

Level of Risk	**Type of Prison Housing**		**Total**
	Individual Housing	Dormitory Housing	
Low	8	26	34
Medium	14	16	30
High	31	7	38
Total	53	49	102

If the IV is categorical and DV is continuous, it may include the use of a *t*-test. The purpose of conducting a *t*-test is to determine the differences between two means. For example, as indicated in Table 7.8, suppose one is interested in determining whether 1- or 10-year officers receive the highest number of complaints within a juvenile correctional facility. Since the IV is nominal, composed of two categories (1- and 10-year officers), and the DV is continuous (number of complaints), a *t*-test would be used. If the aforementioned included an additional IV, say, 20-year officers, a total of three categories would exist. This would require the use of the analysis of variance test (ANOVA), which is used to determine the mean differences between three or more groups or categories.

TABLE 7.8 **Officer Experience and Complaints**

Number of Years (Experience)	**Total Number of Officers**	**Total Number of Complaints (1 Year)**
1	5	16
10	5	8
Number of Years (Experience)	**Total Number of Officers**	**Total Number of Complaints (1 Year)**
1	5	16
10	5	8
20	4	3

If the IV and DV are continuous, it may call for the use of a correlation test. The purpose of a correlation test is to determine if linear relationships exist between variables. Suppose one is interested in determining whether an increase in the number of health-care staff is associated with lower numbers of lawsuits filed by inmates against a correctional facility. A correlation test would be used to identify the association of such, as well as the strength of that association. Both associations are identified in Table 7.9.

TABLE 7.9 **Number of Health-Care Staff and Number of Lawsuits/Amount of Lawsuits**

Number of Prison Health-Care Staff	Total Number of Lawsuits
1	27
5	14
10	5
Number of Prison Health-Care Staff	**Total Amount of Expenses From Lawsuits**
1	75,000
5	25,000
10	1,800

Chapter Learning Assessment Questions

To gauge your learning, provide answers to the following questions:

1. If we had a $p < 0.0045$, the interpretation would be written in the following manner:
   a. If we conducted a hypothesis test 10,000 times, we would commit a type I error 45 times.
   b. If we conducted a hypothesis test 1,000 times, we would commit a type I error 450 times.
   c. If we conducted a hypothesis test 1,000 times, we would commit a type I error 4.5 times.
   d. If we conducted a hypothesis test 10,000 times, we would commit a type I error 0.045 times.
2. The extent to which a researcher is willing to be incorrect is known as ________.
   a. level of risk
   b. statistical estimate
   c. significance ratio
   d. none of the above
3. The most common levels of risks are ________.
   a. $p < 0.05$
   b. $p < 0.01$
   c. $p < 0.001$
   d. all of the above

4. When a researcher is willing to be incorrect, they are willing to engage in ________.
   a. a type I error
   b. a type II error
   c. either a type I or type II error
   d. none of the above
5. When determining what type of statistical test to use, a researcher must determine the ________.
   a. levels of measurement for the independent and dependent variables
   b. number of independent variables and dependent variables
   c. number of dependent variables
   d. none of the above
6. If a researcher desires to use a chi-square test, which of the following must exist?
   a. The independent variable must be categorical.
   b. The dependent variable must be continuous.
   c. The sample size must include at least 200 cases or subjects.
   d. Both the independent and dependent variables must be categorical.
7. Which of the following types of hypothesis testing is used to determine differences in which the independent variable is categorical and the dependent variable is continuous?
   a. A chi-square test
   b. A *t*-test
   c. A correlation test
   d. None of the above

Answers

1. a
2. a
3. d
4. a
5. a
6. d
7. b

For our next section, we will examine the further details of hypothesis testing. This includes (1) computing a hypothesis test, (2) determining statistical significance, and (3) making a decision regarding the null hypothesis.

Engage in Calculating a Hypothesis Test, Determining Statistical Significance, and Making a Decision Regarding the Null Hypothesis

At this point, we've discussed the following steps of the hypothesis testing process:

1. State the hypotheses.
2. Establish the level of risk.
3. Determine the appropriate statistical test.

We have yet to discuss the following remaining steps:

1. Compute the STV and CDV.
2. Determine statistical significance.
3. Make a decision regarding the null hypothesis.

To provide context, we will combine all the steps into one single hypothesis test, which will include Steps 4–6. Furthermore, we will use a *t*-test statistic, which will be covered in a subsequent chapter. As an example, we will refer to our previous illustration based on the intervention measured employed by our statistics professor at the beginning of the chapter

Step 1—Establish Hypotheses

Hypotheses: The professor believes that exposing her students to a guest speaker will result in an increase in their test grades.

1. H_1 = Exposing students to a guest speaker will result in an increase in their test grades.
2. H_0 = Exposing students to a guest speaker will not result in an increase in their test grades.

Since the professor believes that the test scores of one group will be greater than the test scores of the other group, she is conducting a one-tailed hypothesis test (directional). If she simply stated that there would be a difference between the two groups, her test would be considered a type of two-tailed test (nondirectional).

Step 2—Establish Level of Risk

1. Level of risk: The professor is willing to be wrong (commit a type I error) 5 times out of 100. In other words, if the professor conducts this same test 100 times, she is willing to commit a type I error 5 times. Thus, her probability of committing a type I error is less than 5%, which is denoted as $p < 0.05$.
2. Compared to the level of risk noted above, suppose the professor is more confident in her expectations. In particular, if she conducts this test 100 times, she is willing to commit a type I error 1 time. To that end, her level of risk is 1%, which is displayed as $p < 0.01$.

Step 3—Determine Appropriate Statistical Test

To determine the appropriate statistical test, the professor engages in the following steps:

1. She must determine the levels of measurement for the independent and dependent variables in the hypothesis test.
2. In this process, the professor separated her students into two groups. As revealed in Table 7.10, one group (Group A) of students was exposed to the guest speaker, and the other group (Group B) was not exposed to the guest speaker.

TABLE 7.10 **Groups of Students and the Impact of Their Exposure as Demonstrated Through Test Scores**

Group	Number of Students	Mean Test Scores (Observed)	Exposure to Guest Speaker	Mean Test Scores (Expected)
A	9	69	Yes	79
B	9	66	No	66

TABLE 7.11 **Groups of Students and the Impact of Their Exposure as Demonstrated Through Test Scores**

Before		After	
Group A	Group B	Group A	Group B
68	67	79	67
73	70	81	70
69	67	76	67
70	69	85	69
65	65	86	65
68	67	87	67
63	60	79	60
72	59	73	59
73	71	68	71
$\bar{x} = 69$	$\bar{x} = 66$	$\bar{x} = 79$	$\bar{x} = 66$

1. In this scenario, the independent variables represent students who were either exposed or not exposed to the intervention (guest speaker). Table 7.11 includes students in Group A and Group B.
2. This separation of students into two different groupings is consistent with a nominal level of measurement, which is based on data that falls within a category that does not possess any ranking. Students placed in Group A are no different than students placed in Group B. Regardless of group, both categories of students are in the same course and exposed to the same expectations and academic assignments.
3. The dependent variables represent the actual exam grades of both groups of students. Since the characteristics of grades are continuous, they are aligned with the interval level of measurement.
4. Since the independent variables are nominal and the dependent variables are interval, we refer to the previous table (Table 7.6), which calls for the use of a *t*-test.

Step 4—Compute STV and Determine CDV

To determine STV, we must compute the actual test statistic. In this case, we are using an independent sample *t*-test statistic (which will be covered in detail in another chapter of this textbook).

1. As we refer to Table 7.10, we observed the following:
   a. Students in both Group A and Group B possess a mean test score of 68.
   b. Based on the hypothesis of the professor, students in Group A are expected to demonstrate an improvement in their test grades as a result of their exposure to the guest speaker.
   c. More specifically, the professor believes she will observe a 10-point increase in grades when comparing the test results of students in Group A with those in Group B.
2. Once our observations (and expectations) are established, we use the appropriate test statistic formula:
   a. Formula for independent sample t-test
   b. $$t = \frac{\overline{X}_1 - \overline{X}_2}{\sqrt{\left[\frac{(n_1 - 1)s_1^2 + (n_2 - 1)s_2^2}{n_1 + n_2 - 2}\right]\left[\frac{n_1 + n_2}{n_1 n_2}\right]}}$$
3. At this point, we include our numbers in the formula. Given that we will examine the details of such in the future, we will not engage in this process at this time. However, we can assume that the numbers applied to the *t*-test formula will include the mean test scores derived from Table 7.11.
4. Once the computation process is complete, suppose our *t*-test statistic is 5.86.
5. Despite the number of steps, our calculation process is not complete. We must identify the standard that enables one to determine statistical significance. This includes discovering the CDV.

To identify CDV, we must consider the following as it relates to our test statistic:

With a t-test, as well as other types of statistical tests, we must identify what is referred to as degrees of freedom (df) in determining our CDV. Overall, degrees of freedom provide the basis for uncovering the "critical value" of identifying statistical significance. We will further discuss the use of degrees of freedom in the remaining chapters of this textbook.

1. To compute df, using a *t*-test statistic, this includes adding the number of scores in each group and subtracting the sum by 2. In our example, this includes:
   a. df = Group A (n = 9) + Group B (n = 9)
   b. df = 9 + 9 = 18
   c. df = 18 - 2
   d. df = 16
2. Once the degrees of freedom are computed (df = 16), we locate the degrees of freedom number in a table located near the end of the text. As revealed in Table 7.12, this includes the number located in the far-left column. Once this is complete, we then locate the corresponding level of risk (0.05), which is in the top row of the table. Once both numbers are identified,

we locate the number where both the df and level of risk intersect. This is our CDV. If you recall, this process is slightly similar to what we covered in the previous chapter in which we located the area of the z-score under the curve by using a table.

TABLE 7.12 **Critical Region Table for *t*-Test**

df	0.10	0.05	0.01
1	3.078	6.134	31.82
2	1.886	2.92	6.965
3	1.638	2.353	4.541
4	1.533	2.132	3.747
5	1.476	2.015	3.365
6	1.44	1.943	3.143
7	1.415	1.895	2.998
8	1.397	1.86	2.897
9	1.383	1.833	2.822
10	1.372	1.813	2.764
11	1.364	1.796	2.718
12	1.356	1.783	2.681
13	1.35	1.771	2.651
14	1.345	1.762	2.625
15	1.341	1.753	2.603
16	1.337	1.746	2.584

Step 5—Determine Statistical Significance

1. Now that we have identified our STV (5.86) and CDV (1.74), we must determine the difference between the two values. To determine statistical significance, we compare the STV to the CDV based on the following criterion:
   a. If STV > CDV = statistical significance is achieved
   b. If STV < CDV = statistical significance is not achieved
2. Since our STV (5.86) is greater than our CDV (1.74), our statistical test provides evidence that there is a statistically significant difference between the values.
3. In short, there is a statistically significant difference between the mean test scores among the two groups of students.

Step 6 – Make a Decision regarding the Null Hypothesis

1. Our final decision requires that we make a decision regarding the null hypothesis. This includes the following criteria:
   a. If STV > CDV = reject the null hypothesis
   b. If STV < CDV = fail to reject the null hypothesis
2. Since our STV (5.86) is greater than our CDV (1.74), we must reject the null hypothesis.

3. In other words, our statistical test provides evidence that fails to support the assumption that there is no difference between the test scores of students who experienced the intervention process and those who did not.

Chapter Learning Assessment Questions

To gauge your learning, provide answers to the following questions:

1. Suppose a researcher believes that inmates who experience visitation opportunities with family members are less likely to engage in aggressive behavior. Which of the following is the null hypothesis of this claim?
   a. Inmates who experience visitation opportunities with family members are less likely to engage in aggressive behavior.
   b. Inmates who experience visitation opportunities with family members are not less likely to engage in aggressive behavior.
   c. Inmates who fail to experience visitation opportunities with family members are less likely to engage in aggressive behavior.
   d. None of the above
2. In hypothesis testing, level of risk refers to ______________.
   a. one's willingness to be incorrect
   b. one's willingness to commit a type II error
   c. one's willingness to be correct
   d. none of the above
3. If the STV is less than the CDV, which of the following decisions should be made?
   a. The null hypothesis should be rejected.
   b. The null hypothesis should not be rejected.
   c. The alternative hypothesis should be accepted.
   d. None of the above

Answers

1. b
2. a
3. b

As indicated in our results, statistical significance was achieved. To that end, let's examine the role of confidence intervals and levels in the study of statistics.

Confidence Intervals and Confidence Levels

First, confidence intervals and confidence levels are two very different concepts within the study of statistics. It is important not to confuse the terms and their meanings. *Confidence intervals* are always *expressed as a range*. Within the specified range, we predict (using a sample) the location of a population parameter. On the other hand, a *confidence level* is *stated as a percentage*. With data, a confidence level is used to illustrate the probability of a predicted data point to lie with a confidence interval (Henkel, 1976). For example, consider the following statement:

I am 95% (⟵ confidence level) sure that the population mean falls between 8 and 16 (⟵ confidence interval).

As noted in the definitions of both confidence level and confidence interval, the term parameter is used. The best, *but not precise*, manner to define the concept of parameter is to envision it as a descriptive statistic for a population. In short, *parameters* are the mathematical entities within a population, while *statistics* is the term used for data in a sample. As we further explore the use of the confidence interval, the heart of understanding the use of such is based on the existence of a sampling error. As previously discussed, a sampling error is the measurable distance between a sample mean and the population parameter (e.g., population mean). The greater the distance between the sample mean and the population mean, the greater the error.

confidence interval The range in which the predicted parameters of a population mean is located.

confidence level A probability that is used to describe how sure a person can be in approximating the location of a population parameter. It is often stated as a percentage.

Confidence Intervals

Confidence intervals are available for both parametric and nonparametric statistics. The confidence interval formulas are based on a particular test statistic. Thus, for every statistical test, there exists a unique formula for confidence intervals.

A practical example of the confidence interval (and confidence level) is provided below:

Suppose a university administrator is interested in determining the mean IQ score of 3,000 incoming freshman students. In general, the population mean of an IQ score is 100, and the standard deviation is 15. To determine the mean score, the administrator does not have the time (or the resources) to examine each student's academic record. To that end, the administrator decides to randomly select a sample from the population of students. This includes a total of 30 students. Once the sample has been collected, the students ($n = 30$) are encouraged to complete an IQ test. The mean IQ test of the sample is $\bar{x} = 103$. Despite the results, the administrator is keenly aware that the sample mean does not exactly represent the population mean IQ score. This discrepancy is due to sampling error.

standard error of the mean The term that reveals how much distance is estimated (on average) between the sample mean and the population mean.

At this point, the administrator realizes that the sample mean will fall within 68.2% of the true population mean.

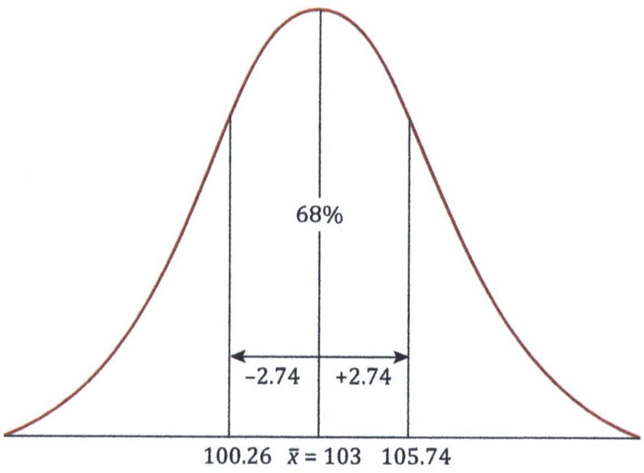

FIGURE 7.4 Estimated Population Mean IQ Score of 3,000 University Freshman

The administrator computes what is referred to as the standard error of the mean. A standard error of the mean is a process that measures the distance between a sample and a population mean.

The formula of the standard error of the mean is provided below:

$$\sigma_{\bar{x}} = \frac{\sigma}{\sqrt{N}}$$

The application of values within the formula results in the following steps:

$$\sigma_{\bar{x}} = \frac{15}{\sqrt{30}} = \frac{15}{5.47} = 2.74$$

Since $\bar{x} = 103$ is an estimate of what may exist in the population. By adding (and subtracting) 2.74 with 103, we establish a range (or the confidence interval). This includes (100.26 – 105.74). Thus, the confidence interval (CI) is written as

$$68\%\ \text{CI} = 103 \pm 2.74.$$

The interpretation of this process is based on the following:

The administrator is 68% confident that the mean IQ score for the university population of incoming freshmen is 103 ± 2.74. In other words, if someone randomly selected 68 students out of a total of 100 students, those students would likely possess an IQ score that falls between 100.26 and 105.74. In this example, 68% represents the confidence level.

Confidence Levels

As identified in the illustration, confidence levels are used to describe how sure a person can be in approximating the location of a population parameter. As an illustration, let's play a game called "guess the number of pennies." For $5, you are entitled to guess the correct number of pennies in the jar and win $50. What are the chances of winning the $50 under those circumstances?

Let's play the game again but with different rules. The new rule: Pay $5 and win $50 if the guess is within 10 of the true number of pennies in the jar.

Another scenario: pay $5 and win $50 if the guess is within 50 of the true number of pennies in the jar.

Another scenario: pay $5 and win $50 if the guess is within 100 of the true number of pennies in the jar.

Another scenario: pay $5 and win $50 if the guess is within 500 of the true number of pennies in the jar.

Thus, we have a choice among five games:

A. Win $50 for guessing the exact number.
B. Win $50 for guessing within 10 pennies of the exact number.
C. Win $50 for guessing within 50 pennies of the exact number.
D. Win $50 for guessing within 100 pennies of the exact number.
E. Win $50 for guessing within 500 pennies of the exact number.

Which game would you choose? If you selected E, you're well on your way to understanding confidence levels. If you selected any other option, you should never play poker.

The key element is: As confidence increases, as one moves from option A to E (then selecting option E), the room for error grows. In option E, you can "miss the mark" by 500 pennies and still win $50.

Ultimately, there is a type of trade-off between acceptable error and the level of confidence. From this standpoint, when predicting (and the requirement calls for precision), confidence decreases. On the other hand, if leeway for error is given, confidence in predicting increases.

This logic is the basis for understanding confidence levels and is closely connected to what we know about confidence intervals.

IMAGE 7.1

Let's say that you are predicting a population mean, and you are 99% confident that the mean lies between 25 and 100. How helpful is that? Not much. The distance or confidence interval is too wide to be practical. In reducing the confidence interval, we now have:

IMAGE 7.2

Would it be better if we stated that we are 95% confident that the mean is between 45 and 50? Our confidence interval is smaller (better), but our confidence level has been reduced (from 99% to 95%). In other words, we are less confident.

Suppose we reduce our confidence interval to 46.1 and 46.6 (which is very small), but we only have a 3% chance (confidence level) that the population mean is between these two points.

IMAGE 7.3

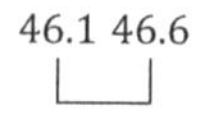

As we reduce the size of our confidence interval, we reduce the chances of being accurate (confidence level) in our prediction. As we increase the size of our confidence interval, we increase our chances of being accurate (confidence level). As mentioned previously, there is no single formula for determining confidence intervals and confidence levels. These formulas are married to the specific statistical test used in hypothesis testing.

Chapter Learning Assessment Questions

To gauge your learning, provide answers to the following questions:

1. The range in which the predicted parameters of a population mean is located is referred to as a(n):
   a. confidence interval
   b. confidence level
   c. estimate range
   d. estimate level
2. The term "parameter" is used in association with a ______________.
   a. population
   b. sample
   c. either a or b
   d. none of the above
3. As a confidence level increases,
   a. confidence interval increases.
   b. confidence interval decreases.
   c. either a or b
   d. none of the above
4. The heart of understanding the value of confidence interval and confidence level is based on one's understanding of ______________.
   a. sampling error
   b. standard error of the mean
   c. sample statistics
   d. none of the above
5. The first step in computing the standard error of the mean is to ______________.
   a. determine the square root of the sample size
   b. divide the sample size by the standard deviation of the population

c. divide the sample size by the standard deviation of the sample
d. none of the above

6. After reviewing the final exam scores of her students, a professor includes the following statement in a report.

$$95\%\ \text{CI} = 97 \pm 3$$

Which of the following is the appropriate interpretation of the statement provided by the professor?
a. If someone randomly selected 95 students (out of a total of 100 students), those students would likely possess a final exam score that falls between 94 and 100.
b. If someone randomly selected 90 students (out of a total of 95 students), those students would likely possess a final exam score that falls between 94 and 100.
c. If someone randomly selected 90 students (out of a total of 97 students), those students would likely possess a final exam score that falls between 94 and 100.
d. None of the above

Answers

1. a
2. a
3. a
4. a
5. a
6. a

Now that we have discussed the role of confidence levels and intervals, let's redirect our attention to additional matters of significance. This includes power analysis and the protocol for written statistical results.

Additional Matters of Significance

Power Analysis

Because of the American Statistical Association's policy statement on p-values and statistical significance, the study of power analysis is moving to the forefront of statistical analysis. Essentially, the term "power in statistics" generally refers to the probability that the researcher will correctly reject the null hypothesis. As an alternative way of understanding, we can state that power is the probability that we will correctly obtain

power analysis The probability that the researcher will correctly reject the null hypothesis. The probability of correctly obtaining a small p-value.

a small p-value. If we have a high probability of correctly obtaining a small p-value (and rejecting the null hypothesis), we have a large amount of power.

If we failed to reject our null hypothesis because our p-value is greater than 0.05 (like 0.0599), but we have a strong theory to support the alternative hypothesis, could we just increase our sample size? The answer is no. To engage in such is unethical by the standards established by the American Statistical Association. As a remedy, we are encouraged to collect data that represents a new sample population. The problem could be prevented if we conduct a power analysis to determine what sample size will ensure a high probability that we correctly reject the null hypothesis.

Given that nonparametric statistical tests are less powerful than parametric statistical tests, power analysis are generally used for parametric statistics. Thus, power analysis is not used with nonparametric statistics.

How to Illustrate the Answer in Statistics

In the world of statistics, a standardized protocol has been established to exhibit the results of a statistical analysis. We learn the protocol by example and use it for future illustrations.

For centuries, we have seen a never-ending debate on the Transylvania hypothesis (a term coined by Geller & Shannon, 1976). Essentially, the Transylvania hypothesis proposes that the lunar cycle has an influence on human behavior. The hypothesis stresses that admissions to psychiatric facilities are influenced by the full moon. Marson (1975) tested this hypothesis with admissions to an inpatient alcoholic rehabilitation center. He matched the date of admissions to the cycles of the moon and discovered that there was a disproportionate number of admissions during the full moon cycle. It is *unlikely* that this relationship is the result of random chance. To that end, he employed the standard method (written response) to illustrate the results:

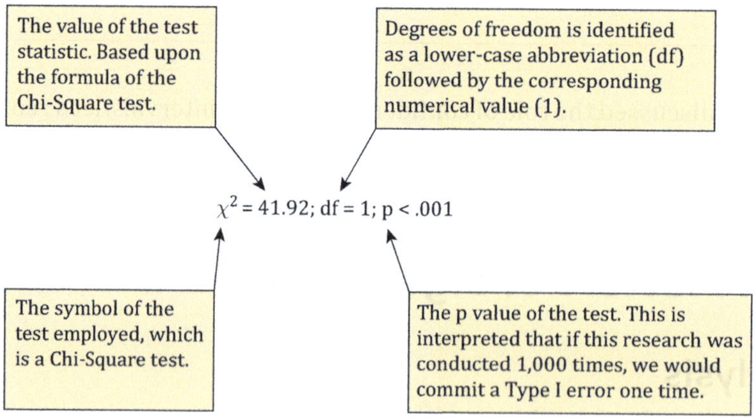

FIGURE 7.5 Written Results of a Chi-Square Test

In comparison to Figure 7.5. one caveat exists. The result of a test for significance is influenced by the sample size. Thus, in the text of a statistical manuscript, one is ethically mandated to report the sample size in this manner: $n = 316$. A thoughtful reader will question the results when the sample size is not reported. Lastly, although not part of the standard protocol, there is nothing wrong with including the sample size, as indicated in the following:

$$X^2 = 41.92;\ df = 1;\ p < 0.001;\ n = 316$$

As revealed, the sample size is designated by a lowercase n.

Chapter Learning Assessment Questions

To gauge your learning, provide answers to the following questions:

1. If a researcher conducts a hypothesis test in which a power analysis is used, the researcher may desire to meet all the following goals except
   a. increase the probability that the null hypothesis is rejected.
   b. increase the probability that their study will result in obtaining a small p-value.
   c. increase the probability that their study will result in obtaining a large p-value.
   d. none of the above
2. A power analysis test is often used with a __________.
   a. parametric test
   b. nonparametric test
   c. both a and b
   d. none of the above

For Questions 3–5, consider the following written statement:

$$X^2 = 15.13;\ df = 6;\ p < 0.05;\ n = 173$$

3. In the statement above, X^2 represents __________.
   a. the symbol of the test
   b. the value of the test
   c. the degrees of freedom
   d. none of the above
4. In the statement above, the value of 6 represents __________.
   a. the symbol of the test
   b. the value of the test
   c. the degrees of freedom
   d. none of the above
5. In the statement above, 15.13 represents __________.
   a. the value of the test
   b. the number of cases (or subjects) in the sample
   c. the number of cases (or subjects) in the population
   d. none of the above

6. Which of the following may serve as evidence that a power analysis was used?
   a. $p < 0.05$
   b. $p < 0.0025$
   c. $p > 0.01$
   d. all of the above

Answers

1. c
2. a
3. a
4. c
5. a
6. d

Final Thoughts

As with any statistical process, there are rules that must be adhered to achieve appropriate outcomes. Just as the level of measurement associated with each value determines the type of statistical test used, the level of risk will determine if the results of a statistical test are significant. In most cases, the latter is often determined by the researcher. In this respect, contrary to popular belief, statistics is not exclusively "a hands-off" topic. Finally, on exposure to information that indicates the existence of significant differences, consider asking yourself whether the differences are *actual differences* or *the result of sampling errors*. In addition, don't be afraid to question the research findings (statistical conclusions) of others. This will demonstrate your level of commitment to integrity and ethics within research as it relates to the use of statistics.

Discussion

A study reveals that a significant difference exists between youth based on age and the probability of being waived to the adult court. Youth between the ages of 13–15 are less likely to have their cases waived to the adult court compared to youth between the ages of 16–17. As you examine the details of the study, you notice that the independent and dependent variables are both continuous. In addition, you discover that a chi-square test was used. What is your response to this study? Do you agree or disagree with the test that was used and the results of the study? Explain.

Chapter Summary

This chapter emphasizes the following information:

Objective 1 – Define and explain the use of sample and population.

- A sample is a subset of a population composed of the actual group of research participants.
- A population is the actual group of reference that the sample data (or statistic) represents.

Objective 2 – Define and explain the use of sampling error and true differences.

- A sampling error is a value that represents an occurrence due to chance.
- A true difference is a value that represents an occurrence that is not due to chance.

Objective 3 – Describe the role and steps of hypothesis testing.

- A hypothesis is an idea (or a claim) about a phenomenon that is often verified through testing.
- Hypothesis testing is the process of steps designed to produce evidence that either supports (or fails to support) a hypothesis.
- The steps in conducting a hypothesis test include (1) identifying the null and alternative hypothesis, (2) identifying the level of risk, (3) choosing the appropriate test, (4) computing the STV, (5) identifying the CDV, (6) comparing the STV to the CDV, and (7) rejecting (or failing to reject) the null hypothesis.

Objective 4 – Define and explain critical aspects of hypotheses.

- A null hypothesis is a statement that proposes a lack of difference (or relationship) between variables. An alternative hypothesis is a statement that proposes that a difference (or relationship) between variables exists.
- A directional alternative hypothesis proposes a difference (or relationship) in a specific direction. A nondirectional alternative hypothesis proposes a difference (or relationship) in a nonspecific direction.
- A type I error is the mistake of rejecting a true null hypothesis. A type II error is the mistake of failing to reject a false null hypothesis.

Objective 5 – Explain the level of risk in selecting the appropriate test.

- Level of risk (or level significance) is the probability that a statistician is willing to be incorrect (i.e., reject a true null hypothesis). The most common levels of risk are 0.05 (5%) and 0.01 (1%).
- Selecting the appropriate test is based on the levels of measurement as identified in the independent and dependent variables.

Objective 6 – Engage in calculating a hypothesis test, determining statistical significance, and making a decision regarding the null hypothesis.

- If the STV is greater than the CDV, statistical significance is achieved, and one must reject the null hypothesis.
- If the STV is not greater than the CDV, statistical significance is not achieved, and one must fail to reject the null hypothesis.

Objective 7 – Discuss the role of confidence intervals and confidence levels.

- A confidence level is used to describe how sure a person can be in approximating the location of a population parameter. It is often stated as a percentage. A confidence interval is used to estimate a range where the population parameter is located.

Objective 8 – Explore additional matters of significance.

- Power analysis is the probability that a researcher will correctly reject the null hypothesis. It is the probability of correctly obtaining a small p-value.
- Written statistical results require a protocol.

Terms

Sample
Population
Null hypothesis
Nondirectional alternative hypothesis
Type 1 error
Type 2 error
Alternative hypothesis
Directional alternative hypothesis
Statistical significance
Level of risk
Sampling error
True difference
Hypothesis
Confidence levels
Confidence intervals
Hypothesis testing
Power analysis
Standard error of the mean

Chapter Review Questions

1. Rejecting a null hypothesis assumes which of the following:
   a. The difference between means is not significant.
   b. The difference between means is significant.
   c. There is no difference between sample means.
   d. There is no difference between population means.
2. As a researcher, you are interested in discovering the amount of confidence minorities have in the police in their communities. You select a total of 248 minorities to complete a survey, which reveals that 68% support their local police. The statistic (68%) was derived from which of the following?
   a. The population
   b. The sample
   c. The mean
   d. The majority
3. A graduate student has just read an article that reveals that police officers who experience difficulty encountering paradoxical experiences (PE) are more likely to leave the profession. To that end, the student is curious as to whether college education or law enforcement

experience serves as a protective factor among police who encounter PE. Examples of PE, which include faulty assumptions that police officers may embrace, include the belief that officers will spend the majority of their time actually fighting crime as opposed to engaging in noncrime fighting responsibilities (i.e., addressing minor disputes, submitting paperwork, etc.). The student engages in survey data research in which she receives a total of 478 completed surveys. Over 90% of surveys reveal that both education (at least a 4-year degree) and years of law enforcement experience (at least 5 years) are associated with lower probabilities of leaving the profession. The statistic (90%) reflects (or represents) which of the following?

a. The population
b. The sample
c. The mean
d. The majority

4. A study reveals that greater levels of frustration among police is associated with greater levels of involvement in a police subculture. In an effort to replicate this study, you have received authorization to conduct research with a local law enforcement agency. To begin the data collection process, you decide to only distribute surveys to officers who have at least 10 years of experience. The aforementioned scenario is an example of the need of ______________ in research:

a. Nondirectional alternative hypothesis
b. Directional alternative hypothesis
c. Random selection
d. Sample

5. Among first-time offenders, the following data represents the findings of a study in which Black arrestees are less likely to receive equitable plea agreements from prosecutors compared to White arrestees.

Race of Arrestee	Number of Arrestees	Offense Charge	Potential Maximum Years of Confinement	Average Plea Agreement Offer (Years of Confinement)
Black	15	Aggravated Robbery	10	7
White	20	Aggravated Robbery	15	3

This study is an example of a(n):

a. Null hypothesis
b. Alternative hypothesis
c. Nondirectional alternative hypothesis
d. Directional alternative hypothesis

6. One is interested in examining the relationship between harsh parental discipline and delinquency among youth between the ages of 8 and 13. The independent variable is categorical,

and the dependent variable is continuous. Which of the following is the appropriate type of test that should be used?

a. Chi-square test
b. *T*-test
c. Correlation test
d. ANOVA test

7. A study reveals an association between lax parental discipline and delinquency among female youth. The independent and dependent variables are both continuous. Which of the following is the appropriate type of test that should have been used?
   a. Chi-square test
   b. *T*-test
   c. Correlation test
   d. ANOVA test
8. Studies suggest that the early onset of drug abuse, early sexual involvement, and hyperactivity are related to instances of delinquency. The independent variables (which include three categories) are categorical, and the dependent variable is continuous. Which of the following is the appropriate type of test that should have been used?
   a. Chi-square test
   b. *T*-test
   c. Correlation test
   d. ANOVA test
9. ____________ refers to any differences between variables (or groups) that are not based on chance.
   a. Statistical significance
   b. Confidence intervals
   c. Level of risk
   d. Degrees of freedom
10. ____________ represents the degree to which a statistician is willing to reject a true null hypothesis.
    a. Statistical significance
    b. Confidence intervals
    c. Level of risk
    d. Degrees of freedom
11. Which of the following is the correct interpretation of $p < 0.05$?
    a. If a test is conducted 1,000 times, one is willing to make a type 1 error 5 times.
    b. If a test is conducted 100 times, one is willing to make a type 1 error 50 times.
    c. If a test is conducted 1,000 times, one is willing to make a type 1 error 0.05 times.
    d. If a test is conducted 100 times, one is willing to make a type 1 error 5 times.

12. Which of the following is the correct interpretation of $p < 0.0020$?
    a. If a test is conducted 10,000 times, one is willing to make a type 1 error 2 times.
    b. If a test is conducted 10,000 times, one is willing to make a type 1 error 200 times.
    c. If a test is conducted 10,000 times, one is willing to make a type 1 error 20 times.
    d. If a test is conducted 10,000 times, one is willing to make a type 2 error 2 times.
13. When conducting an inferential statistical test, the step that includes statements that identify the independent and dependent variables is considered:
    a. Step 3
    b. Step 1
    c. Step 2
    d. Step 5
14. When conducting an inferential statistical test, the step that identifies the extent to which the researcher is willing to engage in a type 1 error is considered:
    a. Step 1
    b. Step 4
    c. Step 2
    d. Step 5
15. When conducting an inferential statistical test, the step that requires the use of a table that identifies the value needed for rejecting the null hypothesis is considered:
    a. Step 3
    b. Step 2
    c. Step 4
    d. Step 5
16. When conducting statistical calculations that employ the use of a p-value, it is required that one uses a(n) ___________.
    a. Algorithm
    b. Calculator
    c. Theory
    d. Abacus
17. A confidence level is stated as a ___________.
    a. distribution that includes at least five data points
    b. range
    c. distribution that excludes outliers
    d. percentage
18. Which of the following statements is an example of a confidence interval?
    a. The population mean exists between 9 and 18
    b. The population mean exists between 5 and 10

c. The population mean exists between 6 and 12
d. All of the above

19. ____________ are used to describe how sure a person can be in approximating the location of a population parameter.
   a. Confidence intervals
   b. Confidence levels
   c. Degrees of freedom
   d. Level of risk
20. As one reduces the size of a confidence interval, one also reduces their chances of being accurate, or the ____________.
   a. p-value
   b. confidence level
   c. degrees of freedom
   d. levels of risk

Answers

1. b
2. b
3. a
4. c
5. d
6. b
7. c
8. d
9. a
10. c
11. d
12. c
13. b
14. c
15. d
16. c
17. d
18. d
19. b
20. b

Matching: Place the letter of the following definitions with its corresponding term.

__1. Sample	a. group of reference that the sample data (or statistic) represents
__2. Population	b. proposes a lack of difference (or relationship) between variables
__3. Null hypothesis	c. proposes a difference (or relationship) between variables
__4. Alternative hypothesis	d. subset of a population composed of the actual group of research participants
__5. Nondirectional alternative hypothesis	e. proposes a difference (or relationship) in a specific direction
__6. Directional alternative hypothesis	f. proposes a difference (or relationship) without a specific direction
__7. Type 1 error	g. mistake of failing to reject a false null hypothesis
__8. Type 2 error	h. value that represents an occurrence due to chance
__9. Sampling error	i. value that represents an occurrence that is not due to chance
__10. True difference	j. provides the basis for uncovering the "critical value" of statistical significance and determining confidence intervals and confidence level
__11. Statistical significance	k. describes how sure a person can be in approximating the location of a population parameter
__12. Level of risk	l. the degree to which a statistician is willing to reject a true null hypothesis (type I error)
__13. Confidence intervals	m. always expressed as a range
__14. Confidence levels	n. any differences between variables (or groups) that are not based on chance
__15. Degrees of freedom	o. mistake of rejecting a true null hypothesis

Answers

1. d
2. a
3. b
4. c
5. f
6. e
7. o
8. g
9. i
10. h
11. n
12. l
13. m
14. k
15. j

Bibliography

Feinberg, W. E. (1971). Teaching the type I and type II errors: The judicial process. *The American Statistician, 25*(3), 30–32.

Geller, S., & Shannon, H. W. (1976). The moon, weather, and mental health contacts: Confirmation and explanation of the Transylvania effect. *Journal of Psychiatric Nursing and Mental Health Services, 14*(1), 13–17.

Henkel, R. E. (1976). *Tests of significance.* SAGE Publications.

Marson, S. M. (1975). *Identifying variables related to successful treatment in an in-patient alcoholic rehabilitation facility* [Master's thesis, Ohio State University].

Chapter 7 SPSS and Workbook Questions

SPSS and Confidence Interval

In order to compute a confidence interval using SPSS, consider the following steps:

A criminologist is interested in whether college students experience fear of crime. To gauge such fear, he encourages students to complete an inventory assessment tool. The scores derived from this tool are measured between 0 and 10. More specifically, scores closest to 10 indicate a high degree of victimization anxiety among respondents. Identified below are the reported scores of 20 students.

Student	Fear of Crime
1	10
2	9
3	8
4	9
5	8
6	7
7	9
8	5
9	6
10	7
11	5
12	7
13	5
14	6
15	7
16	8
17	7
18	8
19	9
20	10

Based on the data provided, compute the mean and confidence interval using SPSS.

Entry of Data—SPSS

1. Select variable view to include information associated with the variable of interest. In our example, this would include *fear*.
2. In the first row, include the term *fear* under the column identified as name.
3. In the column identified as label, you might choose to include a more specific description of the variable.
4. In the column identified as measure, select the scale option.

5. Select data view to include the scores in the corresponding column.

IMAGE 7.4

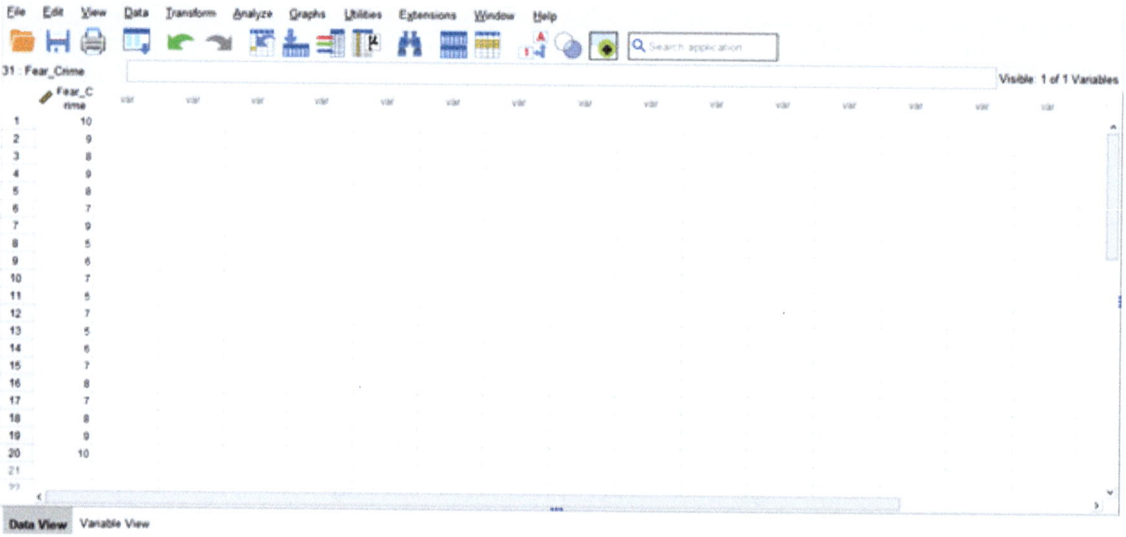

IMAGE 7.5

Analysis of Data—SPSS

1. Select analyze, descriptive statistics, and explore.
2. At this point, you will see a box (located on the left) that includes the variable fear. Select this variable and move it to the box located to the right, which is identified as dependent list.
3. Within the statistics section, under the term identified as descriptives, be sure to select the appropriate confidence level percentage. The option provided should include 95%. Once completed, select continue.
4. Once all desired functions have been selected and completed, select OK.

Output of Data Analysis—SPSS

The data analysis in the output section includes a total of two tables. Table 1 includes details related to the sample data. This includes the total number of scores along with the number of missing scores. In addition, the corresponding percentages for each category of scores are included.

The final table includes more specific information in relation to the descriptive statistics of the sample. As identified, this includes data related to both measures of central tendency (e.g., mean, median) and dispersion (e.g., variance, standard deviation). When observing the mean statistic (e.g., 7.50), we are also able to observe the standard error (SE) of 0.352. By adding the SE of 0.352 to the mean (7.50), the upper bound of the CI is 8.24. By subtracting the SE from the mean, the lower bound of the CI is 6.76. Overall, we are 95% confident that the mean statistic (7.50) will exist between 6.76 and 8.24 in the population.

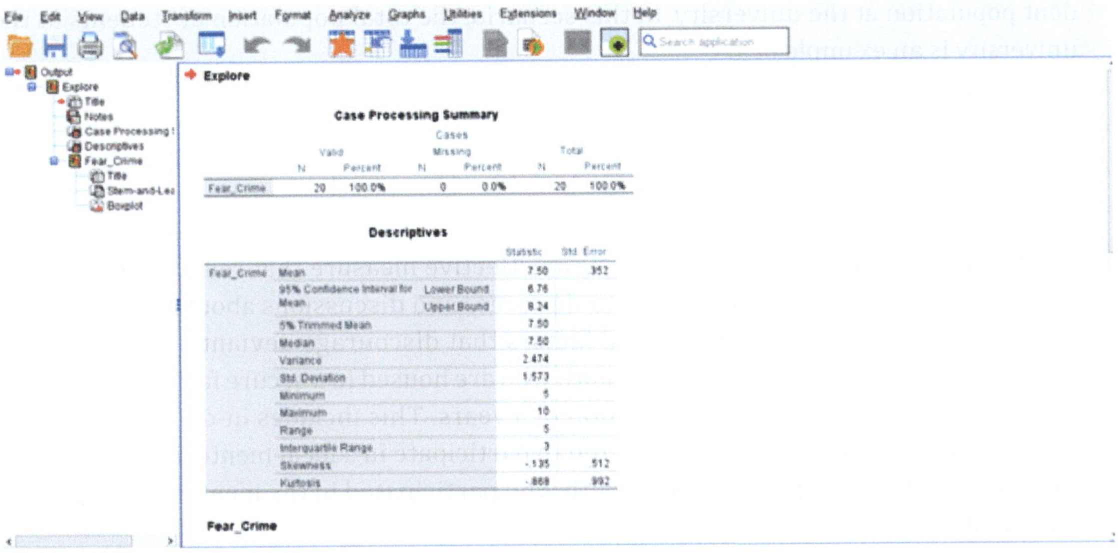

IMAGE 7.6

Workbook Questions

Objective 1—Define and Explain the Use of Sample and Population

- A sample is a subset of a population composed of the actual group of research participants.
- A population is the reference group that the sample data (or statistic) represents.

Corresponding Questions

1. A criminology professor is interested in whether students in his course believe that certain ecological factors might explain the existence of crime. For instance, seasons of the year, as well as temperatures, might explain an increase (or decrease) in the commission of certain offenses. To determine if the students understand the relationship between outside temperatures and the existence of crimes during summer months, the professor decides to investigate the opinions of students at the university. This includes a total of

200 students, which reflects the total amount of students enrolled in the four courses that the professor is required to teach. In this scenario, the aforementioned 200 students are an example of a:

a. sample
b. population
c. both a and b
d. none of the above

2. While discussing the differences between culture and society, a sociology professor believes that her students would prefer to communicate with others using technology as opposed to face-to-face interaction. In an effort to determine whether her hypothesis is valid, she distributes a total of 300 surveys to her students, which represents 10% of the total student population at the university. In this scenario, the total population of students at the university is an example of a:

a. sample
b. population
c. both a and b
d. none of the above

3. A data analyst believes that mentoring is an effective measure that reduces delinquency among youth. More specifically, the actual process and discussions about mentoring may offer significant insight into the actual factors that discourage deviant behavior among youth. In order to gain the opinions of youth who are housed in a secure facility, the analyst conducts a series of interviews for a total of 3 years. This includes in-depth discussions with a total of 50 youth who were selected to participate in a local mentoring program. In this scenario, the total population of youth who participated in the mentoring program is an example of a:

a. sample
b. population
c. both a and b
d. none of the above

4. Based on the previous scenario, suppose the results of the interviews reveal that 85% of the youth reported that their relationship with their mentor discouraged them from engaging in delinquent behavior at school. The statistic of 85% represents what is expected within the ____________.

a. sample of those who participated in the mentoring program
b. the total population of youth in the secure facility
c. both a and b
d. none of the above

Answers

1. a
2. b
3. a
4. b

Objective 2—Define and Explain the Use of Sampling Error and True Differences.

- A sampling error is a value that represents an occurrence due to chance.
- A true difference is a value that represents an occurrence that is not due to chance.

Corresponding Questions

1. The evaluation of delinquency prevention measures is both common and important. Without such, the selection and use of effective solutions would likely not exist, resulting in increased rates of delinquency, status offenses, and potential criminal offenses. As a researcher, you have been given the task of recommending programs in response to the commission of youth offenses by a state agency. While reviewing various government reports and studies, you observe a promising program. In particular, the program states that the use of their delinquency prevention techniques has a probability of success at 99.9%. In response to such, you are skeptical about the probability statistic. To that end, you decide to continue your research and discover a program that offers a probability of success between 70%–80%. Based on this scenario, the probability of 99.9% is an example of a:
   a. sampling error
   b. true difference
   c. probability error
   d. false difference
2. Suppose a recent annual report reveals an increase in the use of zero-tolerance policies that have resulted in an increase in expulsion among minority students in a local school district. As a potential remedy, a researcher believes that the use of restorative justice practices might offer a reasonable alternative. To gauge the attitudes related to the use of restorative justice, the researcher distributed a survey to 12 school counselors. After an initial analysis, over 99% of the counselors reported support for the use of restorative justice. Despite the promising results, the researcher believes that the statistic is reflective of a chance occurrence. Potential explanations of this chance occurrence may include
   a. gathering data from subjects who are not counselors.
   b. gathering data from a small sample size of counselors.
   c. gathering data from counselors who represent a certain age or experience.
   d. all of the above

Answers

1. a
2. d

Objective 3—Describe the Role and Steps of Hypothesis Testing

- A hypothesis is an idea (or a claim) about a phenomenon that is often verified through testing.
- Hypothesis testing is the process of steps designed to produce evidence that either supports (or fails to support) a hypothesis (or a claim).

Corresponding Questions

1. A hypothesis is ____________.
   a. an idea
   b. a claim
   c. tested
   d. all of the above
2. In hypothesis testing, the researcher is expected to ____________.
   a. select the appropriate statistical test
   b. compute a statistical value
   c. locate the CDV
   d. all of the above
3. A graduate school student is interested in whether individuals who have experienced crimes in the past believe they will likely experience crimes in the future. The first step in this research process should include
   a. identifying the level of risk.
   b. identifying the null and alternative hypothesis.
   c. choosing the appropriate test.
   d. making a decision whether to reject or fail to reject the null hypothesis.
   e. computing and identifying the STV.
   f. identifying the CDV.
4. A published study entitled *Situational Crime Theory* by Robert Clarke (1995) describes conditions in which certain items are more likely to become the targets of thieves. After reviewing the study, a graduate student decides to replicate a similar study within a local community. The third step in this potential research project should include:
   a. choosing the appropriate test.
   b. identifying the level of risk.
   c. identifying the null and alternative hypothesis.

d. identifying the CDV.
e. computing and identifying the STV.
f. making a decision whether to reject or fail to reject the null hypothesis.

5. In an effort the reduce crime at a local school, the administrative personnel within a school district decide to consult the expertise of a local crime prevention expert. This includes the process of conducting preliminary survey research on the attitudes of both faculty and staff with respect to their choice of certain crime prevention measures. More specifically, the specific crime prevention measures include the use of either (1) locking mechanisms or (2) biometrics (e.g., facial recognition) at various entry points in the school building. The final step of this research project should include
   a. identifying the level of risk.
   b. identifying the null and alternative hypothesis.
   c. making a decision whether to reject or fail to reject the null hypothesis.
   d. computing and identifying the STV.
   e. choosing the appropriate test.
   f. identifying the CDV.
6. Studies associated with student behavioral problems in school settings reveal that early intervention is associated with diffusing conflict among youth. This often involves the use of de-escalation techniques as well as nonverbal measures among school resource officers (Steinberg et al., 2011). In light of such, a delinquency expert believes that teachers, instead of school resource officers, who receive training in de-escalation measures are more likely to use such within their classrooms. To that end, the expert decides to gauge the opinions of faculty at a middle school to determine their interest in the prospect of receiving training. The second step of this research project should include
   a. identifying the level of risk.
   b. identifying the null and alternative hypothesis.
   c. making a decision whether to reject or fail to reject the null hypothesis.
   d. computing and identifying the STV.
   e. choosing the appropriate test.
   f. identifying the CDV.

Answers

1. d
2. d
3. b
4. a
5. c
6. a

Objective 4—Define and Explain the Critical Aspects of Hypothesis

- A null hypothesis is a statement that proposes a lack of difference (or relationship) between variables.
- An alternative hypothesis is a statement that proposes that a difference (or relationship) between variables exists.
- A directional alternative hypothesis proposes a difference (or relationship) in a specific direction.
- A nondirectional alternative hypothesis proposes a difference (or relationship) in a nonspecific direction.
- A type I error is the mistake of rejecting a true null hypothesis.
- A type II error is the mistake of failing to reject a false null hypothesis.

Corresponding Questions

1. A crime report reveals an increase in serious violent offenses, which includes the use of firearms. The report shows an average of two gun-related homicides each week in a particular urban area within a 6-month period. Researcher A believes that a gun buy-back program will likely result in a decrease in gun-related homicides in the area. On the other hand, Researcher B does not believe that the proposed solution will lead to a decrease in gun-related homicides. Based on this scenario, the alternative hypothesis is:
   a. A gun buy-back program will likely result in a decrease in gun-related homicides in the area.
   b. A gun buy-back program will not likely result in a decrease in gun-related homicides in the area.
   c. A decrease in gun-related homicides is based on the number of gun buy-back programs in an urban area.
   d. The number of gun-related homicides is based on the number of gun buy-back programs in an urban area.
2. Based on the previous scenario, the null hypothesis is:
   a. A gun buy-back program will likely result in a decrease in gun-related homicides in the area.
   b. A gun buy-back program will not likely result in a decrease in gun-related homicides in the area.
   c. A decrease in gun-related homicides is based on the number of gun buy-back programs in an urban area.
   d. The number of gun-related homicides is based on the number of gun buy-back programs in an urban area.
3. Research suggests that a lack of cooperation among minorities in the investigation of crimes within minority communities may explain the existence of high crime rates. Crime Justice Expert 1 believes that increasing the cash award amount in exchange for information that leads to the arrest of a suspect will decrease the number of crimes in minority communities. On the other hand, Crime Justice Expert 2 believes that increasing the cash award amount in

exchange for information that leads to the arrest of a suspect will not decrease the number of crimes in minority communities. Based on this scenario, the null hypothesis is:

a. Increasing the cash award amount in exchange for information that leads to the arrest of a suspect will decrease the number of crimes in minority communities.
b. Increasing the cash award amount in exchange for information that leads to the arrest of a suspect will not decrease the number of crimes in minority communities.
c. Increasing the cash award amount in exchange for information that leads to the arrest of a suspect will increase the number of crimes in minority communities.
d. Decreasing the cash award amount in exchange for information that leads to the arrest of a suspect will decrease the number of crimes in minority communities.

4. Based on the previous scenario, the alternative hypothesis is:
   a. Increasing the cash award amount in exchange for information that leads to the arrest of a suspect will decrease the number of crimes in minority communities.
   b. Increasing the cash award amount in exchange for information that leads to the arrest of a suspect will not decrease the number of crimes in minority communities.
   c. Increasing the cash award amount in exchange for information that leads to the arrest of a suspect will increase the number of crimes in minority communities.
   d. Decreasing the cash award amount in exchange for information that leads to the arrest of a suspect will decrease the number of crimes in minority communities.
5. A study reveals a lack of interest in potential law enforcement among minority students, which might undermine any potential community policing efforts. As a potential solution, a researcher suggests the use of a financial incentive, which will likely increase the number of minorities who submit applications for enrollment in a regional police academy. This includes a $3,000 signing bonus, along with the option of reimbursement for those pursuing a college degree. Based on this scenario, the null hypothesis is:
   a. The use of a financial incentive will likely increase the number of minorities who submit applications for enrollment in a regional police academy.
   b. The use of a financial incentive will not likely increase the number of minorities who submit applications for enrollment in a regional police academy.
   c. The use of a financial incentive will not likely increase the number of minorities who are eligible to receive the $3,000 signing bonus.
   d. The use of a financial incentive will likely increase the number of minorities who are eligible to receive the option of reimbursement for those pursuing a college degree.
6. Based on a lack of diversion programs for those alleged of minor offenses, it is not uncommon for overcrowding to exist in local detention centers and jails. A researcher believes that a diversion program that emphasizes the use of psychological assessment and group counseling might lead to a reduction in the use of secure confinement. More specifically, the researcher believes that counseling will result in a 20% reduction in the number of individuals temporarily detained prior to adjudication. Based on this scenario, the alternative hypothesis is:
   a. The use of counseling will not result in a 20% reduction in the number of individuals temporarily detained prior to adjudication.

b. The use of counseling will result in a 20% reduction in the number of individuals temporarily detained prior to adjudication.
c. The use of counseling will result in a 10% reduction in the number of individuals temporarily detained prior to adjudication.
d. The use of counseling will result in a 20% increase in the number of individuals temporarily detained prior to adjudication.

7. A researcher believes that males and females differ in response to stress. If this is true, the results of an independent study may prove beneficial for those who work in high-stress settings, such as correctional officers and first responders. Based on the researcher's belief, which of the following represents a directional alternative hypothesis?
   a. Males respond better to stress compared to females.
   b. Females respond better to stress compared to males.
   c. Males and females respond equally to stress.
   d. Either a or b
8. Based on the previous scenario, the nondirectional alternative hypothesis is:
   a. Males respond better to stress compared to females.
   b. Females respond better to stress compared to males.
   c. Males and females do not respond differently in response to stress.
   d. Males and females respond differently in response to stress.
9. In a rural area, the number of status offenses among juveniles has increased. In response to such, a delinquency expert believes that programs that employ face-to-face interaction between the offender and victim will result in a decrease in status offenses among youth in the area. To test this hypothesis, the expert uses a *t*-test and identifies both the critical region and the *t*-test statistic. As a result of the process, with the t-statistic below the critical region value, the expert rejects the null hypothesis. Based on this scenario, which of the following has occurred?
   a. A type 1 error
   b. A type 2 error
   c. A type 3 error
   d. An error has not occurred
10. After hearing a lecture about crime taking place during certain conditions, a student believes that minor juvenile offenses may take place on October 31. To gain evidence to support his hypothesis, the student conducts a *t*-test in which the t-statistic is above the critical region value. In light of such, the student fails to reject the null hypothesis. Based on this scenario, which of the following has occurred?
    a. A type 1 error
    b. A type 2 error
    c. A type 3 error
    d. An error has not occurred

Answers

1. a
2. b
3. b
4. a
5. b
6. b
7. d
8. d
9. a
10. b

Objective 5—The Level of Risk and Selecting the Appropriate Test

- Level of risk (or level of significance) is an estimate that identifies the extent to which a researcher is willing to be incorrect.

Corresponding Questions

1. Studies reveal that exposure to violence among youth is associated with aggressive behavior. For instance, a researcher believes that male youth—compared to female youth—who watch at least between 20 and 30 hours of violent TV content are more likely to engage in aggressive behavior. To test this hypothesis, the researcher conducts a statistical test using a level of risk of 0.05. The accurate interpretation of the selected level of risk by the research means that
   a. the researcher is willing to be incorrect 0.05 times if the research was conducted 100 times.
   b. the researcher is willing to be incorrect 5 times if the research was conducted 10 times.
   c. the researcher is willing to be incorrect 50 times if the research was conducted 100 times.
   d. the researcher is willing to be incorrect 5 times if the research was conducted 100 times.
2. If the researcher in the above scenario selected a level of risk of 0.0030, the accurate interpretation of the selected level of risk would be
   a. the researcher is willing to be incorrect 3 times if the research was conducted 10,000 times.
   b. the researcher is willing to be incorrect 30 times if the research was conducted 100 times.
   c. the researcher is willing to be incorrect 30 times if the research was conducted 10,000 times.
   d. the researcher is willing to be incorrect 30 times if the research was conducted 1,000 times.
3. Collective efficacy, a term that refers to a commitment to community relationships, has been associated with low numbers of deviant behavior and crime in certain areas. A criminologist who believes that social disorganization explains crime in a metropolitan area

is convinced that collective efficacy may serve as a protective factor in relation to certain serious violent crimes in an impoverished urban area. While attempting to test the strength of his assumption, the criminologist conducts a statical test that uses a level of significance of 1%. This level of significance is consistent with which of the following probability levels?

a. $p < 0.05$

b. $p < 0.01$

c. $p < 0.001$

d. $p \leq 0.05$

4. A criminal justice professor shares the following information with his students who are enrolled in a victimology course. "Victims of crimes often need resources and opportunities in an effort to experience justice. Examples of resources may include victim compensation, such as financial aid, as well as assistance in understanding the processes of the criminal justice system. In terms of opportunities, victims may be able to offer impact statements, which may influence judicial decisions that affect the individual(s) convicted of an offense(s)." To gauge the opinions of the students, the professor conducts a hypothesis test based on their preferences for the most important single type of victim service. This includes either victim compensation or a victim impact statement. The level of significance selected for the hypothesis test is based on the researcher's willingness to be incorrect 0.1% of the time, which is the probability level of:

a. $p < 0.05$

b. $p < 0.01$

c. $p < 0.001$

d. $p \leq 0.05$

5. An educator believes that a relationship exists between exposure to different customs and cultures among students and their level of cultural sensitivity. The independent variable, which measures exposure to different customs and cultures, is categorical. The dependent variable, which measures the level of cultural sensitivity, is also categorical. Which of the following is the appropriate type of statistical test that should be used?

a. ANOVA test

b. Chi-square test

c. Correlation test

d. T-test

6. A psychologist who specializes in educational psychology is convinced that conditioning is related to positive learning outcomes among students. For instance, the psychologist believes that middle school students who are expected to read more than two books a week will likely demonstrate higher levels of reading comprehension compared to students who are not expected to read two books a week. Reading comprehension represents the dependent variable; the number of books a student is expected to read during the week is the independent variable. In this scenario, both variables are continuous. Which of the following is the appropriate type of statistical test that should be used?

a. ANOVA test
b. Chi-square test
c. Correlation test
d. T-test

7. A researcher who has a background in sociology believes the income level of families that live in impoverished urban areas is associated with the possibility of experiencing crime victimization. More specifically, families that earn no more than $16,000 a year and reside in communities with a low property tax value are more likely to experience (or witness instances of) serious violent crimes. In this scenario, the independent variables, which include no more than two variables, are categorical; the dependent variable is continuous. Which of the following is the appropriate type of statistical test that should be used?
   a. ANOVA test
   b. Chi-square test
   c. Correlation test
   d. T-test
8. Groupthink, which refers to an outcome in which individuals of a group tend to agree with each other for the sake of consensus, is a topic that is discussed among students with a sociology professor. When the professor is asked to provide an example of groupthink, the professor responds by sharing with students the likelihood of groupthink taking place during jury deliberations. To combat the potential of such among students, the professor is convinced that the experience of sharing opposing opinions in the form of classroom debates is essential. Based on this assumption, he requires classroom debates in three of the four courses that he is required to teach during the semester. In short, the professor believes that the activity of engaging in classroom debates (which includes three groups of students) is associated with greater levels of confidence and self-expression among students. In this scenario, the independent variables are categorical, and the dependent variable is continuous.
   a. ANOVA test
   b. Chi-square test
   c. Correlation test
   d. T-test

Answers

1. d
2. c
3. b
4. c
5. b
6. c
7. d
8. a

Objective 6—Engage in Calculating a Hypothesis Test, Determining Statistical Significance, and Making a Decision Regarding the Null Hypothesis

Corresponding Questions

1. A researcher believes that police officers who possess an undergraduate degree are less likely to violate the civil rights of a citizen. This researcher's hypothesis is considered an example of a ______________.
   a. one tail hypothesis
   b. directional hypothesis
   c. two tail hypothesis
   d. either a or b
2. Once a STV has been computed, the next step is to ______________.
   a. determine the CDV
   b. determine whether the STV is less than the CDV
   c. determine whether the null hypothesis should be rejected
   d. none of the above
3. Which of the following steps must immediately take place once the levels of measurement for the independent and dependent variables have been identified?
   a. select the appropriate test
   b. compute the CDV
   c. compute the STV
   d. either b or c
4. If the STV is greater than the CDV, this indicates that ______________________.
   a. The researcher should reject the null hypothesis
   b. The researcher should accept the alternative hypothesis
   c. The researcher should fail to reject the null hypothesis
   d. None of the above

Answers

1. d
2. a
3. a
4. a

Objective 7—Define and Explain the use of CIs and Confidence Levels

- A CI is the range in which the predicted parameters of a population mean is located.
- A confidence level is a probability that is used to describe how sure a person can be in approximating the location of a population parameter. It is often stated as a percentage.

Corresponding Questions

1. Which of the following statements is an example of a CI
   a. the population mean exists between 12 and 16
   b. the population mean exists between 7 and 11
   c. the population mean exists between 4 and 8
   d. all of the above
2. A CI is often expressed as a(n) ___________.
   a. percentage
   b. range
   c. outlier
   d. none of the above
3. The use and formula of a confidence interval depends on ___________.
   a. the number of statistical tests used
   b. the type of statistical test used
   c. both a and b
   d. none of the above
4. Which of the following is an example of a confidence level?
   a. the researcher is 95% confident that the population mean will exist between the confidence range of 3 and 7
   b. the researcher is 99% confident that the population mean will exist between the confidence range of 4 and 8
   c. the researcher is 99.9% confident that the population mean will exist between the confidence range of 3 and 7
   d. all of the above
5. As the size of a confidence ___________ decreases, the confidence ___________ also decreases.
   a. interval, level
   b. level, interval
   c. Both a and b
   d. None of the above

Answers

1. d
2. b
3. b
4. d
5. a

Objective 8—Additional Matters of Significance

- A power analysis is the probability that the researcher will correctly reject the null hypothesis.

Corresponding Questions

1. When writing the results of a statistical test, one is likely required to provide all of the following details except:
   a. the test statistic (number)
   b. the number which reflects the degrees of freedom
   c. the symbol which represents the type of statistical test used
   d. the p-value
   e. all of the details above are likely required in writing the results of a statistical test
2. In order to lower the likelihood of someone questioning the results of a statistical test, one is encouraged to provide: ___________
   a. the sample size
   b. the population size
   c. the estimated population size
   d. the estimated sample size

Answers

1. e
2. a

Credits

CHAPTER 8

z-Test (One Sample)

Maturity is the capacity to endure uncertainty.
— John Finley

Objectives

1. Define and explain the use of a one-sample z-test.
2. Identify the formula for computing a one-sample z-test.
3. Compute examples that call for the use of a one-sample z-test.
4. Explain the value of a one-sample z-test within criminal justice.

Differences and the Pursuit of Funding

Suppose you discover a research grant opportunity that is interested in funding law enforcement agencies that wish to lower arrest rates among minority youth. After reviewing statewide arrest data, you discover that the annual mean age of arrest among Black youth in a certain urban location is 15. Based on this information, you are curious as to whether the annual mean age (15) reflects the same mean age among Black youth in your state over the past 10 years. If the annual mean age of arrest in the urban area is lower than the mean age of arrest in the state, the local law enforcement agency (within the urban location) might be eligible to receive grant funding. To discover whether a difference exists, a one-sample z-test is required.

One-Sample z-Test

A **one-sample z-test** is a statistical test that is used to determine if the mean of a sample reflects the mean of a population. In our example, the annual mean age of Black youths arrested in the urban location represents the sample, while the mean age of Blacks arrested in the state (within a 10-year period) reflects the population.

> **One-sample z-test** A statistical test that is used to determine if the mean of a sample reflects the mean of a population.

In general, hypothesis tests include assumptions. In short, assumptions (or requirements) serve as the basis for determining whether certain types of statistical tests can be used under certain circumstances. In other words, the assumptions of one test do not apply to the use of another type of statistical test.

The assumptions of the one-sample z-test:

1. The sample size must include at least 30 items (or subjects).
2. The population must be normally distributed.
3. The standard deviation of the population must be identified.

Chapter Learning Assessment Questions

To gauge your learning, provide answers to the following questions:

1. A researcher is interested in conducting a one-sample z-test. In order to use a one-sample z-test, the sample size must include at least ______ subjects.
   a. 40
   b. 25
   c. 30
   d. none of the above
2. A professor believes that the mean exam scores ($\bar{x}$ = 84) of her students in one class (Introduction to Sociology), (n = 18), is significantly higher than the mean scores ($\bar{x}$ = 83.1) of all the students (n = 278) who were previously enrolled in the course in the past 5 years. In order to conduct a one-sample z-test, which of the following additional information is needed?
   a. Sample size
   b. Population size
   c. Standard deviation of the sample
   d. None of the above

Answers

1. c
2. d

Formula for Computing the One-Sample z-Test

The formula for computing a one-sample z-test is as follows:

$$z = \frac{\bar{x} - \mu}{\frac{\sigma}{\sqrt{n}}},$$

where

$\bar{x}$ = mean of the sample population

μ = mean of the population

σ = standard deviation for the population

n = size (number) of the sample

As noted in the formula, within the numerator section, the mean of the population (μ) (which represents our expected value) is subtracted from the mean of the sample ($\bar{x}$) (which represents our observed value). Within the denominator section, the difference between the expected and observed value ($\bar{x} - \mu$) is divided by the standard error of the mean (which is $\sigma/\sqrt{n}$).

Since the one-sample z-test can be used as a type of hypothesis test, it is important to review the following steps, as described in detail in Chapter 7:

1. Identify the null and alternative hypotheses.
2. Identify the level of risk (or significance).
3. Choose the appropriate test.
4. Compute and identify the statistical test value (STV).
5. Identify and compare the critical decision value (CDV) to the STV.
6. Make a decision regarding the null hypothesis.

Chapter Learning Assessment Questions

To gauge your learning, provide answers to the following questions:

1. Within the formula for the one-sample z-test, the standard error of the mean includes ________________.
   a. dividing the standard deviation by the sample size
   b. dividing the standard deviation by the population size
   c. subtracting the standard deviation from the sample size
   d. none of the above
2. Within the formula for the one-sample z-test, the square root of the ________________ is used.
   a. sample size
   b. population size
   c. standard deviation
   d. none of the above

Answers

1. d
2. a

Computing the One-Sample z-Test

To develop your understanding and application of the one-sample z-test, consider the following scenarios.

One-Sample z-Test (Example 1)

As an example, let's refer to the previous illustration: determining if the mean age of arrest of Black youth in an urban area is reflective of the mean age of arrest of Black youth in the state. This includes the following details:

The sample (which is an urban area) includes a total number of 41 arrests, with a mean age of 15 and a standard deviation of 3.0. The population (which includes the state) includes a total of 7,500 arrests, with a mean age of 16 and a standard deviation of 2.5.

Let's use the steps discussed in the previous chapter in computing the one-sample z-test statistic:

1. Identify the null and alternative hypotheses.

   With respect to the application of the null hypothesis, our example indicates that there is no difference between the annual mean arrest age of Black youth in the urban area in comparison to the 10-year mean arrest age of Black youth in the state. The application of the alternative hypothesis states there is a difference between the annual mean arrest age of Black youth in the urban area in comparison to the 10-year mean arrest age of Black youth in the state. As indicated in our alternative hypothesis, we did not choose a specific direction in terms of whether the mean arrest age is higher (or lower) in one geographic location (the state) than the mean arrest age in another geographic location (urban area). To that end, we will employ a nondirectional alternative hypothesis test.

$$H_0\text{: } \bar{x} = \mu$$
$$H_1\text{: } \bar{x} \neq \mu$$

2. Identify the level of risk or significance.

   We will choose our level of risk of being incorrect (engaging in a type I error) at 0.05.
3. Choose the appropriate test.

   Based on our desire to determine if the mean of the sample is reflective of the mean of the population, we selected the one-sample z-test.
4. Compute and identify the STV.

   At this point, consider the following numbers from our example in relation to the z-test formula:

$$z = \frac{15 - 16}{\frac{2.5}{\sqrt{41}}}$$

a. Our first calculation step is to compute the standard error of the mean:

$$\frac{2.5}{\sqrt{41}} = \frac{2.5}{6.40} = 0.39$$

b. Our final calculation step is to compute the STV:

$$z = \frac{15 - 16}{0.39} = \frac{-1}{0.39} = -2.56$$

c. Our STV is −2.56

5. Identify and compare the CDV to the STV.
Identifying the CDV requires the use of a table that identifies the values needed for rejecting the null hypothesis. Since the alternative hypothesis did not identify a specific direction, we will use ±1.96 as the value in which to reject the null hypothesis. Since our STV is −2.56, we compare this value with the CDV, which is ±1.96. Table 8.1 represents a portion of a table (located near the end of this textbook) that identifies the critical values for the one-sample z-test.

TABLE 8.1

z	0.00	0.01	0.02	0.03	0.04	0.05	0.06	0.07	0.08	0.09
1.5	0.4332	0.4345	0.4357	0.4370	0.4382	0.4394	0.4406	0.4418	0.4429	0.4441
1.6	0.4452	0.4463	0.4474	0.4484	0.4495	0.4505	0.4515	0.4525	0.4535	0.4545
1.7	0.4554	0.4564	0.4573	0.4582	0.4591	0.4599	0.4608	0.4616	0.4625	0.4633
1.8	0.4641	0.4649	0.4656	0.4664	0.4671	0.4678	0.4686	0.4693	0.4699	0.4706
1.9	0.4713	0.4719	0.4726	0.4732	0.4738	0.4744	**0.4750**	0.4756	0.4761	0.4767

6. If the STV > CDV, reject the null hypothesis.
As revealed in Figure 8.1, given that the STV (−2.56) extends beyond the CDV (±1.96), we must reject the null hypothesis. Thus, we have enough evidence to support the claim (alternative hypothesis) that there is a difference between the annual mean arrest age of Black youth in an urban area compared to the 10-year mean arrest age of Black youth in the state.

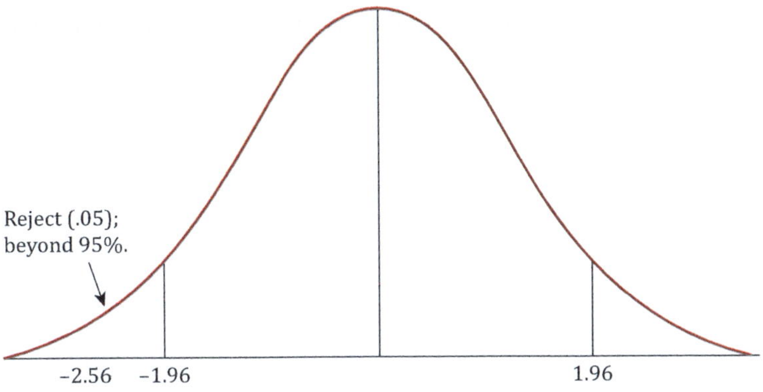

FIGURE 8.1 Location of Statistical Decision Value and CDV

One-Sample z-Test (Example 2)

Suppose we are interested in whether hate crimes in a specific area are different in comparison to a larger population (Cheng et al, 2013).

This includes the following details:

The sample (which is a single state) includes a total number of 18 incidents, a mean of 5.3, and a standard deviation of 5.0. The larger population (which includes 49 states) includes a total of 120 incidents, a mean of 5.5, and a standard deviation of 4.5.

As a researcher, you believe that the single-state mean is *significantly lower* than the mean number of the 49 states.

Let's use our steps:

1. Identify the null and alternative hypotheses.

   In relation to the null hypothesis, our example indicates there is no difference between the annual mean number of hate crimes in a single state in comparison to the 10-year mean number of hate crimes in 49 states. The alternative hypothesis states that the annual mean number of hate crimes in a single state is lower in comparison to the 10-year mean number of hate crimes in 49 states. In line with our alternative hypothesis, we chose a specific direction by indicating the belief that the mean number of hate crimes is higher in one area (a single state) in comparison to another area (49 states). Thus, we will employ a directional alternative hypothesis test.

   $$H_0: \bar{x} = \mu$$
   $$H_1: \bar{x} < \mu$$

2. Identify the level of risk or significance.

   We will choose our level of risk of being incorrect (engaging in a type I error) at 0.05.
3. Choose the appropriate test.

   Based on the desire to determine if the mean of the sample is lower than the mean of the population, we selected the one-sample z-test.
4. Compute and identify the STV.
   a. At this point, we include the numbers from our example in the z-test formula:

   $$z = \frac{5.3 - 5.5}{\frac{4.5}{\sqrt{18}}}$$

   b. Our first calculation step is to compute the standard error of the mean:

   $$\frac{4.5}{\sqrt{18}} = \frac{4.5}{4.24} = 1.06$$

   c. Our final calculation step is to compute the STV:

   $$z = \frac{5.3 - 5.5}{1.06} = \frac{-0.2}{1.06} = -0.18$$

   d. Our STV is −0.18

5. Identify and compare the CDV to the STV.
   By using the table, which identifies the values needed for rejecting the null hypothesis, we will use the value that corresponds to the specific direction identified in the alternative hypothesis. To that end, we will use +1.64 as the value in which to reject the null hypothesis.

Since our STV is −0.18, we compare this value with the CDV, which is +1.64. Table 8.2 is a portion of the table that identifies the critical values for the one-sample z-test.

TABLE 8.2

z	0.00	0.01	0.02	0.03	0.04	0.05	0.06	0.07	0.08	0.09
0.0	0.0000	0.0040	0.0080	0.0120	0.0160	0.0199	0.0239	0.0279	0.0319	0.0359
0.1	0.0398	0.0438	0.0478	0.0517	0.0557	0.0596	0.0636	0.0675	0.0714	0.0753
0.2	0.0793	0.0832	0.0871	0.0910	0.0948	0.0987	0.1026	0.1064	0.1103	0.1141
0.3	0.1179	0.1217	0.1255	0.1293	0.1331	0.1368	0.1406	0.1443	0.1480	0.1517
0.4	0.1554	0.1591	0.1628	0.1664	0.1700	0.1736	0.1772	0.1808	0.1844	0.1879
0.5	0.1915	0.1950	0.1985	0.2019	0.2054	0.2088	0.2123	0.2157	0.2190	0.2224
0.6	0.2257	0.2291	0.2324	0.2357	0.2389	0.2422	0.2454	0.2486	0.2517	0.2549
0.7	0.2580	0.2611	0.2642	0.2673	0.2704	0.2734	0.2764	0.2794	0.2823	0.2852
0.8	0.2881	0.2910	0.2939	0.2967	0.2995	0.3023	0.3051	0.3078	0.3106	0.3133
0.9	0.3159	0.3186	0.3212	0.3238	0.3264	0.3289	0.3315	0.3340	0.3365	0.3389
1.0	0.3413	0.3438	0.3461	0.3485	0.3508	0.3531	0.3554	0.3577	0.3599	0.3621
1.1	0.3643	0.3665	0.3686	0.3708	0.3729	0.3749	0.3770	0.3790	0.3810	0.3830
1.2	0.3849	0.3869	0.3888	0.3907	0.3925	0.3944	0.3962	0.3980	0.3997	0.4015
1.3	0.4032	0.4049	0.4066	0.4082	0.4099	0.4115	0.4131	0.4147	0.4162	0.4177
1.4	0.4192	0.4207	0.4222	0.4236	0.4251	0.4265	0.4279	0.4292	0.4306	0.4319
1.5	0.4332	0.4345	0.4357	0.4370	0.4382	0.4394	0.4406	0.4418	0.4429	0.4441
1.6	0.4452	0.4463	0.4474	0.4484	**0.4495**	0.4505	0.4515	0.4525	0.4535	0.4545
1.7	0.4554	0.4564	0.4573	0.4582	0.4591	0.4599	0.4608	0.4616	0.4625	0.4633
1.8	0.4641	0.4649	0.4656	0.4664	0.4671	0.4678	0.4686	0.4693	0.4699	0.4706
1.9	0.4713	0.4719	0.4726	0.4732	0.4738	0.4744	0.4750	0.4756	0.4761	0.4767

6. If the STV > CDV, reject the null hypothesis.
   Given that the STV (−0.18) is less than the CDV (+1.64), we fail to reject the null hypothesis.

   Thus, as indicated in Figure 8.2, we do not have enough evidence to support the claim that there is a difference between the annual mean number of hate crimes (in a single state) in comparison to the 10-year mean number of hate crimes in 49 states.

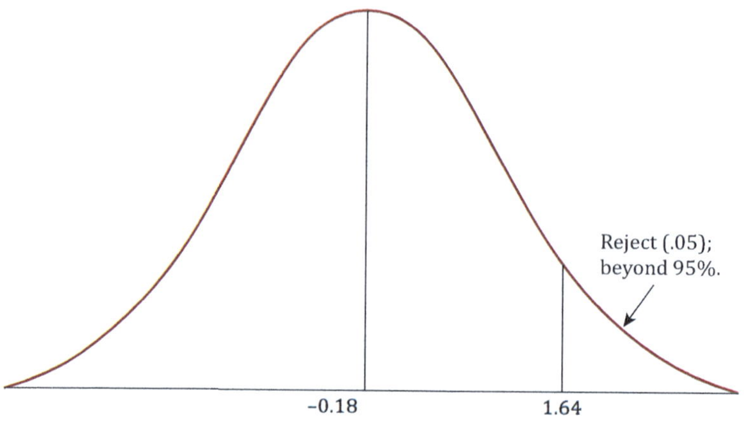

FIGURE 8.2 Location of Statistical Decision Value and CDV

One-Sample z-Test (Example 3)

A candidate for the position of district attorney claims that his opponent, who has held the position of district attorney for the past 15 years, is soft on crime. He states that his opponent, who is a proponent of treatment programs, is responsible for a considerable number of homicides in the county. In fact, the candidate claims that under the leadership of his opponent, the average homicide number was greater than 70 reported incidents. To investigate the candidate's claim, a criminal justice student randomly selects the following 15 homicide numbers in the county. This includes reported incidents of homicide during the tenure of the current district attorney for the past 15 years.

TABLE 8.3 **Number of Reported Homicides Between 2000 and 2014**

Year	Number of Homicides
2000	11
2001	20
2002	22
2003	24
2004	34
2005	50
2006	56
2007	60
2008	61
2009	66
2010	74
2011	74
2012	80
2013	82
2014	83

Based on the information provided, is there enough evidence to support the candidate's claim? With a standard deviation of 24.8, compute a one-sample z-test.

1. Identify the null and alternative hypotheses.

   Based on the example, the null hypothesis indicates that there is no difference between the sample and the population mean. In other words, the mean number of homicides is no greater than the mean number of homicides within a 15-year period. On the other hand, the alternative hypothesis declares a statement that contradicts the null hypothesis. This is the claim offered by the opponent of the current district attorney. The mean number of homicides in the sample is higher in comparison to the 15-year mean number of homicides in the county. In essence, the candidate made the claim that the mean homicide number during his opponent's tenure is higher than 70 reported incidents. Given that the opponent claims that the population mean number of homicides is higher than the sample mean number, we will employ a directional alternative hypothesis test.

$$H_0: 70 = \mu$$
$$H_1: 70 < \mu$$

2. Identify the level of risk or significance.

   We will choose our level of risk of being incorrect (engaging in a type I error) at 0.05.
3. Choose the appropriate test.

   Based on the desire to determine if the mean of the sample is higher (or lower) than the mean of the population, we selected the one-sample z-test.
4. Compute and identify the STV.

   a. Include the numbers from Table 8.3 in the z-test formula:

$$z = \frac{53 - 70}{\frac{24.8}{\sqrt{15}}}$$

   b. Our first calculation step is to compute the standard error of the mean:

$$\frac{24.8}{\sqrt{15}} = \frac{24.8}{3.87} = 6.40$$

   c. Our final calculation step is to compute the STV:

$$z = \frac{53 - 70}{6.40} = \frac{-17}{6.40} = -2.65$$

   d. Our STV is −2.65
5. Identify and compare the CDV to the STV.

   By using Table 8.4, we will locate the value that corresponds to the specific direction identified in the alternative hypothesis. This includes +1.64 as the value in which to reject the null hypothesis. With −2.65 as our STV, we compare −2.65 with our CDV (+1.64). Details of this process are provided in Table 8.4.

TABLE 8.4

z	0.00	0.01	0.02	0.03	0.04	0.05	0.06	0.07	0.08	0.09
0.0	0.0000	0.0040	0.0080	0.0120	0.0160	0.0199	0.0239	0.0279	0.0319	0.0359
0.1	0.0398	0.0438	0.0478	0.0517	0.0557	0.0596	0.0636	0.0675	0.0714	0.0753
0.2	0.0793	0.0832	0.0871	0.0910	0.0948	0.0987	0.1026	0.1064	0.1103	0.1141
0.3	0.1179	0.1217	0.1255	0.1293	0.1331	0.1368	0.1406	0.1443	0.1480	0.1517
0.4	0.1554	0.1591	0.1628	0.1664	0.1700	0.1736	0.1772	0.1808	0.1844	0.1879
0.5	0.1915	0.1950	0.1985	0.2019	0.2054	0.2088	0.2123	0.2157	0.2190	0.2224
0.6	0.2257	0.2291	0.2324	0.2357	0.2389	0.2422	0.2454	0.2486	0.2517	0.2549
0.7	0.2580	0.2611	0.2642	0.2673	0.2704	0.2734	0.2764	0.2794	0.2823	0.2852
0.8	0.2881	0.2910	0.2939	0.2967	0.2995	0.3023	0.3051	0.3078	0.3106	0.3133
0.9	0.3159	0.3186	0.3212	0.3238	0.3264	0.3289	0.3315	0.3340	0.3365	0.3389
1.0	0.3413	0.3438	0.3461	0.3485	0.3508	0.3531	0.3554	0.3577	0.3599	0.3621
1.1	0.3643	0.3665	0.3686	0.3708	0.3729	0.3749	0.3770	0.3790	0.3810	0.3830
1.2	0.3849	0.3869	0.3888	0.3907	0.3925	0.3944	0.3962	0.3980	0.3997	0.4015
1.3	0.4032	0.4049	0.4066	0.4082	0.4099	0.4115	0.4131	0.4147	0.4162	0.4177
1.4	0.4192	0.4207	0.4222	0.4236	0.4251	0.4265	0.4279	0.4292	0.4306	0.4319
1.5	0.4332	0.4345	0.4357	0.4370	0.4382	0.4394	0.4406	0.4418	0.4429	0.4441
1.6	0.4452	0.4463	0.4474	0.4484	**0.4495**	0.4505	0.4515	0.4525	0.4535	0.4545
1.7	0.4554	0.4564	0.4573	0.4582	0.4591	0.4599	0.4608	0.4616	0.4625	0.4633
1.8	0.4641	0.4649	0.4656	0.4664	0.4671	0.4678	0.4686	0.4693	0.4699	0.4706
1.9	0.4713	0.4719	0.4726	0.4732	0.4738	0.4744	0.4750	0.4756	0.4761	0.4767

6. If the STV > CDV, reject the null hypothesis.
   Given that the STV (−2.65) is less than the CDV (+1.64), we are required to not reject (or retain) the null hypothesis. Thus, we do not have enough evidence to support the claim that there is a difference between the mean number of homicides in the sample in comparison to the 15-year mean number of homicides during the current district attorney's tenure. In short, the claim of the opponent for the position of the district attorney is not supported.

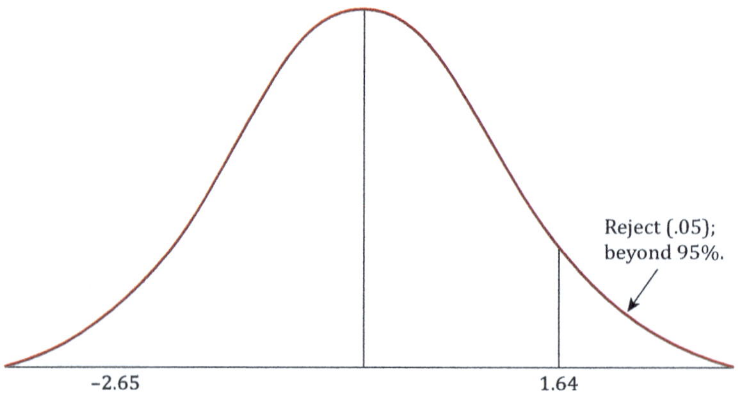

FIGURE 8.3 Location of Statistical Decision Value and CDV

One-Sample z-Test (Example 4)

The following data includes the number of robberies in a highly populated city. Based on the information provided, is there a significant mean difference between the number of robberies reported in 2017 compared to the mean reported number of robberies between 2011 and 2020? With a population standard deviation of 12.9, compute a one-sample z-test.

TABLE 8.5 **Number of Reported Homicides Between 2000 and 2014**

Year	Number of Robberies
2011	113.9
2012	111.2
2013	105
2014	101.3
2015	102.9
2016	102.9
2017	98.1
2018	86.1
2019	81.8
2020	73.9

1. Identify the null and alternative hypotheses.

   In our example, the null hypothesis indicates that there is no difference between the sample and the population mean. This assumes that there are no significant differences between the mean number of robberies in 2017 compared to 2011–2020. The alternative hypothesis claims that a difference does exist between the mean number of robberies as identified in the two time periods. Considering that the alternative hypothesis failed to provide a specific direction, we will employ a nondirectional alternative hypothesis test.

$$H_0: \bar{x} = \mu$$
$$H_1: \bar{x} \neq \mu$$

2. Identify the level of risk or significance.

   We will choose our level of risk of being incorrect (engaging in a type I error) at 0.01.

3. Choose the appropriate test.

   Based on the desire to determine if the mean of the sample is different from the mean of the population, we selected the one-sample z-test.

4. Compute and identify the STV.

   a. Include the numbers from Table 8.5 in the z-test formula:

$$z = \frac{98.1 - 97.7}{\frac{12.3}{\sqrt{168}}}$$

b. Our first calculation step is to compute the standard error of the mean:

$$\frac{12.3}{\sqrt{168}} = \frac{12.3}{12.96} = 0.94$$

c. Our final calculation step is to compute the STV:

$$z = \frac{98.1 - 97.7}{0.94} = \frac{0.4}{0.94} = 0.42$$

d. Our STV is 0.42

5. Identify and compare the CDV to the STV.
Using Table 8.6, we will locate the value that corresponds to the specific direction identified in the alternative hypothesis. This includes ±2.58 as the value in which to reject the null hypothesis. With 0.42 as our STV, we compare it with our CDV (±2.58). Details of this process are provided in Table 8.6.

TABLE 8.6

z	0.00	0.01	0.02	0.03	0.04	0.05	0.06	0.07	0.08	0.09
1.1	0.3643	0.3665	0.3686	0.3708	0.3729	0.3749	0.3770	0.3790	0.3810	0.3830
1.2	0.3849	0.3869	0.3888	0.3907	0.3925	0.3944	0.3962	0.3980	0.3997	0.4015
1.3	0.4032	0.4049	0.4066	0.4082	0.4099	0.4115	0.4131	0.4147	0.4162	0.4177
1.4	0.4192	0.4207	0.4222	0.4236	0.4251	0.4265	0.4279	0.4292	0.4306	0.4319
1.5	0.4332	0.4345	0.4357	0.4370	0.4382	0.4394	0.4406	0.4418	0.4429	0.4441
1.6	0.4452	0.4463	0.4474	0.4484	0.4495	0.4505	0.4515	0.4525	0.4535	0.4545
1.7	0.4554	0.4564	0.4573	0.4582	0.4591	0.4599	0.4608	0.4616	0.4625	0.4633
1.8	0.4641	0.4649	0.4656	0.4664	0.4671	0.4678	0.4686	0.4693	0.4699	0.4706
1.9	0.4713	0.4719	0.4726	0.4732	0.4738	0.4744	0.4750	0.4756	0.4761	0.4767
2.0	0.4772	0.4778	0.4783	0.4788	0.4793	0.4798	0.4803	0.4808	0.4812	0.4817
2.1	0.4821	0.4826	0.4830	0.4834	0.4838	0.4842	0.4846	0.4850	0.4854	0.4857
2.2	0.4861	0.4864	0.4868	0.4871	0.4875	0.4878	0.4881	0.4884	0.4887	0.4890
2.3	0.4893	0.4896	0.4898	0.4901	0.4904	0.4906	0.4909	0.4911	0.4913	0.4916
2.4	0.4918	0.4920	0.4922	0.4925	0.4927	0.4929	0.4931	0.4932	0.4934	0.4936
2.5	0.4938	0.4940	0.4941	0.4943	0.4945	0.4946	0.4948	0.4949	**0.4951**	0.4952

6. If the STV > CDV, reject the null hypothesis.
Given that the STV (0.42) is less than the CDV (±2.58), we are required to not reject (or retain) the null hypothesis. Thus, we do not have enough evidence to support the claim that there is a difference between the mean number of robberies in the sample (2017) in comparison to the population (2011–2020).

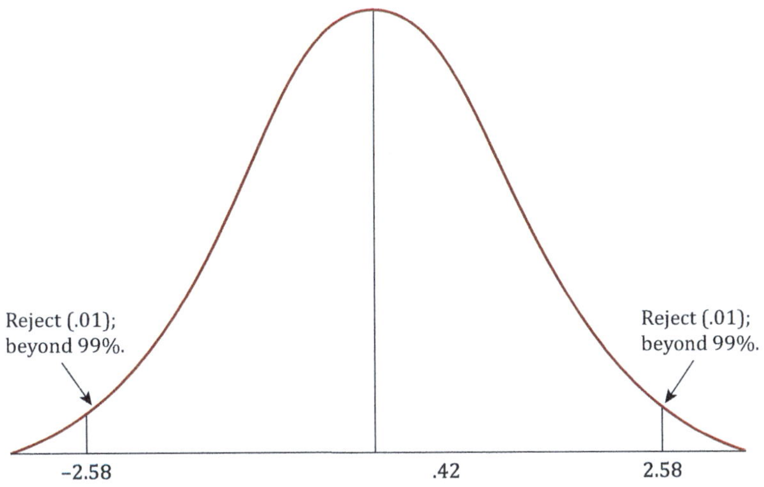

FIGURE 8.4 Location of Statistical Decision Value and CDV

Before we address our final area of discussion, one might be curious as to how a CDV is determined when using a z-test. The following information (in Table 8.7) serves as the basis for answering such a question.

TABLE 8.7 **Criteria for Identifying the CDV**

Level of Significance (or Risk)	Confidence Level	Direction of Alternative Hypothesis	CDV (Critical Decision Value)
0.05	95%	Directional	1.64
0.05	95%	Nondirectional	±1.96
0.01	99%	Directional	2.33
0.01	99%	Nondirectional	±2.58
0.001	99.9%	Directional	3.09
0.001	99.9%	Nondirectional	±3.30

As revealed, the process of determining the CDV includes identifying the level of risk, which includes a corresponding confidence level. It is also based on the direction of the alternative hypothesis.

Chapter Learning Assessment Questions

To gauge your learning, provide answers to the following questions:

1. A researcher believes that those who experience stressful circumstances are more likely to experience a higher blood pressure level compared to those who do not experience stressful circumstances. This is an example of a ______________.
   a. directional alternative hypothesis

b. nondirectional alternative hypothesis
c. directional null hypothesis
d. none of the above

2. Suppose a one-sample z-test includes the following: (1) a level of risk at 0.01, (2) a nondirectional alternative hypothesis, and (3) a STV of 2.16. Which of the following is not the correct choice?
   a. The STV is below the CDV.
   b. The STV is above the CDV.
   c. One must reject the null hypothesis.
   d. Either a or c

Answers

1. a
2. b

Effect Size

In order to determine the extent of differences between two groups, one is able to use what is referred to as the **effect size**. For instance, based on the results of Example 1, our findings revealed that the mean age of arrest of Black youth in an urban area is significantly different from the mean age of arrest of Black youth in a particular state. By calculating the effect size, we are able to identify the magnitude of such differences. The use of effect size is common within many types of inferential tests.

effect size A calculation that reveals the extent (or magnitude) of significant differences between variables of interest.

One of the most commonly used types is referred to as Cohen's *d*. Introduced by Jacob Cohen, the formula for computing Cohen's d, with regard to a one-sample z-test, is identified below:

$$d = \frac{\bar{x} - \mu}{\sigma},$$

where

$\bar{x}$ = mean (sample)

μ = mean (population)

σ = standard deviation (population)

By including the data in the formula from Example 1, we have the following:

$$d = \frac{15 - 16}{2.5}$$

$$d = \frac{-1}{2.5}$$

$$d = -0.04$$

In order to interpret the effect size, the following criteria are used: range (0–0.2) = effect size is small; range (0.2–0.5) = effect size is medium; range (0.5+) = effect size is large.

Based on d = −0.04, which is categorized as less than a small effect size, we conclude that the relative differences between the two groups are not significant. In fact, we could argue that there is an overlap between the two groups (i.e., they are very similar).

The Practical Application of the One-Sample z-Test

You might wonder why it is important to conduct a one-sample z-test in the study of criminal or juvenile justice. To answer that question, consider the following possibilities:

Law Enforcement

- The z-test can be used to address the existence of serious crimes in local communities. Let's assume that the mean arrest number for a certain type of crime (e.g., drug trafficking) appears to be higher in a local community compared to a larger area (such as a region or state). A z-test (and its statistical findings) may be used to justify the need for additional drug intervention resources. Examples of such include additional local, state, and federal law enforcement officers, as well as financial support (Anderson and Kavanaugh, 2017).

Courts

- By using a z-test, let's assume that the mean conviction number for drug possession is higher in a specific jurisdiction compared to the mean statewide conviction number. This statistical disparity, as derived from a z-test, may be used to conduct numerous investigations to determine the basis of such offenses. In addition, the statistical findings may also be used to establish drug courts or diversion-based drug treatment programs (Gallagher et al., 2022; Lundgren et al., 2010).

Corrections

- The z-test can be used to ensure the provision of safety measures among officers and inmates in a prison setting. Let's assume that the mean inmate-officer assault number is lower at one specific prison in comparison to the mean statewide assault number of all seven prisons in a region. This statistical disparity is not a one-time event; rather, this trend has existed for the past 15 years. The statistical findings within the prison might elevate the institution as a model prison for safety training at state, regional, national, and international conferences (Jenness et al., 2010).

Final Thoughts

Being able to explore mean differences between a sample and a population is a valuable skill set. When engaging in this investigation, it is highly recommended that one ensures that the characteristics of both groups are similar. For instance, assuming that all persons sentenced to prison either did not have legal representation or were represented by public defenders is not wise. In fact, many of them might have retained counsel and paid for their services. By keeping an open mind to the influence of numerous factors in relation to important decisions, this practical approach will likely lower the *probability* of "comparing apples with oranges."

Discussion

An organization is offering a grant award to any law enforcement agency that provides high quality academic training to recruits in their police academy. A local law enforcement agency submitted a proposal that includes a study that compared their annual mean number of exam scores to a 10-year statewide mean number. By using a one-sample z-test, the results revealed a significant difference between the local law enforcement agency mean in comparison to the state law enforcement agency mean. Considering such, would you recommend that the local law enforcement agency be considered for a grant award? Explain.

Chapter Summary

This chapter emphasized the following general information:

Objective 1 – Define and explain the use of a one-sample z-test.

- A one-sample z-test is a statistical test that is used to determine if the mean of a sample reflects the mean of a population.

Objective 2 – Identify the formula for computing a one-sample z-test.

- See corresponding pages for details of the chapter.

Objective 3 – Compute a one-sample z-test.

- See corresponding pages for details of the chapter.
- An effect size is a calculation that reveals the extent (or magnitude) of significant differences between variables of interest.

Objective 4 – Explain the value of a one-sample z-test within criminal justice.

- See corresponding pages for details of the chapter.

Terms

One-sample z-test
Effect size

Chapter Review Questions

1. A one-sample z-test is a statistical test that is used to determine if the ________ of a sample reflects the mean of a population.
   a. median
   b. mean
   c. mode
   d. both a and b
2. The formula for computing a one-sample z-test involves
   a. subtracting the mean of the population from the mean of the sample population.
   b. subtracting the mean of the sample population from the mean of the population.
   c. dividing the mean of the sample population from the mean of the population.
   d. adding the mean of the population to the mean of the sample population.
3. The formula for computing a one-sample z-test involves
   a. dividing the standard deviation for the population by the size of the sample.
   b. dividing the standard deviation for the population by the mean of the population.
   c. dividing the standard deviation for the population by the median of the population.
   d. adding the standard deviation for the population by the size of the sample.
4. According to data provided by the UCR, the mean age of police officers killed in 2010 was 38 (FBI, 2011). This includes a total of 55 officers and a standard deviation of 4. Between 2010 and 2019, the mean age of officers killed was 39. This included a total of 511 officers and a standard deviation of 3.5. To what extent does the mean age in 2010 reflect the mean age between 2010 and 2019? Is the 2010 mean age significantly different than the 2010–2019 mean?
5. Annual DWI arrests in one county (n = 425) averaged eight per week. Within the state, the weekly mean was 8.1, and the standard deviation was 12.1. Is the annual DWI arrests in the county significantly different from the state mean?
6. The table below identifies the number of youth who were referred to the juvenile justice system in 2019. The standard deviation was 49. In January 2020, there was a mean amount of 198 (out of a total of 225) youth referred to the juvenile justice system. Is the 2020 mean amount of youth referred to the juvenile justice system significantly different from the 12-month mean amount in 2019?

January	236
February	215
March	179
April	210
May	241
June	289
July	332

August	312
September	289
October	251
November	200
December	179

7. Research associated with 911 calls for service has been conducted (Lersch, 2020). The table below identifies the number of calls for service that did not require law enforcement personnel in 12 counties in 2015. The standard deviation was 63. In 2020, out of a total of 348 calls, there was a mean amount of 214 calls from County 1. When comparing both areas (2015 and 2020), is there a significant difference between the mean number of calls?

County 1	161
County 2	202
County 3	104
County 4	115
County 5	211
County 6	244
County 7	308
County 8	267
County 9	221
County 10	170
County 11	154
County 12	104

8. Studies have examined and identified the influence of various factors related to school-based violence prevention in schools (Messman et al., 2022). Within a local school district in 2017, the mean number of violent incidents among a total of 75 at-risk youth was 10. Within the state, the mean number of violent incidents was 8.91, with a standard deviation of 4.1. Is there a significant difference between the mean number of violent incidents when comparing both areas?

Answers

1. b
2. a
3. a
4. With a z-test score of –2.11, there is a statistically significant difference between the 2010 and 2010–2019 mean age of officers killed in 2010.
5. With a z-test score of –0.17, a statistically significant difference does not exist between the county and the state DWI arrests.

6. With a z-test score of –13.45, there is a statistically significant difference between the 2019 and 2020 mean number of youth referred to the juvenile justice system.
7. With a z-test score of 7.69, there is a statistically significant difference between the 2015 and 2020 mean number of calls.
8. With a z-test score of 2.32, there is a statistically significant difference between the mean number of violent incidents in a local school district in 2017 compared to the state.

Bibliography

Anderson, T. L., & Kavanaugh, P. R. (2017). Women's evolving roles in drug trafficking in the United States: New conceptualizations needed for 21st-century markets. *Contemporary Drug Problems, 44*(4), 339–355.

Cheng, W., Ickes, W., & Kenworthy, J. B. (2013). The phenomenon of hate crimes in the United States. *Journal of Applied Social Psychology, 43*(4), 761–794.

FBI. (2011, October 24). UCR law enforcement officers killed in the line of duty [Press release]. https://ucr.fbi.gov/leoka/leoka-2010/fbi-releases-2010-statistics-on-law-enforcement-officers-killed-and-assaulted

Gallagher, J. R., Wahler, E. A., & Nordberg, A. (2022). Predictors of graduation and criminal recidivism: Findings from a drug court that primarily serves African Americans. *Journal of Ethnic & Cultural Diversity in Social Work, 31*(1), 40–50.

Jenness, V., Maxson, C. L., Sumner, J. M., & Matsuda, K. N. (2010). Accomplishing the difficult but not impossible: Collecting self-report data on inmate-on-inmate sexual assault in prison. *Criminal Justice Policy Review, 21*(1), 3–30.

Lersch, K. M. (2020). COVID-19 and mental health: An examination of 911 calls for service. *Policing: A Journal of Policy and Practice, 14*(4), 1112–1126.

Lundgren, L. M., Curtis, M. A., & Oettinger, C. (2010). Post-incarceration policies for those with criminal drug convictions: A national policy review. *Families in Society, 91*(1), 31–38.

Messman, E., Heinze, J., Hsieh, H. F., Hockley, N., Pomerantz, N., Grodzinski, A., Scott, B., Goldstein, N. & Zimmerman, M. (2022). Anonymous reporting systems for school-based violence prevention: a systematic review. *Health Education & Behavior*, 51(1), 62–70. https://doi.org/10.1177/10901981211073734

Chapter 8 Workbook Questions

The use of SPSS will not be included in this chapter.

Workbook Questions

Objective 1 – Define and explain the use of a one-sample z-test.
Objective 2 – Identify the formula for computing a one-sample z-test.

- **One-sample z-test** is a statistical test that is used to determine if the mean of a sample reflects the mean of a population.

Corresponding Questions

1. According to information in Chapter 8, the practical use of a one-sample z-test may include which of the following examples?
   a. A z-test may be used to determine if the mean number of crimes in a local setting (e.g., county) is higher or lower than the mean number of crimes in the state.
   b. A z-test may be used to determine if the mean number of convictions for certain crimes in a local court (e.g., municipal) is higher or lower than the mean number of convictions for certain crimes in the state or region.
   c. A z-test may be used to determine if the mean number of inmate-officer assaults in a specific setting (e.g., state prison) is higher or lower than the mean number of inmate-officer assaults in multiple state jails in a state.
   d. All of the above are practical examples of how a one-sample z-test can be used in the criminal justice system
2. The use of a one-sample z-test is based on whether the mean of a sample reflects the mean of a ____________.
   a. population
   b. state population
   c. community population
   d. regional population
3. The formula for computing a one-sample z-test includes finding the standard error of the mean. This includes which of the following?
   a. Determining the square root of the sample
   b. Determining the square root of the population
   c. Determining the square root of the population mean
   d. Determining the square root of the sample mean
4. Another step associated with finding the standard error during the process of computing a one-sample z-test includes:
   a. dividing the standard deviation of the population by the square root of the sample size

b. dividing the standard deviation of the sample by the square root of the sample size
c. dividing the standard deviation of the population by the square root of the population size
d. none of the above

5. If a population has a mean of 12 and the mean of a sample population is 10, using the formula for computing a one-sample z-test would result in which of the following:
   a. −22
   b. 22
   c. −2
   d. 2
6. Suppose the results of a one-sample z-test based on a level of significance at 0.05 in which the alternative hypothesis did not specify a direction reveal a test value of 3.18. Which of the following CDVs is needed to reject the null hypothesis?
   a. ± 1.96
   b. $+ 1.64$
   c. ± 1.69
   d. ± 1.64

Answers

1. d
2. a
3. a
4. a
5. c
6. a

Objective 3 – Computing a one-sample z-test.

Corresponding Questions

1. Research has examined the influence of programs and policies designed to reduce recidivism among youth (Crane, 2010). The table below reveals the number of youth who engaged in recidivism as a result of participating in a local after-school program in 2016. This includes a standard deviation of 1.40. In January of 2017, out of a total of 76 youth, a mean amount of 6.3 youth engaged in recidivism. Is the 2017 mean amount of recidivism, which occurred in the month of January, significantly different from the 12-month mean amount of recidivism in 2016?

January	6
February	4
March	8
April	6
May	7
June	5
July	8
August	4
September	6
October	5
November	8
December	7

2. The following table reveals the number of speeding citations distributed to individuals within a 6-month period in a suburban area of a city in 2018. This includes a standard deviation of 2.98. In 2019, out of a total of 103 individuals, a mean amount of 16.8 citizens were cited for speeding. Is the 2019 mean amount of those cited for speeding, which occurred in the month of December, significantly different from the 6-month mean amount of those who received speeding citations in 2018?

July	20
August	16
September	21
October	19
November	17
December	12

3. A researcher believes that restorative justice practices, in comparison to traditional punitive measures, are more effective in reducing property crimes among offenders (Sherman et al., 2015). In particular, the researcher is convinced that victim-offender mediation will likely reduce recidivism among males between the ages of 18–24. In an effort to test his assumption, the researcher was provided an opportunity to implement his idea as part of a diversion program for first-time offenders. Provided below are the results of the researcher's program after 1 year of implementation, which began in 2012. This includes the number of incidents in which young adults engaged in recidivism before and after participation in the program. In 2012, the standard deviation was 4.39. In 2013, toward the end of the second year, the researcher was required to present evidence of whether his program was effective. This included a recidivism report for the month of December, which included a total of 265 individuals. Based on the information below, is there a significant difference in recidivism between 2012 and 2013? If so, how much?

	2012	2013
January	16	?
February	24	?
March	18	?
April	16	?
May	17	?
June	25	?
July	28	?
August	24	?
September	26	?
October	25	?
November	18	?
December	27	21
Total	264	265

4. As a professor who teaches statistics in higher education, you have noticed that a significant number of students struggle with their understanding of the subject matter. This difficulty may stem from their fear of the subject, especially among those who are not strong in math (Levpuscek and Cukon, 2022). Among students who perform well, you notice that many of them have access to resources associated with the use of statistics. This includes hardware, such as laptop computers, as well as statistical software. Provided below is a table that identifies the mean grades of students enrolled in a statistics course who were able to gain access to certain desired resources. This includes a standard deviation score of 6.82. Unfortunately, not all students have access to such resources. In fact, in one of your courses, which includes a total of 36 students, the majority of students come from impoverished communities. Despite that, they have a mean score of 84. To that end, you decide to write a grant proposal for the purpose of securing resources for students who may not have the means to purchase such items. As with any grant proposal, you are required to provide evidence that demonstrates a need in which you decide to use the following information. Does the information provided reflect a significant difference between the mean grades of the two categories of students?

January	87
February	79
March	83
April	96
May	89
June	92
July	95
August	78

September	86
October	84
November	82
December	72

5. Research related to police recruitment challenges after notable law enforcement events exist (Copeland et al., 2022). Thus, a law enforcement recruiter seeking to encourage undergraduate students to consider a career in law enforcement claims that academy recruits will earn an average annual salary of $45,600. The recruiter claims that this salary amount is the result of a 10-year annual increase in pay, which includes a standard deviation of $3,292. After hearing such, along with TV news accounts that report the lack of equitable pay for local police officers, a university professor decides to investigate the claim made by the recruiter. Upon reviewing personnel records, the mean salary of 100 police officers during their first year of service is $45,000. Based on the information provided, is there a significant difference between the salaries identified?

Answers

1. –0.875, is not significantly different
2. –2.5, is significantly different
3. –3.7, is significantly different
4. –1.10, is not significantly different
5. –1.82, is significantly different

Bibliography

Copeland, C., del Carmen, A., & Semukhina, O. B. (2022). Revisiting the Ferguson effect: Law enforcement perception of recruitment in the post George Floyd era. *International Journal of Police Science & Management*, https://doi.org/10.1177/14613557221074988

Crane, C. E. (2010). An after school program to reduce teen violence, recidivism, and prepare teens for the workplace in Douglas County, Georgia [Master's thesis, Georgia State University].

Levpušček, M. P., & Cukon, M. (2022). That old devil called 'statistics': Statistics anxiety in university students and related factors. *Center for Educational Policy Studies Journal*, *12*(1), 147–168.

Sherman, L. W., Strang, H., Mayo-Wilson, E., Woods, D. J., & Ariel, B. (2015). Are restorative justice conferences effective in reducing repeat offending? Findings from a Campbell systematic review. *Journal of Quantitative Criminology*, *31*(1), 1–24.

CHAPTER 9

t-Test

Although it is well known that the method of using the normal curve is only trustworthy when the sample is "large," no one has yet told us very clearly where the limit between "large" and "small" samples is to be drawn.
—Student (William S. Gosset)

Objectives

1. Define and explain the use of a *t*-test and the types of *t*-tests (independent and dependent).
2. Determine which type of *t*-test to use (pooled and separate variances).
3. Explain the *f*-test and when it should be used.
4. Identify the formulas for computing a *t*-test (independent and dependent).
5. Understand how to compute a *t*-test (independent and dependent).
6. Define and explain the use of effect size with a *t*-test.

Introduction—CJ Topics and the *t*-Test

Suppose you are interested in determining whether male or female detectives are more effective at gaining a confession from a youth suspected of a serious violent crime (Alderden and Ullman, 2012). With regard to pretrial detention, you'd like to know whether there is a difference between male and female youth with respect to how long they are detained before adjudication (Guereva and Spohn, 2006). Finally, you're curious as to whether the political affiliation (i.e., Democrat, Republican) of a criminal court judge is related to the number of years to which defendants are sentenced based on race (Peck and Beaudry-Cyr, 2016).

t-Test and Types of *t*-Tests

To answer these questions, a *t*-test is needed. A ***t*-test** is a statistical test that is used to determine mean differences between two groups and includes a categorical independent variable and a continuous dependent variable. Overall, there are two types of *t*-tests: an independent sample and a dependent sample *t*-test. An **independent sample *t*-test** is a test in which members of two samples (or groups) are not related. For instance, in determining whether gender plays a role in

***t*-test** A statistical test that is used to determine mean differences between two groups and includes a categorical independent variable and a continuous dependent variable.

independent sample *t*-test A test in which members of two samples (or groups) are not related.

dependent sample *t*-test A test in which members of the two samples (or groups) are related to some degree.

Side Bar

The independent sample *t-test* is also called the unmatched pair *t-test*. The dependent sample *t-test* is also called the matched *t-test*. In criminal justice, the unmatched *t*-test is more likely to be used.

how long youth are detained before adjudication, a sample subject cannot exist as both a male and female.

On the other hand, a **dependent sample *t*-test** is a test in which members of the two samples (or groups) are related to some degree. This type of test is often used in measuring the effectiveness of a decision, strategy, or policy. For example, suppose you desire to study the awareness among police officers of a policy associated with the use of choke holds (Bozeman et al., 2022). More specifically, you want to know whether officers who possess a college degree are more likely to retain policy information compared to officers who do not possess a college degree. Both groups would be asked to complete a short exam that includes questions regarding policies and laws related to the use of choke holds. Scores from the exam would be recorded and identified as a baseline mark for future assessment. This is commonly referred to as a *pretest measure*.

On completion of the pretest measure, both groups of officers participate in a 6-week training period associated with the use of choke holds by law enforcement personnel. After training, both groups of officers complete a second exam that includes questions regarding policies and laws related to the use of choke holds. Scores from the second exam are recorded and compared to scores from the previous exam. The second exam is referred to as a *posttest measure,* which is designed to measure the impact of the training. In this example, the pretest and posttest measures involve the use of the same members within both groups, as well as the same measuring instrument (e.g., an exam). Based on the pretest (Exam 1) and posttest (Exam 2) measures, you are able to determine (via exam scores) the extent to which officers who possess a college degree are more likely to retain policy information compared to officers who do not possess a college degree.

Assumption of the *t*-Test

The use of any statistical test requires certain assumptions (or requirements). To that end, it's important that we identify the assumptions related to the use of a *t*-test. In general, there are a total of three assumptions.

1. The independent variables are composed of two groups. Independent variables that include three or more groups are required to use a test referred to as analysis of variance (ANOVA).
2. The dependent variable is designated at the continuous (i.e., interval, ratio) level. If you are not certain about the information related to levels of measurement, please refer to Chapter 2.
3. The dependent variables must be normally distributed. In instances where normal distribution is not satisfied, you might consider using a Wilcoxin-Mann-Whitney U-test.

Chapter Learning Assessment Questions

To gauge your learning, provide answers to the following questions:

1. Which of the following assumptions are not related to the use of a *t*-test?
   a. The independent variables are composed of two or more groups.
   b. The dependent variable is designated at the continuous level.
   c. The dependent variables must be normally distributed.
   d. None of the above
2. A professor is interested in determining whether gender is associated with social media activity and depression among middle school students. Gender is measured by two categories and depression is measured by a score based on the completion of a numerical scale. Which of the following statistical tests should be conducted?
   a. z-test
   b. One-sample z-test
   c. *t*-test
   d. None of the above

Answers

1. a
2. c

Pooled and Separate Variance *t*-Tests

In addition to the independent and dependent *t*-tests, the calculation of a *t*-test includes the pooled variance and separate variance *t*-tests (Figure 9.1). A **pooled variance *t*-test** is used with independent samples in which population variances are equal. The **separate variance *t*-test** is used with independent samples in which population variances are unequal. More specifically, the population variances in both the pooled and separate *t-tests* must be either statistically similar or statistically different. The basis for this distinction is important when computing the *t-test*. If two population samples have similar variances (pooled variance), they can be calculated in the form of an estimate. However, if two population variances are not similar (separate variance), they must be manipulated prior to calculation.

pooled variance *t*-test A test that is used with independent samples in which population variances are equal.

separate variance *t*-test A test that is used with independent samples in which population variances are unequal.

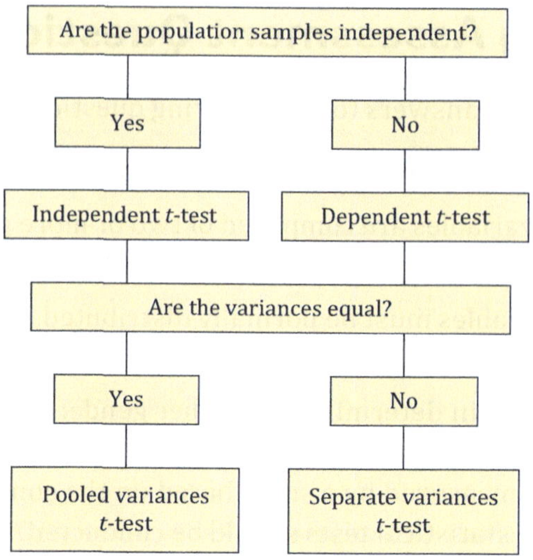

FIGURE 9.1 Pooled and Variances *T*-Test

f-Test

To determine which *t*-test to use (pooled or separate variances), it is important to conduct an *f*-test. An ***f*-test** is used to determine if the variances of two independent samples are equal or unequal. This includes calculating the variances of the two independent samples. If the p-value of an *f*-test is less than 0.05 (or any other threshold, such as 0.01), the separate variance *t*-test should be used. On the other hand, if the *f*-test value is greater than 0.05, the pooled variance *t*-test should be used. As an example, consider the following, which represents the average number of days a young person (on the basis of gender) was detained prior to adjudication.

> ***f*-test** A test that is used to determine if the variances of two independent samples are equal or unequal.

Step 1 – Establish a hypothesis and level of significance (or threshold).

Based on the information provided below, we believe that males, compared to females, are more likely to experience longer periods of time in detention prior to adjudication. Our level of significance/threshold is ($p < 0.05$).

H_0: Males = Females
H_1: Males > Females
Gender and Time Periods of Detention:
Males: 4, 6, 5, 7, 5, 8, 9, 5, 7, 7 = variance (2.45)
Females: 3, 4, 5, 6, 7,5, 8, 4, 4, 4 = variance (2.44)

Step 2 – Determine the variances for each group.

Step 3 – Divide the variance of our alternative hypothesis group (males) by the variance of our null hypothesis group (females). This will provide our *f*-test value.

$$2.45/2.44 = 1.005 = 0.49$$

Step 4 – Determine the p-value and decide which *t*-test to use.

$$p < 0.49$$

As revealed, the p-value (0.49) is greater than 0.05. Thus, we fail to reject the null hypothesis. In other words, compared to females, males are not more likely to experience longer time periods of detention prior to adjudication. Since our p-value was greater than our established threshold ($p < 0.05$), we are required to use the pooled variance *t*-test.

Chapter Learning Assessment Questions

To gauge your learning, provide answers to the following questions:

1. Which of the following is associated with conducting an *f*-test?
   a. If the p-value of an *f*-test value is greater than 0.05, the pooled variance *t-test* should be used.
   b. To determine if the variances of two independent samples are equal or unequal.
   c. If the p-value of an *f*-test is less than 0.05, the separate variance *t-test* should be used.
   d. All of the above
2. When conducting an *f*-test, one must:
   a. establish a hypothesis
   b. establish level of significance
   c. determine the variances for each group
   d. all of the above

Answers

1. d
2. d

Despite the information provided, we will assume that the following examples for conducting independent sample *t*-tests include similar (equal) variances.

Formula for Computing the Independent Sample *t*-Test

The formula for computing the independent sample *t*-test is based on the following:

$$t = \frac{\bar{x}_1 - \bar{x}_2}{\sqrt{\left[\frac{(n_1 - 1)s_1^2 + (n_2 - 1)s_2^2}{n_1 + n_2 - 2}\right]\left[\frac{n_1 + n_2}{n_1 n_2}\right]}},$$

where

$\bar{x}_1$ = represents the mean for Sample 1

$\bar{x}_2$ = represents the mean for Sample 2

n_1 = represents the number of subjects in Sample 1

n_2 = represents the number of subjects in Sample 2

s_1^2 = the variance for Sample 1

s_2^2 = the variance for Sample 2

Independent Sample *t*-Test (Example 1)

Number of Delinquent Incidents Among Youth

Sample 1: 1, 0, 1, 1, 2, 0, 0, 2, 1, 0, 3, 3, 2, 0
Sample 2: 4, 1, 5, 5, 4, 6, 2, 5, 3, 6, 2, 5, 1, 4

Suppose one is interested in whether mentoring leads to a reduction in delinquency among youth (Tolan et al., 2014). The values above reflect the number of reported incidents of delinquency among two samples of youth. Both Samples participated in behavioral modification programs designed to prevent delinquency. The youth in Sample 1 experienced mentoring in which they were given the opportunity to select their own mentors. They were also required to receive academic support through tutoring provided by their mentors. Those youth in Sample 2 also experienced mentoring but were not given the option of selecting their mentors. In addition, they were also required to take medication and undergo therapy.

Suppose you believe that the mean number of reported incidents of delinquency in Sample 1 is significantly different when compared to the mean number of such incidents in Sample 2.

Let's use these steps to find out:

1. Identify the null and alternative hypotheses.

   Based on our example, the null hypothesis states there is no difference between the mean number of reported incidents of delinquency in Sample 1 when compared to the mean number of reported incidents of delinquency in Sample 2. On the other hand, our alternative hypothesis states there is a difference between those numbers within the two aforementioned samples.

$$H_0\colon \mu_1 = \mu_2$$
$$H_1\colon \bar{x}_1 \neq \bar{x}_2$$

2. Identify the level of risk or significance.
   We will choose the acceptable level of risk of being incorrect (engaging in a type I error) as 0.05.
3. Choose the appropriate test.
   Given the level of measurement with the independent variable (categorical) and dependent variable (continuous) and the subjects in both samples are not related to each other, we selected an independent sample *t*-test.
4. Compute and identify the statistical test value (STV).
   We include the numbers from each sample in the independent sample *t*-test formula:

$$t = \frac{1.14 - 3.78}{\sqrt{\left[\frac{(14-1)1.2 + (14-1)2.9}{14+14-2}\right]\left[\frac{14+14}{14 \times 14}\right]}} = -5.07$$

   Our STV is −5.07
5. Identify and compare the critical decision value (CDV) to the STV.
   a. Before using the table, which identifies the values needed for rejecting the null hypothesis, we must first identify the degrees of freedom.
   b. This is computed by using the formula ($n_1 + n_2 - 2$), which is $28 - 2 = 26$
   c. Since our degrees of freedom is 26, we will locate that number (in the appropriate table near the end of this text) under the degrees of freedom column that corresponds to the nondirectional column at the 0.05 level of risk. The nondirectional column was selected given that we did not identify a specific direction in terms of the expected difference between the sample means.
   d. We will use ±2.056 as the value in which to reject the null hypothesis.
   e. Since our STV is −5.07, we compare this value with the CDV, which is ±2.056. Provided in the appendix is a table that identifies the critical values for the *t*-test distribution.
6. If the STV > CDV, reject the null hypothesis.
   As revealed in Figure 9.2, given that the STV (−5.07) extends beyond the CDV (±2.056), we reject the null hypothesis. Thus, the alternative hypothesis is true, which states that there is a difference between the mean (or average) number of reported incidents of delinquency in Sample 1 in comparison to the mean (or average) number of reported incidents of delinquency in Sample 2.

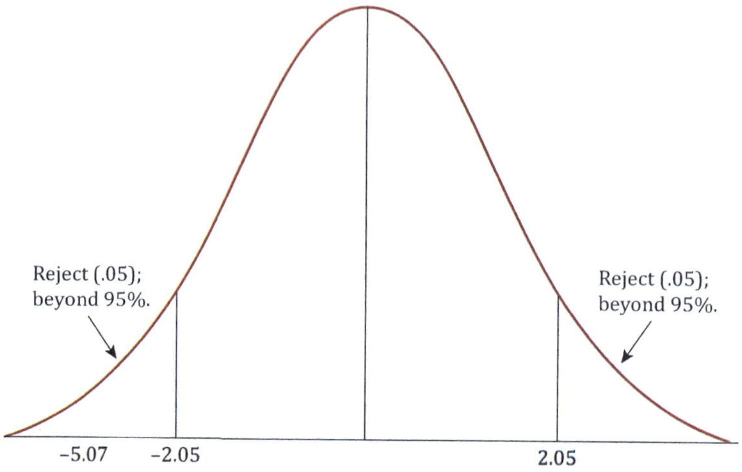

FIGURE 9.2 Normal Curve Illustration of Test Results

The formal results are displayed in this manner:

$$t = -5.07;\ \text{df} = 26;\ p < 0.05^*$$

*If we ran the research 100 times, we could make a type 1 error 5 times

Testing for Confidence Intervals

As addressed in Chapter 7, confidence intervals and confidence levels are critical components in the evaluation of statistical significance. There is no universal formula for calculating confidence intervals. Such formulas are linked to a particular significance test. The following is the formula for the independent *t*-test:

Based on the formula, the computation of the CI for the independent t-test is as follows:

$$= (3.78 - 1.14) \pm 2.06\sqrt{\frac{1.2}{14} + \frac{2.9}{14}}$$

$$= (3.78 - 1.14) \pm 2.06\sqrt{.08 + .20}$$

$$= (3.78 - 1.14) \pm 2.06\sqrt{.28}$$

$$= 2.64 \pm 2.06\ (.5)$$

$$= 2.64 \pm 1.03 = 1.61 \text{ to } 3.67$$

According to our calculations, we can say that if you completed this research 95 times (from our confidence level), our data point (the difference between the means) would fall between 1.61 and 3.67. Our calculated difference between the two means falls inside of our confidence interval.

Independent Sample *t*-Test (Example 2)

Our final example related to the use of the independent sample *t*-test is provided below:

Number of Deaths and Stand-Your-Ground Laws
Sample 1 (12 States): 20, 12, 11, 9, 7, 10, 9 14, 7, 7, 16, 14
Sample 2 (12 States): 5, 7, 12, 5, 15, 8, 6, 5, 7, 9, 11, 6

The values above provide two samples that represent states that either have or do not have stand-your-ground laws (SYGL). Sample 1 includes states that possess SYGL, and Sample 2 includes states that do not. Identified with each state is the number of deaths associated with cases in which a self-defense claim was used to justify the killing of an individual. As a criminologist, it is your assumption that the mean number of deaths in states with SYGL (Sample 1) is greater than the mean number of deaths in states without SYGL (Sample 2) (Guis, 2016).

Let's use our steps:

1. Identify the null and alternative hypotheses.

   Based on our example, the null hypothesis states there is no difference between the mean number of deaths in states with SYGL (Sample 1) compared to states without SYGL (Sample 2). The alternative hypothesis states that the mean number of deaths in states with SYGL (Sample 1) is greater in comparison to the states without SYGL (Sample 2).

$$H_0: \mu_1 = \mu_2$$
$$H_1: \bar{x}_1 > \bar{x}_2$$

2. Identify the level of risk or significance.

   We will choose our level of risk of being incorrect (engaging in a type I error) at 0.05.

3. Choose the appropriate test.

   Given the level of measurement with the independent variable (categorical) and dependent variable (continuous) and the subjects in both samples are not related to each other, we selected an independent sample *t*-test.

4. Compute and identify the STV.

   We include the numbers derived from our example in the independent sample *t*-test formula:

$$t = \frac{11.3 - 8}{\sqrt{\left[\frac{(12-1)16.4 + (12-1)10.1}{12+12-2}\right]\left[\frac{12+12}{12 \times 12}\right]}} = 2.24$$

Our STV is 2.24

5. Identify and compare the CDV to the STV.

   a. The degrees of freedom, computed by using the formula ($n_1 + n_2 - 2$), is $24 - 2 = 22$

   b. With the degrees of freedom at 22, we will locate that number under the degrees of freedom column that corresponds to the directional column. This category (directional column) is selected given that we did identify a specific direction in terms of the expected difference between the sample means.

c. Under the level of risk at 0.05, the value identified is 1.71.
d. We will use 1.71 as the value in which to reject the null hypothesis.
e. Since our STV is 2.24, we compare this value with the CDV, which is 1.71. As stated in our previous example, a table that identifies the critical values for the *t*-test distribution is located in the appendix.

6. If the STV > CDV, reject the null hypothesis.
   Given that the STV (2.24) is greater than the CDV (+1.71), we reject the null hypothesis. Thus, the alternative hypothesis is true, which states that there is a difference between the mean number of deaths in states with SYGL (Sample 1) compared to states without SYGL (Sample 2).

   The results of our test are displayed in the following manner:

$$t = 2.24;\ \text{df} = 22;\ p < .05^{*}$$

*If we ran the research 100 times, we could make a type 1 error 5 times.

Now, let's compute a dependent sample *t*-test. The formula for such is based on the following:

Formula for Computing the Dependent Sample *t*-Test

The formula for computing the dependent *t*-test is based on the following:

$$t = \frac{\Sigma D}{\sqrt{\dfrac{n\Sigma D^2 - (\Sigma D)^2}{n-1}}},$$

where

D = represents the difference between scores
ΣD = represents the sum of all the differences between sample scores
ΣD^2 = represents the sum of the differences squared between samples of scores
n = the number of pairs of observations

Dependent Sample *t*-Test (Example 1)

TABLE 9.1 **Test Scores of School Shooting Responses**

Pretest (P_1)	Posttest (P_2)	Difference ($P_1 - P_2$)	D^2
6	7	1	1
3	7	4	16
7	8	1	1
5	7	2	4

	Pretest (P_1)	Posttest (P_2)	Difference ($P_1 - P_2$)	D^2
	3	9	6	36
	2	10	8	64
	4	8	4	16
	3	7	4	16
	6	4	−2	1
	7	8	1	1
	6	9	3	9
	8	8	0	0
	5	9	4	16
	3	10	7	49
	4	9	5	25
	3	10	7	49
	6	5	−1	1
	7	9	2	4
	5	10	5	25
Sum	93	154	61	334
Mean	4.89	8.11	3.21	17.58

Table 9.1 provides the results of two exams that were completed by faculty and staff at a local high school. The exam was based on one's knowledge of how to respond during an actual school shooting (Huskey and Connell, 2021). Out of a maximum of 10 points, the pretest scores represent the grades earned before the participants were exposed to the policies related to required responses to school shootings as determined by the school district. The posttest scores reflect the grades earned after exposure to the policies by faculty and staff. As a statistician, you are convinced that the mean posttest scores *are significantly higher* than the mean pretest scores.

1. Identify the null and alternative hypotheses.

   The null hypothesis, based on our example, posits there is no difference between the mean posttest scores compared to the mean pretest scores. To the contrary, the alternative hypothesis states that the mean posttest scores are significantly higher than the mean pretest scores.

$$H_0: \mu_{p2} = \mu_{p1}$$
$$H_1: \bar{x}_{p2} > \bar{x}_{p1}$$

2. Identify the level of risk or significance.

   Our selected level of risk is 0.05.

3. Choose the appropriate test.

   Given the level of measurement with the independent variable (categorical) and dependent variable (continuous) and the subjects in both samples are related to each other, we selected a dependent sample *t*-test.

4. Compute and identify the STV.
   At this point, we include the numbers from Table 9.1 in the dependent sample *t*-test formula:

$$t = \frac{61}{\sqrt{\frac{(19 \times 334) - 61^2}{19 - 1}}} = -4.99$$

   The STV is −4.99
5. Identify and compare the CDV to the STV.
   a. The degrees of freedom, computed by using the formula $(n_1 + n_2 - 1)$, is $19 - 1 = 18$.
   b. Since our degrees of freedom is 18, we will locate that number under the degrees of freedom column that corresponds to the directional column at the 0.05 level of risk.
   c. The directional column was selected given that we did identify a specific direction in terms of the expected difference between the sample means.
   d. We will use 1.73 as the value in which to reject the null hypothesis.
   e. Since our STV is −4.99, we compare this value with the CDV, which is 1.73. Provided in the appendix is information that identifies the critical values for the (one-tailed) *t*-test distribution.
6. If the STV > CDV, reject the null hypothesis.
   Given that the STV (−4.99) is less than the CDV (+1.73), we are required to fail to reject (or retain) the null hypothesis. Thus, the null hypothesis is true, which states that the mean posttest scores are not significantly higher than the mean pretest scores.

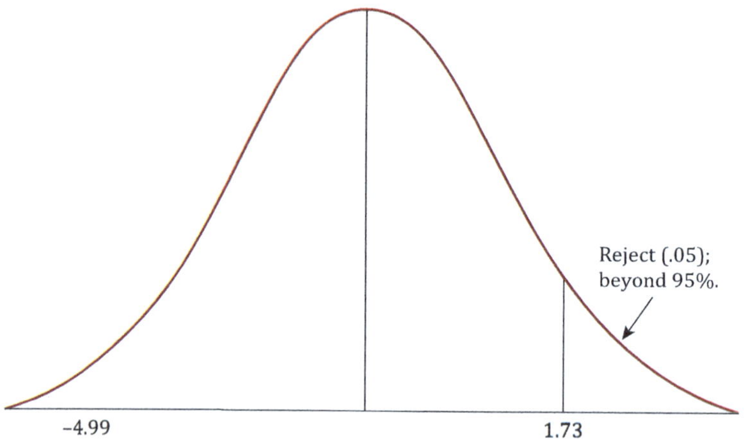

FIGURE 9.3 Normal Curve Illustration of Test Results

Consider the following written results of the test. Do you recognize any differences from the previous test results? Do you see the difference in how the p-value is identified?

$$t = -4.99;\ df = 18;\ p > 0.05$$

Dependent Sample *t*-Test (Example 2)

Our final example related to the use of the dependent sample *t*-test is provided as follows:

TABLE 9.2 **Math Test Scores of Elementary Youth**

	Pretest (P1)	Posttest (P2)	Difference ($P_1 - P_2$)	D^2
	5	8	3	9
	6	7	1	1
	5	9	4	16
	7	10	3	9
	6	9	3	9
	9	12	4	16
	8	11	3	9
	8	10	2	4
	7	6	−1	1
	5	9	4	16
Sum	66	91	26	90
Mean	6.6	9.1	2.6	9

Table 9.2 identifies the scores of a standardized math test given to elementary school students. The values in the pretest column represent the individual scores of students who did not eat breakfast prior to school (Jeong, 2019). The values in the posttest column represent the scores of students who received breakfast before school. As a school administrator, you must decide whether the program responsible for providing breakfast to students should continue to receive funding from the school district. You believe there is a significant difference between the mean pretest scores and the mean posttest scores. To that end, it is your desire to use statistics (results of a dependent *t*-test) as a means of justifying the decision to provide funding for the breakfast program.

1. Identify the null and alternative hypotheses.

   The null hypothesis indicates there is no difference between the mean posttest scores compared to the mean pretest scores. The alternative hypothesis states that the mean posttest scores are significantly different in comparison to the mean pretest scores.

$$H_0\colon \mu_{p2} = \mu_{p1}$$
$$H_1\colon \bar{x}_{p2} \neq \bar{x}_{p1}$$

2. Identify the level of risk or significance.

   Our selected level of risk is 0.05.

3. Choose the appropriate test.

   Given the level of measurement with the independent variable (categorical) and dependent variable (continuous) and the subjects in both samples are related to each other, we selected a dependent sample *t*-test.

4. Compute and identify the STV.
   At this point, we include the numbers from Table 9.2 in the dependent sample *t*-test formula:

$$t = \frac{26}{\sqrt{\frac{(10 \times 90) - 26^2}{10 - 1}}} = -5.24$$

   The STV is −5.24
5. Identify and compare the CDV to the STV.
   a. The degrees of freedom, computed by using the formula (n – 1), is 10 – 1 = 9
   b. Since our degrees of freedom is 9, we will locate that number under the degrees of freedom column that corresponds to the nondirectional column at the 0.05 level of risk.
   c. As indicated in the table (appendix?), we will use ±2.26 as the value in which to reject the null hypothesis.
   d. Since our STV is −5.24, we compare this value with the CDV, which is ±2.26.
6. If the STV > CDV, reject the null hypothesis.
   Since the STV (−5.24) extends beyond the CDV (±2.26), we reject the null hypothesis. Thus, the alternative hypothesis is true, which states that there is a difference between the mean posttest scores compared to the mean pretest scores.

The results of our test are written in the following manner:

$$t = -5.24;\ df = 9;\ p < 0.05$$

Confidence Interval

The formula for confidence intervals for the dependent or match *t*-test is very different than the independent or unmatched *t*-test that was introduced earlier.

Based on the formula, the computation of the CI for the dependent t-test is as follows:

$$= 2.6 \pm 2.26 \frac{1.57}{\sqrt{9}}$$

$$= 2.6 \pm 2.26 \frac{1.57}{3}$$

$$= 2.6 \pm 2.26\ (.52)$$

$$= 2.6 \pm 1.17 = 1.43 \text{ to } 3.77$$

According to our calculations, we can say that if you completed this research 95 times (from our confidence level), our data point (the mean of the distribution of differences) would fall between 1.43 and 3.77. Our calculated difference between the means falls inside of our confidence interval. If the number 0 was identified within our confidence interval (or any confidence interval), our statistically significant t-value finding would be questionable.

Chapter Learning Assessment Questions

To gauge your learning, provide answers to the following questions:

1. Within the *t*-test formula, $x_1 - x_2$ represents ________.
   a. the difference between sample means in an independent sample *t*-test
   b. the difference between sample variances in an independent sample *t*-test
   c. the difference between sample sizes in an independent sample *t*-test
   d. none of the above
2. When conducting a confidence interval with an independent sample *t*-test, one should engage in the following steps except:
   a. include the difference of the sample means
   b. include the t critical value
   c. divide the sample size by each variance within each sample
   d. none of the above

Answers

1. a
2. c

Effect Size and the *t*-Test

Just as we calculated the effect size with the one-sample z-test (Chapter 8), let's consider the process of calculating the effect size with a *t*-test. In this chapter, the purpose of determining effect size is to measure the *extent of the difference* between the two groups.

Suppose we are interested in whether "in-person" classes are more effective in meeting academic goals (i.e., good grades, etc.) than online classes among first-year students. We believe that students who experience in-person learning will achieve a higher grade point average compared to students who experience online learning. To test our hypothesis, a total of 20 first-year students are randomly placed in two groups. One group is required to take in-person courses, while students in the other group are required to take online courses. After four academic semesters, the grade point averages of students from each group are compared, which includes 10 students in each group. The results of the study are provided below:

In-person classes: Mean (3.13) Standard Deviation (0.25)
Online classes: Mean (2.39) Standard Deviation (0.33)

In order to compute the effect size, we divide the difference between the means by one of the standard deviations listed. Consider the following:

$$ES = \frac{\bar{x}_1 - \bar{x}_2}{s},$$

where

ES = effect size

$\bar{x}_1$ = the mean for Group 1

$\bar{x}_2$ = the mean for Group 2

s = the standard deviation from either group

By including the data in the formula from the table, we have the following:

$$ES = \frac{3.13 - 2.39}{0.33}$$

$$d = \frac{0.74}{0.33}$$

$$d = 2.24$$

In order to interpret the effect size, the following criteria is used:

With a range between 0 to 2, the effect size is small. A range between 0.2 to 0.5, the effect size is medium. Finally, a range of 0.5+ corresponds to a large effect size.

Based on $d = 2.24$, which is categorized as greater than a large effect size, we conclude that the relative differences between the two groups are significant.

Chapter Learning Assessment Questions

To gauge your learning, provide answers to the following questions:

1. With regard to problem #2 (independent sample *t*-test), the effect size is ____________.
   a. 11.3
   b. 1.03
   c. 0.81
   d. either b or c
2. In relation to problem #4 (dependent sample *t*-test), the effect size is ____________.
   a. 1.43
   b. 2.6
   c. 1.45
   d. none of the above

Answers

1. d
2. c

Final Thoughts

As discussed in this chapter, a dependent sample *t*-test involves members of one group being tested twice, the latter test following exposure to a stimulus (i.e., treatment, training, etc.). The intent of this process is to determine whether changes will take place because of exposure. As students enrolled in college courses, you might be a participant in a dependent sample *t*-test among those who believe in your potential (e.g., parents, professors).

Discussion

A research team is interested in determining the impact of a training session for police officers with respect to interacting with adolescents in the community (Cleary and Warner, 2016). Topics discussed during the training session include cultural diversity and behavioral development. Prior to the beginning of the training, officers completed an exam (in which their individual scores were recorded). The exam identified their level of knowledge of cultural diversity and the process of adolescent development. In duration, the training included nearly 5 hours of shared information and open discussions. On completion of the training, the officers completed the same exam, and their scores were recorded a second time. By utilizing an independent sample *t*-test, the results revealed a significant difference between scores on the first exam and scores on the second exam. What is your response to the results of the *t*-test? Do you agree or disagree with the results? Explain.

Chapter Summary

Chapter 9 discussed the following information:

Objective 1 – *t*-test and types of *t*-tests

- *t*-test is used to determine mean differences between two groups that include categorical independent and continuous dependent variables.
- Independent sample *t*-test refers to a test in which members of two samples are not related.
- Dependent sample *t*-test is a test in which members of two samples are related.

Objective 2 – Determine which type of *t*-test to use

- A pooled variance *t*-test is a test used with two independent samples in which the population variances are equal.
- A separate variance *t*-test is a test used with two independent samples in which the population variances are unequal.

Objective 3 – F-test

- F-test is used to determine if the variances of two independent samples are equal or unequal.

Objective 4 – Formulas for *t*-test

- See the corresponding pages in the chapter.

Objective 5 – Example problem(s) and the *t*-test

- See the corresponding pages in the chapter.

Objective 6 – Effect size

- To determine the extent of a difference between two samples, one may conduct what is referred to as the effect size.

Terms

t-test
Independent sample *t*-test
Dependent sample *t*-test
Pooled variance *t*-test
Separate variance *t*-test
F-test

Chapter Review Questions

1. The ___________ is used to determine mean differences between two groups and includes a categorical independent variable and a continuous dependent variable.
   a. *t*-test
   b. independent *t*-test
   c. dependent *t*-test
   d. two sample test
2. The ___________ is used in which members of two samples (or groups) are not related.
   a. *t*-test
   b. independent *t*-test
   c. dependent *t*-test
   d. two sample test
3. The ___________ is used in which members of two samples (or groups) are related.
   a. *t*-test
   b. independent *t*-test
   c. dependent *t*-test
   d. two sample test
4. Based on the following, determine if an independent or dependent sample *t*-test is needed:
   a. A researcher is interested in determining which type of counseling leads to higher mean academic grades between two groups of juveniles who experienced counseling. One group received cognitive behavioral therapy, and the other received complex family trauma counseling.
   b. Training within a law enforcement agency is being used to increase mean police response time to 911 calls. Mean response times were recorded before and after the training to determine the impact of the training.

c. Research was conducted to determine if advanced CPR training given to correctional officers lowers the mean number of accidental deaths in prisons within the state. Out of two groups, one group of corrections officers received advanced CPR training, and the other group did not.

d. Access to the use of telephones among prisoners might be associated with lower mean numbers of depression and anxiety. To test this assumption, two groups of inmates (in which one group has access to a telephone) are given a test after 6 months. The test reveals mean levels of depression and anxiety among the two groups.

5. By reviewing the *t*-test table information, near the end of the text, determine if the following STVs (based on a two-tailed test) support the decision to reject the null hypothesis:

Level of Significance	Statistical Test Value	Degrees of Freedom	Critical Decision Value	Reject the Null Hypothesis
.05	4.21	3	3.18	
.05	3.26	6	2.44	
.01	2.89	16	2.92	
.05	3.07	19	2.09	
.05	3.11	4	2.77	
.01	4.25	12	3.05	
.01	10.04	2	9.92	
.01	4.2	7	3.5	
.05	2.45	18	2.10	

6. The following includes the scores of exams completed by attorneys before and after they received training in relation to the juvenile justice system. They were tested regarding their knowledge of the transfer of youth to the adult criminal justice system within the state where they practice law. Choose the appropriate test (at 0.05 level of risk) and determine if a significant difference in knowledge (as measured by exam scores) occurred as a result of the training.

Before Training	After Training
58	63
67	74
71	74
66	59
71	79
68	78
76	82
77	85
69	76
61	69
72	74

7. Provided below are the number of traffic stops among 2 groups of 10 youths based on race. Choose the appropriate test and determine if a significant difference (at 0.05 level of risk) exists.

Blacks	Whites
3	2
1	2
2	3
1	2
2	1
2	1
1	2
3	2
2	1
4	5
5	2

8. In an effort to serve as mentors for first-year college students, several members of a female sorority agreed to receive training at a university. This process is consistent with similar research objectives designed to prevent harm on college campuses (Mancini et al., 2016). The training consists of the policies and procedures of reporting incidents to campus police. To determine their knowledge of the reporting procedures, each member of the sorority completed a series of exams. The administrator of the training believes that those who complete the training will increase their scores from their previous attempt. The data below reflects the pretest and posttest scores of their exam results. Using a significance level of 0.01, determine if a significant difference exists between the two scores. Determine whether the administrator's hypothesis is supported.

Pretest	Posttest
70	80
60	65
65	70
55	50
75	70
55	65
80	85
75	90
60	85
50	55
55	60
65	65

Based on Questions 13–15, conduct an *f*-test and determine which type of *t*-test (pooled variances *t*-test or separate variances *t*-test) should be used:

9. With respect to citizenship and families in the United States, a study might reveal that children whose parents are not U.S.-born citizens are more likely to graduate from college compared to children whose parents are U.S.-born citizens. Identified below is the mean number of children who have graduated from college between 2015 and 2021.

Citizenship of Parents

Year	Non-United States	United States
1997	3	3
1998	2	4
1999	3	3
2000	4	5
2001	5	4
2002	5	3
2003	6	2
2005	5	3
2005	7	1
2006	5	3
2007	6	1
2008	4	2
2009	5	1
2010	7	2
2012	6	1
2013	7	3
2014	5	2
2015	6	1
2016	4	3
2017	6	1
2018	5	2
2019	6	1
2020	5	1
2021	7	2
2022	5	1

10. An advocacy group believes that bail decisions are associated with the ethnicity of an alleged offender. In particular, they believe that Hispanics (compared to Whites) are more likely to experience the denial of bail for the same alleged offense. The following data represents the mean number of alleged offenders who experience the denial of bail within a specific geographical location.

Ethnicity and Denial of Bail

Year	Hispanic	Non-Hispanic
2000	15	5
2001	15	8
2002	12	4
2003	10	3
2004	12	8
2005	8	4
2006	7	4
2007	8	5
2008	9	3
2009	12	5
2010	17	9
2012	18	12
2013	21	12
2014	20	11
2015	18	8
2016	13	6
2017	12	6
2018	21	9

11. In an effort to address racial disparities, a state-level law enforcement executive believes that the inclusion of racial impact policies (RIPS) will have an impact in lowering levels of racial disparity as reflected in the arrest data (Manski and Nagin, 2017). The data provided below reflects the number of arrests among Blacks within local law enforcement agencies that either use (or fail to use) RIPS within 20 service area locations areas in the state.

Inclusion of RIPS

Area	Employed	Not Employed
1	14	28
2	12	25
3	15	27
4	19	25
5	16	27
6	17	30
7	12	29
8	12	31
9	10	33
10	12	34
11	19	36
12	18	37

Area	Employed	Not Employed
13	13	36
14	19	35
15	20	40
16	15	42
17	13	39
18	22	40
19	18	45
20	10	48

12. Studies associated with marriage point to the value of communication in relationships. In light of such, a researcher believes that high levels of communication (at least 30 minutes) are associated with high levels of marital stability among couples. To that end, to what extent is communication (at least 30 minutes/week) associated with marital stability among couples in which one person is incarcerated? To test the researcher's hypothesis, conduct an *f*-test and a *t*-test, with a (0.05) level of significance based on the following details:

At least 30 min.	Less than 30 min.
8	5
8	6
7	4
6	5
8	5
6	4
7	2
8	4
9	6
6	4
9	4
8	3
9	4
7	5
8	4
9	4
8	6
6	3
8	5
9	2
8	5
9	3
10	6

13. A nonprofit organization that provides resources for at-risk youth believes that exposure to restorative justice practices is better than exposure to nonrestorative justice activities (i.e., traditional legal measures). In particular, the head of the organization is convinced that victim mediation experiences are associated with greater levels of understanding (as measured by using a scale from 1 to 5) among youth, especially in relation to the impact of their offenses on the lives of others. To test this hypothesis, conduct an *f*-test and a *t*-test with a (0.05) level of significance based on the following details:

Type of Justice

Restorative	Traditional
5	3
4	4
5	2
4	2
4	4
5	3
4	1
3	1
4	2
5	1
4	3
5	2
5	1
4	4
3	1
5	1
4	2
5	1
5	2
4	1
5	3

14. Within criminology, the social strain theory serves as an explanation of crime. An assumption of the theory includes the process in which individuals choose to retreat from the goal (and method) of obtaining success in society. Often referred to as retreatists, they may engage in mind-altering activities in order to escape the demands of societal success while simultaneously living under substandard conditions. As a researcher, you are convinced that those who must reside in low-income settings (based on certain annual income levels) are more likely to engage in mind-altering criminal activities as a coping mechanism. More specifically, you believe that those who earn $12,000/year (compared to those who earn $16,000/year) are more likely to experience arrests as a result of excessive drug use. In this scenario, drug use is measured by the number of times a person engaged in drug use within

a 10-year period. To test your hypothesis, conduct an *f*-test and a *t*-test with a (0.01) level of significance based on the following details:

Annual Income

$12,000	$16,000
15	8
17	5
12	6
11	5
14	3
19	6
11	7
13	5
18	8
11	3
15	5
16	2
17	4
13	6
15	3

15. A study suggests that youth who have parents who consistently express an intolerant attitude toward deviance (compared to parents who fail to consistently express such) are less likely to engage in deviant behavior. For numerical purposes, consistent parental expression of intolerance (as identified in the table below) is measured on the basis of how many times a young person is able to recall the number of times their parents have shared their views regarding deviant behavior on a monthly basis. Examples of such may include the expression of threats, reasoning, frustration, etc. Parents who are considered expressive are designated as those who share their opinions with their children at least 10 times each month. To test the hypothesis in the study, conduct an *f*-test and a *t*-test (with a 0.05 level of significance), along with a test to measure the effect size (if applicable) based on the following:

Parental Approach to Deviant Behavior

Month	Consistently Expressive	Inconsistently Expressive
January	12	8
February	15	6
March	10	4
April	10	3
May	16	4
June	19	3
July	22	5

August	24	5
September	12	3
October	13	4
November	11	5
December	16	7

16. In the area of immigration and law enforcement relations with minorities in the United States, studies have indicated that the federal enforcement of immigration policies may lead to further distrust between minorities and local law enforcement agencies. As revealed in the data below, certain local law enforcement agencies are likely to provide assistance in the enforcement of federal immigration policies. Levels of trust directed toward local law enforcement among minorities, especially those who have family members in Latin America, are measured on a scale between 1 and 5. To test the study-based hypothesis, conduct an *f*-test and a *t*-test (with a 0.05 level of significance), along with a test to measure the effect size (if applicable) based on the following:

Local Law Enforcement Agencies

Provide Federal Support	Fail to Provide Federal Support
2	4
1	5
2	5
1	4
1	3
2	5
1	5
1	4
1	3
1	4
2	3
3	4

Answers

1. a
2. b
3. c
4.
   a. independent
   b. dependent
   c. independent
   d. dependent

5.

Level of Significance	Statistical Test Value	Degrees of Freedom	Critical Decision Value	Reject the Null Hypothesis
0.05	4.21	3	3.18	Y
0.05	3.26	6	2.44	Y
0.01	2.89	16	2.92	N
0.05	3.07	19	2.09	Y
0.05	3.11	4	2.77	Y
0.01	4.25	12	3.05	Y
0.01	10.04	2	9.92	Y
0.01	4.2	7	3.5	Y
0.05	2.45	18	2.10	Y

6. A dependent sample *t*-test was employed. With a t-statistic of 2.23 and a p-value of 0.004, there is evidence that a statistically significant difference exists between the scores identified.
7. An independent sample *t*-test was employed. With a t-statistic of 0.53 and a p-value of 0.06, there is no evidence that a statistically significant difference exists between the number of traffic stops between the groups.
8. A dependent sample *t*-test was employed. With a t-statistic of 2.61 and a p-value of 0.012, there is evidence that a statistically significant difference exists between the exam scores provided. The hypothesis of the administrator of the training is supported.
9. With an *f*-test score of 1.3 and a p-value of 0.26, a pooled variance *t*-test should be used.
10. With an *f*-test score of 2.24 and a p-value of 0.04, a separate variance *t*-test should be used.
11. With an *f*-test score of 0.28 and a p-value of 0.004, a separate variance *t*-test should be used.
12. With an *f*-test score of 0.99 and a p-value of .49, a pooled variance *t*-test was used. To that end, an independent sample t-test was employed. With a t-statistic of 9.43 and a p-value of 0.001, there is enough evidence that a statistically significant difference exists between the two time frames of communication. The researcher's hypothesis is supported.
13. With an *f*-test score of 0.37 and a p-value of 0.01, a separate variance t-test was used. To that end, an independent sample *t*-test was employed. With a t-statistic of 7.98 and a p-value of 0.001, there is enough evidence that a statistically significant difference exists between the two measures of understanding among the youth. This includes differences based on the type of justice (e.g., restorative, traditional) each youth was exposed to. The hypothesis of the head of the nonprofit organization is supported.
14. With an *f*-test score of 2.03 and a p-value of 0.09, a pooled variance *t*-test was used. To that end, an independent sample *t*-test was employed. With a t-statistic of 11.4 and a p-value of 0.001, there is enough evidence that a statistically significant difference exists between the two amounts of annual income and corresponding drug use. The identified hypothesis in the scenario is supported.
15. With an *f*-test score of 8.35 and a p-value of .001, a separate variance *t*-test was used. To that end, an independent sample *t*-test was employed. With a t-statistic of 7.2 and a p-value of 0.001, there is enough evidence that a statistically significant difference exists between

the expressive and nonexpressive parents. The hypothesis of the research is supported. The corresponding effect size, which is 6.7, is considered a large amount of difference between the impact of the listed parenting approaches.

16. With an *f*-test score of 0.72 and a p-value of 0.29, a pooled variance *t*-test was used. To that end, an independent sample *t*-test was employed. With a t-statistic of 8.5 and a p-value of 0.001, there is enough evidence that a statistically significant difference exists between those who support and those who failed to support federal law enforcement efforts. The hypothesis of the research is supported. The corresponding effect size, which is 3.4, is considered a large amount of difference between the categories provided.

Matching: Place the letter of the following definitions with its corresponding term.

____1. ***t***-test
____2. Independent sample ***t***-test
____3. Dependent sample ***t***-test
____4. Pooled variances ***t***-test
____5. Separative variances ***t***-test
____6. *F*-test

a. test in which members of two samples are not related
b. used to determine mean differences between two groups
c. test used with two independent samples in which the population variances are equal
d. test used with two independent samples in which the population variances are unequal
e. test in which members of two samples are related
f. used to determine if the variances of two independent samples are equal or unequal

Answers

1. b
2. a
3. e
4. c
5. d
6. f

Biblography

Alderden, M. A., & Ullman, S. E. (2012). Gender difference or indifference? Detective decision making in sexual assault cases. *Journal of Interpersonal Violence, 27*(1), 3–22.

Bozeman, W. P., Vilke, G. M., Hall, C., Klinger, D. A., Ross, D. L., Bennell, C., Petit, N. P., Miller, D. L., Ford, K. K., Hiestand, B., & Stopyra, J. P. (2022). Safety of vascular neck restraint applied by law enforcement officers. *Journal of Forensic and Legal Medicine, 92*, 102446–102446.

Cleary, H., & Warner, T. C. (2016). Police training in interviewing and interrogation methods: A comparison of techniques used with adult and juvenile suspects. *Law and Human Behavior, 40*(3), 270.

Gius, M. (2016). The relationship between stand-your-ground laws and crime: A state-level analysis. *The Social Science Journal, 53*(3), 329–338.

Guevara, L., Herz, D., & Spohn, C. (2006). Gender and juvenile justice decision making: What role does race play? *Feminist Criminology, 1*(4), 258–282.

Huskey, M. G., & Connell, N. M. (2021). Preparation or provocation? Student perceptions of active shooter drills. *Criminal Justice Policy Review*, *32*(1), 3–26.

Jeong, E. Y. (2019). The influence of breakfast on the academic performance of school-age adolescents: systematic review. *Journal of Nutrition and Health*, *52*(2), 119–128.

Mancini, C., Pickett, J. T., Call, C., & Roche, S. P. (2016). Mandatory reporting (MR) in higher education: College students' perceptions of laws designed to reduce campus sexual assault. *Criminal Justice Review*, *41*(2), 219–235.

Manski, C. F., & Nagin, D. S. (2017). Assessing benefits, costs, and disparate racial impacts of confrontational proactive policing. *Proceedings of the National Academy of Sciences*, *114*(35), 9308–9313.

Peck, J. H., & Beaudry-Cyr, M. (2016). Does who appears before the juvenile court matter on adjudication and disposition outcomes? The interaction between client race and lawyer type. *Journal of Crime and Justice*, *39*(1), 131–152.

Tolan, P. H., Henry, D. B., Schoeny, M. S., Lovegrove, P., & Nichols, E. (2014). Mentoring programs to affect delinquency and associated outcomes of youth at risk: A comprehensive meta-analytic review. *Journal of Experimental Criminology*, *10*(2), 179–206.

Chapter 9 SPSS and Workbook Questions

SPSS and the *t*-Test

To compute a *t*-test using SPSS, perform the following steps:

As an example, let's refer to our previous information on page 13. This includes determining whether differences exist between groups (as measured by math scores) on the basis of whether breakfast should be provided for students. This requires the use of a dependent sample *t*-test.

Entry of Data—SPSS

1. Select variable view to include information associated with the variables of interest. In our example, this would include both pretest and posttest scores.
2. In the first row, include the term *pretest* under the column identified as name.
3. In the column identified as label, you might choose to include a more specific description of the variable, such as *pretest score*.
4. For the second group, *posttest scores*, follow the same procedure as noted above.
5. Select data view to include the corresponding scores (which are identified in the sample) in each corresponding column. Be sure to include only one score in each cell.

IMAGE 9.1

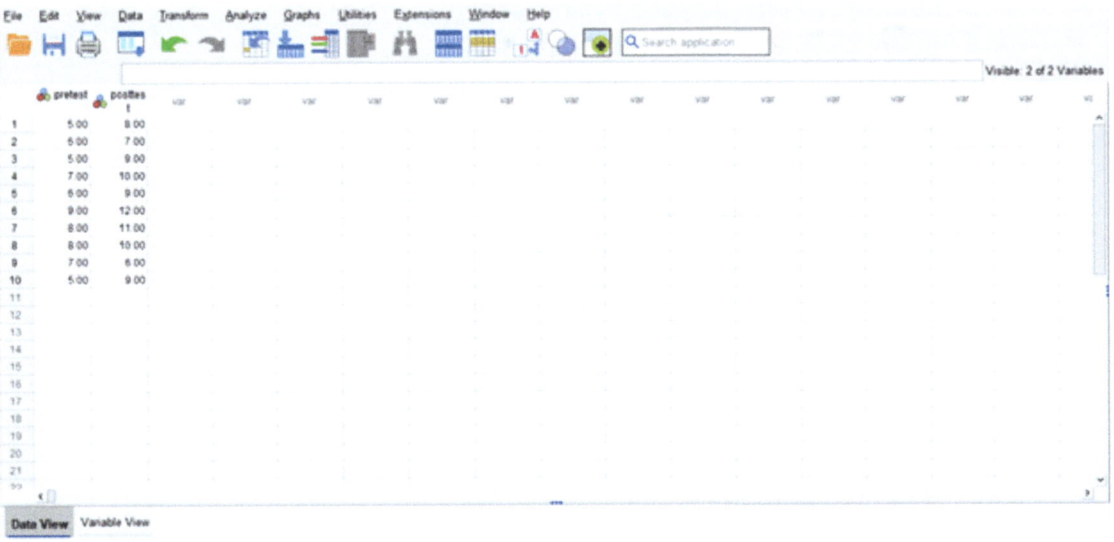

IMAGE 9.2

Analysis of Data—SPSS

1. Select analyze, select compare means and proportions, and choose paired samples *t*-tests.
2. Select the pretest set of scores and move it to the paired variables box. Once completed, it should be identified as Variable 1. In the same manner, select the posttest set of scores and move them to the paired variables box, which should be identified as Variable 2.
3. In the options section, one is able to adjust the confidence interval percentage, which is automatically set at 95%.
4. Once all desired functions have been selected and completed, select OK.

Output of Data Analysis—SPSS

The output of the data analysis includes a total of four tables. Table 1 includes information that identifies the mean, sample size, as well as standard deviation, and standard error for each group of scores. Details associated with the correlation between group scores, as well as the significance of differences, are included in Table 2. Table 3 identifies the mean differences between the groups, *t*-test statistic, and level of significance, along with the corresponding confidence interval of the difference. Finally, Table 4 includes details associated with the effect size of the difference between the two groups.

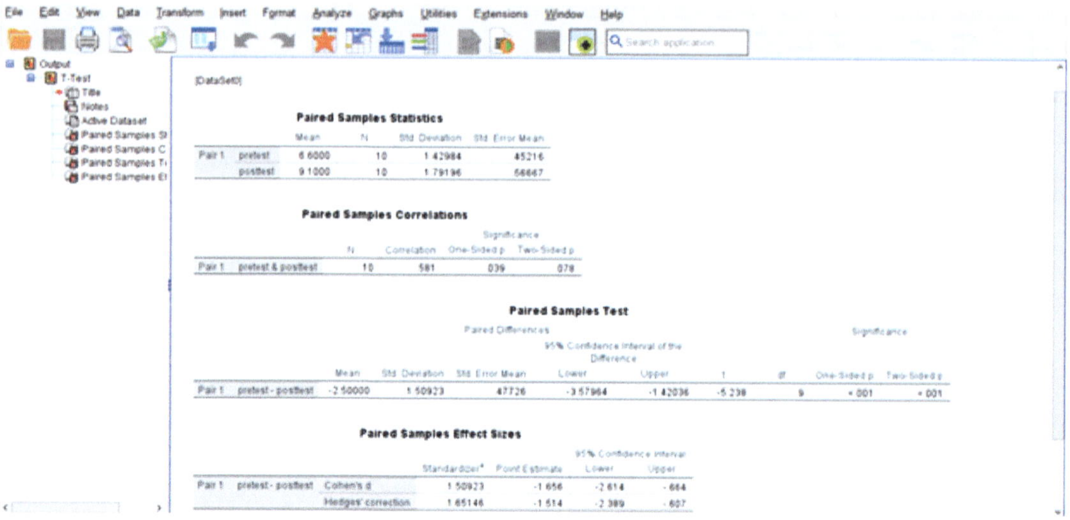

IMAGE 9.3

Workbook Questions

Objective 1—t-Test and Types of t-Tests

- A *t*-test is used to determine mean differences between two groups that include categorical independent and continuous dependent variables.
- Independent sample *t*-test refers to a test in which members of two samples are not related.
- Dependent sample *t*-test is a test in which members of two samples are related.

Corresponding Questions

1. A *t*-test is used to determine mean differences between two groups that include independent and ___________ dependent variables.
   a. categorical/continuous
   b. continuous/categorical
   c. nominal/ordinal
   d. ratio/continuous
2. Which of the following represents the appropriate use of a *t*-test?
   a. A study that examines the relationship between gender and the number of days a suspect is detained in jail.
   b. Research that investigates an association between criminal history and the number of prison years an individual receives during sentencing. Criminal history, which is composed of two categories, is identified in terms of whether or not an individual has at least one felony conviction prior to sentencing.
   c. A teacher who is curious as to whether the race of her students is associated with the number of detention referrals they receive in a school year.
   d. All of the above

3. Which of the following represents the inappropriate use of a *t*-test?
   a. A study that examines the relationship between the time in which a suspect accepts a plea agreement and the number of days a suspect is detained in jail. In this study, time is measured by the number of weeks a suspect is detained in jail.
   b. Research that investigates an association between criminal history and the number of prison years an individual receives during sentencing. Criminal history, which is composed of two categories, is identified in terms of whether or not an individual has at least one misdemeanor conviction prior to sentencing.
   c. A teacher who is curious as to whether the gender of her students is associated with the number of detention referrals they receive in a school year.
   d. None of the above
4. Based on the following, identify which requires the use of either an independent or dependent *t*-test.
   a. A researcher believes that youth who develop meaningful relationships with an authority figure are more likely to experience higher mean academic grades compared to students who do not develop meaningful relationships with an authority figure. This study involves two separate groups of youth.
   b. In a local community, two mentoring programs were used in an effort to decrease the mean number of school-based disciplinary referrals among at-risk youth. This included both a police and religious-based mentoring program.
   c. A local chief prosecutor believes that caseload management among junior-level attorneys is associated with lower mean numbers of absenteeism and resignation. This process included gathering feedback from junior-level attorneys before and after the caseload management policy was used.
   d. After reviewing financial expenses associated with litigation in relation to allegations of police misconduct, a police chief decides to implement a training session for the local police. This includes sharing the loss of financial resources with respect to police misconduct, which has significantly impacted the annual salaries of the officers. To gauge feedback, the chief requires that each officer completes a survey before and after the training.

Answers

1. a
2. d
3. a
4.
   a. independent
   b. independent
   c. dependent
   d. dependent

Objective 2—Determine Which Type of t-Test to Use

- A pooled variance *t*-test is a test used with two independent samples in which the population variances are equal.
- A separate variance *t*-test is a test used with two independent samples in which the population variances are unequal.

Objective 3—F-Test

- The *f*-test is used to determine if the variances of two independent samples are equal or unequal.

Corresponding Questions

1. The first step in conducting an *f*-test includes computing the __________ for each group.
   a. mean
   b. median
   c. variance
   d. standard deviation
2. When conducting an *f*-test, one is required to divide the __________ hypothesis group by the variance of the __________ hypothesis group.
   a. null/alternative
   b. alternative/null
   c. either a or b
   d. None the above
3. If the p-value of an *f*-test is __________ 0.05, the separate variance *t*-test should be used.
   a. less than
   b. greater than
   c. equal to
   d. equal to or less than
4. After teaching an introductory level criminal justice course to first-year students, a professor believes that class A performed significantly better than class B. Based on the following, conduct an *f*-test to determine if the variances of the two samples are equal and select the correct answer.

Class A	Class B
89	12
81	26
78	48
92	52
76	61
88	71
65	23

Class A	Class B
69	53
77	81
72	17

a. The variances are equal, which requires the use of a pooled variance *t*-test.
b. The variances are unequal, which requires the use of a pooled variance *t*-test.
c. The variances are equal, which requires the use of a separate variance *t*-test.
d. The variances are unequal, which requires the use of a separate variance *t*-test.

5. The following information reveals the results of a stress level test between male and female police officers. In light of such, a student is convinced that males are able to respond to stress at a higher level compared to females (Bonner and Brimhall, 2022). Based on the following, conduct an *f*-test to determine if the student's assumption is accurate and select the correct answer.

Males	Females
8	7
9	7
10	8
10	6
9	7
10	8
8	6
9	5
10	6
10	4

a. The variances are equal, which requires the use of a pooled variance *t*-test; therefore, the student's assumption is not accurate.
b. The variances are unequal, which requires the use of a pooled variance *t*-test; therefore, the student's assumption is accurate.
c. The variances are equal, which requires the use of a separate variance *t*-test; therefore, the student's assumption is not accurate.
d. The variances are unequal, which requires the use of a separate variance *t*-test; therefore, the student's assumption is accurate.

6. A legal scholar believes that prosecutors who have at least 10 years of trial experience will have a higher conviction rate compared to prosecutors who have less than 10 years of trial experience (Goncalves Jr., 2022). Identified below are the years of trial experience between two groups of prosecutors. Conduct an *f*-test to determine if the legal scholar's assumption is accurate and select the correct answer.

> 10 Years	< 10 Years
8	7
9	7
10	8
10	6
9	7
10	8
8	6
9	5
10	6
10	4

a. The variances are equal, which requires the use of a pooled variance *t*-test; therefore, the legal scholar's assumption is not accurate.

b. The variances are unequal, which requires the use of a pooled variance *t*-test; therefore, the legal scholar's assumption is accurate.

c. The variances are equal, which requires the use of a separate variance *t*-test; therefore, the legal scholar's assumption is not accurate.

d. The variances are unequal, which requires the use of a separate variance *t*-test; therefore, the legal scholar's assumption is accurate.

Answers

1. c
2. b
3. a
4. d
5. a
6. a

Objective 4—Formulas for t-Test

- See the corresponding pages in the chapter.

Objective 5—Example Problem(s) and the t-Test

- See the corresponding pages in the chapter.

Corresponding Questions

Based on the following exercises, be sure to include the null and alternative hypotheses within your answer.

1. Because of a shortage of correctional officers, administrators at a correctional facility offered the opportunity for officers to work overtime. During this time period, the majority of officers who volunteered were over the age of 50. Unfortunately, the amount of complaints against these officers also increased. In response to such, the administration believes that the age of an officer (e.g., those over the age of 50) is associated with higher numbers of inmate complaints. Based on the following data, which includes the number of complaints reported against an officer on the basis of their age, compute a *t*-test (with a risk level of 0.05) to determine if the administration's hypothesis is supported.

> 50 Years	< 50 Years
9	3
9	7
8	6
7	4
9	5
8	2
8	7
6	5
8	3
6	5
9	2
12	7
10	4
8	3
7	5

2. In general, a probation officer is responsible for managing a vast number of individuals who have been sentenced to probation by the courts. In some cases, a probation officer may be responsible for at least 75 individuals at one time. When probation officers are required to manage a high number of individuals, there is the likelihood that probation violations may increase (Fox et al., 2022). To prevent this possibility, a state-level probation department believes that the ideal number of individuals a probation officer can effectively manage is no more than 50 individuals. Based on the following data, which includes the number of probation violations on the basis of the number of individuals a probation officer is required to manage, compute a *t*-test (with a risk level of 0.05) to determine if the probation department's hypothesis is supported.

> 50 Individuals	< 50 Individuals
9	3
9	10

8	2
7	11
9	1
8	15
8	13
6	2
8	12
6	3
9	15
12	4
14	8
8	13
7	16

3. Proponents of the cash bail system argue that the purpose of bail is to ensure that an individual charged with a crime will appear in court. Those who advocate against the use of cash bail argue that individuals who are arrested are innocent until proven guilty; therefore, they will appear in court (Monaghan et al., 2020). Identified below are individuals who were either released as a result of cash bail or their own recognizance. This includes a corresponding number of failure-to-appear charges for each category. Based on the following data, compute a *t*-test (with a risk level of 0.05) to determine if the hypothesis of proponents of the cash bail system is supported.

Year	Bail	No bail
2011	15	18
2012	22	16
2013	19	14
2014	16	9
2015	18	10
2016	21	24
2017	16	15
2018	14	9
2019	26	8
2020	14	7

Answers

1.
H_0: Officers who are at least 50 years old = Officers who are less than 50 years old
H_1: Officers who are at least 50 years old > Officers who are less than 50 years old
t = 6.26; df = 28; p < 0.05 (the results indicate that the administration's hypothesis is supported)

2.
H_0: Officers with at least 50 individuals = Officers with less than 50 individuals

H_1: Officers with at least 50 individuals > Officers with less than 50 individuals
$t = 0$; $df = 18$; $p < 0.5$ (the results indicate that the probation department's hypothesis is not supported)

3.
H_0: The use of a cash bail system = The use of a noncash bail system
H_1: The use of a cash bail system ≠ The use of a noncash bail system
$t = 2.41$; $df = 18$; $p < 0.05$ (the results indicate that the hypothesis of the proponents of the cash bail system is supported)

Objective 6—Effect Size

- To determine the extent of a difference between two samples, one may conduct what is referred to as the effect size.

Corresponding Question

1. Suppose we are interested in whether "in-person" training classes are more effective in meeting instructional goals (i.e., understanding, retention of information, etc.) compared to online training classes among first responders. We believe that first responders who experience in-person training will achieve a higher grade point average compared to those who experience online training. To test our hypothesis, we randomly place a total of 30 first responders into two groups. One group is required to take in-person training courses, while the other group is required to take online training courses. After 16 weeks of training, the grade point averages of the first responders from each group are compared, which includes 15 individuals in each group. The results of the study are provided below:

	In-Person Training	Online Training
Mean	2.98	2.15
Standard Deviation	0.22	.31

Based on the data provided, compute an effect size to determine if the differences between the groups are significant.

Answers

1.

$$ES = \frac{2.98 - 2.15}{0.31}$$

$$d = \frac{0.83}{0.31}$$

$$d = 2.67$$

Based on $d = 2.67$, which is categorized as greater than a large effect size, we conclude that the relative differences between the two groups are significant.

Bibliography

Bonner, H. S., & Brimhall, A. (2022). Gender differences in law enforcement officer stress and coping strategies. *Police Quarterly*, *25*(1), 59–89.

Fox, C., Harrison, J., Hothersall, G., Smith, A., & Webster, R. (2022). A rapid evidence assessment of the impact of probation caseloads on reducing recidivism and other probation outcomes. *Probation Journal*, *69*(2), 138–158.

Goncalves Jr., W. I. (2022). "How much time am I looking at?": Plea bargains, harsh punishments, and low trial rates in southwest border districts. *American Criminal Law Review*, *59*, 293.

Monaghan, J., van Holm, E. J., & Surprenant, C. W. (2020). Get jailed, jump bail? The impacts of cash bail on failure to appear and re-arrest in Orleans Parish. *American Journal of Criminal Justice*, *47*(5), 1–19.

Credits

CHAPTER 10

ANOVA Test

The analysis of variance is not a mathematical theorem, but rather a convenient method of arranging the arithmetic.
—Ronald Fisher

Objectives

1. Define and explain the use of the ANOVA test.
2. Identify the formula for computing an ANOVA test.
3. Computing an ANOVA test(s).
4. Define and explain the use of a post hoc test.
5. Discuss the significance of effect size.

Sentencing of Youth and the ANOVA Test

As a student of juvenile justice, you are interested in determining whether there are differences between youth (who have been waived to the adult system) based on race and the amount of time they received during sentencing. To answer this question, an analysis of variance test is recommended. An analysis of variance test (or **ANOVA test**) is a statistical test that is used to determine mean differences between three or more groups and includes categorical independent variables and a continuous dependent variable. In some instances, the test is often referred to as a one-way or single-factor ANOVA test. For example, suppose a researcher is interested in determining if differences exist in race/ethnicity with regard to the amount of time in sentencing. When examining differences on the basis of two categories, say Blacks and Whites, the use of a *t*-test is required. However, if the researcher observes more than two categories (e.g., Blacks, Whites, and Hispanics) an ANOVA test is required.

ANOVA test A statistical test that is used to determine mean differences between three or more groups and includes a categorical independent variable and a continuous dependent variable.

The Two-Factor ANOVA Test

An extension of the ANOVA, referred to as a **two-factor ANOVA test (or a factorial analysis)**, employs the use of an additional factor. Building on the previous

two-factor ANOVA test A statistical test that has the same characteristics as the ANOVA test that includes two independent variables.

between-group variance A measurement that identifies the extent to which differences exist between groups or samples.

within-group variance A measurement that identifies the extent to which differences exist between subjects or individuals within a group or sample.

F-distribution A measurement that identifies the between and within-group variance; the test statistic of ANOVA.

illustration, consider the following, which includes the additional variable of gender. In this case, the researcher is now interested in determining whether differences exist between race (e.g., Black, White, Hispanic) and gender (e.g., male, female) with regard to the amount of time in sentencing.

As identified, both ANOVA and factorial analysis share many of the same characteristics of a *t*-test. This includes the use of categorical variables (e.g., race, gender) as independent variables, as well as the use of a continuous variable (e.g., amount of time served) as the dependent variable. The logic behind computing the ANOVA test is based on the use of a proportion (ratio). It also includes the division of the between-group variance by the within-group variance. A **between-group variance** is a measurement that identifies the extent to which differences exist between groups or samples. A **within-group variance** is a measurement that identifies the extent to which differences exist between subjects or individuals within a group or sample. The test statistic of ANOVA is referred to as the **F-distribution**.

Assumptions of the ANOVA

As with any inferential statistical test, conducting an ANOVA has limitations. Consider the following:

1. It should only be used with samples that include three or more groups.
2. The dependent variable is designated at the continuous (i.e., interval, ratio) level and should be normally distributed. However, it is not uncommon to use ordinal-level data with ANOVA, which is often provided as a result of gathering survey data using a Likert scale.
3. Because of the use of three or more groups, a two-tailed test should be used. Imagine computing an ANOVA test in which a statistically significant difference occurs ($p < 0.05$). In response to such, how is one able to determine which groups represent the basis of such differences?
4. In the event of discovering a statistically significant difference, a post hoc test must be used to determine the source of the group differences. The most commonly used post hoc is referred to as Tukey's honestly significant difference (HSD) test, which we will discuss later.
5. Finally, the variances in each group must be derived from populations that include equal variances. This is referred to as homogeneity of variances.

For the problems in this chapter, we will assume that the variances in each group are equal.

The Logic of the ANOVA in Comparison to the *t*-Test

If we are interested in identifying whether statistically significant differences occur between three groups, why not simply conduct three independent *t*-tests (as opposed to the ANOVA test)? The problem with conducting three independent *t*-tests is that each time a *t*-test (or any other hypotheses test) is conducted with a risk (or significance level) of 0.05, the likelihood of error increases. Instead of a 1 in 20 chance (5%) of making a type 1 error, based on the use of a *t*-test, one will experience a 3 in 20 chance (15%) of making a type 1 error as a result of conducting three independent *t*-tests.

Chapter Learning Assessment Questions

To gauge your learning, provide answers to the following questions:

1. Which of the following assumptions are related to the use of an ANOVA test?
   a. The independent variables are comprised of three or more groups
   b. The dependent variable is designated at the continuous level
   c. A nondirectional (two-tailed) test must be used
   d. All of the above
2. A sociologist is interested in whether gender is associated with social media activity among college students. Gender is measured by three categories, which include male, female, and other. Social media is measured by the amount of time (hours during the week) one spends using a social media platform (i.e., Facebook, etc.). Which of the following statistical tests should be conducted?
   a. One sample z-test
   b. *t*-test
   c. ANOVA test
   d. None of the above

Answers

1. d
2. c

Formula for Computing the ANOVA Test

$$F = \frac{MS_{between}}{MS_{within}},$$

where

$MS_{between}$ = variance between the samples

MS_{within} = variance between the samples

ANOVA Test (Example 1)

In Table 10.1, the amount of time (in years) is provided for 3 samples of 10 youths based on the following:

TABLE 10.1 **Youth Sentenced as Adults by Race and Time**

Blacks	Latinx	Whites
5	4	4
7	6	3
6	5	5
8	7	4
6	6	2
9	5	3
8	7	2
6	5	4
7	4	5
3	1	6

As a proponent of critical race theory, you believe there is a significant difference between the mean number of years of the three different samples.

1. Identify the null and alternative hypotheses.

   The null hypothesis indicates there is no difference between the mean number of years of the three different samples. The alternative hypothesis states that there is a difference between the mean number of years of the three different samples (Berkbolatkyzy et al., 2019).

$$H_0: \mu_1 = \mu_2 = \mu_3$$
$$H_1: \bar{x}_1 \neq \bar{x}_2 \neq \bar{x}_3$$

2. Identify the level of risk or significance.

   Our selected level of risk is 0.05.

3. Choose the appropriate test.

   Given the level of measurement with the independent (categorical) and dependent (continuous) variables, along with examining mean differences with at least three groups, we selected an ANOVA test.

TABLE 10.2 **Amount of Years by Race**

Blacks	X^2	Latinx	X^2	Whites	X^2
5	25	4	16	4	16
7	49	6	36	3	9
6	36	5	25	5	25

Blacks	X^2	Latinx	X^2	Whites	X^2
8	64	7	49	4	16
6	36	6	36	2	4
9	81	5	25	3	9
8	64	7	49	2	4
6	36	5	25	4	16
7	49	4	16	5	25
3	9	1	1	6	36
n = 10		n = 10		n = 10	
$\Sigma X = 65$	$\Sigma X^2 = 449$	$\Sigma X = 50$	$\Sigma X^2 = 278$	$\Sigma X = 38$	$\Sigma X^2 = 160$
$\bar{x} = 6.5$		$\bar{x} = 5$		$\bar{x} = 3.8$	

4. Compute and identify the statistical test value (STV).
   At this point, we include the numbers from Table 10.1 into the ANOVA test formula using the following information from Table 10.2
   a. To begin, we must compute the total sum of squares:
      $= (449 + 278 + 160) - (65 + 50 + 38)^2/30$
      $= 887 - (153)^2/30$
      $= 887 - 23{,}409/30$
      $= 887 - 780.3$
      $= 106.7$
   b. A cumulative mean is computed:
      $= 65 + 50 + 38/30 = 153/30 = 5.1$
   c. Compute the between groups sum of squares:
      $= 10(6.5 - 5.1)^2 + 10(5 - 5.1)^2 + 10(3.8 - 5.1)^2$
      $= 10(1.4)^2 + 10(-0.1)^2 + 10(-1.3)^2$
      $= 10(1.96) + 10(0.01) + 10(1.69)$
      $= 19.6 + 0.1 + 16.9$
      $= 36.6$
   d. Compute the within-group sum of squares:
      $106.7 - 36.6 = 70.1$
   e. Compute the means square based on the following formulas:

$$MS_B = \frac{ss_B}{k - 1}$$

$$MS\_B = 36.6 / (3 - 1) = 36.6 / 2 = 18.3$$

$$MS_W = \frac{ss_W}{N - k}$$

$$MS_W = \frac{70.1}{30 - 3} = \frac{70.1}{27} = 2.59$$

f. Determine the obtained (F-distribution) value by using the formula:

$$F = \frac{MS_{between}}{MS_{within}} F = \frac{18.3}{2.59} F = 7.06$$

The STV, referred to as an F-distribution, is 7.06

5. Identify and compare the critical decision value (CDV) to the STV.
There are two degrees of freedom with ANOVA, which are computed by using the following:

$$df_B = k - 1,$$

$$df_W = N - k,$$

where
N = represents the total sample size
k = the total number of samples (groups)

Based on our information, we include our computed information:

$$df_B = 3 - 1,$$

$$df_W = 30 - 3 = 27,$$

a. Since our degrees of freedom are 2 and 27, we will locate the number 2 under the degrees of freedom column for df_B. We will also locate 27 under the column for df_W. Both numbers will be located at the 0.05 level of risk.

b. As indicated in the table, we will use ±3.35 as the value in which to reject the null hypothesis.

c. Since our STV is 7.06, we compare this value with the CDV, which is ±3.35. Provided in the appendix is the table that identifies the critical values for the ANOVA distribution.

6. If the STV > CDV, reject the null hypothesis.
As indicated in Figure 10.1, given that the STV (7.06) is greater than the CDV (±3.35), we reject the null hypothesis. Thus, the alternative hypothesis, which states that there is a difference between the mean number of years of the three different samples, is accepted.

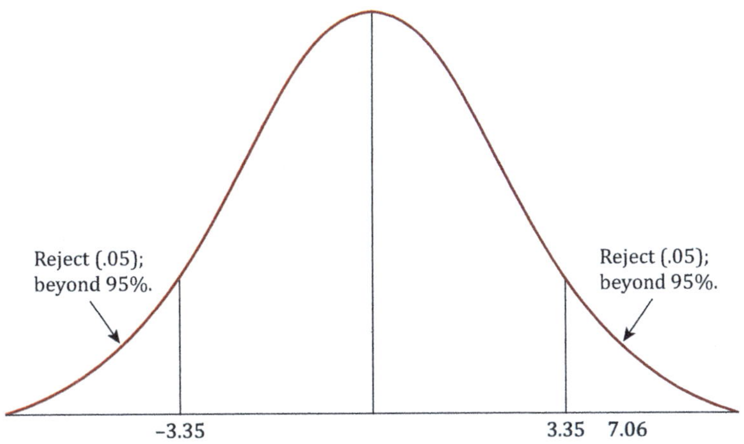

FIGURE 10.1 Normal Curve Illustration of Test Results

In our answer provided, notice the difference in comparison to the results of the *t*-test (in the previous chapter). In particular, the degrees of freedom identified for the between group and within group are listed.

The results of the test are displayed in this manner:

$$F_{(2,27)} = 7.06; p < 0.05$$

ANOVA Test (Example 2)

For our second and final example, consider the following with respect to sources of delinquency and length of therapy among youth.

TABLE 10.3 **Sources of Delinquency and Months of Therapy**

Family	X^2	Abuse	X^2	Drugs	X^2	Trauma	X^2
4	16	9	81	12	144	10	100
3	9	12	144	14	196	8	64
4	16	13	169	15	225	6	36
2.5	6.25	11	121	14	196	7.5	56.25
3.5	12.25			10	100	10	100
4	16			13	169		
2	4						
n = 7		n = 4		n = 6		n = 5	
$\Sigma X = 23$	$\Sigma X^2 = 79.5$	$\Sigma X = 45$	$\Sigma X^2 = 515$	$\Sigma X = 78$	$\Sigma X^2 = 1030$	$\Sigma X = 41.5$	$\Sigma X^2 = 356$
$\bar{x} = 3.3$		$\bar{x} = 11.2$		$\bar{x} = 13$		$\bar{x} = 8.3$	

As an expert in identifying delinquency risk factors, you believe there is a significant difference between the mean number of months of therapy among the four different samples.

1. Identify the null and alternative hypotheses.

   The null hypothesis indicates there is no difference between the mean number of months of therapy among the four different samples. The alternative hypothesis states that there is a difference between the mean number of months of therapy among the four different samples.

$$H_0: \mu_1 = \mu_2 = \mu_3 = \mu_4$$
$$H_1: \bar{x}_1 \neq \bar{x}_2 \neq \bar{x}_3 \neq \bar{x}_4$$

2. Identify the level of risk or significance.

   Our selected level of risk is 0.05.

3. Choose the appropriate test.

   Given the level of measurement with the independent (categorical) and dependent (continuous) variables, along with examining mean differences with at least three groups, we selected an ANOVA test.

4. Compute and identify the STV.

   a. Include the numbers from Table 10.3 into the ANOVA test formula using the following calculation steps:

   b. To begin, we must compute the total sum of squares:

      $= (79.5 + 515 + 1030 + 356.3) - (23 + 45 + 78 + 41.5)^2/22$

      $= 1980 - (187.5)^2/22$

      $= 1980 - 35{,}156/22$

      $= 1980 - 1598$

      $= 382$

   c. A cumulative mean is computed:

      $= 23 + 45 + 78 + 41.5/22 = 187.5/22 = 8.5$

   d. Compute the between-groups sum of squares:

      $= 7(3.3 - 8.5)^2 + 4(11.3 - 8.5)^2 + 6(13 - 8.5)^2 + 5(8.3 - 8.5)^2$

      $= 7(-5.2)^2 + 4(2.8)^2 + 6(4.5)^2 + 5(-0.2)^2$

      $= 7(27.04) + 4(7.84) + 6(20.25) + 5(0.04)$

      $= 189.2 + 31.36 + 121.5 + 0.2$

      $= 342.26$

   e. Compute the within-group sum of squares:

      $382 - 342.26 = 39.74$

Compute the means square based on the following formulas:

$$MS_B = \frac{ss_B}{k-1}$$

$$MS_B = \frac{342.26}{4-1} = \frac{342.26}{3} = 114$$

$$MS_W = \frac{ss_W}{N-k}$$

$$MS_W = \frac{39.74}{22-4} = \frac{39.74}{18} = 2.2$$

Determine the obtained (F-distribution) value by using the formula:

$$F = \frac{MS_{between}}{MS_{within}} \quad F = \frac{114}{2.2} \quad F = 51.08$$

The STV, referred to as an F-distribution, is 51.08

5. Identify and compare the CDV to the STV.
   a. There are two degrees of freedom with ANOVA, which are computed by using the following:

$$df_B = k - 1,$$

$$df_W = N - k,$$

   where
   N = represents the total sample size
   k = the total number of samples (groups)

   Based on our information, we include our computed information:

$$df_B = 4 - 1 = 3$$

$$df_W = 22 - 4 = 18$$

   b. Since our degrees of freedom are 3 and 18, we will locate 3 under the degrees of freedom column for df_B. We will also locate 18 under the column for df_W. Both numbers will be located at the 0.05 level of risk.
   c. As indicated in the table, we will use 3.16 as the value in which to reject the null hypothesis.
   d. Since our STV is 51.08, we compare this value with the CDV, which is 3.16. As mentioned previously, provided in the appendix is the table that identifies the critical values for the ANOVA distribution.
6. If the STV > CDV, reject the null hypothesis.
   Given that the STV (51.08) is greater than the CDV (3.16), we reject the null hypothesis. Thus, the alternative hypothesis, which states that there is a difference between the mean number of months of the four different samples, is true. See Figure 10.2 for visual details.

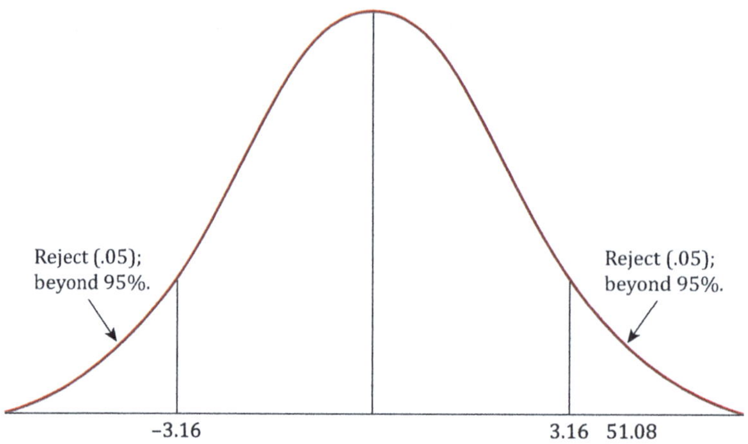

FIGURE 10.2 Normal Curve Illustration of Test Results

The results are displayed in this manner:

$$F_{(3, 18)} = 51.08; p < 0.05$$

Chapter Learning Assessment Questions

To gauge your learning, provide answers to the following questions:

1. Based on the following results:

$$F_{(2, 12)} = ?; p < 0.05$$

   Which of the following is the correct *f*-test statistic?
   a. 3.89
   b. 4.1
   c. 3.98
   d. none of the above
2. To determine the degrees of freedom between groups, one must ___________.
   a. subtract 1 from the total number of samples
   b. add the total number of samples together and divide by 1
   c. divide the total number of samples by 1
   d. none of the above

Answers

1. a
2. a

Post Hoc Tests With ANOVA

Despite the benefit of being able to determine mean differences between three or more groups, the exclusive use of ANOVA does not identify the source of any actual group differences. For example, consider the following mean values for each group: Group 1 (4), Group 2 (1), and Group 3 (1).

To determine whether means differences exist between the groups, the information in Table 10.4 reveals the results of AVONA:

TABLE 10.4 **ANOVA Results**

ANOVA (One Way)						
Groups	**Count**	**Sum**	**Average**	**Variance**		
Group 1	5	20	4	1.5		
Group 2	5	5	1	1.5		
Group 3	5	5	1	1		
Source of Variation	**SS**	**df**	**MS**	**F**	**P-Value**	**F crit**
Between Groups	30	2	15	11.25	0.001771	3.885294
Within Groups	16	12	1.33			
Total	46	14				

Despite the indication ($p < 0.05$) of a statistically significant difference between groups, we are not able to identify the exact source of the group differences. Does the difference exist between:

Group 1 and Group 2?
Group 1 and Group 3?
Group 2 and Group 3?

To address this problem, we use what is referred to as a post hoc test. A **post hoc test** (or posttests) is a test designed to identify the location of the actual mean differences between groups. In light of such, the post hoc test is used (1) once an ANOVA test has been conducted and (2) when a statistically significant difference is observed between groups. A commonly used type of post hoc test in the social sciences includes Tukey's HSD Test.

post hoc test A test designed to identify the location of the actual mean differences between groups.

Tukey's HSD Test

Tukey's honesty significant difference test, often referred to as Tukey's HSD, allows one to compute the means of values between groups. More specifically, the test provides a single value that determines the minimum difference between means, which indicates statistical significance. Referred to as HSD, this value is then compared to the different group means. Any difference that is greater than the HSD is an indication of a statistically significant difference between the two groups. Based on the information in our example, consider the following:

$$HSD = q\sqrt{\text{MS}_{\text{within}} / \text{n}}$$

where:

q = the studentized range statistic
$\text{MS}_{\text{within}}$ = variance within the samples
n = the number of values in each group

To determine the value of *q*, one must use a Tukey Q table, which is located near the end of the text. This includes identifying (a) the total number of groups (which is 3), (b) the degrees of freedom for $\text{MS}_{\text{within}}$ /df for the error term (which is 12), and (3) selecting the level of significance (0.05) (which is 3.77).

When including the numbers (from our example), we identify the following:

$$\text{HSD} = 3.77\sqrt{1.33 / 5}$$

$$\text{HSD} = 3.77\sqrt{.26}$$

$$\text{HSD} = 3.77\ (.515) = 1.94$$

Any value (computed from the mean differences between two samples) that is greater than 1.94 is considered significant.

Tukey's honesty significant difference A type of test designed to identify the location of the actual mean differences between groups. It provides a single value that determines the minimum difference between means, which indicates statistical significance.

For instance:

- The mean differences between Group 1 (4) and Group 2 (1) = (4 – 1) = 3
- The mean differences between Group 1 (4) and Group 3 (1) = (4 – 1) = 3
- The mean differences between Group 2 (1) and Group 3 (1) = (1 – 1) = 0

Based on the calculations, there are significant differences between Groups 1 and 2, as well as Groups 1 and 3.

Effect Size Eith ANOVA

As mentioned in previous chapters, once a statistically significant difference occurs, it might be wise to determine the extent of variability between the values among the three groups. When using ANOVA, this includes discovering what is referred to as the percentage of variance, which is designated as η^2. By referring to the data in Example 1, calculating the percentage of variance includes dividing the $\text{SS}_{\text{between}}$ by the SS_{total}.

$$\eta^2 = \text{SS}_{\text{between}} / \text{SS}_{\text{total}}$$

$$\eta^2 = 36.6/106.7$$

$$\eta^2 = 36.6/106.7 = 0.343\ (34\%)$$

The percentage of variance accounted for between the groups is 34%.

Chapter Learning Assessment Questions

To gauge your learning, provide answers to the following questions:
In the following formula:

$$HSD = q\sqrt{MS_{within} / n}$$

1. *n* represents which of the following?
   a. The number of values in each group subtracted from 1
   b. The number of values in each group divided by 1
   c. All of the above
   d. None of the above
2. To determine the effect size, one must ________________.
   a. divide the SS_{total} by the $SS_{between}$
   b. divide the $SS_{between}$ by the SS_{total}
   c. subtract the $SS_{between}$ from the SS_{total}
   d. none of the above

Answers

1. d
2. b

Final Thoughts

The purpose of the ANOVA test is to determine mean differences between three or more groups. Yet, it is possible that the existence of significant differences may stem from group differences that the researcher may not be aware of. For this reason, it is important to keep an open mind with regard to group characteristics along with direct, indirect, and interactive influences and outcomes.

Discussion

As a researcher, you are interested in examining whether the number of establishments that sell alcohol is associated with homicide rates within communities. For the required analysis, communities are coded with respect to the actual number of alcohol establishments located in their specific areas:

Number of Alcohol Establishments	Community Code	Number of Homicides
1–3	0	2
4–6	1	4
7–10	2	7
11+	3	8

In addition, you are also interested in whether gender plays a role with respect to the victims of alcohol-related homicide. Is the use of an ANOVA appropriate? If not, explain.

Chapter Summary

This chapter emphasized the following information:

Objective 1 – Define and explain the use of the ANOVA test

- ANOVA test is used to determine mean differences between three or more groups, as well as other important terms.
- Factorial analysis refers to an ANOVA test that employs the use of an additional independent variable. It is often used to identify interactive effects on the dependent variable by multiple independent variables.
- Between-group variance is a measurement that identifies the extent to which differences exist between groups or samples.
- Within-group variance is a measurement that identifies the extent to which differences exist between subjects or individuals within a group or sample.
- F-distribution is the test statistic of ANOVA.

Objective 2 – Formula for ANOVA test

- See the corresponding pages in the chapter.

Objective 3 – Example problem(s) and the ANOVA test

- See the corresponding pages in the chapter.

Objective 4 – Post hoc test for ANOVA test

- Post hoc test is a test designed to identify the location of the actual mean differences between groups.
- Tukey's HSD is a type of post hoc test used to identify the location of actual mean differences between groups.

Objective 5 – Effect size for ANOVA test

- To determine the extent of a difference between three or more samples, one may conduct what is referred to as the effect size.

Terms

ANOVA test
Two-factor ANOVA test
Between-group variance
Within-group variance
F-distribution
Post hoc test
Tukey's HSD

Chapter Review Questions

1. In order to determine mean differences between groups, a researcher is provided the option of conducting multiple *t*-tests or an ANOVA test. Why should the researcher select the ANOVA test instead of multiple *t*-tests?
   a. The use of multiple *t*-tests will increase a type I error.
   b. The use of multiple *t*-tests will increase a type II error.
   c. The use of multiple *t*-tests will involve the use of too many post hoc tests.
   d. The use of multiple *t*-tests will increase a type II error if a post hoc test is performed.
2. All of the following are considered assumptions of the ANOVA test *except*:
   a. It should only be used with samples that include three or more groups.
   b. The dependent variable is designated at the nominal level.
   c. A two-tailed test should be used.
   d. In the event of discovering a statistically significant difference, a post hoc test must be used to determine the source of the group differences.
3. A researcher is curious as to what types of alcoholic beverages (beer, wine, liquor) bear influence on the number of DWIs in a jurisdiction. To that end, answer the following questions:
   a. What is the independent variable?
   b. What is the dependent variable?
   c. What is the level of measurement for the independent and dependent variables?
   d. What is the null and alternate hypothesis that should be used?
4. A researcher is interested in whether the experience of a police officer (less than 12 months, between 1 and 10 years, 11+ years) impacts the number of arrests in a community. In light of such, provide answers to the following questions:
   a. What is the independent variable?
   b. What is the dependent variable?
   c. What is the level of measurement for the independent and dependent variables?
   d. What is the null and alternate hypothesis that should be used?
5. A researcher desires to determine if the type of disciplinary action imposed against youth (as measured by detention, short-term expulsion, or long-term expulsion) affects how

many days they attend school (Monahan et al., 2014). In light of such, provide answers to the following questions:

a. What is the independent variable?

b. What is the dependent variable?

c. What is the level of measurement for the independent and dependent variables?

d. What is the null and alternate hypothesis that should be used?

6. A researcher is interested in determining whether the race (White, Black, Asian) of an alleged offender bears influence on the number of charges filed by a district attorney. In light of such, provide answers to the following questions:

a. What is the independent variable?

b. What is the dependent variable?

c. What is the level of measurement for the independent and dependent variables?

d. What is the null and alternate hypothesis that should be used?

7. A researcher is interested in determining whether the security risk of inmates (minimum, medium, maximum) affects the number of disciplinary infractions within a state prison (Cunningham and Sorensen, 2006). In light of such, provide answers to the following questions:

a. What is the independent variable?

b. What is the dependent variable?

c. What is the level of measurement for the independent and dependent variables?

d. What is the null and alternate hypothesis that should be used?

8. Based on the following, determine if an ANOVA test or factorial analysis is warranted:

a. A researcher desires to investigate whether the type of response used by a school police officer reduces the number of delinquent acts among youth. Officer responses include (1) speaking with the youth in private, (2) speaking with the youth in the presence of a school administrator, and (3) speaking with the youth in the presence of their parents and a school administrator.

b. You are interested in whether the gender of a judge affects the sentence given to defendants who are convicted of the following offense categories: (1) assault, (2) aggravated assault, and (3) robbery.

c. A study examines the extent to which annual household income results in delinquency among youth. This includes the delinquency number of youth from the following categories of households: (1) \$9,000–\$18,000/year, (2) \$19,000–\$22,000/year, (3) \$24,000–\$26,000/year, and (4) \$27,000–\$35,000/year.

d. A government report reveals that gender and childhood trauma are associated with aggression among elementary school children. Aggression is measured using a psychological scale with scores between 0 and 15 (Del Pozzo et al., 2021).

9. Review the ANOVA table information near the end of the text and determine if the following STVs support the decision to reject the null hypothesis:

Level of Significance	Statistical Test Value	Degrees of Freedom (b/w)	Critical Decision Value	Reject the Null Hypothesis
0.05	12.15	3/3	9.28	
0.01	5.98	5/9	6.06	
0.05	4.12	2/12	3.89	
0.01	8.12	4/7	7.85	
0.05	4.18	5/8	3.69	
0.01	12.67	1/8	11.26	
0.01	14.25	2/5	13.27	
0.05	3.26	6/8	3.58	
0.05	21.56	4/2	19.25	

10. Crime is often identified as a social dilemma that is affected by the seasons of the year (Siegel, 2015). The following represents the number of crimes within certain months between 1990 and 2020. By using the risk level of 0.01, determine whether a significant difference exists between the number of reported crimes on the basis of the months provided.

Years	January-April	May-August	September-December
1970	78	89	73
1975	84	97	89
1980	81	101	91
1985	58	69	64
1990	48	58	53
1995	76	91	82
2000	51	62	53
2005	43	59	48
2010	39	56	48
2015	34	41	40
2020	72	97	83

11. "Aging out" is a term based on the assumption that as an individual increases in age, they are less likely to engage in crime or delinquency. The following represents the number of crimes among 12 individuals within certain time periods of their lives. By using the risk level of 0.05, determine whether a significant difference exists between the number of reported crimes on the basis of the following age categories.

13-18	19-30	31+
15	9	4
14	8	3
16	6	4
21	8	2
12	5	1

13	6	0
14	4	2
11	8	0
17	3	1
18	9	2
19	6	1
20	7	3

12. A study indicates that age is associated with delinquent behavior among youth. Listed below is the number of youth who were referred to the juvenile justice system by law enforcement officers from 2000 to 2019. This includes three categories of youth on the basis of age. Choose the appropriate test and determine if a significant difference (at 0.01 level of risk) exists.

Youth Referrals and Age

Year	8–10	11–13	14–16
2000	10	29	67
2001	12	25	58
2002	8	34	66
2003	12	44	75
2004	10	43	68
2005	8	51	56
2006	9	39	65
2007	5	48	78
2008	8	41	77
2009	8	42	70
2010	9	37	64
2011	12	36	59
2012	11	42	62
2013	9	48	64
2014	8	39	75
2015	11	27	64
2016	9	28	69
2017	8	29	70
2018	10	42	71
2019	9	32	76

13. For an act to be considered a crime, it is common that intent must be proved. In some states, there are varying types of intent. This includes carrying out an act intentionally, knowingly, and willingly. Provided below are the number of charges on the basis of the type of intent (as filed by a local district attorney). Choose the appropriate test and determine if a significant difference (at 0.05 level of risk) exists.

Year	Intentionally	Knowingly	Willingly
2000	2	6	3
2001	3	7	4
2002	2	6	4
2003	4	8	6
2004	2	6	4
2005	1	9	5
2006	3	8	4
2007	2	7	4
2008	5	9	7
2009	3	8	5
2010	4	7	5
2011	2	8	5
2012	5	7	6
2013	4	6	5
2014	2	7	5
2015	5	8	6
2016	3	7	5
2017	2	9	5
2018	4	7	5
2019	2	8	4
2020	5	7	6

14. In a victimology course, students are exposed to data that reveals the likelihood of crime victimization. In many instances, the data revealed information that defied their preconceived notions about crime-related victimization. For instance, they learned that (1) crime is often committed by individuals who are young; (2) crime often occurs among individuals of similar racial backgrounds (i.e., intraracial); (3) crime often occurs among individuals who are not considered strangers (Siegel 2015). At the completion of the course, each student was required to provide an in-depth presentation of the single factor they believed to be the strongest factor associated with crime victimization in their hometowns. Identified below is the number of student selections based on the aforementioned three factors about crime victimization. Choose the appropriate test and determine if a significant difference (at 0.05 level of risk) exists.

Factors Associated With Reported Crime Victimization

Number of Students in the Class	Youth	Intraracial	Nonstranger
25	8	8	9
25	6	7	12
25	9	5	11
25	7	8	10

Number of Students in the Class	Youth	Intraracial	Nonstranger
25	6	4	15
25	4	6	15
25	6	3	16
25	7	6	12
25	5	3	17
25	7	4	14
25	3	5	17
25	8	6	11
25	5	2	19
25	6	7	12
25	7	6	12

Answers

1. a
2. b
3.
   a. The independent variable is the types of alcoholic beverages.
   b. The dependent variable is the number of DWIs.
   c. The level of measurement for the independent variable is categorical. The level of measurement for the dependent variable is continuous.
   d. The null hypothesis is based on the assumption that there is no difference between the types of alcohol consumed and the number of DWIs. The alternative hypothesis is based on the assumption that there is a difference between the types of alcohol consumed and the number of DWIs.
4.
   a. The independent variable is the experience level of a police officer.
   b. The dependent variable is the number of arrests.
   c. The level of measurement for the independent variable is categorical. The level of measurement for the dependent variable is continuous.
   d. The null hypothesis is based on the assumption that there is no difference between the experience level of a police officer and the number of arrests. The alternative hypothesis is based on the assumption that there is a difference between the experience level of a police officer and the number of arrests.
5.
   a. The independent variable is the type of disciplinary action imposed against youth.
   b. The dependent variable is the number of days of school attendance.
   c. The level of measurement for the independent variable is categorical. The level of measurement for the dependent variable is continuous.
   d. The null hypothesis is based on the assumption that there is no difference between the type of disciplinary action imposed against youth and the number of days of school attendance. The alternative hypothesis is based on the assumption that there is a difference between the type of disciplinary action imposed against youth and the number of days of school attendance.

6.
  a. The independent variable is the race (White, Black, Asian) of an alleged offender.
  b. The dependent variable is the number of charges filed by a district attorney.
  c. The level of measurement for the independent variable is categorical. The level of measurement for the dependent variable is continuous.
  d. The null hypothesis is based on the assumption that there is no difference between the race (White, Black, Asian) of an alleged offender and the number of charges filed by a district attorney. The alternative hypothesis is based on the assumption that there is a difference between the race (White, Black, Asian) of an alleged offender and the number of charges filed by a district attorney.

7.
  a. The independent variable is the security risk of inmates.
  b. The dependent variable is the number of disciplinary infractions within a state prison.
  c. The level of measurement for the independent variable is categorical. The level of measurement for the dependent variable is continuous.
  d. The null hypothesis is based on the assumption that there is no difference between the security risk of inmates and the number of disciplinary infractions within a state prison. The alternative hypothesis is based on the assumption that there is a difference between the security risk of inmates and the number of disciplinary infractions within a state prison.

8.
  a. ANOVA
  b. factorial analysis
  c. ANOVA
  d. factorial analysis

9.

Level of Significance	Statistical Test Value	Degrees of Freedom (b/w)	Critical Decision Value	Reject the Null Hypothesis
0.05	12.15	3/3	9.28	Y
0.01	5.98	5/9	6.06	N
0.05	4.12	2/12	3.89	Y
0.01	8.12	4/7	7.85	Y
0.05	4.18	5/8	3.69	Y
0.01	12.67	1/8	11.26	Y
0.01	14.25	2/5	13.27	Y
0.05	3.26	6/8	3.58	N
0.05	21.56	4/2	19.25	Y

10. Given that the *f*-test value of (1.51) is not greater than the CDV (5.39), there is no statistically significant difference between the categories of months identified and the number of crimes reported.
11. Given that the *f*-test value of (113) is greater than the CDV (3.28), there is a statistically significant difference between the number of crimes reported and the age categories identified.
12. Given that the *f*-test value of (501.7) is greater than the CDV (4.99), there is a statistically significant difference between the number of individuals (on the basis of age) with regard to juvenile court referrals.

13. Given that the *f*-test value of (85) is greater than the CDV (3.1), there is a statistically significant difference between the three different types of intent.
14. Given that the *f*-test value of (61.7) is greater than the CDV (3.21), there is a statistically significant difference between the three different types of victimization factors as provided by the students.

Matching: Place the letter of the following definitions with its corresponding term.

____1. ANOVA test	a. a type of post hoc test used to identify the location of actual mean differences between groups
____2. Two-factor ANOVA	b. used to determine mean differences between three or more groups
____3. Between-group variance	c. an ANOVA test that employs the use of an additional independent variable
____4. Within-group variance	d. a measurement that identifies the extent to which differences exist among subjects or individuals within a group or sample
____5. F-distribution	e. the test statistic of ANOVA
____6. Post hoc test	f. a measurement that identifies the extent to which differences exist between groups or samples
____7. Tukey's HSD	g. a test designed to identify the location of the actual mean differences between groups

Answers

1. b
2. c
3. f
4. d
5. e
6. g
7. a

Bibliography

Bekbolatkyzy, D. S., Yerenatovna, D. R., Maratuly, Y. A., Makhatovna, A. G., & Beaver, K. M. (2019). Aging out of adolescent delinquency: Results from a longitudinal sample of youth and young adults. *Journal of Criminal Justice, 60*, 108–116.

Cunningham, M. D., & Sorensen, J. R. (2006). Nothing to lose? A comparative examination of prison misconduct rates among life-without-parole and other long-term high-security inmates. *Criminal Justice and Behavior, 33*(6), 683–705.

Del Pozzo, J., Walsh-Messinger, J., & Antonius, D. (2021). The influence of childhood trauma on aggression and violent behavior in first episode psychosis: a critical review. *Aggression and violent Behavior, 61*, 101677.

Monahan, K. C., VanDerhei, S., Bechtold, J., & Cauffman, E. (2014). From the schoolyard to the squad car: School discipline, truancy, and arrest. *Journal of Youth and Adolescence, 43*(7), 1110–1122.

Siegel, L. J. (2015). *Criminology: Theories, patterns, and typologies.* Cengage Learning.

Chapter 10 SPSS and Workbook Questions

SPSS and ANOVA Test

In order to compute the ANOVA test using SPSS, use the following example:

A professor introduces the use of restorative justice practices in response to deviant behavior among youth. In order to gauge an understanding of the content provided, the professor distributes a survey to students. Overall, the survey includes information that identifies each student's opinion regarding the effectiveness of restorative justice. More specifically, one question offers students the option of selecting which type of restorative justice practice they would prefer to experience. Listed below is an example of the question:

As one who prefers the use of restorative justice practices (in response to the commission of an offense), which type of restorative justice practice would you consider participating in?

a. Victim-offender mediation (VOM)
b. Restorative boards (RB)
c. Peacemaking circles (PC)
d. None of the above

Identified below are the results that reveal how the students responded to the question:

VOM	RB	PC
4	2	2
5	3	3
4	2	2
5	1	4

In general, VOM uses an approach that includes a minimal amount of participants. This includes the offender, victim, and mediator. Comparatively, both RB and PC involve a greater number of participants. In light of such, you believe that students, who might be more concerned with how others view them, are likely to select the VOM in comparison to RB or PC. In order to test your assumption, through the use of SPSS, compute an ANOVA test.

Entry of Data—SPSS

1. Select variable view to include information associated with the variables of interest. In our example, this would include the three types of restorative justice practices: (1) VOM, (2) RB, and (3) PC.
2. In the first row, include the term *VOM* under the column identified as name.
3. For the remaining groups, which include *RB* and *PC*, follow the same procedure as noted above.
4. Select data view to include the scores for each group in each corresponding column.
5. Once the scores have been added in each column, return to the variable view and include values that correspond to each score.

IMAGE 10.1

IMAGE 10.2

IMAGE 10.3

Analysis of Data—SPSS

1. Select analyze, select compare means and proportions, and choose one-way ANOVA.
2. Select the variable *source* and move it to the box identified as factor. In the same manner, select the variable *preference* and move it to the box identified as dependent list.
3. In the options section, under the term "statistics," select the descriptive in order to reveal the statistics of the sample.
4. After all desired functions have been selected, select OK.

Output of Data Analysis—SPSS

The output of the data analysis includes a total of two tables. Table 1 includes information that identifies the descriptive statistics of each independent variable. This includes the mean and sample size, as well as the standard deviation and standard error for each variable. Table 2 identifies the results of the ANOVA test. This includes the SS (sum of squares), degrees of freedom (df), mean square, and *f*-test. Finally, the table also includes details associated with the p-value (0.005), which demonstrates a statistically significant difference between the three types of preferences.

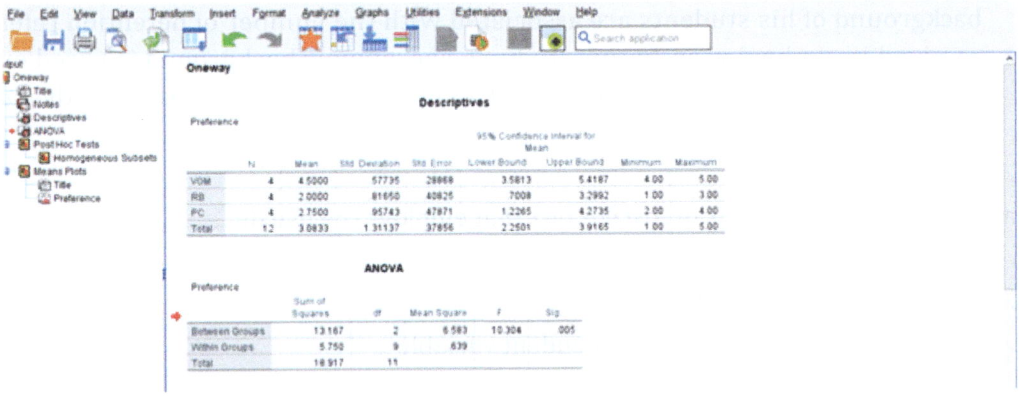

Oneway

Descriptives

Preference

	N	Mean	Std. Deviation	Std. Error	95% Confidence Interval for Mean: Lower Bound	95% Confidence Interval for Mean: Upper Bound	Minimum	Maximum
VOM	4	4.5000	.57735	.28868	3.5813	5.4187	4.00	5.00
RB	4	2.0000	.81650	.40825	.7008	3.2992	1.00	3.00
PC	4	2.7500	.95743	.47871	1.2265	4.2735	2.00	4.00
Total	12	3.0833	1.31137	.37856	2.2501	3.9165	1.00	5.00

ANOVA

Preference

	Sum of Squares	df	Mean Square	F	Sig.
Between Groups	13.167	2	6.583	10.304	.005
Within Groups	5.750	9	.639		
Total	18.917	11			

IMAGE 10.4

Workbook Questions

Objective 1—Define and Explain the Use of the ANOVA Test

- ANOVA test is used to determine mean differences between three or more groups.
- Factorial analysis refers to an ANOVA test that employs the use of an additional independent variable. It is often used to identify interactive effects on the dependent variable by multiple independent variables.
- Between-group variance is a measurement that identifies the extent to which differences exist between groups or samples.
- Within-group variance is a measurement that identifies the extent to which differences exist between subjects or individuals within a group or sample.
- F-distribution is the test statistic of ANOVA.

Corresponding Questions

1. An ANOVA test is used to determine mean differences between groups that include categorical independent and continuous dependent variables.
   a. two
   b. two or more
   c. three
   d. three or more
2. Which of the following represents the appropriate use of an ANOVA test?
   a. A study that examines the relationship between gender, race, and the number of months a suspect is detained in a correctional facility.
   b. Research that investigates an association between criminal offense category and the number of years an individual receives during sentencing. The criminal offense category is based on whether an individual was convicted of a drug, property, or public disorder offense.
   c. A middle school teacher is curious as to whether the race, gender, and socioeconomic background of his students are associated with the number of detention referrals received in a school year. In this study, socioeconomic background is based on the annual income of each student's parents. This includes parents who earned either above or below $25,000 each year.
   d. All of the above
3. Factorial analysis refers to an ANOVA test that employs the use of ________ variable.
   a. an additional independent variable
   b. an additional dependent variable
   c. an additional independent or dependent variable
   d. All of the above
4. Factorial analysis is often used to identify interactive effects on the ________ variable by multiple ________ variables.
   a. dependent/independent
   b. independent/dependent
   c. independent/independent
   d. dependent/dependent
5. Based on the following, identify which requires the use of an ANOVA or a factorial analysis test.
   a. In a program designed to prevent drug use among youth, a researcher believes that youth who engage in certain activities will likely result in a decreased number of drug-related arrests. These activities include active listening, effective communication, and self-control techniques.
   b. Studies reveal the attempt by law enforcement to reduce crime in communities (Pizza et al., 2019). In an effort to prevent crime in a small community, a local police department uses several measures within a 6-month period, which results in a decrease in serious

violent crime. This includes the use of CCTV, additional street lighting, and metal detectors. During the last month (of the 6-month period), the police department included the use of computers in their patrol cars to determine its impact on the amount of serious violent crime in the community.

c. After a 2-week discussion related to the use of discretion among police officers, a professor is interested in whether students are able to comprehend the amount of information they received. This includes administering a total of 5 exams among a total of 300 students. Once the exams are completed, the professor determines whether student classification (e.g., freshman, sophomore) is associated with passing grades, which is any grade above 70 points.

d. A local nonprofit agency offers a diversion program for individuals accused of certain offenses. This program, which includes anger management, restitution, and community service, has resulted in a decrease in detention costs and recidivism within a jurisdiction.

e. Within a 10-year period, a state probation office used certain intermediate measures, which resulted in the reduction of costs associated with the use and construction of jails within a specific region. More specifically, these intermediate measures included restitution, house arrest, and GPS. In a more recent time period, the state probation office used the same approach in determining whether the intermediate measures were associated with cost reductions, but in this case, they included the gender of each probationer.

Answers

1. d
2. d
3. a
4. a
5.
   a. ANOVA
   b. factorial analysis
   c. ANOVA
   d. ANOVA
   e. factorial analysis

Objective 2—Formula for ANOVA Test

- See the corresponding pages in the chapter.

Objective 3—Example Problem(s) and the ANOVA Test

- See the corresponding pages in the chapter.

Corresponding Questions

Based on the following exercises (if applicable), be sure to include the null and alternative hypotheses within your answer.

1. After teaching over 400 students about theories associated with juvenile delinquency, a professor decided to spend a considerable amount of time discussing the routine activities theory. Overall, the theory posits that criminal victimization will likely take place under certain conditions. This includes (1) the availability of a suitable target, (2) the absence of a capable guardian, and (3) a motivated offender (Cohen and Felson, 1979). After discussing the theory, the professor is curious as to which single condition is believed to be more likely associated with crime victimization. He then polls all the students in each of his classes. Based on the following data, which includes the number of selections associated with each factor of the routine activities theory, compute an ANOVA test (with a risk level of 0.05) to determine if there is a significant difference between the selections.

Target	Guardian	Offender
1	9	12
3	7	11
5	8	12
3	6	14
5	9	12
4	6	14
6	8	11
4	9	12
5	6	14
2	5	15
3	6	17
1	6	16
5	8	17
3	9	18
6	7	15

2. After hearing a university-wide presentation associated with risk factors and juvenile delinquency, three different groups of students (with nearly 200 students in each class) shared their opinions with their professors. Students in Classroom 1 are convinced that community-based factors serve as the basis of the greatest number of arrests among youth. On the other hand, students in Classroom 2 believe that school-related factors are responsible for the rising amount of arrests among youth. Finally, students in Classroom 3 support the notion that family-related factors are significantly associated with high arrest numbers among youth. Based on the following data, which includes the number of selections associated with each factor of support, compute an ANOVA test (with a risk level of 0.05) to determine if there is a significant difference between the classrooms.

Classroom 1	Classroom 2	Classroom 3
16	11	7
15	13	9
14	14	7
16	12	9
15	13	8
16	14	13
13	10	15
12	8	17
14	8	8
16	9	4
19	7	19
12	9	18
16	14	21
19	15	17
18	16	12

3. During the first week of their Introduction to Corrections course, students were exposed to information related to the importance of classification within prison settings. This includes the process of inmates completing a battery of tests related to a number of individual factors (Tahamont, 2019). Examples of such include psychological, educational, and health-related information. Their professor is curious as to which factor is considered the most important among the students. To gain student feedback, students were required to complete a survey. Identified below are the results of the survey which reveal student support for three classification factors. Based on the following data, compute an ANOVA test (with a risk level of 0.05) to determine if there is a significant difference between the factors.

Educational	Health	Psychological
4	7	2
6	8	4
5	7	3
7	9	5
8	7	7
6	8	5
7	5	4
4	9	8
5	8	6
7	9	3

Answers

1. Given that the STV (124.3) is greater than the CDV (3.21), there is a statistically significant difference between the selected categories among the students.
2. Given that the STV (4.64) is greater than the CDV (3.21), there is a statistically significant difference between the classrooms.
3. Given that the STV (9.75) is greater than the CDV (3.35), there is a statistically significant difference between the selection of the factors.

Objective 4—Post Hoc Test for ANOVA Test

- Post hoc test is a test designed to identify the location of the actual mean differences between groups.
- Tukey's HSD is a type of post hoc test used to identify the location of actual mean differences between groups.

Objective 5—Effect Size for ANOVA Test

- To determine the extent of a difference between three or more samples, one may conduct what is referred to as the effect size.

Corresponding Question

1. A researcher believes that students have different levels of support in relation to the use of certain measures designed to address cybercrime. This approach is consistent with previous research measures (Brewer et al., 2019). To assess such differences, the researcher distributed surveys among three classes of students enrolled in a cybersecurity course. Listed below are the survey results of nearly 170 students, which identify each cybersecurity measure option along with corresponding student support:

Software Piracy	Copyright Infringement	Identity Theft
1	4	6
2	5	9
2	4	8
5	6	9
4	7	7
2	5	10
4	6	7
5	4	9
6	5	7
3	8	9

ANOVA: Single Factor						
SUMMARY						
Groups	***Count***	***Sum***	***Average***	***Variance***		
Software Piracy	10	34	3.4	2.711111111		
Copyright Infringement	10	54	5.4	1.822222222		
Identity Theft	10	81	8.1	1.655555556		
ANOVA						
Source of Variation	***SS***	***df***	***MS***	***F***	***P-value***	***F crit***
Between Groups	111.2667	2	55.63333	26.96768402	3.66052E-07	3.354131
Within Groups	55.7	27	2.062963			
Total	166.9667	29				

Based on the data provided, compute an effect size to determine if the differences between the groups are significant.

Answers

1.

$$\eta^2 = SS_{between}/SS_{total}$$

$$\eta^2 = 111.26/166.9$$

$$\eta^2 = 0.666 = 66.6\ (67\%)$$

The percentage of variance accounted for between the groups is 67%.

Bibliography

Brewer, R., de Vel-Palumbo, M., Hutchings, A., Holt, T., Goldsmith, A., & Maimon, D. (2019). *Cybercrime prevention: Theory and applications*. Springer Nature.

Cohen, L. E., & Felson, M. (1979). Social change and crime rate trends: A routine activity approach. *Crime: Critical Concepts in Sociology, 1*, 316.

Piza, E. L., Welsh, B. C., Farrington, D. P., & Thomas, A. L. (2019). CCTV surveillance for crime prevention: A 40-year systematic review with meta-analysis. *Criminology & Public Policy, 18*(1), 135–159.

Tahamont, S. (2019). The effect of facility security classification on serious rules violation reports in California prisons: A regression discontinuity design. *Journal of Quantitative Criminology, 35*(4), 767–796.

Credits

CHAPTER 11

Two-Factor ANOVA Test

Facts are stubborn, but statistics are more pliable.
—Mark Twain

Objectives

1. Define and explain the use of the two-factor ANOVA test
2. Identify the formula for computing a two-factor ANOVA test
3. Compute a two-factor ANOVA test(s)
4. Discuss the significance of effect size

Gender,Military Experience and Simulation Scores

Within law enforcement training, you discover that training cadets are exposed to shooting simulation exercises. As a researcher, you believe cadets, on the basis of gender and military experience, are more likely to achieve higher simulation shooting scores compared to cadets who do not have military experience (Johnson, 1998).

The Two-Factor ANOVA Test

To investigate your claim, a two-factor analysis of variance (or two-factor ANOVA) is suggested. As mentioned in the previous chapter, an analysis of variance test is a statistical test that is used to determine mean differences between three or more groups. It often employs the use of single categorical independent variables and multiple continuous dependent variables. The **two-factor ANOVA** (or factorial analysis), on the other hand, utilizes two independent categorical variables (e.g., gender, military experience) and a continuous dependent variable (e.g., simulation score). In most cases, a two-factor ANOVA is used to determine the interactive effects of at least two independent variables on a single dependent variable.

two-factor ANOVA test A test used to determine mean differences between three or more groups that includes at least two independent variables. It is often used to determine the interactive effects on the dependent variable by multiple independent variables.

Assumptions of the Two-Factor ANOVA Test

As indicated in the previous chapter, the assumptions of the two-factor ANOVA test are consistent with the ANOVA test.

As indicated, the **two-factor ANOVA test** shares the same characteristics of an ANOVA test and a *t*-test. This includes the use of categorical variables as independent variables and the use of a continuous variable as the dependent variable. In our example, the categorical variables of gender and military experience serve as the independent variables. The continuous variable of simulation scores represents the dependent variable. What is unique about this technique is that a researcher can either (1) observe whether each independent variable has an impact on the dependent variable or (2) observe whether both independent variables have an interactive impact on the dependent variable. For instance, in the study of medicine and pharmacology, the availability and use of drugs are often examined in relation to certain factors (i.e., age, gender, etc.) to determine their impact under various conditions. A similar example examines the impact of both diet and exercise in relation to weight loss.

Based on our example, the two-factor ANOVA test is used to answer the following questions:

1. Is there a difference between shooting simulation scores and gender?
2. Is there a difference between shooting simulation scores and military experience?
3. Is the effect of military experience different on the basis of gender?

In short, the two-factor ANOVA test is used to determine mean differences within one analysis based on the use of a proportion.

Formula for the Two-Factor ANOVA Test

Formula for computing the two-factor ANOVA test:

$$\omega^2 = \frac{SS_B - (df_B)(MS_w)}{MS_w + SS_T},$$

where

ω^2 = the value of the effect size

SS_B = the sum of the squares between treatments

df_B = total degrees of freedom

MS_w = the mean sum of squares within treatments

SS_T = the corrected total sum of squares

Chapter Learning Assessment Questions

To gauge your learning, provide answers to the following questions:

1. In comparison to the use of an ANOVA test, the two-factor ANOVA test enables one to determine
   a. differences between the independent and dependent variables.

   b. whether independent variables have an interactive impact on the dependent variable.
   c. differences between variables in which the independent variable is categorical, and the dependent variable is continuous.
   d. All of the above
2. Which of the following topics are suitable for a two-factor ANOVA test?
   a. To what extent are gender and race associated with numerical grades in a particular course? Gender is measured by male, female, or other. Race is measured by Black, White, or Asian.
   b. Is criminal history and gender related to the amount of time a person must remain in custody within a local detention facility? Criminal history is measured by whether the defendant has at least two prior offenses.
   c. Does a defendant's citizenship status and socioeconomic background bear influence on the number of months they receive when sentenced to probation? Citizenship status is measured by American or non-American.
   d. All of the above

Answers

1. d
2. d

Computing Two-Factor ANOVA Tests

To test your understanding and application of the two-factor ANOVA test, consider the following scenarios.

Two-Factor ANOVA Test (Example 1)

As an example, in Table 11.1, the shooting simulation scores are provided for two samples of cadets based on the following:

TABLE 11.1 **Simulation Scores by Gender and Military Experience**

	Military Experience	Nonmilitary Experience
Males	The mean simulation score among males with military experience is 8.	The mean simulation score among males without military experience is 4.
Females	The mean simulation score among females with military experience is 6.	The mean simulation score among females without military experience is 3.

As a proponent of military experience, you believe there is a significant difference between the mean number of scores of the two different samples.

1. Identify the null and alternative hypotheses.

   The null hypothesis indicates there is no difference between gender (male or female), as well as military experience and the mean number of simulation scores among the two samples. Furthermore, there is no difference in the mean number of simulation scores owing to the interaction effect of gender and military experience status. The alternative hypothesis states that there is a difference between the mean number of scores of the two different samples.

$$H_0: \mu_{\text{Males}} = \mu_{\text{Females}}$$

$$H_0: \mu_{\text{Military Exp}} = \mu_{\text{No Military Exp}}$$

$$H_0: \mu_{\text{Gender/Military Exp}} = \mu_{\text{Simulation Score}}$$

$$H_1: x_{\text{Males}} \neq x_{\text{Females}}$$

$$H_1: x_{\text{Military Exp}} \neq x_{\text{No Military Exp}}$$

$$H_1: x_{\text{Gender/Military Exp}} \neq x_{\text{Simulation Score}}$$

2. Identify the level of risk or significance.

   Our selected level of risk is 0.05.

3. Choose the appropriate test.

   Given the level of measurement with the independent (categorical) and dependent (continuous) variables, along with examining mean differences and interactive effects with at least two groups, we selected a two-factor ANOVA test. Consider the following description in Table 11.2.

TABLE 11.2 **Simulation Scores by Gender and Military Experience**

		Factor B-Military Experience			
		Military Experience			
		Yes	No		
	Male	7	4		
		9	5		
		7	3		
		9	4		
		8	4		
Factor A - Gender		SS = 4	SS = 2		
		Total = 40	Total = 20	Total row 60	N = 20
		Mean = 8	Mean = 4		G = 105
	Female	5	3		$\Sigma X^2 = 637$
		7	4		
		6	3		
		7	3		
		5	2		

SS = 4	SS = 2	
Total = 30	Total = 15	Total row 45
Mean = 6	Mean = 3	
Total col. 70	Total col. 35	

4. Compute and identify the statistical test value (STV).
Stage 1 of this process involves creating a visual illustration of the research question, along with computing several items. This includes (a) the sum of values, (b) the sum of squares, and (c) the mean in each of the four groups. In addition, the total amount of values, the grant total, and the total sum of squares.

At this point, we include the numbers from Table 11.2 in the following steps and formulas:

a. To begin, we must compute the total sum of squares and degrees of freedom for total variability:

$$
\begin{aligned}
SS_{\text{total}} &= \Sigma x^2 - \frac{G^2}{N} \\
&= 637 - (105)2/20 \\
&= 637 - 11{,}025/20 \\
&= 637 - 551.3 \\
&= 85.7
\end{aligned}
$$

The formula for determining the degrees of freedom is $df_{\text{total}} = N - 1$, thus:

$$
\begin{aligned}
df_{\text{total}} &= 20 - 1 \\
&= 19
\end{aligned}
$$

b. Compute the within-group sum of squares. This includes commuting the *SS* of each individual treatment, along with the corresponding degrees of freedom:

$$
\begin{aligned}
SS_{\text{within treatments}} &= 4 + 4 + 2 + 2 \\
&= 12 \\
df_{\text{within treatments}} &= 4 + 4 + 4 + 4 \\
&= 16
\end{aligned}
$$

c. Compute the between-group sum of squares. This includes subtracting the SS_{within} from the SS_{total} and computing the degrees of freedom:

$$
\begin{aligned}
SS_{\text{between treatments}} &= SS_{\text{total}} - SS_{\text{within}} \\
SS_{\text{between treatments}} &= 85.7 - 12 \\
&= 73.7
\end{aligned}
$$

The between-treatment value of df is computed by the number of cells minus 1:

$$df_{\text{between treatements}} = \text{number of cells} - 1$$
$$df_{\text{between treatements}} = 4 - 1$$
$$= 3$$

Stage 2 of this process involves identifying the between-treatment differences for Factors A, B, and the interaction.

Factor A

The main effect of Factor A involves evaluating the mean differences between rows (as revealed in Table 11.2). This involves calculating a between-treatment *SS* using the row totals in the same manner we previously computed $SS_{\text{between treatments}}$ using the treatment total. For Factor A, the row totals are 60 and 45, which were obtained by adding 10 scores.

$$SS_A = \sum \frac{T^2_{ROW}}{n_{ROW}} - \frac{G^2}{N}$$
$$= 60^2/10 + 45^2/10 - 105^2/20$$
$$= 360 + 203 - 551$$
$$= 12$$

Computing the *df* for Factor A is based on:

$$dfA = \text{number of rows} - 1$$
$$= 2 - 1$$
$$= 1$$

Factor B

The main effect of Factor B involves evaluating the mean differences between rows using the same process as Factor A. The difference is that this involves calculating a between-treatment *SS* using the column instead of row totals. To that end, the column totals are 70 and 35.

$$SSB = \sum \frac{T^2_{COL}}{n_{COL}} - \frac{G^2}{N}$$
$$= 70^2/10 + 35^2/10 - 105^2/20$$
$$= 490 + 122.5 - 551$$
$$= 61.5$$

Computing the *df* for Factor B is based on:

$$dfB = \text{number of columns} - 1$$
$$= 2 - 1$$
$$= 1$$

A × B Interaction

The function of A × B interaction is to reveal the differences not accounted for by the main effects of Factors A and B. To identify the corresponding *SS* and *df* interaction values ($SS_{A \times B}$), we subtract the SS_A and SS_B from the $SS_{between\ treatments}$ accordingly:

$$SS_{A \times B} = SS_{\text{between treatments}} - SS_A - SS_B$$
$$= 73.7 - 12 - 61.5$$
$$= 0.2$$

Computing the $df_{A \times B}$ is based on:

$$df_{A \times B} = df_{\text{between treatments}} - df_A - df_B$$
$$= 3 - 1 - 1$$
$$= 1$$

Stage 3 of this process involves identifying the mean squares and F-ratios.

This requires the development of F-ratios in which the denominator of each is designed to identify variance at the expense of no treatment effects. The within-treatments variance is identified as the mean square and is based on the following:

$$MS_{\text{within treatments}} = SS_{\text{within treatments}}/df_{\text{within treatments}}$$
$$= 12/16$$
$$= 0.75$$

The numerators of the F-ratio are derived from the information from Factor A, B, and the interaction of A × B

$$MS_A = SS_A/df_A \qquad MS_B = SS_B/df_B \qquad MS_{A \times B} = SS_{A \times B}/df_{A \times B}$$
$$MS_A = 12/1 \qquad MS_B = 61.5/1 \qquad MS_{A \times B} = .2/1$$

F-ratio information includes:

$$F_A = MS_A/MS_{\text{within treatments}} = 12/.75 = 16$$

$$F_B = MS_B/MS_{\text{within treatments}} = 61.5/.75 = 82$$

$$F_{A \times B} = MS_{A \times B}/MS_{\text{within treatments}} = .2/.75 = .26$$

1. Identify and compare the critical decision value (CDV) to the STV.

   Now that the F-ratios are identified, we determine if each value is statistically significant by looking at the critical values for *F* in the F-distribution table. Since the degrees of freedom for all factors are 1, our numerator (within the table) is 1. Our degrees of freedom for our denominator, based on our within treatments, is 16. The details of this process stem from the F-distribution table, which is located in the appendix.

   a. Since our degrees of freedom are 1 and 16, we will locate the number 1 under the degrees of freedom column for the numerator. We will then locate 16 under the column for the degrees of freedom for the denominator. Both numbers will be located at the 0.05 level of risk.
   b. As indicated in the table, we will use 4.49 as the value in which to reject the null hypothesis.

   Since our STV(s) are 16, 82, and 0.02, we compare these values with the CDV, which is 4.49.

2. If the STV > CDV, reject the null hypothesis.

   Given that the STVs (16 and 82) are greater than the CDV (4.49), we reject the null hypothesis. Thus, the alternative hypothesis, which states that there is a difference between the mean number of simulation scores of the two different groups, is true. However, given that the STV (0.02) is not greater than 4.49, we fail to reject the null hypothesis. To that end, there is no evidence of an interactive effect (gender x military experience) on the shooting simulation scores.

   For additional details, consider the following:

   As revealed below (Table 11.3), we obtained F = 16 for the main effect of A, which is gender. This main effect is significant because it is greater than the CDV of 4.49. A similar pattern is identified with the main effect of B. This includes an F-ratio of 82, which is military experience, which is also greater than the CDV of 4.49. Both findings suggest that gender and military experience have a significant impact on shooting simulation scores. Finally, the interactive effect of A × B revealed F = 0.26, which is not greater than the CDV (4.49). To that end, the interaction between gender and military experience does not have a significant impact on shooting simulation scores. Consider the final results of the two-factor ANOVA test in Table 11.3 and Figure 11.1.

TABLE 11.3 **Final Results**

Source	SS	df	MS	F
Between treatments	73.7	3		
Factor A	12	1	12	16
Factor B	61.5	1	61.5	82
A x B	0.2	1	0.2	0.26
Within treatments	12	16	0.75	
Total	159.4	22		

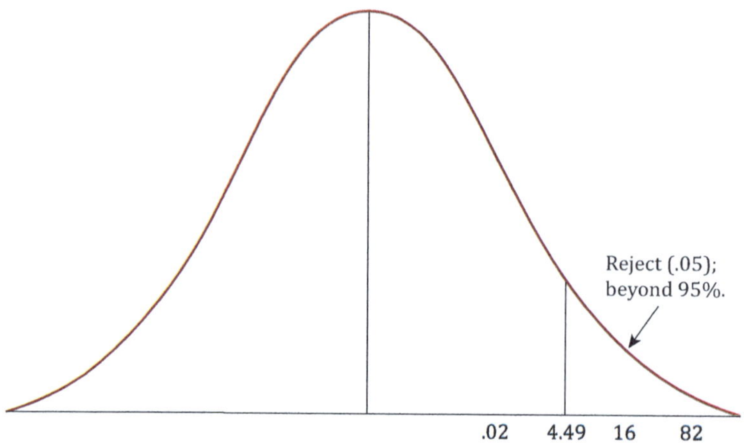

FIGURE 11.1 Normal Curve Illustration of Test Results

When providing the written results, include the *df* for interactive variables (A × B) and the *df* for the within-treatments value. This includes 1 and 16. The results of the test are displayed in this manner:

$$F_{(1, 16)} = 0.26; p > 0.05$$

Two-Factor ANOVA Test (Example 2)

For our second example, consider the following information in Table 11.4. In prisons, risk assessment tools are used to determine how individuals are housed in secure settings. This includes the use of certain factors, such as type of crime and criminal history.

Based on our example, the two-factor ANOVA test is used to answer the following questions:

1. Is there a difference between risk assessment scores and offense type?
2. Is there a difference between risk assessment scores and criminal background?
3. Is the effect of offense type different on the basis of criminal background?

As an example, let's use a revised version of the information from Table 11.4. In Table 11.4, the risk assessment scores are provided for two samples of convicted inmates. Risk assessment scores range between 1 and 5, with 1 being the lowest and 5 as the highest. Those with a score of 5 are considered a risk in relation to acts of violent behavior; those with a score of 1 are considered a lower risk in relation to committing acts of violence. Criminal background is based on the history of criminal behavior and conviction by the inmate. Consider the following in Table 11.4:

TABLE 11.4 **Risk Assessment Scores by Offense Type and Criminal Background**

	Criminal Background	Noncriminal Background
Violent	The mean risk assessment score among those convicted of a violent offense with a criminal background is 4.2.	The mean risk assessment score among those convicted of a violent offense without a criminal background is 3.4.
Nonviolent	The mean risk assessment score among those convicted of a nonviolent offense with a criminal background is 2.6.	The mean risk assessment score among those convicted of a nonviolent offense without a criminal background is 1.6.

After taking a course that reveals the impact of an individual's criminal background, you believe there is a significant difference between the mean number of scores of the two different samples (Hamilton, 2015).

1. Identify the null and alternative hypotheses.

   The null hypothesis indicates there is no difference between offense type (violent or nonviolent) and criminal background and the mean number of risk assessment scores among the two samples. Furthermore, there is no difference in the mean number of risk assessment scores owing to the interaction effect of offense type and criminal background status. The alternative hypothesis states that there is a difference between the mean number of scores of the two different samples.

$$H_0: \mu_{\text{Violent}} = \mu_{\text{NonViolent}}$$

$$H_0: \mu_{\text{Criminal Background}} = \mu_{\text{Noncriminal Background}}$$

$$H_0: \mu_{\text{Offense Type/Background}} = \mu_{\text{Risk Assessment Score}}$$

$$H_1: x_{\text{Violent}} \neq x_{\text{NonViolent}}$$

$$H_1: x_{\text{Criminal Background}} \neq x_{\text{Noncriminal Background}}$$

$$H_1: x_{\text{Offense Type/Background}} \neq x_{\text{Risk Assessment Score}}$$

2. Identify the level of risk or significance.

   Our selected level of risk is 0.01.

3. Choose the appropriate test.

   Given the level of measurement with the independent (categorical) and dependent (continuous) variables, along with examining mean differences and interactive effects with at least two groups, we selected a two-factor ANOVA test. Consider the following in Table 11.5:

TABLE 11.5 **Risk Assessment Scores by Offense Type and Criminal Background**

		Factor B-Criminal Background			
		Criminal Background			
		Yes	No		
Factor A - Offense Type	Violent	4	4		
		5	3		
		3	3		
		5	4		
		4	3		
		SS = 2.8	SS = 1.2		
		Total = 21	Total = 17	Total row 38	N = 20
		Mean = 4.2	Mean = 3.4		G = 59
	Nonviolent	3	1		$\Sigma X^2 = 205$
		3	2		
		2	1		
		1	1		
		4	3		
		SS = 5.2	SS = 3.2		
		Total = 13	Total = 8	Total row 21	
		Mean = 2.6	Mean = 1.6		
		Total col. 34	Total col. 25		

4. Compute and identify the STV.
Stage 1 of this process involves creating a visual illustration of the research question, along with computing several items. This includes (a) the sum of values, (b) the sum of squares, and (c) the mean in each of the four groups. In addition, the total amount of values, the grant total, and the total sum of squares.

At this point, we include the numbers from Table 11.2 in the following steps and formulas:

a. To begin, we must compute the total sum of squares and degrees of freedom for total variability:

$$SS_{\text{Total}} = \Sigma x^2 - \frac{G^2}{N}$$

$$= 205 - (59)^2/20$$

$$= 205 - 3{,}481/20$$

$$= 205 - 174.05$$

$$= 30.9$$

The formula for determining the degrees of freedom is $df_{total} = N - 1$, thus:

$$df_{total} = 20 - 1$$
$$= 19$$

b. Compute the within-group sum of squares. This includes commuting the *SS* of each individual treatment along with the corresponding degrees of freedom:

$$SS_{within\ treatments} = 2.8 + 5.2 + 1.2 + 3.2$$
$$= 12.4$$
$$df_{within\ treatments} = 4 + 4 + 4 + 4$$
$$= 16$$

c. Compute the between-group sum of squares. This includes subtracting the SS_{within} from the SS_{total} and computing the degrees of freedom:

$$SS_{between\ treatments} = SS_{total} - SS_{within}$$
$$SS_{between\ treatments} = 30.9 - 12.4$$
$$= 18.5$$

The between-treatment value of *df* is computed by the number of cells minus 1:

$$df_{between\ treatements} = \text{number of cells} - 1$$
$$df_{between\ treatements} = 4 - 1$$
$$= 3$$

Stage 2 of this process involves identifying the between-treatment differences for Factors A, B, and the interaction.

Factor A

The main effect of Factor A involves evaluating the mean differences between rows (as revealed in Table 11.2). This involves calculating a between-treatment *SS* using the row totals in the same manner we previously computed $SS_{between\ treatments}$ using the treatment total. For factor A, the row totals are 38 and 21, which were obtained by adding 10 scores.

$$SS_A = \sum \frac{T^2_{ROW}}{n_{ROW}} - \frac{G^2}{N}$$

$$= 38^2/10 + 21^2/10 - 59^2/20$$

$$= 144.4 + 44.1 - 174$$
$$= 14.5$$

Computing the *df* for Factor A is based on:

$$df_A = \text{number of rows} - 1$$
$$= 2 - 1$$
$$= 1$$

Factor B

The main effect of Factor B involves evaluating the mean differences between rows using the same process as Factor A. The difference is that this involves calculating a between-treatment *SS* using the column instead of row totals. To that end, the column totals are 34 and 25.

$$SS_B = \sum \frac{T_{COL}^2}{n_{COL}} - \frac{G^2}{N}$$
$$= 34^2/10 + 25^2/10 - 59^2/20$$
$$= 115.6 + 62.5 - 174$$
$$= 4.1$$

Computing the *df* for Factor B is based on:

$$df_B = \text{number of columns} - 1$$
$$= 2 - 1$$
$$= 1$$

A x B Interaction

The function of A × B interaction is to reveal the differences not accounted for by the main effects of Factors A and B. To identify the corresponding *SS* and *df* interaction values ($SS_{A \times B}$), we subtract the SS_A and SS_B from the $SS_{between\ treatments}$ accordingly:

$$SS_{A \times B} = SS_{\text{between treatments}} - SS_A - SS_B$$
$$= 18.5 - 14.5 - 4.1$$
$$= -0.1$$

Computing the $df_{A \times B}$ is based on:

$$df_{A \times B} = df_{\text{between treatments}} - df_A - df_B$$

$$= 3 - 1 - 1$$
$$= 1$$

Stage 3 of this process involves identifying the mean squares and F-ratios.

This requires the development of F-ratios in which the denominator of each is designed to identify variance at the expense of no treatment effects. The within-treatments variance is identified as the mean square and is based on the following:

$$MS_{\text{within treatments}} = SS_{\text{within treatments}} / df_{\text{within treatments}}$$
$$= 12.4/16$$
$$= .77$$

The numerators of the F-ratio are derived from the information from Factor A, B, and the interaction of A × B

$MS_A = SS_A/df_A$ $\quad$ $MS_B = SS_B/df_B$ $\quad$ $MS_{A\times B} = SS_{A\times B}/df_{A\times B}$

$MS_A = 14.5/1$ $\quad$ $MS_B = 4.1/1$ $\quad$ $MS_{A\times B} = -0.1/1$

F-ratio information includes:

$$F_A = MS_A/MS_{\text{within treatments}} = 14.5/0.77 = 18$$
$$F_B = MS_B/MS_{\text{within treatments}} = 4.1/0.77 = 5$$
$$F_{A\times B} = MS_{A\times B}/MS_{\text{within treatments}} = -1/0.77 = -1$$

1. Identify and compare the CDV to the STV.

   Now that the F-ratios are identified, we determine if each value is statistically significant by looking at the critical values for *F* in the F table, which is located in the appendix of this textbook. Since the degrees of freedom for all factors are 1, our numerator (within the table) is 1. Our degrees of freedom for our denominator, based on our within treatments, is 16.

   a. Since our degrees of freedom are 1 and 16, we will locate the number 1 under the degrees of freedom column for the numerator. We will then locate 16 under the column for the degrees of freedom for the denominator. Both numbers will be located at the 0.01 level of risk.
   b. As indicated in the table, we will use 8.53 as the value in which to reject the null hypothesis.

   Since our STV(s) are 18, 5, and –1, we compare these values with the CDV, which is 8.53.

2. If the STV > CDV, reject the null hypothesis.
   Given that the STV of 18 is greater than the CDV (8.53), we reject the null hypothesis. Thus, the alternative hypothesis, which states that there is a difference between the mean number of risk assessment scores of the two different groups, is true. However, since the values of 5 and –1 are not greater than 8.53, there is no evidence of an interactive effect (offense type x criminal background) on risk assessment scores.

   For additional details, consider the following:

   As revealed in Table 11.6, we obtained F = 18 for the main effect of A, which is offense type. This main effect is significant because it is greater than the CDV of 8.53. However, a similar pattern is not identified with the main effect of B. This includes an F-ratio of 5, which is criminal background, that is less than the CDV of 8.53. Both of these findings suggest that only offense type and not criminal background have a significant impact on risk assessment scores. Finally, the interactive effect of A x B revealed F = –1, which is not greater than the CDV (8.53). To that end, the interaction between offense type and criminal background does not have a significant impact on risk assessment scores.

TABLE 11.6 **Final Results**

Source	SS	df	MS	F
Between treatments	18.5	3		
Factor A	14.5	1	14.5	18
Factor B	4.1	1	4.1	5
A X B	−0.1	1	−0.1	−1
Within treatments	12.4	16	0.77	
Total	49.4	22		

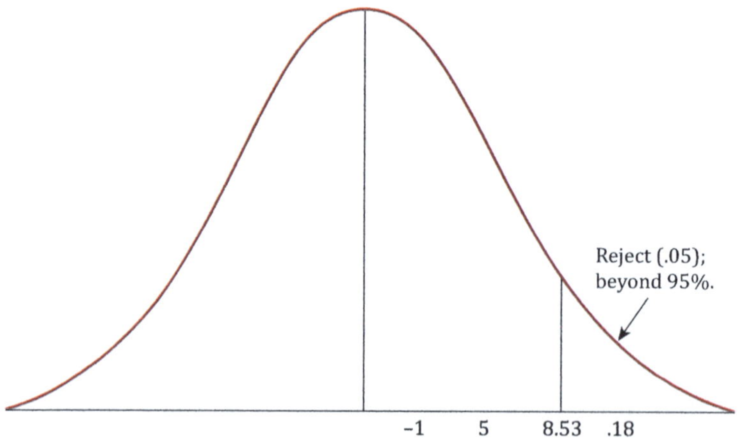

FIGURE 11.2 Normal Curve Illustration of Test Results

As stated in the previous example, the *df* for the interactive variables (A × B) and the *df* for the within-treatments value include 1 and 16. The results of the test are displayed in this manner:

$$F_{(1,16)} = -0.1; p > 0.05$$

Chapter Learning Assessment Questions

To gauge your learning, provide answers to the following questions:

1. Based on the following results:

   $$F_{(2,16)} = ?; p < 0.05$$

   Which of the following is the correct *f*-test statistic:

   a. 6.16
   b. 4.9
   c. 3.19
   d. none of the above

2. The function of the A × B interaction is to reveal the differences ________ main effects of Factors A and B.

   a. not accounted for by the
   b. along with the
   c. that are consistent with the
   d. none of the above

Answers

1. d
2. a

Effect Size With the Two-Factor ANOVA

As mentioned in previous chapters, once a statistically significant difference is identified, one might be interested in determining the extent of the variability between the groups. When using a two-factor ANOVA, this includes computing three separate values, which correspond to each factor. The formulas are provided below:

$$\text{Factor A: } \eta^2 = SS_A/SS_A + SS_{\text{within treatments}}$$

$$\text{Factor B: } \eta^2 = SS_B/SS_B + SS_{\text{within treatments}}$$

$$\text{Factor A} \times \text{B: } \eta^2 = SS_{A\times B}/SS_{A\times B} + SS_{\text{within treatments}}$$

Based on information in Example 2, calculating the percentage of variance includes dividing the following:

$$\text{Factor A: } \eta^2 = 14.5/14.5 + 12.4$$

$$\eta^2 = 14.5/26.9$$

$$\eta^2 = 0.53\ (53\%)$$

$$\text{Factor B: } \eta^2 = 4.1/4.1 + 12.4$$

$$\eta^2 = 4.1/16.5$$

$$\eta^2 = 0.24\ (24\%)$$

$$\text{Factor A} \times \text{B: } \eta^2 = -0.1/-0.1 + 12.4$$

$$\eta^2 = -0.1/12.3$$

$$\eta^2 = 0.01\ (1\%)$$

Given that each value reflects a percentage that is not based on the total variability, each value of the effect size is referred to as a partial eta.

In terms of providing a written response, consider the following (for each factor):

$$F_{(1,16)} = 18;\ p > 0.05,\ \eta^2 = 0.53$$

$$F_{(1,16)} = 5;\ p > 0.05,\ \eta^2 = 0.24$$

$$F_{(1,16)} = -1;\ p > 0.05,\ \eta^2 = 0.01$$

Final Thoughts

As indicated in this chapter, the purpose of the two-factor ANOVA test is to determine mean differences between three or more groups by using two independent variables. Despite the value of this approach, it is important to use data that corresponds to the use of a two-factor ANOVA test.

This includes categorical independent variables and continuous dependent variables. In relation to such, would the following research information qualify as a study that would call for the use of a two-factor ANOVA test? Explain?

A researcher believes that juveniles who are consistently exposed to (1) mentoring and (2) after-school tutoring are less likely to skip school. Mentoring is measured as to whether a juvenile has a mentor during a specific time-period. This includes the designation of a mentor as either yes or no. After-school tutoring is measured in a similar manner. Finally, skipping school is measured based on the number of days a student failed to attend school.

Discussion

A legal scholar is interested in determining whether gender and trial litigation experience are associated with the number of successful convictions in a month. This includes the following information, which identifies the litigation experience and gender of each attorney, along with their case conviction record for the month of June:

		Factor B Gender	
		Male	**Female**
	Experience (0–10)	17	19
		14	12
		16	16
		15	14
Factor A		18	19
Litigation Experience	Experience (11+)	17	18
		15	16
		18	17
		14	16
		17	19

Is the use of a two-factor ANOVA appropriate? Explain?

Chapter Summary

Chapter 11 discussed the following information:

Objective 1 – Define and explain the use of the two-factor ANOVA test.

- Two-factor ANOVA test (or factorial analysis) refers to a test used to determine mean differences between three or more groups that include at least two independent variables. It is often used to determine the interactive effects on the dependent variable by multiple independent variables.

Objective 2 – Identify the formula for computing a two-factor ANOVA test.

- See the corresponding pages in the chapter.

Objective 3 – Compute a two-factor ANOVA test(s).

- See the corresponding pages in the chapter.

Terms

Two-factor ANOVA test

Chapter Review Questions

1. Based on the following, determine if an ANOVA test or two-factor ANOVA analysis is warranted:
   a. A researcher desires to investigate the relationship between positive parental-youth relationships and academic achievement among adolescent students (Panaoura, 2021). Evidence of academic achievement is based on semester grade point average. Indicators of positive relationships consist of the types of conversations (e.g., directional or interactive communication) parents have with their offspring, as well as the gender of each parent.
   b. A graduate student desires to conduct research related to police-youth interaction in an educational setting. More specifically, the study focuses on interaction between school resource officers and at-risk youth at an alternative school. The factors within the study will determine whether the officer engages in supportive or authoritative use of their discretion. The impact of such is based on the number of disciplinary infractions the student receives as a result of their contact with the officer.
   c. After working in a private law firm for over 20 years, an attorney decides to review his work. In over 475 legal cases, the attorney discovered that the race of his clients was significantly associated with the amount of reduced time based on the plea deal they received from the district attorney's office. In other words, compared to non-White clients, White clients received higher amounts of reduced time during plea agreement negotiations. This association included the factors of race and socioeconomic status.
   d. A research study reveals that the length of prison sentences imposed by a criminal court judge may stem from the type of offenses (e.g., drug trafficking, theft by fraud, kidnapping) an individual is convicted of.
   e. As an expert in criminal justice reform, you believe that treatment is needed among those incarcerated in prison, especially those who are convicted of serious violent crimes (Houser et al., 2019). Before making a recommendation, you decide to conduct a pilot study in order to determine if cognitive behavioral therapy is an effective deterrent to violence and aggression among inmates. In your study, you decide to offer cognitive behavioral therapy on the basis of gender and criminal history. The impact of your

approach is measured by the number of violent complaints within the prison during a 2-year period.

2. Based on the following, compute the total in each section.
    a. Males
        i. Detained: 18, 25, 16, 12, 19, 22
        ii. Not detained: 12, 19, 10, 8, 12,12
    b. Females
        i. Detained: 9, 7, 12, 7, 8, 10
        ii. Not detained: 13, 11, 16, 11, 15, 13
3. Based on the following, compute the total and mean in each section.
    a. Minorities
        i. Arrested: 16, 23, 12, 9, 14, 16
        ii. Not arrested: 8, 15, 5, 4, 10,12
    b. Nonminorities
        i. Arrested: 6, 9, 5, 7, 6, 4
        ii. Not arrested: 18, 18, 17, 19, 21, 24
4. Based on the following, compute the total, mean, and SS in each section.
    a. >$50,000
        i. Private Attorney: 20, 27, 15, 13, 18, 21
        ii. Court-Appointed Attorney: 10, 17, 6, 6, 11, 13
    b. <$50,000
        i. Private Attorney: 8, 5, 10, 9, 8, 5
        ii. Court-Appointed Attorney: 21, 22, 21, 23, 25, 27
5. Based on the following, compute the row total
    a. Criminal History
        i. Vocational Training: Total = 199
        ii. Nonvocational Training: Total = 46
        iii. Total Row = 245
    b. No Criminal History
        i. Vocational Training: Total = 33
        ii. Nonvocational Training: Total = 150
        iii. Total Row = 183
6. Based on the following, compute the row total and grand total
    a. Parents with a college degree

   i. Pursuit of a college degree: Total = 132
   ii. Failure to pursue a college degree: Total = 55
   iii. Total Row = 187

b. Parents without a college degree

   i. Pursuit of a college degree: Total = 55
   ii. Failure to pursue a college degree: Total = 121
   iii. Total Row = 176
   iv. Grand Total = 363

7. Researcher (A) believes that youth who are reared in single-parent homes are more likely to engage in delinquency. Researcher (B) believes that youth raised in single-parent homes in which their parents earn below $25,000 a year are likely to engage in delinquency. The numbers within each sample represent the number of delinquent acts within a 6-month period. Based on this scenario, (1) complete the information below, (2) determine which researcher is correct by including your answer in a completed ANOVA table, and (3) use a risk level of 0.05.

	Factor B-Income			
	Above 25, 000/Year			
	Yes	**No**		
	4	7		
	3	8		
1 Parent	5	7		
	4	6		
	4	8		
Factor A-Household	SS = 3	SS = 2		
	Total = 21	Total = 17	Total row 38	N = 20
	Mean = 4	Mean = 3		G = 59
	1	3		$\Sigma X^2 = 205$
	0	2		
2 Parents	2	4		
	2	3		
	1	2		
	SS = 6	SS = 4		
	Total = 13	Total = 8	Total row 21	
	Mean = 3	Mean = 2		
	Total col. 34	Total col. 25		

8. Imagine a study that examines the relationship between police and youth. The study includes two research questions. Question 1: To what extent does the race of the youth impact an

officer's decision to refer a youth to the juvenile court system? Question 2: To what extent does the demeanor (e.g., respectful) of a youth impact an officer's decision to refer a youth to the juvenile court system? The numbers within each sample represent the number of youth who were referred to the juvenile court system in the past 18 months. Based on this scenario, identify whether there is an interactive association between the variables in the research questions identified. This includes (1) completing the information below, (2) providing your answer in a completed ANOVA table, and (3) using a risk level of 0.05.

		Factor B–Demeanor			
		Respectful			
		Yes	No		
		9	12		
		8	13		
	Black	10	12		
		9	14		
		6	15		
Factor A–Race		SS =	SS =		
		Total =	Total =	Total row	N = 20
		Mean =	Mean =		G =
		6	8		ΣX^2 =
		2	7		
	White	7	9		
		7	8		
		6	7		
		SS =	SS =		
		Total =	Total =	Total row	
		Mean =	Mean =		
		Total col.	Total col.		

9. As a member of a state parole board, you are responsible for reviewing inmate information in order to determine eligibility for parole. In making such important decisions, the board is required to develop an assessment tool to determine who is likely to achieve success if granted parole. Upon review of the numerous files of those who were previously granted parole and achieved success by avoiding recidivism, you notice the existence of two factors: vocational training and counseling. Along with your fellow members of the board, you believe that prison disciplinary records reveal the extent to which an inmate might be truly reformed and ready for community reentry. The numbers within each sample represent the number of disciplinary infractions among inmates who are seeking parole eligibility in the past 24 months. For the purpose of developing a reliable assessment tool, identify whether there is an interactive association between vocational training and counseling. This includes

(1) completing the information below, (2) providing your answer in a completed ANOVA table, and (3) using a risk level of 0.05.

		Factor B-Counseling			
		Completed Counseling			
		Yes	**No**		
		3	7		
		4	8		
	Yes	4	9		
		3	7		
		3	8		
		2	8		
Factor A-Vocational Training		SS =	SS =		
		Total =	Total =	Total row	N = 20
		Mean =	Mean =		G =
		8	11		ΣX^2 =
		9	13		
	No	10	13		
		9	12		
		10	14		
		12	15		
		SS =	SS =		
		Total =	Total =	Total row	
		Mean =	Mean =		
		Total col.	Total col.		

Answers

1.
   a. two-factor ANOVA
   b. ANOVA
   c. two-factor ANOVA
   d. ANOVA
   e. two-factor ANOVA
2.
   a.i. Total = 112
   a.ii. Total = 73
   b.i. Total = 53
   b.ii. Total = 79

3.
a.i. Total = 90; Mean = 15
a.ii. Total = 54; Mean = 9
b.i. Total = 37; Mean = 6.16
b.ii. Total = 117; Mean = 19.5

4.
a.i. Total = 114; Mean = 19; SS = 122
a.ii. Total = 63; Mean = 10.5; SS = 89.5
b.i. Total = 45; Mean = 7.5; SS = 21.5
b.ii. Total = 139; Mean = 23.1; SS = 28.8

5. 199 + 46 = Total Row of 245; 33 + 150 = Total Row of 183
6. 132 + 55 = Total Row of 187; 55 + 121 = Total Row of 176; G = 363
7.

Researcher (B) is correct based on the following:

ANOVA						
Source of Variation	*SS*	*df*	*MS*	*F*	*P-value*	*F crit*
Sample	14.45	1	14.45	18.64516	0.00053	4.493998
Columns	4.05	1	4.05	5.225806	0.036228	4.493998
Interaction	0.05	1	0.05	0.064516	0.802731	4.493998
Within	12.4	16	0.775			
Total	30.95	19				

8.

There is no interactive effect based on the following:

ANOVA						
Source of Variation	*SS*	*df*	*MS*	*F*	*P-value*	*F crit*
Sample	84.05	1	84.05	37.35556	1.50036E-05	4.493998
Columns	61.25	1	61.25	27.22222	8.46289E-05	4.493998
Interaction	8.45	1	8.45	3.755556	0.07048641	4.493998
Within	36	16	2.25			
Total	189.75	19				

9.

There is no interactive effect based on the following:

ANOVA						
Source of Variation	*SS*	*df*	*MS*	*F*	*P-value*	*F crit*
Sample	204.1667	1	204.1667	163.3333	4.4318E-11	4.351244
Columns	96	1	96	76.8	2.77199E-08	4.351244
Interaction	2.666667	1	2.666667	2.133333	0.15965933	4.351244
Within	25	20	1.25			

Biblography

Hamilton, M. (2015). Back to the future: The influence of criminal history on risk assessments. *Berkeley Journal of Criminal Law, 20*, 75.

Houser, K. A., Vîlcică, E. R., Saum, C. A., & Hiller, M. L. (2019). Mental health risk factors and parole decisions: Does inmate mental health status affect who gets released. *International Journal of Environmental Research and Public Health, 16* (16), 2950.Johnson, T. A. (1998). *The effects of higher education/military service on achievement levels of police academy cadets.* Texas Southern University.

Panaoura, R. (2021). Parental involvement in children's mathematics learning before and during the period of the COVID-19. *Social Education Research*, 2(1), 65–74. https://doi.org/10.37256/ser.212021547

Chapter 11 SPSS and Workbook Questions

SPSS and Two-Factor ANOVA Test

To compute the two-factor ANOVA test using SPSS, consider the following:

Research examines the impact of individual characteristics and career advancement on various components of the criminal justice system. For instance, suppose one is interested in determining the impact of education and gender on promotional opportunities among law enforcement officers (Todak et al., 2021). To achieve a particular rank in law enforcement, officers must often complete a series of assessment measures and processes. Examples include review boards, interviews, and examinations. Identified in Table 11.7 are the examination results of officers (as measured between 0 and 20) who desire the position of sergeant within a local metropolitan law enforcement agency.

TABLE 11.7 **Education, Gender, Promotion Scores**

	Degree	Diploma
Males (n = 15)	20	14
	19	12
	19	12
	17	14
	18	13
	16	12
	19	11
		9
Females (n = 15)	20	17
	20	17
	19	14
	20	
	20	
	19	
	19	
	20	
	16	
	14	
	14	

As a proponent of education, you are convinced that officers who possess post-secondary education are more likely to achieve higher examination scores in comparison to those with a high school diploma. You are curious, however, as to whether gender and educational status influence the examination scores of officers. Through the use of SPSS, compute a two-factor ANOVA test.

Entry of Data—SPSS

1. Select variable view to include information associated with the variables of interest. In our example, this would include gender, education, and score.
2. In the first row, include the term *gender* under the column identified as name.
3. For the remaining groups, which include *education* and *score*, follow the same procedure as noted above.
4. Select data view to include the scores for each group in each corresponding column.
5. Once the scores have been added in each column, return to the variable view and include values that correspond to each score. Consider the examples below.

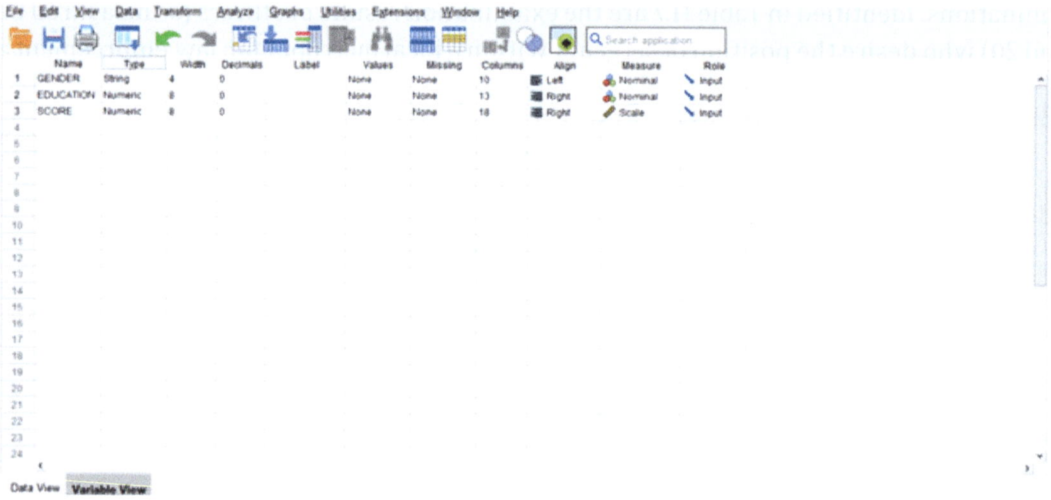

IMAGE 11.1

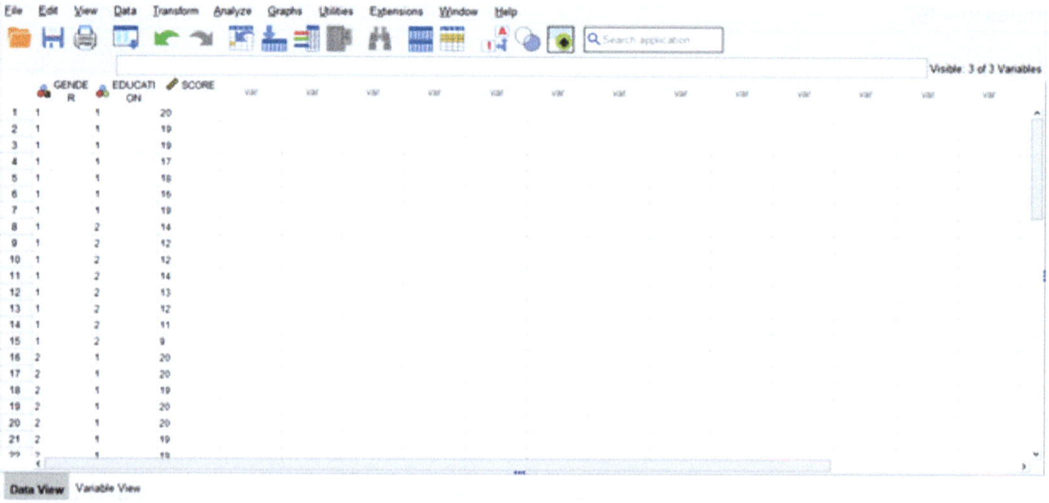

IMAGE 11.2

IMAGE 11.3

Analysis of Data—SPSS

1. Select analyze, select general linear module, and select univariate.
2. Select the variables *gender* and *education* and move them to the box identified as fixed factor(s). In the same manner, select the variable *score* and move it to the box identified as dependent list.
3. In the options section, under the term *display*, select descriptive in order to reveal the descriptive statistics of the sample.
4. After all desired functions have been selected, select OK.

Output of Data Analysis—SPSS

As revealed in the screenshot below, the results of the data analysis consist of two tables. Table 1 reveals the descriptive statistics of each independent variable, which includes gender and level of education. This includes the mean and sample size, as well as the standard deviation of both groups. The results of the two-factor ANOVA test are identified in Table 2. This includes the SS (sum of squares), degrees of freedom (df), mean square, f-test, and levels of significance (p-values). Based on the results, significant statistical differences exist between gender (0.019) and education (0.001) in association with examination scores. When observing the interactive influence of both independent variables on the dependent variable, we observe a significant statistical difference of (0.027).

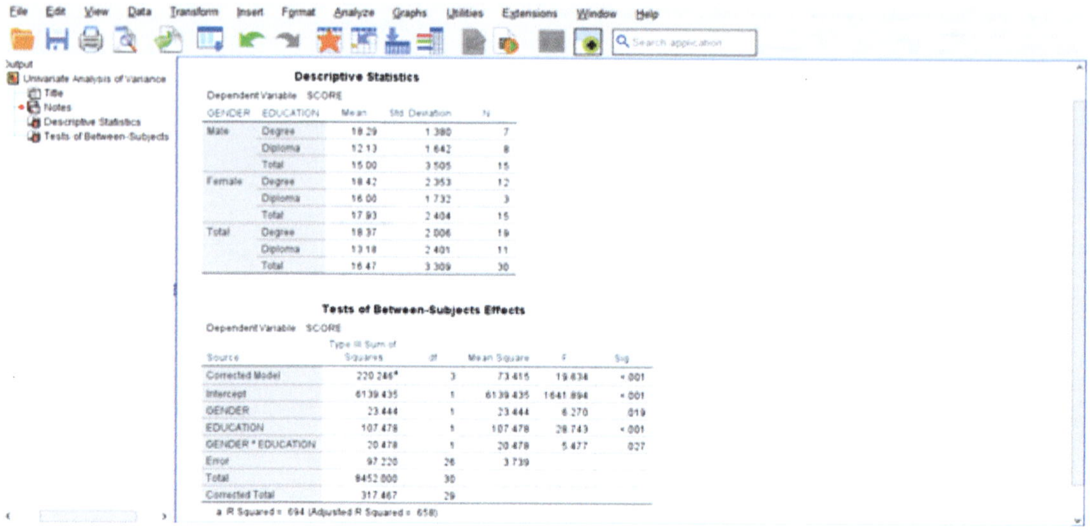

Descriptive Statistics

Dependent Variable SCORE

GENDER	EDUCATION	Mean	Std. Deviation	N
Male	Degree	18.29	1.380	7
	Diploma	12.13	1.642	8
	Total	15.00	3.505	15
Female	Degree	18.42	2.353	12
	Diploma	16.00	1.732	3
	Total	17.93	2.404	15
Total	Degree	18.37	2.006	19
	Diploma	13.18	2.401	11
	Total	16.47	3.309	30

Tests of Between-Subjects Effects

Dependent Variable SCORE

Source	Type III Sum of Squares	df	Mean Square	F	Sig.
Corrected Model	220.246[a]	3	73.415	19.634	<.001
Intercept	6139.435	1	6139.435	1641.894	<.001
GENDER	23.444	1	23.444	6.270	.019
EDUCATION	107.478	1	107.478	28.743	<.001
GENDER * EDUCATION	20.478	1	20.478	5.477	.027
Error	97.220	26	3.739		
Total	8452.000	30			
Corrected Total	317.467	29			

a. R Squared = .694 (Adjusted R Squared = .658)

IMAGE 11.4

Workbook Questions

Objective 1—Define and Explain the Use of the Two-Factor ANOVA Test

- A two-factor ANOVA test is a statistical test that is used to observe whether each independent variable has an impact on the dependent variable or whether both independent variables have an interactive impact on the dependent variable.

Corresponding Questions

1. What is unique about the ______________ is that a researcher can either (1) observe whether each independent variable has an impact on the dependent variable or (2) whether both independent variables have an interactive impact on the dependent variable.
   a. two-factor ANOVA test
   b. one-factor ANOVA test
   c. correlation test
   d. linear regression test
2. A researcher is interested in whether the race and gender of a suspect are associated with the number of hours they are interrogated by detectives (Blair, 2005). Race is measured by whether the suspect is either Black, White, or Asian. Gender is measured by the distinction of male or female. Based on these details, the researcher would likely use a __________ test.
   a. linear regression test
   b. one-factor ANOVA test
   c. two-factor ANOVA test
   d. a two-sample *t*-test

2. Studies point to the use of restorative justice measures among youth (Anfara et al., 2013). For example, restitution is recognized as a viable measure. Identified in the table below is the gender of middle school students who have been identified as high-risk youth, along with the corresponding mean number of conduct violations at a local public school. In light of such, consider the following:
   a. Researcher (A) believes that there is a difference between the number of conduct violations and the use of restitution practices.
   b. Researcher (B) believes that there is a difference between the number of conduct violations and gender.
   c. Researcher (C) believes that there is a difference between the number of conduct violations that stem from the interactive association between gender and the use of restitution practices.
   d. Researcher (D) believes that there is no difference between the number of conduct violations and the use of restitution practices or gender.

   Based on the following data, compute a two-factor ANOVA (with a risk level of 0.05) to determine if any of the assumptions offered by the researchers are accurate.

	Restitution	**No Restitution**
Males	2	5
	3	4
	2	5
	4	3
	3	5
	4	4
	2	6
Females	1	3
	2	4
	3	3
	2	5
	1	4
	2	5
	1	3

3. Research documents the existence of risk and protective factors associated with juvenile delinquency (Bean et al., 2006). Examples of protective factors include academic achievement, school attendance, and parental support of academic achievement among youth. A researcher believes that parents who consistently read in the presence of their children actually model support for activities related to academic achievement, which may indirectly serve as a protective factor for juvenile delinquency. On the other hand, in terms of a risk factor for delinquency, studies suggest that low socioeconomic status is associated with juvenile delinquency. However, the researcher is convinced that parental examples of

reading will interact with low socioeconomic status in order to serve as a viable protective factor. The following includes information includes the reading scores of youth, along with socioeconomic status and reports of reading examples exhibited by their parents. Based on the data provided, compute a two-factor ANOVA (with a risk level of 0.01) to determine if any of the assumptions offered by the researcher are accurate.

	Reading Example	No Reading Example
Less than 20,000/year	90	80
	85	81
	93	84
	87	81
	85	79
	95	79
	84	76
More than 20,000/year	88	81
	92	82
	86	73
	91	76
	79	82
	98	81
	81	77

Answers

1. Given that both F-ratios (4.43 and 4.14) of the victim-offender relationship and race extend beyond the F-critical value of 4.14, the assumption of Researcher (A) is supported. However, the F-ratio of the interactive association between victim-offender relationship and race is (0.49), which does not extend beyond (4.14). This finding does not support the assumption of Researcher (B).
2. The results reveal that the F-ratios of gender (7.68) and the use of restitution (33.13) extend beyond the F-critical value of 4.25, which indicates statistically significant differences between the variables. This supports the assumptions of Researchers (A) and (B) and fails to support the assumption of Researcher (D). Finally, since the interactive association between gender and the use of restitution reveals an F-ratio of 0.40, which does not extend beyond 4.25, the assumption of Researcher (C) is not supported.
3. Among the F-ratios of socioeconomic status and parental reading example, only the latter (26.49) extends beyond the F-critical value of 7.82. This provides partial support for the assumption of the researcher. In terms of the interactive association between the independent variables and the reading scores, the F-ratio of 0.02 does not extend beyond 7.82, thus, the assumption of the researcher is not supported.

Bibliography

Anfara Jr., V. A., Evans, K. R., & Lester, J. N. (2013). Restorative justice in education: What we know so far. *Middle School Journal, 44*(5), 57–63.

Bean, R. A., Barber, B. K., & Crane, D. R. (2006). Parental support, behavioral control, and psychological control among African American youth: The relationships to academic grades, delinquency, and depression. *Journal of Family Issues, 27*(10), 1335–1355.

Blair, J. P. (2005). What do we know about interrogation in the United States? *Journal of Police and Criminal Psychology, 20*(2), 44–57.

DeLisi, M., Jones-Johnson, G., Johnson, W. R., & Hochstetler, A. (2014). The aftermath of criminal victimization: Race, self-esteem, and self-efficacy. *Crime & Delinquency, 60* (1), 85–105.

Messina, N., Grella, C. E., Cartier, J., & Torres, S. (2010). A randomized experimental study of gender-responsive substance abuse treatment for women in prison. *Journal of Substance Abuse Treatment, 38* (2), 97–107.

Todak, N., Leban, L., & Hixon, B. (2021). Are women opting out? A mixed methods study of women patrol officers' promotional aspirations. *Feminist Criminology, 16* (5), 658–679.

Credits

CHAPTER 12

Chi-Square Test

The aim of science is to seek the simplest explanation of complex facts. ...
Seek simplicity and distrust it.
—A. N. Whitehead

Objectives

1. Define and explain the use of the chi-square test
2. Identify the formula for computing the chi-square test
3. Computing the chi-square test
4. Discuss the significance of effect size

Introduction—Parametric and Nonparametric Tests

At this point, we have previously discussed the *t*-test and the ANOVA test, which are referred to as types of hypothesis tests that fall under the category of parametric tests. In other words, these two types of tests are only used under certain conditions or assumptions. The assumptions of a parametric test are based on the characteristics of data that might become part of a sample within a research study (Sedgwick, 2015). More specifically, the data (within a parametric test) must

1. reflect normal distribution,
2. be independent,
3. have approximate equal distance (variance) from each other,
4. reflect random selection,
5. not include extreme values (i.e., outliers), and
6. include interval or ratio data.

There are occasions in which access to certain types of data may not provide the opportunity to use a parametric test. For instance, consider the following two statements:

1. Researcher (A) is interested in determining whether the *proportion* of youth who major in criminal justice is related to individuals who have criminal justice experience as a law enforcement officer.

2. Researcher (B) is interested in determining whether the *number* of youth who major in criminal justice is related to individuals who have criminal justice experience as a law enforcement officer.

Notice the term "proportion," which is not the same as number. Within a parametric test, numbers are often used; within a nonparametric test, proportions may be used. If a researcher desires to investigate a difference in relation proportions (or relative frequencies), they might consider using a nonparametric test. For this reason, the use of a nonparametric test requires the use of categorical data. In our example (with Researcher (A)), students (who are criminal justice majors) are either categorized as those who (1) have a relative who has criminal justice experience or (2) do not have a relative who has criminal justice experience. Upon comparison of the assumptions between a parametric and nonparametric test, a parametric test is more powerful. A common type of nonparametric test is known as the chi-square test.

Chi-Square Test

As a student who is interested in the impact of race within criminal case processing, you are curious as to whether criminal defendants experience differential treatment by prosecutors based on their race. In particular, you believe that minority criminal defendants (compared to nonminority criminal defendants) are less likely to be offered plea agreements by the local district attorney's office. In order to produce evidence that supports (or fails to support) your expectations, a chi-square test is required. A **chi-square test** is a statistical test that is used to determine differences between expected and observed outcomes (or values) and includes categorical independent and dependent variables. There are two types of chi-square tests, which are used based on the number of samples. A single sample requires the use of a chi-square test referred to as a **goodness of fit test**. The required chi-square test for two samples is known as a **test of independence**.

goodness of fit test A chi-square test used for a single sample.

test of independence A chi-square test used for two samples.

Assumptions of the Chi-Square Test

Before we discuss the two major types of the chi-square test, the assumptions of this nonparametric test are as follows:

1. It should be used with randomly selected populations. In fact, all types of hypothesis testing should involve gathering data from randomly selected populations.
2. The use of a chi-square should not be used to calculate variables that are related. For instance, suppose one is curious as to whether a single population (such as a class of students) exposed to certain information will lead to an increase in demonstrated knowledge among individuals of the same population. In short, chi-square cannot be used with multiple test measures (i.e., pretest and posttest, time series data) with the same population.

3. The test statistic should be used with large samples. The criteria of what is designated as a large number is generally 30 or more cases. As with most inferential-based hypothesis tests, larger samples will likely produce reduced margins of error.
4. A chi-square test should be used with a minimum number of expected frequencies of cells. All calculated expected values should have a value of at least 5. Any calculated value that is below 5 will distort the observed results of a test. Consider the following examples:

   a. $\text{Cell (A)} = \frac{(f_0 - f_e)^2}{f_e} = \frac{(5-1)^2}{1} = \frac{(4)^2}{1} = 16$

   In Cell (A), the observed frequency is 5, and the expected frequency is 1. By subtracting the expected frequency (1) from the observed frequency (5), the result is $4^2 = 16$.

   b. $\text{Cell (B)} = \frac{(f_0 - f_e)^2}{f_e} = \frac{(20-16)^2}{16} = \frac{(4)^2}{16} = 1$

   In Cell (B), the observed frequency is 20, and the expected frequency is 16. By subtracting the expected frequency (16) from the observed frequency (20), the result is $4^2 = 36$.

   In both examples, subtracting the expected frequency from the observed frequency resulted in the same difference (4); however, the results clearly demonstrate a significant difference (16 and 1). For this reason, it is highly recommended to use large sample sizes.

Formula for Computing the Chi-Square Test

$$\chi^2 = \Sigma \frac{(0 - E)^2}{E},$$

where

Σ = represents sum of values
0 = represents observed values
E = represents expected values

Chapter Learning Assessment Questions

To gauge your learning, provide answers to the following questions:

1. In this chapter, there are ________ types of chi-square tests discussed.
   a. 4
   b. 3
   c. 2
   d. none of the above
2. Which of the following are considered assumptions of the chi-square test?
   a. Must use randomly selected populations

b. Must use a minimum number of expected frequencies of cells
c. Should not be used to calculate variables that are related
d. All of the above

Answers

1. c
2. d

Goodness of Fit

The objective of conducting a goodness of fit chi-square test is to determine whether the observed data (or frequencies) *fits with* the expected frequencies. An observed frequency is the individual value in a sample that is designated in a particular category. Consider the following example of observed frequencies based on a total of 40 students who applied for graduation in a sample. This includes 18 who applied before the deadline, 12 pending applications, and 10 applications that were accepted (because of special circumstances) beyond the deadline.

On the other hand, an expected frequency is a value that is *expected from the proportions in the null hypothesis and sample size.* In short, the expected frequency represents an ideal distribution that would likely exist if the sample proportions aligned in agreement identified in the null hypothesis. In short, expected outcomes *are values that correspond to the null hypothesis.*

1. As noted in the example, to discover the actual expected frequency in each category, divide each observed frequency by the total number of observed frequencies (40). This results in those who applied (18/40) = 0.45; pending applications (12/40) = 0.30; submission beyond the deadline (10/40) = 0.25.
2. Based on the calculated information, our expected frequency for each category is 0.45 (45%), 0.30 (30%), and 0.25 (25%).

Chi-Square Test (Example 1)

As indicated in the definition, the purpose of the chi-square test is to determine the differences between expected and observed outcomes. For example, suppose one is interested in determining if the following number of youth arrests (also known as observed outcomes) is equally distributed across the listed racial categories in a sample (Mears et al, 2014). This includes Blacks ($n = 67$), Latinx ($n = 41$), and Whites ($n = 37$) for a total of 145. This is an example of a goodness of fit test.

Let's use our statistical steps:

As a criminal justice expert, you believe there is a significant difference between the frequencies (number of arrests) in each category.

1. Identify the null and alternative hypotheses.

   The null hypothesis indicates there is no difference between the frequencies in each category. The alternative hypothesis states that there is a difference between the frequencies in each category.

$$H_0: P_1 = P_2 = P_3$$
$$H_1: P_1 \neq P_2 \neq P_3$$

2. Identify the level of risk or significance.
   Our selected level of risk is 0.05.
3. Choose the appropriate test.
   Given that the categorical level of measurement of the independent and dependent variables is nominal, we selected the use of a chi-square test.
4. Compute and identify the statistical test value (STV).
   Consider the numbers in Table 12.1, which includes the calculation outcomes of a chi-square test:

TABLE 12.1 **Youth Arrests by Race**

Category	Observed	Expected	Difference	Difference^2	D2/Expected
Blacks	67	48.3	18.7	349.69	7.23
Latinx	41	48.3	7.3	53.29	1.10
Whites	37	48.3	11.3	127.69	2.64
Total	145				10.97

The aforementioned involved the following steps:

a. Identify the categories along with their observed values (frequencies)
b. Identify the expected values. This requires dividing the sum of the categories (145) by the number of categories (3), which is (145/3 = 48.3)
c. Identify the differences between the observed and expected values. This involves subtracting the observed from the expected values.
d. Identify the squared differences.
e. Divide the squared differences by the expected frequencies.
f. Find the sum of the values in the final column, which is the chi-square value of 10.97.

The STV, referred to as a chi-square value, is 10.97

5. Identify and compare the critical decision value (CDV) to the STV.
   a. The degrees of freedom with a one-sample chi-square test is computed by r – 1, in which r represents the number of rows.
   b. Based on our numbers, this is 3 – 1 = 2
   c. At this point, we will use the table that identifies the critical values for the chi-square distribution, which is located in the appendix of this textbook.
   d. Since our degrees of freedom is 2, we will locate that number under the degrees of freedom column and under the 0.05 level of risk.

e. As indicated in the table, we will use 5.99 as the value in which to reject the null hypothesis.

f. Since our STV (chi-square value) is 10.97, we compare this value with the CDV, which is 5.99.

6. If the STV > CDV, reject the null hypothesis.

Given that the STV (10.97) is greater than the CDV (5.99), we reject the null hypothesis. Thus, the alternative hypothesis is true, which states that there is a difference between the frequencies in each category. Visual details of this process are included in Figure 12.1.

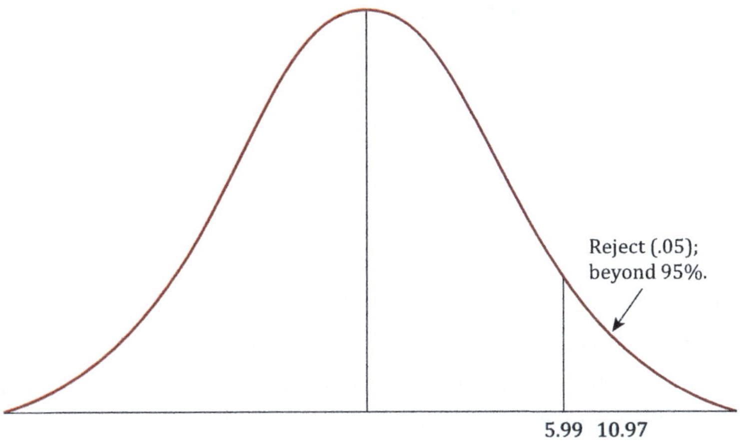

FIGURE 12.1 Normal Curve Illustration of Test Results

In our answer provided, notice how the degrees of freedom are listed. The results of the test are displayed in this manner:

$$\chi^2(2) = 10.97, p < 0.05$$

Chi-Square Test (Example 2)

Suppose a researcher believes there is a significant difference between the frequencies (number of arrests) in each location of a particular area. This includes those arrested in the South ($n = 23$), Northwest ($n = 26$), and East ($n = 45$) for a total of 94.

Let's use our statistical steps:

1. Identify the null and alternative hypotheses.

The null hypothesis indicates there is no difference between the frequencies in each category. The alternative hypothesis states that there is a difference between the frequencies in each category.

$$H_0: P_1 = P_2 = P_3$$
$$H_1: P_1 \neq P_2 \neq P_3$$

2. Identify the level of risk or significance.
   Our selected level of risk is 0.05.
3. Choose the appropriate test.
   Given that the categorical level of measurement of the independent and dependent variables is nominal, we selected the use of a chi-square test.
4. Compute and identify the STV.
   Consider the numbers in Table 12.2, which includes the details of a chi-square test:

TABLE 12.2 **Youth Arrests by Location**

Category	Observed	Expected	Difference	Difference^2	D2/Expected
South	23	32	−9	81	2.53125
Northwest	26	32	−6	36	1.125
East	45	32	13	169	5.28125
Total	96				8.93

The aforementioned involved the following steps:

a. Identify the categories, along with their observed values (frequencies).
b. Identify the expected values. This requires dividing the sum of the categories (96) by the number of categories (3), which is (96/3 = 32).
c. Identify the differences between the observed and expected values. This involves subtracting the observed from the expected values.
d. Identify the squared differences.
e. Divide the squared differences by the expected frequencies.
f. Find the sum of the values in the final column, which is the chi-square value of 8.93.

The STV, referred to as a chi-square value, is 8.93

5. Identify and compare the CDV to the STV.
   a. The degrees of freedom with a one-sample chi-square test is computed by r – 1, in which r represents the number of rows.
   b. Based on our numbers, this is 3 – 1 = 2
   c. As previously, we will now use the table which identifies the critical values for the chi-square distribution.
   d. Since our degrees of freedom is 2, we will locate that number under the degrees of freedom column and under the 0.05 level of risk.
   e. As indicated in the table, we will use 5.99 as the value in which to reject the null hypothesis.

   Since our STV (chi-square value) is 8.93, we compare this value with the CDV, which is 5.99.
6. If the STV > CDV, reject the null hypothesis.
   Given that the STV (8.93) is greater than the CDV (5.99), we reject the null hypothesis. Thus, the alternative hypothesis is true, which states that there is a difference between the frequencies in each category.

The results of the test are displayed in this manner:

$$\chi^2(2) = 8.93, p < 0.05$$

Now, as previously identified, the required chi-square test for two samples is known as a test of independence. Consider the following:

Chi-Square Test (Example 3)

Suppose one is interested in whether support for the use of handguns on college campuses is related to the academic level of a student. Among 289 undergraduate students, this includes 78 who support and 211 who fail to support such a measure. With a total of 70 graduate students, this includes 28 in support and 42 in opposition.

Let's use our statistical steps:

1. Identify the null and alternative hypotheses.
   The null hypothesis indicates there is no relationship between the academic level of a student and their support for handguns on campus. The alternative hypothesis states that there is a relationship between the academic level of a student and their support for handguns on campus.

$$H_0: \chi^2 = 0$$
$$H_1: \chi^2 \neq 0$$

2. Identify the level of risk or significance.
   The selected level of risk is 0.05.
3. Choose the appropriate test.
   Given that the categorical level of measurement of the independent and dependent variables is nominal, we selected the use of a chi-square test.
4. Compute and identify the STV.
   Consider the numbers in Table 12.3, which includes the calculation processes of a chi-square test.

TABLE 12.3 **Student Type and Support for Handguns on Campus**

Observed	Expected	Difference	Difference^2	D^2/Expected
78	85.33	−7.33	53.73	0.63
211	203.67	7.33	53.73	0.26
28	20.67	7.33	53.73	2.60
42	49.33	−7.33	53.73	1.09
Total				4.58

The aforementioned involved the following steps:

a. Identify the categories along with their observed values (frequencies).
b. Identify the expected values. This requires multiplying the row marginal by the column marginal and dividing each value by the total:
   1. $289 \times 106/359 = 85.33$
   2. $289 \times 253/359 = 203.67$
   3. $70 \times 106/359 = 20.67$
   4. $70 \times 253/359 = 49.33$
c. Identify the differences between the observed and expected values. This involves subtracting the observed from the expected values.
d. Identify the squared differences.
e. Divide the squared differences by the expected frequencies.
f. Find the sum of the values in the final column, which is the chi-square value of 4.58.

The STV, referred to as a chi-square value, is 4.58

5. Identify and compare the CDV to the STV.
   a. The degrees of freedom for a two-sample chi-square test are computed by $(r - 1)(c - 1)$; r represents the number of rows, and c represents the number of columns.
   b. This includes $(2 - 1)(2 - 1) = (1)(1) = 1$
   c. We will now use the table (in the appendix area), which identifies the critical values for the chi-square distribution.
   d. Since our degrees of freedom is 1, we will locate that number under the degrees of freedom column and under the 0.05 level of risk.
   e. As indicated in the table, we will use 3.84 as the value in which to reject the null hypothesis.
   f. Since our STV (chi-square value) is 4.58, we compare this value with the CDV, which is 3.84.
6. If the STV> CDV, reject the null hypothesis.
   Given that the STV (4.58) is greater than the CDV (3.84), we reject the null hypothesis. Thus, the alternative hypothesis, which states there is a relationship between the academic level of a student and their support for handguns on campus, is true. Provided below (in Figure 12.2) is a visual example of the aforementioned steps.

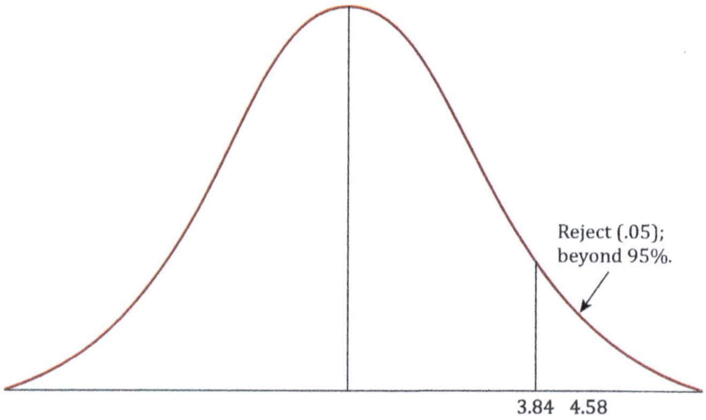

FIGURE 12.2 Normal Curve Illustration of Test Results

The results of the test are displayed in this manner:

$$\chi^2(1) = 4.58, p < 0.05$$

Chi-Square Test (Example 4)

Our final example includes a study that addresses potential criminal victimization among college students. In particular, the question is whether there is a relationship between academic classification and the prospect of experiencing property theft. The details of such include a total of 50 sophomores in which 34 students experienced property theft, and 16 students failed to experience property theft. Among 76 juniors, 55 experienced victimization, and 21 did not experience victimization. Finally, with 67 seniors, 41 encountered, and 26 failed to encounter property theft victimization.

Let's follow our statistical steps:

1. Identify the null and alternative hypotheses.

   The null hypothesis indicates there is no relationship between student classification and their perceived victimization of property theft on campus. The alternative hypothesis states that there is a relationship between student classification and their perceived victimization of property theft on campus.

$$H_0: \chi^2 = 0$$
$$H_1: \chi^2 \neq 0$$

2. Identify the level of risk or significance.

   The selected level of risk is 0.10.
3. Choose the appropriate test.

   Given that the categorical level of measurement of the independent and dependent variables is nominal, we selected the use of a chi-square test.
4. Compute and identify the STV.

   Consider the numbers in Table 12.4:

TABLE 12.4 **Student Classification and Victimization of Property Theft**

Observed	Expected	Difference	Difference^2	D^2/Expected
34	33.68	0.32	0.10	0.00
16	16.32	−0.32	0.10	0.01
55	51.19	3.81	14.52	0.28
21	24.81	−3.81	14.52	0.59
41	45.13	−4.13	17.06	0.38
26	21.87	4.13	17.06	0.78
Total				2.04

The aforementioned involved the following steps:

a. Identify the categories along with their observed values (frequencies).

b. Identify the expected values. This requires multiplying the row marginal by the column marginal and dividing each value by the total:

1. $50 \times 130/193 = 33.68$
2. $50 \times 63/193 = 16.32$
3. $76 \times 130/193 = 51.19$
4. $76 \times 63/193 = 24.81$
5. $67 \times 130/193 = 45.13$
6. $67 \times 63/193 = 21.87$

c. Identify the differences between the observed and expected values. This involves subtracting the observed from the expected values.

d. Identify the squared differences.

e. Divide the squared differences by the expected frequencies.

f. Find the sum of the values in the final column, which is the chi-square value of 2.04.

The STV, referred to as a chi-square value, is 2.04

5. Identify and compare the CDV to the STV.

a. The degrees of freedom for a two-sample chi-square test are computed by (r – 1)(c – 1); r represents the number of rows, and c represents the number of columns.

b. This includes $(3 - 1)(2 - 1) = (2)(1) = 2$

c. Now we will refer to the table that identifies the critical values for the chi-square distribution.

d. Since our degrees of freedom is 2, we will locate that number under the degrees of freedom column and under the 0.10 level of risk.

e. As indicated in the table, we will use 4.00 as the value in which to reject the null hypothesis. Since our STV (chi-square value) is 2.04, we compare this value with the CDV, which is 4.00.

6. If the STV > CDV, reject the null hypothesis.

As revealed in Figure 12.3, given that the STV (2.04) is less than the CDV (4.00), we fail to reject the null hypothesis. Thus, the null hypothesis, which states there is no relationship between student classification and their perceived victimization of property theft on campus, is true.

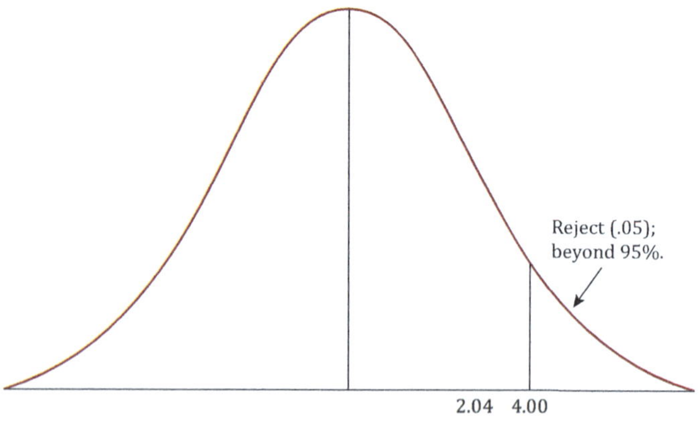

FIGURE 12.3 Normal Curve Illustration of Test Results

The results of the test are displayed in this manner:

$$\chi^2(2) = 2.04, p > 0.05$$

Chapter Learning Assessment Questions

To gauge your learning, provide answers to the following questions:

1. Based on the following results:

$$\chi^2(16) = ?, p < 0.05,$$

   which of the following is the correct χ^2 test statistic?

   a. 6.98
   b. 9.17
   c. 9.19
   d. None of the above

2. Based on the following results:

$$\chi^2(2) = ?, p < 0.01,$$

   which of the following is the correct χ^2 test statistic?

   a. 16.18
   b. 19.17
   c. 26.31
   d. None of the above

Answers

1. d
2. c

Effect Size and Chi-Square Test (Cohen's *w*)

As mentioned in the previous chapters, evidence of statistical differences between groups does not always share the extent to which those differences may exist. Thus, statistically significant differences do not necessarily point to a large effect. For this reason, it is suggested that a statistic, referred to as Cohen's *w*, is used for chi-square tests.

The formula for Cohen's *w* is listed as follows:

$$w = \sqrt{\Sigma \frac{(p_o - p_e)^2}{p_e}},$$

where:

p_0 = observed values (based on dividing each value by the total number of individuals)

p_e = expected values (based on the equal distribution of each category)

The formula requires the following steps:

1. For each category, compute the difference between p_0 and p_e.
2. Square the difference between p_0 and p_e.
3. Divide the squared difference between p_0 and p_e by p_e.
4. Find the sum of values from Step 3.
5. Find the square root of the sum in Step 4.

Consider the following example:

A researcher is interested in determining whether law school students have any preferences among four types of instructional delivery modes at a law school. This includes a sample of 40 students who selected one option from the categories of (1) in-person instruction ($n = 18$), (2) remote instruction ($n = 12$), and (3) hybrid instruction (a combination of remote and in-person instruction) ($n = 10$).

The null hypothesis (expected frequencies) states that there is an equal distribution among the three categories. This is computed by finding the sum of the observed values and finding the sum of each observed value divided by the sum. With respect to the categories, the following identifies the sum of the squared differences divided by the expected frequencies: in person (18/40) = 0.45; remote (12/40) = 0.30; hybrid (10/40) = 0.25.

TABLE 12.5 **Instructional Preferences**

	p_o	p_e	$(p_o - p_e)$	$(p_o - p_e)^2$	$(p_o - p_e)^2/p_e$
In Person	0.45	0.33	0.12	0.01	0.04
Remote	0.30	0.33	−0.03	0.01	0.03
Hybrid	0.25	0.33	−0.08	0.01	0.02
					0.09

Based on our formula:

$$w = \sqrt{\Sigma \frac{(p_o - p_e)^2}{p_e}}$$

$$\Sigma \frac{(p_o - p_e)^2}{p_e} = 0.09 \text{ and since } w = \sqrt{\Sigma \frac{(p_o - p_e)^2}{p_e}} = \sqrt{0.09} = 0.29$$

The effect size (w) of the difference is 0.29

The following serves as a criterion in determining the magnitude of w: value near 0.10 = small effect; value near 0.30 = medium effect; value near 0.50 = large effect.

Given that w is 0.29, the extent of such is considered a medium effect.

Final Thoughts

The use of the chi-square test provides several benefits in relation to identifying potential differences between expectations and actual outcomes. Be sure that you use the correct type of variable (nominal level) in your analysis; incorrect (or faulty) *input* will lead to incorrect (or faulty) *output*.

Discussion

As a researcher, you are interested in whether age is related to traffic accidents among youth. To gather data, you decide to use a self-report survey in which youth identify their age. What is unique about the survey is that it includes a question where the actual number of an individual's age is required. It also identifies whether youth have experienced traffic accidents in the past 3 years. This requires answering yes or no to certain questions. Based on the details provided, can the researcher use a chi-square test to investigate the relationship between age and traffic accidents? Explain?

Chapter Summary

Chapter 12 discussed the following information:

Objective 1– Define and explain the use of the chi-square test

- A chi-square test, which includes the use of categorical data, is used to determine differences between expected and observed outcomes.
- A goodness of fit test is a chi-square test in which a single sample is required.
- A test of independence is a chi-square test in which two samples are required.

Objective 2 – Formula for the chi-square test

- See the corresponding pages in the chapter.

Objective 3 – Example problems(s) and the chi-square test

- See the corresponding pages in the chapter.

Objective 4 – Effect size for chi-square test

- To determine the extent of a difference between two or more samples using a chi-square test, one may conduct what is referred to as Cohen's *w*.

Terms

Chi-square test
Goodness of fit test
Test of independence
Cohen's *w*

Chapter Review Questions

1. A *t*-test is considered a type of
   a. parametric test
   b. nonparametric test
   c. descriptive test
   d. none of the above

2. Identified below are the assumptions of a nonparametric test, *except*
   a. data must reflect normal distribution
   b. data must have approximate equal distance (variance) from each other
   c. a and b
   d. none of the above
3. Listed below are the assumptions of a parametric test
   a. data must reflect random selection
   b. data must not include extreme values (i.e., outliers)
   c. data are designated as either interval or ratio level
   d. all of the above
4. Compared to parametric tests, nonparametric tests
   a. are less powerful
   b. are more powerful
   c. are less powerful depending on the level of data used
   d. are more powerful depending on (1) the level of data used and (2) the desired level of significance
5. Which of the following are considered an assumption of the chi-square test:
   a. large sample sizes
   b. at least two samples
   c. random sampling
   d. all of the above
6. To find the degrees of freedom when conducting a chi-square test, one should
   a. subtract 1 row from the total number of groups and multiply with the total number of columns (rows − 1 × columns)
   b. subtract 1 row from the total number of groups along with the total number of columns and multiply by each other (rows − 1 × columns − 1)
   c. subtract 1 row from the total number of groups and multiply with the total number of columns plus one additional column (rows − 1 × columns + 1)
   d. add 1 row to the total number of groups and multiply with the total number of columns plus one additional column (rows + 1 × columns + 1)
7. Based on the following, determine if a goodness of fit or test of independence is warranted:
   a. A researcher desires to investigate whether a relationship exists between male and female juvenile court judges and support for private or open youth hearings.
   b. A group of 28 high school students (10 Black, 10 White, and 8 Latinx) admitted that they were questioned by police officers. To that end, you are interested in identifying the equal distribution of the aforementioned total amount based on the listed racial categories.
   c. A study examines the extent to which the racial background (Black, Latinx, Asian) of a juvenile is related to police-initiated referral decisions.

d. A total of 24 undergraduate students (8 freshman, 12 juniors, and 4 seniors) completed a criminology course at a local community college. What is the equal distribution of the total amount of students on the basis of classification category?

e. A statistician examined the extent to which two community-based programs (block watches or neighborhood patrols) are related to support (or nonsupport) among members of the community.

f. A researcher is interested in whether gender is related to decisions of guilt or innocence in criminal court trials.

8. By reviewing the chi-square table information near the end of the text, determine if the following STVs support the decision to reject the null hypothesis:

Level of Significance	Statistical Test Value	Degrees of Freedom	Critical Decision Value	Reject the Null Hypothesis
0.05	8.48	3	7.82	
0.05	3.91	1	3.84	
0.01	17.49	7	18.48	
0.05	6.01	2	5.99	
0.05	17.56	10	18.31	
0.01	12.34	4	13.28	
0.01	27.57	12	26.22	
0.01	42.65	23	41.64	
0.05	31.29	19	30.14	

9. A researcher is interested in determining whether a relationship exists between the number of years a police officer has worked in an agency and the number of complaints that an officer has received. Using a random sample of 300 officers, the researcher collects data that identifies the years of experience of each officer, as measured by (0–5), (6–10), and (11+). The number of complaints was also collected from each officer. These were measured on the basis of (0–10), (11–15), (16+).

   a. What is the independent variable?
   b. What is the dependent variable?
   c. What is the level of measurement for the independent and dependent variables?
   d. What is the null and alternate hypothesis that should be used?

10. A government agency is responsible for testing the relationship between age and the use of a waiver in a state. The agency statistician collects data, which includes the ages of the youth and whether the youth were waived to the criminal court system. In this process, the age of youth is designated as those above (or below) the age of 15. Use of the waiver is designated as either yes or no.

   a. What is the independent variable?
   b. What is the dependent variable?

c. What is the level of measurement for the independent and dependent variables?
d. What are the null and alternate hypotheses that should be used?

11. A private agency is responsible for testing the relationship between employment experience and promotional opportunities in a local law enforcement agency. The private agency collects data that includes the work experience of employees (as measured between 5 and 10 or 11+ years) and whether that employee was offered (yes or no) an opportunity for promotion.
    a. What is the independent variable?
    b. What is the dependent variable?
    c. What is the level of measurement for the independent and dependent variables?
    d. What are the null and alternate hypotheses that should be used?
12. As part of an effort to pass legislation to maintain the use of determinate sentencing in state government, several members of a political party decided to use research during a debate. During this process, three individual government officials decide to provide evidence that identifies the need for various types of determinate sentencing. Examples of such included (1) presumptive sentences, (2) mandatory sentences, and (3) flat-time sentences. At the conclusion of their presentation, random members of the state government voted for one of the three types of sentencing. Choose the appropriate test and determine if a significant relationship (at 0.05 level of risk) exists.

Types of Determinate Sentencing

	Presumptive	Mandatory	Flat Time
Democrats	21	18	6
Libertarians	5	13	22
Republicans	25	21	5

13. At an annual prison training session for correctional officers, 179 correctional officers were randomly placed in 3 separate groups. After receiving information about the necessity of inmate classification, each officer completed a survey that revealed their individual support. More specifically, their decisions of support were based on the types of advantages associated with the use of classification. Choose the appropriate test and determine if a significant relationship (at 0.05 level of risk) exists.

Advantages of Classification

	Provides Safety for Officers and Inmates	Reduces or Isolates Gang Activity	Improves Access to Services for Special Needs Inmates
Group 1	15	25	20
Group 2	29	21	7
Group 3	18	30	14

14. Upon release from prison, it is not uncommon for formerly incarcerated individuals to participate in reentry programs. A particular reentry program desires to use numerous

gender-based practices that attempt to address the specific needs of each participant. In order to identify those needs, a total of 100 formerly incarcerated individuals were placed in two groups. The program director of the reentry program believes that gender differences exist in relation to the initial experiences of formerly incarcerated individuals. To test the hypothesis, choose the appropriate test and determine if a significant relationship (at 0.05 level of risk) exists.

Initial Prison Experiences of Inmates

	Individual Treatment May Seem Inhuman	Preoccupied With Learning to Survive	Increased Levels of Depression and Anxiety
Females	20	18	6
Males	15	24	17

15. In an attempt to test whether a certain teaching practice (delivery of content) is more effective than a traditional teaching practice (i.e., lecture), an instructor randomly assigns 70 students to two groups (Group A/Group B). Students in Group A are exposed to academic content through the use of guest speakers, videos, and a field trip to an actual prison. Those in Group B are exposed to lectures and classroom group discussions. In comparison to students in Group B, the instructor is convinced that the students in Group A will likely be able to remember information related to prison inmate social norms. This includes earning a score of at least 75 on an exam at the end of the semester. Identified below are the student final exam scores. Choose the appropriate test and determine if a significant relationship (at 0.05 level of risk) exists. Is the instructor's assumption valid?

Test Results of Prison Inmate Social Norms

	> 75	< 75
Group A	24	11
Group B	17	18

16. Imagine a supervisory officer in a maximum security prison consistently receiving complaints from older inmates who are not satisfied with the services provided by medical personnel in the facility. In a different area of the prison, the supervisor observes what appears to be a lack of adequate mental health services that are available for the inmates with special needs. During the required monthly executive meetings with the warden, you share the aforementioned concerns. This is followed by concerns expressed by other supervisors, which include the lack of drug abuse treatment programs in the facility. With only a certain amount of funding provided for the facility, the warden requires the submission of a report (based on survey findings from 240 randomly selected inmates) to determine how resources will be managed. The information provided below reflects the source of health-care problems in the facility among inmates on the basis of age. The supervisor assumes that most older inmates will express the opinion that the source of health-related problems stems from a

lack of qualified medical/personnel. To test this assumption, choose the appropriate test and determine if a significant relationship (at 0.05 level of risk) exists.

Health-Care Problems Among Prisoners

	Lack of Qualified Medical/Support Personnel	Lack of Treatment for Drug Abuse	Lack of Appropriate Mental Health Services
21-35	29	39	12
36-45	10	26	44
46+	40	30	10

17. Within a 10-year period, an instructor has a local juvenile court judge to serve as a guest speaker in his juvenile justice courses. During the presentation, the guest speaker mentioned that each state has its own juvenile justice system. To that end, each state has its own definition of who is considered a juvenile, which is often based on a type of criteria. In general, the criteria may include the physiological, emotional, and intellectual maturity level of an individual. To determine which type of criteria should be used among the students, the instructor randomly selects 400 students who complete a survey, which includes the following types of criteria. Choose the appropriate test and determine if a significant relationship (at 0.05 level of risk) exists.

Criteria and Juvenile Status

	Physiological	Emotional	Intellectual
Seniors	36	38	48
Juniors	25	28	41
Sophomores	25	39	20

18. Through the use of a randomly distributed survey among 300 students, a researcher posed the following question among second-year law school students at a law school. "Which of the following standards of proof should be used in juvenile proceedings?" The results of a total of 290 completed surveys are identified below, which are composed of first- and third-year students. In comparison to the first-year students (because of their lack of experience), the researcher believes that the third-year students are more likely to select the standard of proof beyond a reasonable doubt (which is the highest legal standard). Choose the appropriate test and determine if a significant relationship (at 0.05 level of risk) exists. Is the researcher's assumption valid?

Standards of Proof in Juvenile Proceedings

	Proof Beyond a Reasonable Doubt	Preponderance of the Evidence	Reasonable Proof
First-year students	20	40	40
Third-year students	40	25	30

19. During a criminology course, a professor discusses the major assumptions of a criminological theory referred to as the routine activities theory (Cohen and Felson, 1979). This theory posits that crime/delinquency will likely exist if the following occurs: (1) a suitable target exists (i.e., an expensive cell phone), (2) a motivated offender (i.e., an individual with a strong desire to possess or gain access to something), and (3) a lack of capable guardian (i.e., no one is available to adequately protect an item that someone desires). To gain feedback from the students, the professor randomly selects 450 students, assigns them to specific groups, and distributes a survey that identifies their support for each of the assumptions of the routine activities theory. Choose the appropriate test and determine if a significant relationship (at 0.05 level of risk) exists. If a significant difference does exist, determine the extent of the difference.

Support for the Assumptions of the Routine Activities Theory

	Suitable Target	Motivated Offender	Lack of Guardian
Group 1	48	55	60
Group 2	41	58	62
Group 3	24	52	50

Answers

1. a
2. d
3. d
4. a
5. d
6. b
7.
    a. test of independence
    b. goodness of fit
    c. test of independence
    d. goodness of fit
    e. test of independence
    f. test of independence
8.

Level of Significance	Statistical Test Value	Degrees of Freedom	Critical Decision Value	Reject the Null Hypothesis
0.05	8.48	3	7.82	Y
0.05	3.91	1	3.84	Y
0.01	17.49	7	18.48	N
0.05	6.01	2	5.99	Y
0.05	17.56	10	18.31	N
0.01	12.34	4	13.28	N

Level of Significance	Statistical Test Value	Degrees of Freedom	Critical Decision Value	Reject the Null Hypothesis
0.01	27.57	12	26.22	Y
0.01	42.65	23	41.64	Y
0.05	31.29	19	30.14	Y

9.
   a. The independent variable is the number of years a police officer has worked at a law enforcement agency.
   b. The dependent variable is the number of complaints that an officer has received.
   c. The level of measurement for the independent variable is categorical. The level of measurement for the dependent variable is categorical.
   d. The null hypothesis is based on the assumption that there is no difference between the number of years a police officer has worked at a law enforcement agency and the number of complaints that an officer has received. The alternative hypothesis is based on the assumption that there is a difference between the number of years a police officer has worked at a law enforcement agency and the number of complaints that an officer has received.

10.
   a. The independent variable is the age of each youth.
   b. The dependent variable is the use of a waiver in a state.
   c. The level of measurement for the independent variable is categorical. The level of measurement for the dependent variable is categorical.
   d. The null hypothesis is based on the assumption that there is no difference between the age of each youth and the use of a waiver in a state. The alternative hypothesis is based on the assumption that there is a difference between the age of each youth and the use of a waiver in a state.

11.
   a. The independent variable is the work experience of employees.
   b. The dependent variable is whether an employee was offered an opportunity for promotion.
   c. The level of measurement for the independent variable is categorical. The level of measurement for the dependent variable is categorical.
   d. The null hypothesis is based on the assumption that there is no difference between the work experience of employees and whether an employee was offered an opportunity for promotion. The alternative hypothesis is based on the assumption that there is a difference between the work experience of employees and whether an employee was offered an opportunity for promotion.

12. With an STV of (32.5) and (a p-value of 0.001), there is a statistically significant difference between political party affiliation and the types of sentencing discussed and voted on.
13. With an STV of (13.11) and (a p-value of 0.001), there is a statistically significant difference between groups and selected types of advantages associated with prison classification systems.
14. With an STV of (5.47) and (a p-value of 0.14), there is no statistically significant difference between gender and initial prison experiences.
15. With an STV of (2.88) and (a p-value of 0.08), there is no statistically significant difference between the types of content delivery and test scores.

16. With an STV of (53.3) and (a p-value of 0.001), there is a statistically significant difference between age categories and types of health-care problems identified among inmates.
17. With an STV of (9.89) and (a p-value of 0.007), there is a statistically significant difference between student academic classification and types of juvenile criteria status.
18. With an STV of (11.4) and (a p-value of 0.009), there is a statistically significant difference between student experience and selected types of proof in juvenile proceedings.
19. With an STV of (4.35) and (a p-value of 0.11), there is no statistically significant difference between student groups and support for certain assumptions of the routine activities theory.

Bibliography

Cohen, L. E., & Felson, M. (1979). Social change and crime rate trends: A routine activity approach. *American Sociological Review*, 588–608.

Mears, D. P., Cochran, J. C., Stults, B. J., Greenman, S. J., Bhati, A. S., & Greenwald, M. A. (2014). The "true" juvenile offender: Age effects and juvenile court sanctioning. *Criminology, 52*(2), 169–194.

Sedgwick, P. (2015). A comparison of parametric and nonparametric statistical tests. *BMJ, 350*.

Chapter 12 SPSS and Workbook Questions

SPSS and Chi-Square Test

In order to compute the **chi-square test** using SPSS, work through the following steps:

Documented research explores the relationship between exposure to media content and interest in career options. For instance, suppose one is interested in determining whether the amount of media exposure to criminal justice information bears a relationship to interest as a potential law enforcement officer among college students. Examples of criminal justice media include television programs, as well as local- and national-level news accounts. To conduct research regarding the relationship between media content and occupational interest, a researcher distributes a survey to nearly 50 students. The researcher hypothesizes that students who know someone who has experience as a law enforcement officer (in comparison to students who are unfamiliar with anyone who has law enforcement experience) will report high levels of interest as a potential law enforcement officer.

Entry of Data—SPSS

1. Select variable view to include information associated with the variables of interest. In our example, this would include familiarity and interest as a law enforcement officer.
2. In the first row, include the term *familiarity* under the column identified as name.
3. For the remaining group, which includes *interest as a law enforcement officer*, follow the same procedure as noted above.
4. Select data view to include the scores for each group in each corresponding column.
5. Once the scores have been added in each column, return to the variable view and include values that correspond to each score.

IMAGE 12.1

IMAGE 12.2

IMAGE 12.3

Analysis of Data—SPSS

1. Select analyze, select descriptive statistics, and select crosstabulation.
2. Select the variable *familiarity* and move it to the box identified as row(s). In the same manner, select the variable *interest as a law enforcement officer* and move it to the box identified as column.
3. In the statistics section, select chi-square and select continue.
4. In the count section, under the term counts, select both the observed and expected. Under the term percentages, select both row and column. When completed, select continue.
5. After all desired functions have been selected, select OK.

Output of Data Analysis—SPSS

The results, which include two tables, reflect the data analysis of the variables. Table 1 reveals the descriptive statistics of the independent variable, which includes the total count for each possible outcome (e.g., yes or no). It also includes the observed and expected counts, along with their corresponding percentages. Table 2 reveals the results of the chi-square test, which includes the values, degrees of freedom (df), and level of significance ($p = 0.003$). Based on the hypothesis of the researcher, a statistically significant relationship exists between the likelihood that a student's familiarity with a person who has law enforcement experience will result in reporting interest in becoming a law enforcement officer.

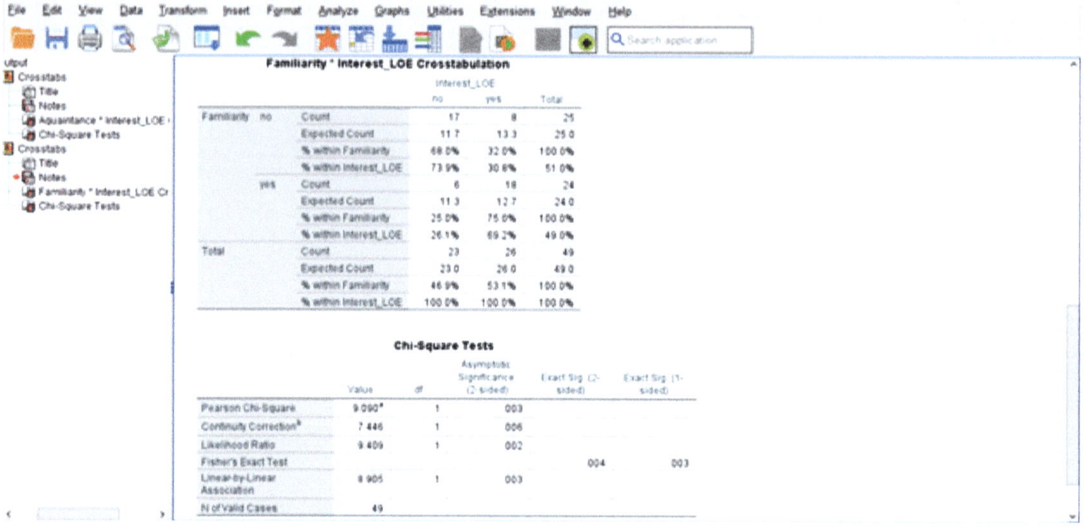

Familiarity * Interest_LOE Crosstabulation

			Interest_LOE no	Interest_LOE yes	Total
Familiarity	no	Count	17	8	25
		Expected Count	11.7	13.3	25.0
		% within Familiarity	68.0%	32.0%	100.0%
		% within Interest_LOE	73.9%	30.8%	51.0%
	yes	Count	6	18	24
		Expected Count	11.3	12.7	24.0
		% within Familiarity	25.0%	75.0%	100.0%
		% within Interest_LOE	26.1%	69.2%	49.0%
Total		Count	23	26	49
		Expected Count	23.0	26.0	49.0
		% within Familiarity	46.9%	53.1%	100.0%
		% within Interest_LOE	100.0%	100.0%	100.0%

Chi-Square Tests

	Value	df	Asymptotic Significance (2-sided)	Exact Sig. (2-sided)	Exact Sig. (1-sided)
Pearson Chi-Square	9.090[a]	1	.003		
Continuity Correction[b]	7.446	1	.006		
Likelihood Ratio	9.409	1	.002		
Fisher's Exact Test				.004	.003
Linear-by-Linear Association	8.905	1	.003		
N of Valid Cases	49				

IMAGE 12.4

Workbook Questions

Objective 1—Define and Explain the Use of the Chi-Square Test

- A chi-square test, which includes the use of categorical data, is used to determine differences between expected and observed outcomes.
- A goodness of fit test is a chi-square test in which a single sample is required.
- A test of independence is a chi-square test in which two samples are required.

Corresponding Questions

1. A chi-square test is used to determine differences between ________________ and observed outcomes.
   a. expected
   b. unexpected
   c. direct
   d. indirect
2. Based on the following types of data, a chi-square test includes the use of __________ level data.
   a. interval
   b. ratio
   c. nominal
   d. ordinal

3. Suppose a researcher is interested in whether gender is associated with detention status. In this analysis, gender (which includes the use of two samples) is defined as male or female, and detention status is defined as detained or not detained. Based on the details of this information, the appropriate statistical test used is:
   a. goodness of fit test
   b. test of independence
   c. *t*-test
   d. z-test
4. Using a single sample, a researcher believes that males, compared to females, achieve higher grades in an undergraduate course. In this analysis, higher grades refer to the number of scores above 90 (e.g., A's) earned in a statistics class. Based on the details of this information, the appropriate statistical test used is:
   a. goodness of fit test
   b. test of independence
   c. *t*-test
   d. z-test
5. Which of the following represents the appropriate use of a chi-square test?
   a. A study that examines the difference between gender and the classification of inmates in a correctional facility. Gender is defined as either male or female, and classification is defined as low, medium, or high-level risk.
   b. Research that investigates the difference between the criminal offense category and the type of punishment an individual receives during sentencing. The criminal offense category is based on whether an individual was convicted of a drug or property offense. The type of punishment received includes prison or probation.
   c. A schoolteacher is curious as to whether a difference exists on the basis of race and the number of detention referrals received in a school year. In this study, racial background is defined as Black or White. The number of detention referrals is based on a student experiencing 5 (or more) within a single school year.
   d. All of the above
6. Based on the following, identify which requires the use of a test of independence or a goodness of fit test.
   a. In an effort to recruit students to consider employment opportunities with a local law enforcement agency, a recruiter discusses the differences between patrol officers and detectives. To determine which type of officer a student might be interested in, the recruiter asks the students to demonstrate their preference by raising their hands. Out of 75 students, 25 selected the prospect of becoming a detective, 45 selected the option of becoming a patrol officer, and only 5 indicated that they were not interested in any of the options.
   b. After hearing a series of lectures related to the importance of reporting crimes, a professor is interested in whether students understood the information that was provided. More specifically, the professor believes that the males, compared to the females, were

more likely to remember crime reporting information that included numerical information. By distributing a single-question survey, which included a question that provided only two options, the results revealed that the professor's assumption was incorrect.

c. A student believes that the proportion of speeding tickets is higher for individuals less than 25 compared to those who are older than 25.

d. After hearing a presentation about the various styles of policing, a professor distributes a survey to students in order to gauge their preferences. After analyzing the data, the males showed a preference for the crime fighter approach. On the other hand, the females demonstrated a preference for the social agent approach.

e. A group of students are able to attend a probation facility. During this period, a senior probation officer shares information related to the numerous intermediate sanctions that are used among those sentenced to probation. This includes a lengthy discussion related to the use of electronic monitoring and house arrest. At the conclusion of speaking with the students, the officer poses a question to determine their single preference from the two types of intermediate sanctions discussed. The probation officer believes that the gender of the students is associated with their preferences.

Answers

1. a
2. c
3. b
4. a
5. d
6.
   a. goodness of fit
   b. test of independence
   c. goodness of fit
   d. test of independence
   e. test of independence

Objective 2—Formula for the Chi-Square Test

- See the corresponding pages in the chapter.

Objective 3—Example Problem(s) and the Chi-Square Test

- See the corresponding pages in the chapter.

Corresponding Questions

1. The following data represents the number of juvenile court cases dismissed among youth on the basis of race/ethnicity. Your professor believes that race plays a significant role in dismissal decisions (Gann, 2019). Based on the following details, in which the total for

each racial/ethnic category is listed, compute a chi-square test (with a risk level of 0.05) to determine if your professor's hypothesis is valid.

	Case Dismissed	Case Not Dismissed
Blacks	2	28
Hispanic	14	16
White	21	9

2. After hearing a report related to an increase in violent crimes in the community, a law enforcement agency decided to use a gun buyback program (Violano et al., 2014). Various officers have differing opinions in relation to which type of gun will be turned in exchange for gift cards and vouchers. Given the rural area in which the opportunity is being offered, the majority of the officers believe that shotguns and rifles will represent the highest category of weapon provided. In fact, they believe that the number of shotguns and rifles will be statistically greater than the other categories of weapons provided by members of the community. Based on the following data, which includes the number of guns and total within each general category, compute a chi-square test (with a risk level of 0.05) to determine if there are significant differences between the categories of guns received.

Semiautomatic Weapons	Shotguns/Rifles	Handguns
8	10	8
7	12	10
7	13	8
8	11	9
15	12	8
16	13	10
7	9	14
6	8	11
14	8	8
8	11	4
8	8	19
6	9	17
8	15	18
9	14	12
7	14	6
134	**167**	**162**

3. Within the topic of victimology, a research team examined the factors associated with the availability of funds for victims of crime (Newmark, 2004). Specifically, the study focused on whether the race of the victim was associated with being awarded financial compensation. Identified below are the results of a survey that reveal the number of allocated awards on the basis of the race of each category of victim. Based on the following data, compute a chi-square test (with a risk level of 0.05) to determine if there are significant differences between the racial categories.

Black	Latino	White
1	5	9
3	7	6
2	6	7
2	8	6
1	6	8
3	5	8
1	8	9
2	7	9
1	8	7
2	3	6
3	2	8
4	5	6
3	7	8
4	6	7
2	2	3
3	3	5
37	**88**	**112**

Answers

1. Given that the STV (25.4) is greater than the CDV (5.99), we reject the null hypothesis. Thus, the alternative hypothesis (your professor's assumption) is true, which states that there is a difference between the frequency of cases dismissed for each racial/ethnic category.
2. Given that the STV (4.1) is not greater than the CDV (5.99), a statistically significant difference between the categories of guns provided does not exist. Therefore, the assumptions of the majority of officers are not valid.
3. Given that the STV (37.1) is greater than the CDV (5.99), there is a statistically significant difference between the selection of the factors.

Objective 4—Effect Size for Chi-Square Test

- To determine the extent of a difference between two or more samples, one may conduct what is referred to as the Cohen's *w*.

Corresponding Question

A researcher is interested in identifying specific career preferences among minority students who are classified as criminal justice majors at a historically Black college and university (Gabbidon et al., 2003).

This includes three categories, which represent the major components of the criminal justice system. Provided below is a sample of 85 students who selected one option from the categories of (1) law enforcement officer, (2) attorney/judge, and (3) corrections/probation officer.

Law Enforcement Officer	Attorney/Judge	Corrections/Probation	Total
25	39	21	85

Answers

1.

	p_o	p_e	$(p_o - p_e)$	$(p_o - p_e)^2$	$(p_o - p_e)^2/p_e$
Law Enforcement	0.29	0.33	−0.04	0.001	0.004
Attorney/ Judge	0.45	0.33	0.12	0.014	0.043
Corrections/ Probation	0.24	0.33	−0.09	0.008	0.024
					0.07

Based on the formula:

$$w = \sqrt{\Sigma \frac{(p_o - p_e)^2}{p_e}}$$

$$\Sigma \frac{(p_o - p_e)^2}{p_e} = 0.07 \text{ and since } w = \sqrt{\Sigma \frac{(p_o - p_e)^2}{p_e}} = \sqrt{0.07} = 0.26$$

The effect size is small.

Bibliography

Gabbidon, S. L., Penn, E. B., & Richards, W. A. (2003). Career choices and characteristics of African-American undergraduates majoring in criminal justice at historically black colleges and universities. *Journal of Criminal Justice Education, 14*(2), 229–244.

Gann, S. M. (2019). Examining the relationship between race and juvenile court decision-making: A counterfactual approach. *Youth Violence and Juvenile Justice, 17*(3), 269–287.

Newmark, L. C. (2004). Crime victims' needs and VOCA-funded services: Findings and recommendations from two national studies (Report 214263). National Institute of Justice. http://www.ncjrs.gov/pdffiles1/nij/grants/214263.pdf.

Violano, P., Driscoll, C., Chaudhary, N. K., Schuster, K. M., Davis, K. A., Borer, E., Winters, J. K., & Hirsh, M. P. (2014). Gun buy-back programs: A venue to eliminate unwanted guns in the community. *Journal of Trauma and Acute Care Surgery, 77* (3), S46–S50.

Credits

CHAPTER 13

Correlation Test

I'm very familiar with how people can confuse correlation with causation.
—Tim Ferriss

Objectives

1. Define and explain the use of the correlation test
2. Identify the formula for computing the correlation test
3. Computing the correlation test

Introduction—DWI and Speeding

Suppose a police officer who observes a vehicle traveling at a high rate of speed responds by pursuing the driver. Once the individual is pulled over, the officer approaches the driver and begins to question him as to why he was speeding. During this interaction, the officer notices a distinct smell as the driver is responding to his questions. At this point, the officer notifies dispatch to send an additional unit to conduct a field sobriety test. Based on the officer's experience, it is his opinion that driving while intoxicated is correlated with the speed at which an individual operates a motor vehicle. In order to test this proposition, this scenario would require the use of a correlation test.

correlation test A statistical test that is designed to determine both the strength and direction of a relationship between variables.

positive correlation test A test that is used to determine whether a relationship in which an increase (or decrease) in the independent variable results in an increase (or decrease) in the dependent variable.

Correlation Test

A **correlation test** is a statistical test that is designed to determine both the strength and direction of a relationship between variables. More specifically, it is used to determine a linear relationship between a continuous independent and dependent variable. There are two types of correlation tests: a positive and a negative correlation test. A **positive correlation** test is used to determine whether a relationship in which an increase (or decrease) in the independent variable results in an increase (or decrease) in the dependent variable.

Overall, both variables are moving in the same direction. On the other hand, a **negative correlation** test is employed for the purpose of determining whether an increase (or decrease) in the independent variable results in the dependent variable moving in the opposite direction. For instance, based on our scenario, let's assume there is a linear relationship between blood alcohol level (BAL) and driving speed. As revealed in Figures 13.1 and 13.2, a positive correlation states that as BAL increases, driving speed also increases. However, a negative correlation would indicate that as BAL increases, driving speed decreases.

negative correlation test A test that is used to determine whether an increase (or decrease) in the independent variable results in the dependent variable moving in the opposite direction.

scatterplot A visual illustration of the relationship between the independent and dependent variables.

In many cases, a correlation test may include a visual illustration of the relationship between the independent and dependent variables. This is referred to as a **scatterplot**. A scatterplot reveals the relationship between variables by using data points that represent the actual numbers reflected in the independent and dependent variables.

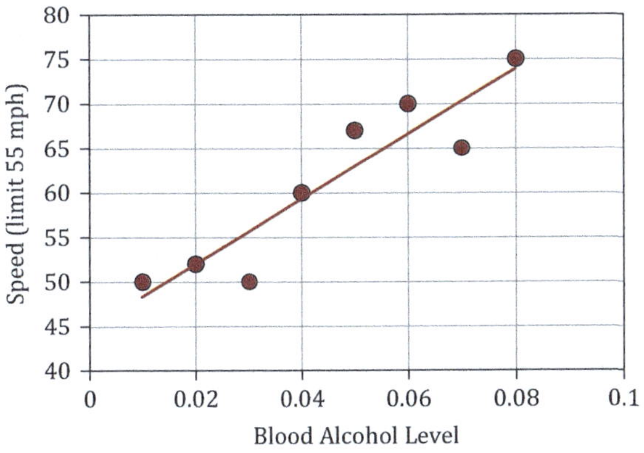

FIGURE 13.1 BAL and Increase of Speed

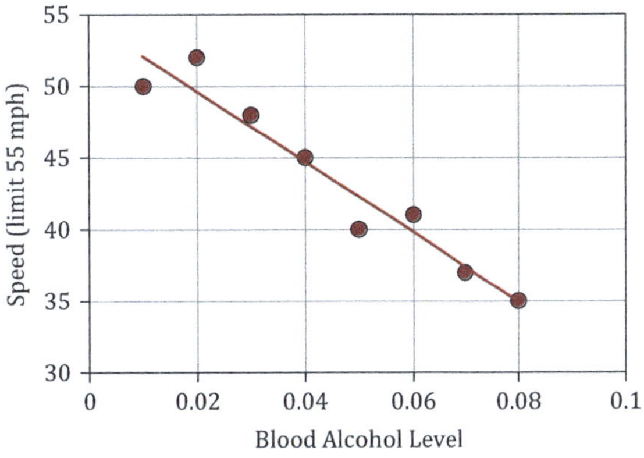

FIGURE 13.2 BAL and Decrease of Speed

Curvilinear Correlation

Despite the goal of determining a perfect straight-line relationship, it is not uncommon to discover relationships between the independent and dependent variables that are curvilinear. A **curvilinear correlation** is a relationship between an independent and dependent variable that either begins in a positive or negative direction or ends in an oppositive direction. For instance, suppose one is interested in determining the impact of age (x) on fear of crime (y)(Braungart et al., 1980). The scatterplot provides a U-shaped line as opposed to a straight line. As indicated in Figure 13.3, fear of crime initially exists at relatively high levels (ages 5–14), tends to decrease as individuals reach a certain age (early 20s–mid-40s), and increases again (between the ages of 60–90).

curvilinear correlation A visual illustration of the relationship between an independent and dependent variable that either begins as a positive or negative direction and ends in an oppositive direction.

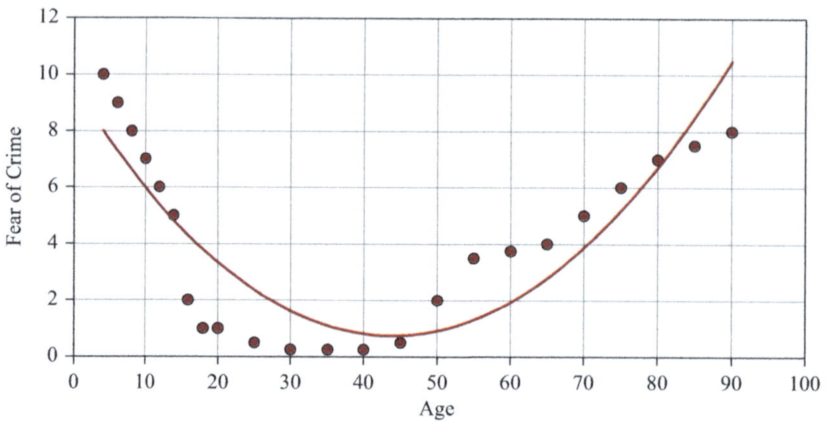

FIGURE 13.3 Curvilinear Correlation, Age, and Fear of Crime

correlation coefficient A statistic used in calculating a correlation test that includes a numerical range between −1 and +1.

A key component in the use of a correlation test is what is referred to as a correlation coefficient. A **correlation coefficient**, the statistic used in calculating the correlation test, is a range between −1 and +1. Values that are close to −1 or +1 indicate a strong relationship between an independent and dependent variable. Values close to (or at) zero reveal either a weak or no relationship between variables.

Provided in Table 13.1 is a continuum of values that identify the strength and direction of a straight-line correlation:

TABLE 13.1 **Correlation Coefficient Scale**

−1.00	Perfect negative correlation
−0.60	Strong negative correlation
−0.30	Moderate negative correlation
−0.10	Weak negative correlation
0.00	No correlation
+0.10	Weak positive correlation
+0.30	Moderate positive correlation
+0.60	Strong positive correlation
+1.00	Perfect positive correlation

Explanations of the Use of the Correlation Test

There are multiple advantages and explanations related to the use of the correlation test. Listed below are a number of applications.

1. It is not uncommon for criminologists to test theories to determine the basis of criminal activity under certain circumstances. This may include making specific predictions on the basis of a relationship between two variables. For instance, a theory that explains deviant

behavior may predict a relationship between the number of days a child fails to attend school and the number of disciplinary infractions a child has accumulated during their middle school years. A developmental theory within the discipline of psychology may predict a relationship between a father and child and its impact on the child's resiliency as an adult. Regardless of discipline or area, the testing of a theory may include testing the relationship between two variables.

2. Let's assume that a new test that measures aggression among youth has just been published in a popular and well-respected journal. How could someone determine if the test truly measures aggression? This is often referred to as validating the findings of a test. One approach is to use correlation. If the new test uses actual measures of aggression, one could compare the results of such with other similar or previously used tests. If the results are similar, one may conclude that the results of the new test are valid.
3. Overall, reliability refers to the consistency of measurement procedures. For instance, if a measurement procedure, let's say an exam, produces the same scores regardless of how many times the exam is administered, that measurement procedure is considered reliable. Imagine a student who scores a 95 on an exam during week 4 in a course and scores a 94 on the same exam during week 8. This is an example of a management procedure that is reliable.
4. An appealing use of the correlation test is its ability to identify a predictive relationship between an independent and dependent variable. For example, suppose one was interested in whether SAT scores (or grade point averages) among high school students could be used to predict how well a student performs academically in college. If both SAT scores (independent variable 1) and grade point averages (independent variable 2) actually correlate with students who perform well in college (dependent variable 1) and graduate in a timely manner (i.e., 4–5 years) (dependent variable 2), we can assume that SAT scores and grade point averages might be used as prediction factors among colleges and universities. This process of using relationships between variables in order to assert predictions is referred to as regression, which will be discussed in more detail in the next chapter.

Assumptions of the Correlation Test

As with any statistical test, within the scope of hypothesis testing, a correlation test has assumptions. The assumptions of the correlation test are as follows:

1. The data must not include outliers.
2. The data must be normally distributed.
3. The variances of the dependent variable are equal for each value of the independent variable. In other words, the data points (which reflect the independent variable and dependent variable) must have a similar amount of space from a trend line. This is referred to as homoscedasticity.
4. The data reflects a relationship that is identified in a straight line.

Chapter Learning Assessment Questions

To gauge your learning, provide answers to the following questions:

1. A correlation coefficient of 0.5 is an indication of a _______________.
   a. moderate positive correlation
   b. perfect negative correlation
   c. moderate negative correlation
   d. none of the above
2. Which of the following are considered assumptions of the correlation coefficient?
   a. Must use data that does not include outliers
   b. Must use data that is normally distributed
   c. Must use data that reflects the existence of homoscedasticity
   d. All of the above

Answers

1. a
2. d

Formula for Computing the Correlation Test

$$r = \frac{SP}{\sqrt{SS_x SS_y}},$$

where

SP = represents sum of products

SS_X = represents the squared deviations of x

SS_Y = represents the squared deviations of y

Correlation Test (Example 1)

As indicated below, suppose one is interested in determining if a correlation exists between the age of a middle school student and the number of instances in which they experienced detention in school. One may be likely to assume that as youth mature, they are less likely to experience detention in school. Consider the following data: ages (13, 13, 14, 12, 12, 12, 12, 14, 13, 14) and number of corresponding detention incidents (3, 4, 3, 4, 3, 4, 2, 2, 1).

Our statistical steps:

1. Identify the null and alternative hypotheses.

   The null hypothesis indicates there is no correlation between the age of the youth and the number of detention experiences. The alternative hypothesis states that there is a correlation between the age of the youth and the number of detention experiences.

$$H_0: \rho = 0$$
$$H_1: \rho \neq 0$$

2. Identify the level of risk or significance.

   Our selected level of risk is 0.05.
3. Choose the appropriate test.

   The continuous level of measurement of the independent and dependent variables requires the use of a correlation test.
4. Compute and identify the statistical test value (STV).

   Consider the following numbers in Table 13.2. This includes the calculation outcomes of the correlation test.

Overall, calculating the STV will include a series of steps. This includes computing the numerator as highlighted in the formula:

$$r = \frac{SP}{\sqrt{SS_x SS_y}}$$

Step 1—Compute *SP*

TABLE 13.2 **Youth Age and School Detention**

Age (x)	Number of Detention Experiences (y)	$(x - M_x)$	$(y - M_y)$	$(x - M_x)(y - M_y)$
13	3	0	0.12	0
13	4	0	1.12	0
14	3	1	0.12	0.12
12	4	−1	1.12	−1.12
12	3	−1	0.12	−0.12
12	4	−1	1.12	−1.12
14	2	1	−0.88	−0.88
13	2	0	−0.88	0
14	1	1	−1.88	−1.88
$M_x = 13$	$M_y = 2.88$			$SP = -5$

The aforementioned process involves the following steps:

a. Identify the means of the independent and dependent values (Columns 1 and 2).
b. Subtract the means from each of the independent and dependent values (Columns 3 and 4).
c. Multiply the values in Columns 3 and 4 (Column 5).
d. Find the sum of the values referred to as SP (Column 5).

As a result of this process, our *SP* is –5.

$$r = \frac{SP}{\sqrt{SS_x SS_y}}$$

Step 2—Compute the remaining steps

Now we will compute the remaining steps (Table 13.3) as identified in the formula. This requires including the squared deviations.

TABLE 13.3 **Youth Age and School Detention**

Age (x)	Number of Detention Experiences s(y)	$(x - M_x)$	$(y - M_y)$	$(x - M_x)^2$	$(y - M_y)^2$	(x – Mx) (y – My)
13	3	0	0.12	0	0.0144	0
13	4	0	1.12	0	1.2544	0
14	3	1	0.12	1	0.0144	0.12
12	4	–1	1.12	1	1.2544	–1.12
12	3	–1	0.12	1	0.0144	–0.12
12	4	–1	1.12	1	1.2544	–1.12
14	2	1	–0.88	1	0.7744	–0.88
13	2	0	–0.88	0	0.7744	0
14	1	1	–1.88	1	3.5344	–1.88
$M_x = 13$	$M_y = 2.88$			$SS_x = 6$	$SS_y = 8.88$	$SP = -5$

Now we will include all of the required numbers within the formula:

$$r = \frac{SP}{\sqrt{SS_x SS_y}}$$

$$r = \frac{-5}{\sqrt{(6)(8.88)}} = \frac{-5}{\sqrt{53.28}} = \frac{-5}{7.29} = -0.68$$

$$r = -0.68$$

Our final step involves calculating the t-statistical significance formula:

$$t = \frac{r - \rho}{\sqrt{\frac{(1 - r^2)}{(n - 2)}}}$$

$$t = \frac{-0.68 - 0}{\sqrt{\frac{(1 - 0.4624)}{(9 - 2)}}} = \frac{-0.68}{\sqrt{\frac{0.5376}{7}}} = \frac{-0.68}{\sqrt{0.0768}} = \frac{-0.68}{\sqrt{0.0768}} = \frac{-0.68}{0.277}$$

$$t = -2.45$$

Based on the aforementioned, our r is −0.68, and our t is −2.48
The STV, referred to as a correlation value, is −2.48

1. Identify and compare the critical decision value (CDV) to the STV.
   a. The degrees of freedom with a correlation test are computed by N − 2.
   b. Based on our numbers, this is 9 − 2 = 7.
   c. By observing these values in the two-tailed *t*-test table, which is in the appendix, we determine if the STV is greater or less than the CDV.
   d. Since our degrees of freedom are 7, we will locate that number under the degrees of freedom column and under the nondirectional 0.05 level of risk.
   e. As indicated in the two-tailed *t*-test table, we will use ±2.36 as the value in which to reject the null hypothesis. Since our STV (correlation value) is −2.48, we compare this value with the CDV, which is ±2.36.
2. If the STV > CDV, reject the null hypothesis.
   Given that the STV (−2.48) extends beyond the CDV (±2.36), we reject the null hypothesis. Thus, the alternative hypothesis, which states that there is a correlation between the age of the youth and the number of detention experiences, is true. Overall, as revealed in Figure 13.4, as age increases, detention experiences decrease.

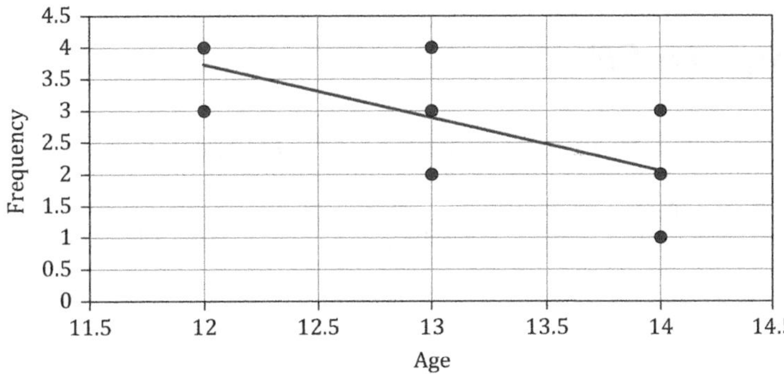

FIGURE 13.4 Age and Detention Decisions

In our answer, consider how the degrees of freedom are listed. This is consistent with the previous chapters in the text.

The results of the test are displayed in this manner:

$$r_{(7)} = -0.68, p < 0.05$$

Correlation Test (Example 2)

Our final example is based on the belief that a correlation exists between the time at which bars close and the number of violent crimes reported. More specifically, the later a bar closes the higher the number of reported assaults will take place. Listed below is information from a 10-year study that includes a total of 8 bars that close at 9 p.m. or at 1 a.m., along with their corresponding reported assault numbers. Closing times: 9, 1, 9, 1, 9, 1, 9, 1; Corresponding Assaults: 30, 36, 14, 21, 10, 12, 16, 19.

Our statistical steps are as follows:

1. Identify the null and alternative hypotheses.

   The null hypothesis indicates there is no correlation between the closing time of a bar and the number of assaults reported. The alternative hypothesis states that closing time positively correlates with the number of assaults reported.

$$H_0: \rho = 0$$

$$H_1: \rho > 0$$

2. Identify the level of risk or significance.

   Our selected level of risk is 0.05.
3. Choose the appropriate test.

   The continuous level of measurement of the independent and dependent variables requires the use of a correlation test.
4. Compute and identify the STV.

   Consider the numbers in Table 13.4. This includes the calculation outcomes of the correlation test:

Step 1—Compute *SP*

TABLE 13.4 **Bar Closing Times and Number of Violent Crimes**

Time (x)	Number of Assaults (y)	$(x - M_x)$	$(y - M_y)$	$(x - M_x)(y - M_y)$
9	30	4	10.25	41
1	36	−4	16.25	−65
9	14	4	−5.75	−23
1	21	−4	1.25	−5
9	10	4	−9.75	−39
1	12	−4	−7.75	31
9	16	4	−3.75	−15
1	19	−4	−0.75	3
$M_x = 5$	$M_y = 19.75$			$SP = -72$

The aforementioned process (as revealed in Table 13.4) involves the following steps:

1. Identify the means of the independent and dependent values (Columns 1 and 2).
2. Subtract the means from each of the independent and dependent values (Columns 3 and 4).
3. Multiply the values in Columns 3 and 4 (Column 5).
4. Find the sum of the values referred to as SP (Column 5).

As a result of this process, our *SP* is –72.

$$R = \frac{SP}{\sqrt{SS_x SS_y}}$$

Step 2—Compute the remaining steps

As indicated in Table 13.5, we will now compute the remaining steps as identified in the formula. This requires including the squared deviations.

TABLE 13.5 **Bar Closing Times and Number of Violent Crimes**

Time (x)	Number of Assaults (y)	$(x - M_x)$	$(y - M_y)$	$(x - M_x)^2$	$(y - M_y)^2$	(x — Mx) (y — My)
9	30	4	10.25	16	105.0625	41
1	36	-4	16.25	16	264.0625	-65
9	14	4	-5.75	16	33.0625	-23
1	21	-4	1.25	16	1.5625	-5
9	10	4	-9.75	16	95.0625	-39
1	12	-4	-7.75	16	60.0625	31
9	16	4	-3.75	16	14.0625	-15
1	19	-4	-0.75	16	0.5625	3
$M_x = 5$	$M_y = 19.75$			$SS_x = 128$	$SS_y = 573.5$	$SP = -72$

Now we will include all of the required numbers within the formula:

$$r = \frac{SP}{\sqrt{SS_x SS_y}}$$

$$r = \frac{-72}{\sqrt{(128)(573.5)}} = \frac{-72}{\sqrt{73408}} = \frac{-72}{270} = -0.026$$

$$r = -0.026$$

Our final step involves calculating the t-statistical significance formula:

$$t = \frac{r - \rho}{\sqrt{\frac{(1 - r^2)}{(n - 2)}}}$$

$$t = \frac{-0.026 - 0}{\sqrt{\frac{(1 - 0.0706)}{(8 - 2)}}} = \frac{-0.026}{\sqrt{\frac{.9238}{6}}} = \frac{-.026}{\sqrt{0.1549}} = \frac{-0.026}{0.39357} = -1.74$$

$$t = -1.74$$

Based on the aforementioned, our r is −0.026, and our t is −1.74
The STV, referred to as a correlation value, is −1.74

1. Identify and compare the CDV to the STV.
   a. The degrees of freedom with a correlation test is computed by N – 2.
   b. Based on our numbers, this is 8 – 2 = 6.
   c. We must now identify these values in the one-tail *t*-test table (e.g., appendix) to determine if the STV is greater or less than the CDV.
   d. Since our degrees of freedom is 6, we will locate that number under the degrees of freedom column and under the directional 0.05 level of risk.
   e. As indicated in the appendix table we will use 1.94 as the value in which to reject the null hypothesis. Since our STV (correlation value) is −1.74, we compare this value with the CDV, which is 1.94.
2. If the STV > CDV, reject the null hypothesis.
   Given that the STV (−1.74) is less than the CDV (1.94), we fail to reject the null hypothesis. Thus, as illustrated in Figure 13.5, the null hypothesis is true, which states that there is no correlation between the closing time of a bar and the number of assaults reported.

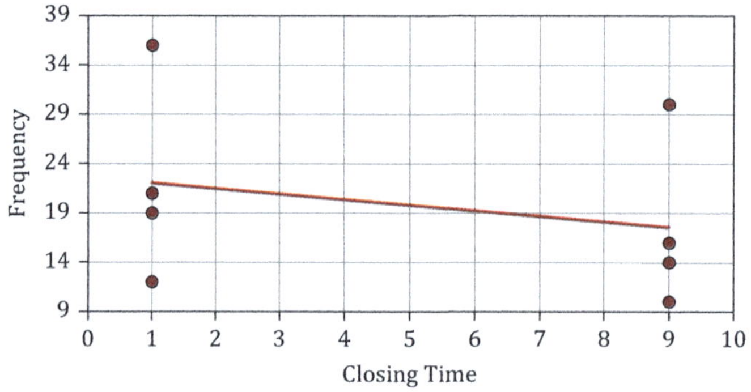

FIGURE 13.5 Bar Closing Times and Number of Assaults

The results of the test are displayed in this manner:

$$r(6) = -0.26, p > 0.05$$

Chapter Learning Assessment Questions

To gauge your learning, provide answers to the following questions:

1. When computing a directional (one-tail) correlation coefficient, with a *df* of 4 and a level of risk $p < 0.01$, which of the following is the correct CDV needed to reject the null hypothesis?
   a. 3.58
   b. 3.78
   c. 2.39
   d. None of the above
2. When computing a nondirectional (two-tail) correlation coefficient, with a *df* of 10 and a level of risk $p < 0.05$, which of the following is the correct CDV needed to reject the null hypothesis?
   a. 2.19
   b. 1.78
   c. 2.23
   d. None of the above

Answers

1. b
2. c

Final Thoughts

Correlation is a popular and yet often misinterpreted term. For instance, how many times have you heard that poverty is correlated with delinquency or crime? Upon hearing this statement, many assume that the term correlation is the same as identifying the actual cause of something. Be sure to avoid this mistake by keeping in mind that correlation is not causation. In short, one can experience correlation without causation, but one cannot experience causation without correlation.

Discussion

Imagine that you are the director of a state-wide youth rehabilitation program. You are responsible for the well-being of over 100,000 youth and their families, as well as the safety of communities and schools. To avoid a reduction of state funding, you decide to provide scientific evidence that supports your approach to addressing the negative impact of trauma among youth. In your efforts, you locate a recent study that reveals that childhood trauma is correlated with delinquency. What is your response to this finding? Do you decide to use the article as evidence to justify avoiding budget cuts within your program? Explain.

Chapter Summary

Chapter 13 discussed the following information:

Objective 1 – The correlation test

- A correlation test is employed to determine if a linear relationship exists between a continuous independent and dependent variable.
- A positive correlation is a relationship in which an increase (or decrease) in the independent variable results in a similar impact on the dependent variable. Both variables are moving in the same direction.
- A negative correlation is a relationship in which an increase (or decrease) in the independent variable results in the dependent variable moving in the opposite direction.
- A correlation coefficient, the statistic used in calculating the correlation test, is a range of values between −1 to +1.
- A curvilinear correlation is a relationship between an independent and dependent variable that either begins in a positive or negative direction and ends in an oppositive direction.
- A scatterplot reveals the relationship between variables by using data points that represent the actual numbers reflected in the independent and dependent variables.

Objective 2 – Formula for the correlation test

- See the corresponding pages in the chapter.

Objective 3 – Example problems(s) and the correlation test

- See the corresponding pages in the chapter.

Terms

Correlation test
Correlation coefficient
Curvilinear correlation
Positive correlation
Negative correlation
Scatterplot

Chapter Review Questions

1. A _______________ is a statistical test that is used to determine a linear relationship between an independent and dependent variable.
   a. correlation test
   b. negative correlation test
   c. positive correlation test
   d. linear regression analysis
2. A correlation test can express the following within a single number.
   a. the strength of the correlation

b. the direction of the correlation
c. both the direction and strength of the correlation
d. the relative value of the correlation

3. If data points in a scatterplot are located closely around a straight line, the correlation is considered ________.
   a. negative
   b. positive
   c. strong
   d. weak
4. A ________ is used to determine whether a relationship in which an increase (or decrease) in the independent variable results in an increase (or decrease) in the dependent variable.
   a. negative correlation test
   b. positive correlation test
   c. correlation coefficient
   d. either a or b
5. When conducting a correlation test, the dependent variable must be designated at which of the following levels of measurement:
   a. nominal
   b. ordinal
   c. continuous
   d. either a or b
6. A ________ is the statistic used in calculating the correlation test.
   a. correlation factor
   b. correlation point
   c. correlation coefficient
   d. correlation range
7. A ________ is a relationship between an independent and dependent variable that either begins in a positive or negative direction and ends in an oppositive direction.
   a. correlation coefficient
   b. correlation range
   c. curvilinear correlation
   d. curvilinear coefficient
8. The statistic used in calculating the correlation test includes a range between
   a. −1 to +1
   b. 0 to 1
   c. −10 to +1
   d. −10 to +10

9. A correlation coefficient of −0.4 is considered:
   a. a moderate negative correlation
   b. between a moderate and a strong negative correlation
   c. between a moderate and a negative correlation
   d. a strong negative correlation
10. A correlation coefficient of −0.68 is considered:
    a. negative and strong
    b. negative and weak
    c. positive and strong
    d. positive and weak
11. A visual illustration of the relationship between the independent and dependent variable is referred to as a ______________.
    a. correlation coefficient
    b. scatterplot
    c. curvilinear correlation
    d. curvilinear coefficient
12. Which of the following is not appropriate for conducting a correlation coefficient?
    a. random sample
    b. normal distribution of data
    c. nominal level data
    d. continuous level data
13. When observing the statistic used in calculating the correlation test, the value of 1 is interpreted as:
    a. a weak relationship between the independent and dependent variable
    b. a moderate relationship between the independent and dependent variable
    c. a strong relationship between the independent and dependent variable
    d. an inconclusive relationship between the independent and dependent variable
14. When observing the statistic used in calculating the correlation test, the value of 0 is interpreted as:
    a. no relationship between the independent and dependent variable
    b. a weak relationship between the independent and dependent variable
    c. a moderate relationship between the independent and dependent variable
    d. either a or b
15. A professor wishes to investigate the hypothesis that conflict resolution programs may decrease the number of violent incidents within a school district. This includes gaining access to data which includes the amount of conflict resolution programs utilized in the schools. The number of violent acts as measured by the number of aggravated assaults reported in the schools.

a. What is the independent variable?
b. What is the dependent variable?
c. What is the level of measurement for the independent and dependent variables?
d. What are the null and alternate hypotheses that should be used?

16. A researcher is interested in testing whether the number of working lights in a high-crime neighborhood will decrease the number of violent crimes in the area (Xu et al., 2018). Based on data provided by the city, the researcher can identify the amount and location of the lights that have been installed and replaced in the neighborhood. Data that identifies the number of crimes is based on reported incidents as collected by the local police department.
    a. What is the independent variable?
    b. What is the dependent variable?
    c. What is the level of measurement for the independent and dependent variables?
    d. What are the null and alternate hypotheses that should be used?
17. A statistician believes that for every number of individuals who experience arrest, a certain number of those individuals are sentenced to prison. Thus, as arrest numbers increase, those sentenced to prison will also increase. Through the use of public access data, individuals who experience arrest and imprisonment are measured in a state on an annual basis.
    a. What is the independent variable?
    b. What is the dependent variable?
    c. What is the level of measurement for the independent and dependent variables?
    d. What are the null and alternate hypotheses that should be used?
18. A criminologist believes that the availability and use of mirrors in public areas may prevent robberies (Calder and Bauer, 1992). To test this hypothesis, the criminologist gains access to data that identifies the number of mirrors within public settings. This information, which is a matter of public record, was provided by a local government entity responsible for providing licenses and permits. Data that identifies the number of robberies is measured based on whether a robbery occurred in an area after a mirror was replaced or installed.
    a. What is the independent variable?
    b. What is the dependent variable?
    c. What is the level of measurement for the independent and dependent variables?
    d. What are the null and alternate hypotheses that should be used?
19. By reviewing the *t*-test table information near the end of the text, determine if the following STVs support the decision to reject the null hypothesis:

Level of Significance	Type of Test	Statistical Test Value	Degrees of Freedom	Critical Decision Value	Reject the Null Hypothesis
0.01	Directional	4.15	4	3.74	
0.05	Directional	1.96	12	1.78	
0.01	Directional	2.38	21	2.58	
0.01	Nondirectional	3.12	15	2.94	

Level of Significance	Type of Test	Statistical Test Value	Degrees of Freedom	Critical Decision Value	Reject the Null Hypothesis
0.05	Nondirectional	3.21	9	2.26	
0.05	Directional	1.68	24	1.71	
0.01	Nondirectional	3.37	40	2.70	
0.05	Directional	2.15	30	1.69	
0.01	Directional	1.78	18	2.55	

20. Determine if the following results indicate a positive or a negative correlation:
    a. The increasing number of schools that decided to resume classes during the early part of September (as opposed to the second week in August) also experienced an increase in the number of incidents of delinquency from last year.
    b. The increasing number of law enforcement agencies that receive implicit bias training within a 5-year period also experienced a reduction in the number of citizen complaints.
    c. A study revealed that as the number of felony convictions in a defendant's criminal history increases, the amount of time they received with respect to sentencing will likely increase.
    d. An increase in the number of violent incidents an inmate engages in is associated with the amount of time they will spend in a secure detention cell.
    e. As the number of individuals who are convicted of a felony offense increases, the number of individuals who are convicted in criminal court increases.
    f. The increasing number of states that passed gun control legislation experienced a lower annual number of gun-related crimes.
    g. As the amount of funding for the number of minority youth mentoring programs in a community decreases, there is an increase in the number of school suspensions among minority youth.
    h. As the number of people who support the legalization of a certain drug in a community increases, the number of arrests associated with the use and possession of that certain drug in the community decreases.
    i. As the number of pretrial diversion programs increases, the graduation rate of youth (who were considered "at-risk") increases.
21. Based on the following series of values, (1) conduct a correlation test (at 0.05 level of risk) to determine if a significant association exists, and (2) assume a directional test. Values for x include 1, 6, 4, 3, 2, 8, 9. Values for y include: 2, 4, 2.5, 2.25, 3, 5, 5.3.
22. Based on the following series of values, (1) conduct a correlation test (at 0.05 level of risk) to determine if a significant association exists, and (2) assume a directional test. Values for x include: 3, 4, 6, 8, 10, 12, 9. Values for y include 5.7, 2.1, 8.9, 12.5, 9.3, 15, 7.3.
23. Based on the following series of values, (1) conduct a correlation test (at 0.05 level of risk) to determine if a significant association exists, and (2) assume a directional test. Values for x include: 2, 3.6, 4.1, 2.7, 4.6, 3, 2. Values for y include 4, 6.2, 8.4, 4.9, 1, 2.8, 7.

24. The following identifies a possible association among youth based on their understanding of the Miranda warning and providing false confessions. This includes the completion of a literacy test (scores ranging from 0 to 10) among youth regarding their knowledge and application of the Miranda warning. It is assumed that a higher test score will result in a lower number of false confessions. Conduct a correlation test (at 0.01 level of risk) to determine if a significant association exists. Values for test scores include 3, 5, 4, 7, 6, 3, 2, 6, 2, 8. Values for false confessions include 6, 4, 5, 3, 2, 3, 5, 3, 4, 2.
25. Provided below is information that identifies an association between crime reporting and property recovery. Victims of property crime provided the actual number of minutes that transpired from the time they realized that they had been victimized and notified the police. They also provided the number of days on which they received notification from the police regarding the recovery of their property. Conduct a correlation test (at 0.05 level of risk) to determine if a significant association exists. Values for minutes include 5, 7, 10, 8, 15, 20, 9, 4. Values for days include 3, 4, 8, 7, 12, 13, 9, 2.
26. Within criminology, the power control theory asserts that as the population of minorities increases in certain areas, social control measures are employed in response to such. Examples of social control measures include arrests, criminal convictions, etc. Identified below are the census population and traffic stop numbers of Whites and Blacks between 2010 and 2019.

	Population			**Traffic Stops**	
	Whites	Blacks		Whites	Blacks
2010	457,512	226,195	2010	67,138	77,418
2011	464,527	233,635	2011	58,638	69,094
2012	473,677	241,746	2012	46,372	55,812
2013	481,755	251,150	2013	53,715	65,288
2014	488,942	258,641	2014	63,473	76,493
2015	498,795	267,099	2015	48,089	60,451
2016	509,073	275,638	2016	34,823	45,306
2017	517,768	283,235	2017	38,156	56,588
2018	524,978	289,553	2018	28,442	42,388
2019	533,038	295,907	2019	35,566	55,256

In light of the aforementioned information, provide answers to the following questions:

a. Which racial category experienced the greatest increase in population growth between 2010 and 2019?
b. Which racial category experienced the greatest decrease in traffic stops between 2010 and 2019?
c. Based on the data provided, is there a sufficient amount of evidence that supports the power control theory? Explain.

27. A researcher is curious to determine whether there is an association between the use of technology and reported aggressive behavior among youth. The following information

represents the amount of time a young person spends surfing the internet. It also includes information related to the number of school disciplinary infractions in relation to aggressive behavior (i.e., fighting, etc.). Conduct a correlation test (at 0.05 level of risk) to determine if a significant association exists. Values for time include 4, 6, 5.5, 3, 4, 7, 6.5, 2, 3, 4, 2, 1, 4. Values for number of infractions include 7, 11, 10, 5, 7, 13, 14, 4, 6, 7, 3, 2, 9.

Time Spent Surfing the Internet (Hours per Day)	Number of Disciplinary Infractions (Within the School Year)
4	7
6	11
5.5	10
3	5
4	7
7	13
6.5	14
2	4
3	6
4	7
2	3
1	2
4	9

28. A researcher is interested in whether there is an association between years of experience and stress (as measured on a scale from 1 to 10) among criminal justice practitioners. Specifically, she believes that newly licensed attorneys are more likely to experience higher levels of stress when compared to attorneys who have at least 5 years of experience. The following data includes the number of years of service as well as the stress level among attorneys. Conduct a correlation test (at 0.05 level of risk) to determine if a significant association exists.

Years of Legal Experience	Level of Stress (1-10)
4	8
8	4
9	4
16	5
10	6
14	3
3	9
4	10
3	9
8	10
21	5
5	6
17	6

29. A researcher believes that consistent interaction among family members plays a role in the behavior of those who are incarcerated (Pierce et al., 2018). More specifically, inmates who receive visitation from their children are less likely to engage in disciplinary infractions within a prison setting. The data below represents the number of visits an inmate receives, along with the number of prison disciplinary infractions within a 6-month time period. Conduct a correlation test (at 0.05 level of risk) to determine if a significant association exists.

Number Visits	Disciplinary Infractions
24	3
3	15
7	6
21	2
8	8
12	6
8	8
1	14
4	9
19	2
3	13
10	5
17	3
2	12
9	9
1	14
3	10
9	12
15	2
6	6

Answers

1. a
2. c
3. c
4. b
5. c
6. c
7. c
8. a
9. b
10. a
11. b
12. c
13. c

14. d
15.
   a. The independent variable is the existence of conflict resolution programs.
   b. The dependent variable is the number of violent incidents within a school district.
   c. The level of measurement for the independent variable is continuous. The level of measurement for the dependent variable is continuous.
   d. The null hypothesis is based on the assumption that there is no association between the existence of conflict resolution programs and the number of violent incidents within a school district. The alternative hypothesis is based on the assumption that there is an association between the existence of conflict resolution programs and the number of violent incidents within a school district.
16.
   a. The independent variable is the number of working lights in a high-crime neighborhood.
   b. The dependent variable is the number of violent crimes in an area.
   c. The level of measurement for the independent variable is continuous. The level of measurement for the dependent variable is continuous.
   d. The null hypothesis is based on the assumption that there is no association between the number of working lights in a high-crime neighborhood and the number of violent crimes in an area. The alternative hypothesis is based on the assumption that there is an association between the number of working lights in a high-crime neighborhood and the number of violent crimes in an area.
17.
   a. The independent variable is the increased number of individuals who experience arrest.
   b. The dependent variable is the increased number of individuals who are sentenced to prison.
   c. The level of measurement for the independent variable is continuous. The level of measurement for the dependent variable is continuous.
   d. The null hypothesis is based on the assumption that there is no association between the increased number of individuals who experience arrest and the increased number of individuals who are sentenced to prison. The alternative hypothesis is based on the assumption that there is an association between the increased number of individuals who experience arrest and the increased number of individuals who are sentenced to prison.
18.
   a. The independent variable is the number of mirrors within public settings.
   b. The dependent variable is the number of robberies that occurred in a public setting after a mirror was replaced or installed.
   c. The level of measurement for the independent variable is continuous. The level of measurement for the dependent variable is continuous.
   d. The null hypothesis is based on the assumption that there is no association between the number of mirrors within public settings and the number of robberies that occurred in a public setting after a mirror was replaced or installed. The alternative hypothesis is based on the assumption that there is an association between the number of mirrors within public settings and the number of robberies that occurred in a public setting after a mirror was replaced or installed.

19.

Level of Significance	Type of Test	Statistical Test Value	Degrees of Freedom	Critical Decision Value	Reject the Null Hypothesis
0.01	Directional	4.15	4	3.74	Y
0.05	Directional	1.96	12	1.78	Y
0.01	Directional	2.38	21	2.58	N
0.01	Nondirectional	3.12	15	2.94	Y
0.05	Nondirectional	3.21	9	2.26	Y
0.05	Directional	1.68	24	1.71	N
0.01	Nondirectional	3.37	40	2.70	Y
0.05	Directional	2.15	30	1.69	Y
0.01	Directional	1.78	18	2.55	N

20.
a. positive
b. negative
c. positive
d. positive
e. positive
f. negative
g. negative
h. negative
i. positive

21. With an $r = 0.94$ and a ($p < 0.05$), there is a statistically significant association between the x and y values identified.
22. With an $r = 0.79$ and a ($p < 0.05$), there is a statistically significant association between the x and y values identified.
23. With an $r = -0.18$ and a ($p > 0.05$), there is no statistically significant association between the x and y values identified.
24. With an $r = -0.71$ and a ($p < 0.01$), there is a statistically significant association between test scores and the number of false confessions.
25. With an $r = 0.93$ and a ($p < 0.05$), there is a statistically significant association between test scores and the number of false confessions.
26. The racial category that experienced the greatest increase in population growth between 2010 and 2019 is Blacks.
The racial category that experienced the greatest decrease in traffic stops between 2010 and 2019 is Whites.
With an $r = -0.84$ and a ($p < 0.05$), there is a statistically significant association between the population increase of minorities and the number of traffic stops experienced by minorities. Thus, based on the data provided, there is a sufficient amount of evidence to support the power control theory.
27. With an $r = 0.97$ and a ($p < 0.05$), there is a statistically significant association between the time spent surfing the internet and the number of disciplinary infractions related to aggressive behavior among youth.
28. With an $r = -0.61$ and a ($p < 0.05$), there is a statistically significant association between the number of years of experience and the level of stress among attorneys.
29. With an $r = -0.86$ and a ($p < 0.05$), there is a statistically significant association between the number of visits and the number of inmate disciplinary infractions in a prison setting.

Matching: Place the letter of the following definitions with its corresponding term.

___1. Correlation test	a. a relationship in which an increase (or decrease) in the independent variable results in a similar impact on the dependent variable
___2. Positive correlation	b. the statistic used in calculating the correlation test
___3. Negative correlation	c. employed to determine if a linear relationship exists between a continuous independent and dependent variable
___4. Correlation coefficient	d. a relationship in which an increase (or decrease) in the independent variable results in the dependent variable moving in the opposite direction
___5. Curvilinear correlation	e. the relationship between variables by using data points which represent the actual numbers reflected in the independent and dependent variables
___6. Scatterplot	f. a relationship between an independent and dependent variable that either begins in a positive or negative direction and ends in an oppositive direction

Answers

1. c
2. a
3. d
4. b
5. f
6. e

Bibliography

Braungart, M. M., Braungart, R. G., & Hoyer, W. J. (1980). Age, sex, and social factors in fear of crime. *Sociological Focus, 13*(1), 55–66.

Calder, J. D., & Bauer, J. R. (1992). Convenience store robberies: Security measures and store robbery incidents. *Journal of Criminal Justice, 20*(6), 553–566.

Pierce, M. B., Freiburger, T. L., Chapin, J. R., Epling, B., & Madden, T. J. (2018). Assessing the impact of visitation on inmate misconduct within a county jail. *Security Journal, 31*(1), 1–20.

Stanford University, *What is BAC?* Office of Substance Use Programs Education & Resources. https://super.stanford.edu/alcohol-drug-info/buzz-buzz/what-bac

Xu, Y., Fu, C., Kennedy, E., Jiang, S., & Owusu-Agyemang, S. (2018). The impact of street lights on spatial-temporal patterns of crime in Detroit, Michigan. *Cities, 79*, 45–52.

Chapter 13 SPSS and Workbook Questions

SPSS and the Correlation Test

To compute the correlation test using SPSS, consider the following:

Studies in criminal justice have examined the role of police officer experience as it relates to public responses.

For example, suppose one is interested in whether the amount of experience that a patrol officer has is significantly associated with the number of complaints they receive from citizens. If an association between experience and complaints exists, then a policy that requires additional training for officers with a certain level of experience might be developed or revised. Shown below is a table that reveals information related to patrol experience and officer complaints.

Officer Experience	Number of Complaints	Officer Experience	Number of Complaints
4	10	10	1
5	6	12	2
3	7	12	1
5	5	13	4
4	6	16	3
6	8	12	2
3	6	12	3
4	7	14	2
7	8	18	1
5	5	19	2
6	6	17	3
4	5	21	2
5	4	25	3
5	4	28	2
6	3	31	4

Entry of Data—SPSS

1. Select variable view to include information associated with the variables of interest. In our example, this would include *officer experience* and *number of complaints*.
2. In the first row, include the term *experience* under the column identified as name.
3. For the remaining group, which includes *complaints*, follow the same procedure as noted above.
4. Select data view to include the scores for each variable in each corresponding column.

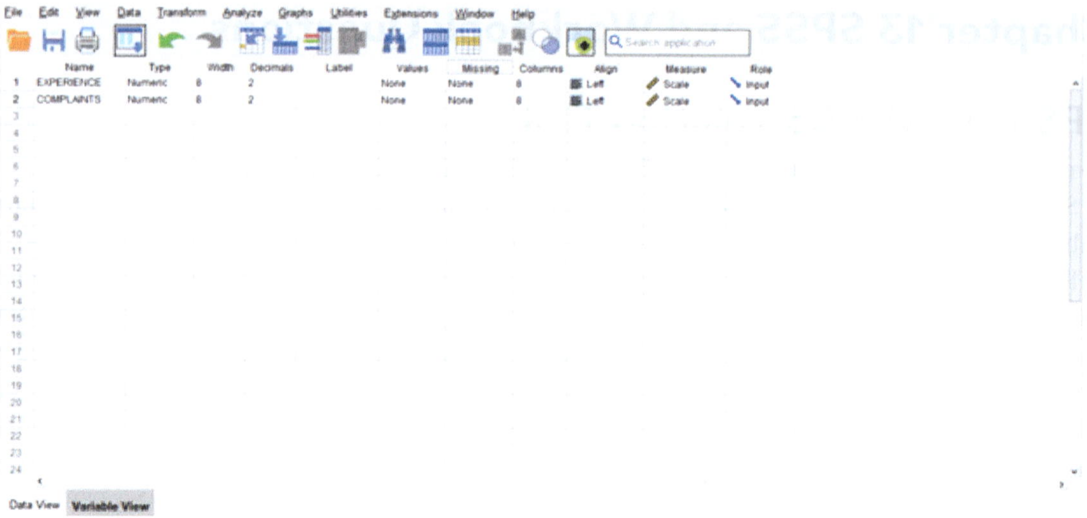

IMAGE 13.1

IMAGE 13.2

Analysis of Data—SPSS

1. Select analyze, select correlate, and select bivariate.
2. Select the variables *experience* and *complaints* and move them to the box identified as variables.
3. Under the section identified as correlation coefficients, select Pearson.
4. Under the section referred to as Test of Significance, select two-tailed (if a specific direction is not expressed) or select one-tailed (if a specific direction is expressed). Since an expressed direction was not provided, select two-tailed.
5. Finally, in order to noticeably identify significant associations between variables, consider selecting the option flag the significant correlations.
6. In the options section, select statistics, and select means and standard deviations in order to include the descriptive statistics of the analysis.
7. After all desired functions have been selected, select OK.

Output of Data Analysis - SPSS

In alignment with previous results, our analysis includes two tables of information. The descriptive statistics, as provided in Table 1, includes the number, standard deviation, and mean of each variable (i.e., experience, complaints). The results of the bivariate correlation are provided in Table 2. This includes the correlation coefficients, sample size, and level of significance (p-value = 0.001). Overall, the results reveal a significant statistical association between the experience of a patrol officer and the extent to which an officer receives a citizen's complaint.

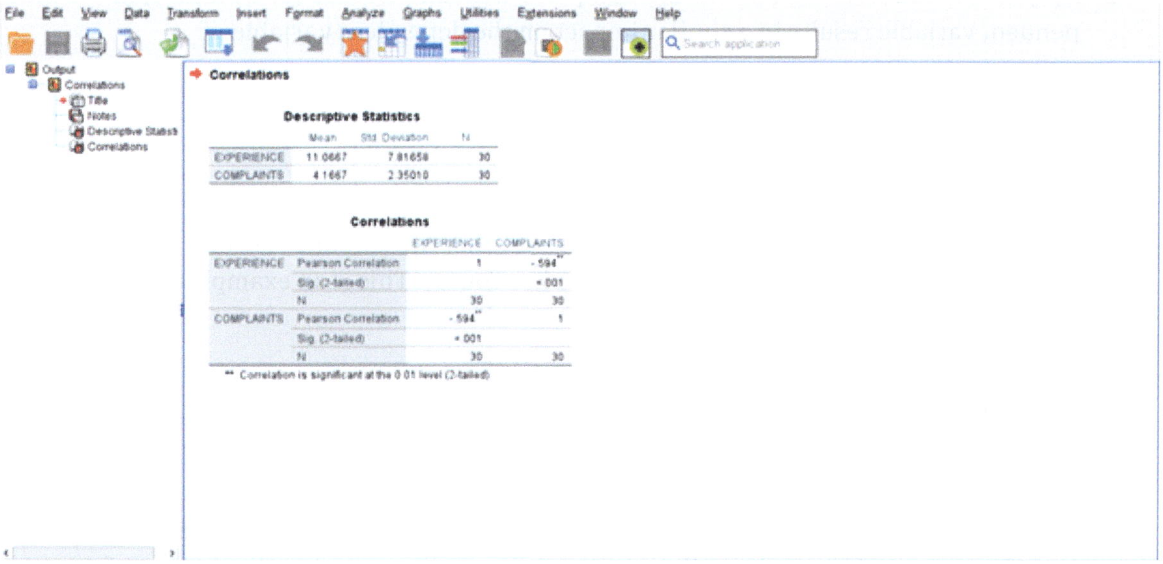

Descriptive Statistics

	Mean	Std. Deviation	N
EXPERIENCE	11.0667	7.81658	30
COMPLAINTS	4.1667	2.35010	30

Correlations

		EXPERIENCE	COMPLAINTS
EXPERIENCE	Pearson Correlation	1	-.594**
	Sig. (2-tailed)		<.001
	N	30	30
COMPLAINTS	Pearson Correlation	-.594**	1
	Sig. (2-tailed)	<.001	
	N	30	30

** Correlation is significant at the 0.01 level (2-tailed).

IMAGE 13.3

Workbook Questions

Objective 1—Define and Explain the Use of the Correlation Test

- A correlation test is employed to determine if a linear relationship exists between a continuous independent and dependent variable.
- A positive correlation is a relationship in which an increase (or decrease) in the independent variable results in a similar impact on the dependent variable. Both variables are moving in the same direction.
- A negative correlation is a relationship in which an increase (or decrease) in the independent variable results in the dependent variable moving in the opposite direction.
- A correlation coefficient, the statistic used in calculating the correlation test, is a range of values between –1 to +1.
- A curvilinear correlation is a relationship between an independent and dependent variable that either begins in a positive or negative direction and ends in an oppositive direction.
- A scatterplot reveals the relationship between variables by using data points that represent the actual numbers reflected in the independent and dependent variables.

Corresponding Questions

1. A correlation test is used to determine if a linear relationship exists between a(n) ________ independent and dependent variable.
   a. nominal level
   b. ordinal level
   c. categorical
   d. continuous
2. A(n) ________ correlation is a relationship in which an increase (or decrease) in the independent variable results in a similar impact on the dependent variable.
   a. positive
   b. negative
   c. inverted
   d. either b or c
3. As a proponent of reading, a researcher believes that the amount of time a student spends studying is related to their numerical grades in a course. This is an example of a(n) ________ correlation.
   a. negative
   b. positive
   c. curvilinear
   d. either b or c
4. A researcher who supports the use of meditation in response to offensive behavior believes that the amount of time a juvenile spends meditating is related to the amount of negative behavioral incidents they engage in at a secure correctional facility (Wongtongkam et al, 2014). This is an example of a(n) ________ correlation.
   a. negative
   b. positive
   c. curvilinear
   d. either b or c
5. A(n) ________ correlation is a relationship in which an increase (or decrease) in the independent variable results in the dependent variable moving in the opposite direction.
   a. positive
   b. negative
   c. inverted
   d. either a or b
6. A ________ is the statistic used in calculating the correlation test.
   a. correlation coefficient
   b. statistical coefficient

c. binomial coefficient

d. multivariate coefficient

7. The statistic used in calculating the correlation test uses a range of values between ________.

a. 0 to +1

b. –1 to 0

c. –1 to +1

d. –1 to 0

8. Suppose a research study based on the relationship between gun possession and homicides in a community reveals a coefficient of 0.35. This would represent a finding that indicates a ________ between gun ownership and homicides.

a. weak positive correlation

b. strong positive correlation

c. moderate positive correlation

d. weak negative correlation

9. A(n) ________ correlation is a relationship between an independent and dependent variable that either begins in a positive or negative direction and ends in an oppositive direction.

a. positive

b. curvilinear

c. negative

d. inverted

10. A ________ reveals the relationship between variables by using data points which represent the actual numbers reflected in the independent and dependent variables.

a. scatterplot

b. point plot

c. data plot

d. numerical plot

11. Which of the following represents an inappropriate use of a correlation test?

a. A researcher believes that the age of an inmate is associated with the number of disciplinary infractions they received while incarcerated in prison.

b. A study that examines the association between gender and the number of juvenile offenders in a secure confinement facility.

c. A research publication journal reveals the association between the number of criminal offenses a defendant has and the number of years they received in sentencing.

d. The principal of an elementary school is curious as to whether an association exists between the number of days a student fails to attend school and their grades at the end of the year. In this example, student grades are represented by numerical criteria (e.g., 90, 85, etc.).

Answers

1. d
2. a
3. b
4. a
5. b
6. a
7. c
8. c
9. b
10. a
11. b

Objective 2—Formula for the Correlation Test

- See the corresponding pages in the chapter.

Objective 3—Example Problem(s) and the Correlation Test

- See the corresponding pages in the chapter.

Corresponding Questions

1. The following information represents the number of individuals who experienced an encounter with a police officer. Your professor believes that age is associated with police encounters (Friedman et al., 2004). More specifically, he believes that younger individuals, compared to older individuals, are more likely to experience interaction with police. Based on the following, compute a correlation test (with a risk level of 0.05) to determine if your professor's hypothesis is valid.

Age	Number of Encounters
14	5
17	4
23	3
32	1
18	3
15	5
27	4
25	4
30	1
24	3
19	3
15	6

14	4
28	2
40	1

2. After hearing a lecture about the advantages and disadvantages of capitalism, a student enrolled in an advanced-level sociological theory course believes that income amount is associated with the conviction of white-collar crimes (Gottschalk and Rundmo, 2014). Based on the following data, which includes the reported incomes and conviction records of individuals accused of white-collar crimes, compute a correlation test (with a risk level of 0.05) to determine if the student's hypothesis is valid.

Income	Convictions
75,000	1
175,000	3
115,000	2
55,000	0
125,000	2
225,000	2
47,300	1
50,000	2
105,000	1
134,000	1
178,000	2
192,000	2
205,000	3
68,500	1
87,500	2

3. Within the topic of criminology, students begin to understand how various factors in society may have an impact on deviant behavior. In fact, one student believes that power outages might be associated with crime (Chaflin et al, 2021). Identified below are the number of reported power outages which includes the time periods of how long citizens did not have electricity. The table also includes the number of burglaries in the same area during the time in which power was not available. Based on the following data, compute a correlation test (with a risk level of 0.05) to determine if there is a significant association between the time periods of power outages and burglaries.

Hours of Power Outage	Number of Burglaries
3	2
6	3
4	2
5	2
4	2

Hours of Power Outage	Number of Burglaries
8	3
8	3
6	2
3	2
4	1
2	1
4	1
7	3
3	2
5	3

Answers

1. With an $r = -0.82$ and a ($p < 0.05$), there is a statistically significant association between age and the number of police encounters. Thus, the alternative hypothesis (your professor's assumption), which states that there is an association between the age of an individual and the number of encounters with the police, is true.
2. With an $r = 0.66$ and a ($p < 0.05$), there is a statistically significant association between the income amounts and the number of convictions for white-collar crimes. Thus, the assumption (alternative hypothesis) of the student is valid.
3. With an $r = 0.74$ and a ($p < 0.05$), there is a statistically significant association between the power outage time and the number of burglaries. Thus, the assumption (alternative hypothesis) of the student is valid.

Bibliography

Chalfin, A., Kaplan, J., & LaForest, M. (2021). Street light outages, public safety and crime attraction. *Journal of Quantitative Criminology*, 1–29.

Friedman, W., Lurigio, A. J., Greenleaf, R., & Albertson, S. (2004). Encounters between police officers and youths: The social costs of disrespect. *Journal of Crime and Justice*, *27*(2), 1–25.

Gottschalk, P., & Rundmo, T. (2014). Crime: The amount and disparity of sentencing–A comparison of corporate and occupational white-collar criminals. *International Journal of Law, Crime and Justice*, *42*(3), 175–187.

Wongtongkam, N., Ward, P. R., Day, A., & Winefield, A. H. (2014). A trial of mindfulness meditation to reduce anger and violence in Thai youth. *International Journal of Mental Health and Addiction*, *12*(2), 169–180.

Credits

CHAPTER 14

Linear Regression Test

Life is ten percent what you experience and ninety percent how you respond to it.
—Dorothy M. Neddermeyer

Objectives

1. Define and explain the use of linear regression tests
2. Identify the formula for computing the linear regression test
3. Compute linear regression test(s)
4. Define and explain the use of a multiple regression test
5. Identify the formula for computing multiple regression tests

Introduction—Mental Status and Judicial Decisions

Judges have an important role in imposing sentences on defendants. Decisions associated with this process often include the consideration of numerous factors. Examples of such may include the number of offenses convicted, a defendant's criminal history, or a defendant's mental status. As a researcher, suppose you are curious to determine whether a defendant's mental status (as measured by completing a psychological test) can be used to predict a sentencing outcome, which is measured by the number of months a defendant is incarcerated. A test that is useful in discovering this kind of relationship is referred to as a linear regression test.

Linear Regression Tests

A **linear regression** test is a statistical test that is used to determine the extent to which a continuous-level independent variable predicts a continuous-level dependent variable. For instance, the test might be used to predict sentencing or monetary fine amounts based on the number of arrests or charges filed against an individual. The use of two variables in a linear regression model is known as the **bivariate**

linear regression test A statistical test that is used to determine the extent to which a continuous-level independent variable predicts a continuous-level dependent variable.

bivariate regression test A statistical test used to determine the extent to which a single independent variable predicts a single dependent variable.

multiple regression test A statistical test used to determine if more than one independent variable predicts a dependent variable.

regression test. The use of more than one independent variable is referred to as the **multiple regression test**.

Assumptions of the Linear Regression Test

As indicated in previous chapters related to inferential statistical tests, the linear regression test includes the following assumptions, which are consistent with the correlation coefficient test:

1. Data within the sample must be selected randomly.
2. Independent and dependent variables are considered interval-level data.
3. Linear regression usage assumes that the data will demonstrate a straight line. For this reason, the data included should demonstrate a correlational relationship.
4. A large sample size is preferred to test for significance.

Formula for Computing the Linear Regression Test

$$\hat{y} = a + bx,$$

where

a = represents the y intercept

b = represents the slope (or slope coefficient)

x = value of the independent variable

To compute b, the formula is as follows:

$$b = \frac{\Sigma XY - (\Sigma X \Sigma Y / n)}{\Sigma X^2 - \left[(\Sigma X)^2 / n\right]}$$

To compute a, the formula is as follows:

$$a = \frac{\Sigma Y - b\Sigma X}{n}$$

Chapter Learning Assessment Questions

To gauge your learning, provide answers to the following questions:

1. Suppose a researcher is interested in determining whether the number of days a student is expelled from school is associated with the number of status offenses they engaged in. This scenario calls for the use of which of the following types of statistical tests?

   a. Independent *t*-test or dependent *t*-test
   b. Bivariate regression test
   c. Multiple regression test
   d. None of the above
2. All of the following are considered assumptions of the linear regression test except:
   a. data within the sample must be selected randomly.
   b. the independent and dependent variables are considered categorical level.
   c. the use of a large sample size is preferred.
   d. all of the above

Answers

1. b
2. b

Computing the Linear Regression Test

To determine your understanding and application of the linear regression test, consider the following scenario:

Linear Regression Test (Example)

Suppose one is interested in determining if the number of violations that a youth has on their record is used to predict the number of privileges revoked in a youth correctional facility. Consider the following details. Violations: 1, 1, 3, 2, 4, 1, 3, 2, 2. Revoke Privileges: 2, 2, 6, 4, 8, 2, 6, 4, 4.

Our statistical steps:

1. Identify the null and alternative hypotheses.
   The null hypothesis indicates there is no relationship between the number of violations and the number of privileges revoked. The alternative hypothesis indicates there is a relationship between the number of violations and the number of privileges revoked.

$$H_0: B = 0$$

$$H_1: B \neq 0$$

2. Identify the level of risk or significance.
   Our selected level of risk is 0.05.
3. Choose the appropriate test.
   The prediction of a continuous-level dependent variable from a continuous-level independent variable requires the use of a bivariate linear regression test.

4. Compute and identify the statistical test value (STV).
   Consider the numbers below in Table 14.1. This includes the calculation outcomes of the correlation test:

TABLE 14.1 **Number of Violations and Revoked Privileges**

Violations (x)	Revoked Privileges (y)	x^2	y^2	(x)(y)
1	2	1	4	2
1	2	1	4	2
3	6	9	36	18
2	4	4	16	8
4	8	16	64	32
1	2	1	4	2
3	6	9	36	18
2	4	4	16	8
2	4	4	16	8
$\Sigma x = 19$	$\Sigma y = 38$	$\Sigma x^2 = 49$	$\Sigma y^2 = 196$	$\Sigma xy = 98$

The aforementioned involves the following steps:

a. Identify the violation values and the sum.
b. Identify the revoked privileges values and the sum.
c. Identify the squared violation values and the sum.
d. Identify the square privileges values and the sum.
e. Multiply and identify the violation and privileges values along with the sum.

Based on Table 14.1, include the numbers within the previously listed formula:

$$b = \frac{\Sigma XY - (\Sigma X \Sigma Y/n)}{\Sigma X^2 - \left[(\Sigma X)^2/n\right]} = \frac{98-(19\times 38/9)}{49-\left[(19)^2/9\right]} = \frac{98-(722/9)}{49-[361/9]} = \frac{98-80.2}{49-40.1} = \frac{17.8}{8.9} = 2$$

$$a = \frac{\Sigma Y - b\Sigma X}{n} = \frac{38-(2\times 19)}{9} = \frac{38-38}{9} = 0$$

Once we include our numbers, we have the following:

$$\hat{y} = 0 + 2x,$$

As an independent variable (for x), let's include 3, representing a total of 3 violations. Consider the trend identified in Figure 14.1.

$$\hat{y} = 0 + 2(3) = 6$$

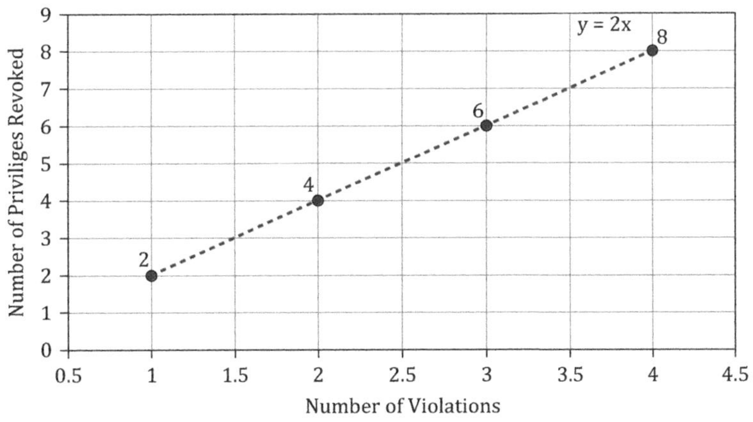

FIGURE 14.1 Number of Violations and Revoked Privileges

Our final step involves calculating the statistical significance formula. This requires two parts (a, b):

Part a involves computing the correlation between x and y (r):

$$r = \frac{N\Sigma xy - \Sigma x\Sigma y}{\sqrt{\left[N\Sigma x^2 - (\Sigma x)^2\right]\left[N\Sigma y^2 - (\Sigma y)^2\right]}} = \frac{9(98) - (19)(38)}{\sqrt{[9(49) - (19)^2][9(196) - (38)^2]}}$$

$$= \frac{882 - 722}{\sqrt{[80][320]}} = \frac{160}{\sqrt{25{,}600}} = \frac{160}{160} = 1$$

Part b involves calculating the standard error of the coefficient formula:

$$SE_b = \frac{S_y}{S_x}\sqrt{\frac{1 - r^2}{N - 2}} = \frac{2.10}{1.05}\sqrt{\frac{1 - 1^2}{9 - 2}} = \frac{2.10}{1.05}\sqrt{\frac{0}{7}} = \frac{2.10}{1.05}\sqrt{0} = \frac{2.10}{1.05} = 2$$

$$t_{obt} = \frac{b}{SE_b} = \frac{2}{2} = 1$$

Based on the aforementioned, our t_{obt} is 1.
The STV is 1.

5. Identify and compare the critical decision value (CDV) to the STV.
   a. The degrees of freedom with a linear regression test is computed by N – 2.
   b. Based on our numbers, this is 9 – 2 = 7.
   c. As a result of this process, we refer to the two-tailed *t*-test table in the appendix to determine the critical value.
   d. Since our degrees of freedom is 7, we will locate that number under the degrees of freedom column and under the nondirectional 0.05 level of risk.
   e. As indicated, we will use ±2.36 as the value in which to reject the null hypothesis.

Since our STV is 1, we compare this value with the CDV, which is ± 2.36

6. If the STV > CDV, reject the null hypothesis.

   Given that the STV (1) is less than the CDV (± 2.36), we fail to reject the null hypothesis. Thus, the null hypothesis, which states that there is no relationship between the number of violations and the number of privileges revoked, is true.

   The written results of the linear regression test are based on the following:

The results of the linear regression test reveal that the number of violations (independent variable) failed to explain the variation of the number of privileges (dependent variable).

$$F\,(1{,}7) = 1,\ p > 0.05$$

As indicated, the F, which was used in ANOVA, is included. In addition, the r^2 value, along with whether the result was significant, is included as well.

Chapter Learning Assessment Questions

To gauge your learning, provide answers to the following questions:

1. When computing a directional (one tail) linear regression test, with a *df* of 18 and a level of risk $p < 0.01$, which of the following is the correct CDV needed to reject the null hypothesis?
   a. 1.58
   b. 2.19
   c. 2.39
   d. none of the above
2. When computing a nondirectional (two-tail) linear regression test with a *df* of 14 and a level of risk $p < 0.05$, which of the following is the correct CDV needed to reject the null hypothesis?
   a. 2.14
   b. 1.78
   c. 1.96
   d. none of the above

Answers

1. d
2. a

Multiple Regression Test

As mentioned previously, a **multiple regression test** is a statistical test that is used to determine the extent to which multiple continuous-level independent variables predict a continuous-level dependent variable. For instance, the test might be used to predict monetary fine amount (dependent variable) based on the number of arrests (independent variable 1) and number of days spent in pretrial detention (independent variable 2).

Formula for Computing the Multiple Regression Test

$$\hat{y} = a + bx_1 + bx_2,$$

where

a = represents the y intercept
b = represents the slope (or slope coefficient)
x_1 = value of independent variable 1
x_2 = value of independent variable 2

Application of the Multiple Regression Test

The practical use of the multiple regression test may be applied in the following areas:

Law Enforcement

- The test can be used for identifying trends in relation to homeland security arrest decisions (Desmarais et al., 2017). In Figure 14.2, let's assume that federal agents are interested in identifying the actual factors (independent variables) associated with the number of arrests (dependent variable) related to acts of potential terrorism. Examples of independent variables might include the number of officers involved in the investigation and apprehension of suspects, the number of questionable activities in which the suspect is involved, and the number of terrorist-related associates the suspect is associated with.

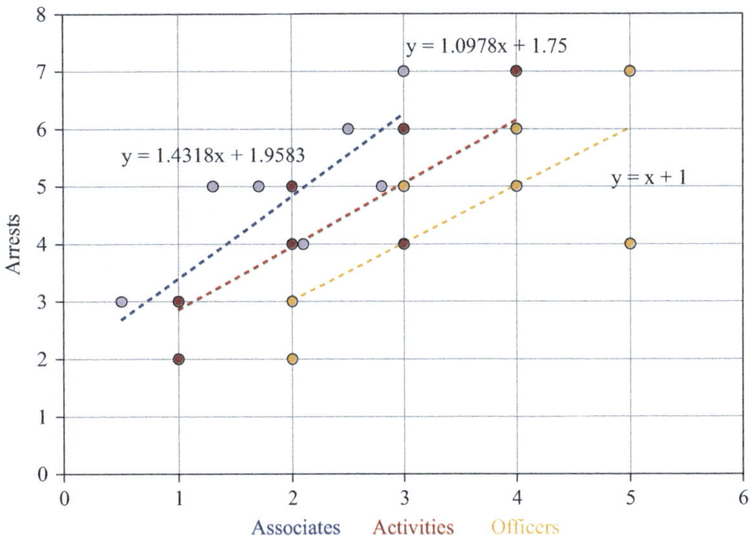

FIGURE 14.2 Factors and Arrest

Courts

- A multiple regression test may be of value in the establishment of specialized courts, such as a drug court, located in Figure 14.3. This could involve identifying multiple factors (independent variables), such as the number of drug convictions and drug-related probation violations in relation to sentencing length (dependent variable). Such distinctions could also be used for specific types of processes and support programs provided (Breno et al., 2022).

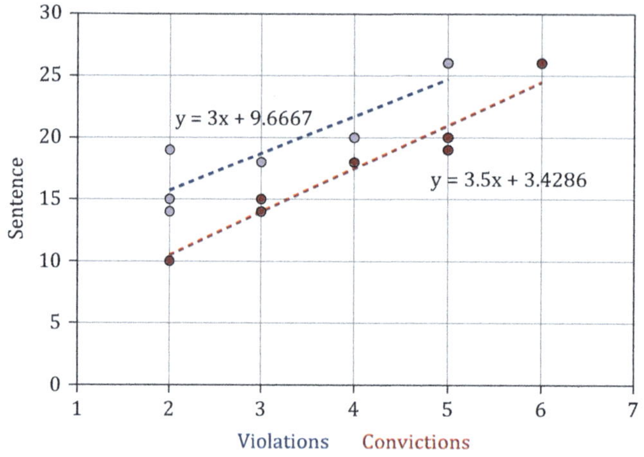

FIGURE 14.3 Factors and Sentencing Length

Corrections

- As revealed in Figure 14.4, the linear regression test can also be used to predict the amount of time (dependent variable) that an inmate will be placed into a separation cell because of acts of violence in prison. Multiple factors (independent variables), such as the number of violence-related offenses, as well as the number of violent incidents within prior detention settings, would be used to determine which inmates are likely to be removed from the general population because of their potential for violence (Wolff et al., 2022).

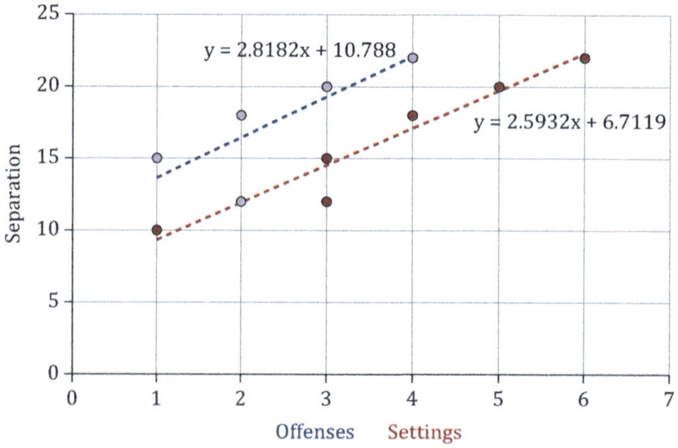

FIGURE 14.4 Factors and Time of Separation

Final Thoughts

A linear regression test is a powerful technique for determining the outcome of a phenomenon that may occur in the future. For those who watch the weather reports, meteorologists rely on regression to predict weather conditions in various locations. In a similar manner, as you become more familiar with the use of the various types of regression models, you will likely experience confidence in the areas of predicting outcomes at the expense of what appears to be (to others) trivial and meaningless.

Discussion

A study reveals that poor academic performance and poor school attendance may predict youth delinquency. What is your response to this finding? Is this enough information to identify the causes of delinquency among the youth? Explain.

Chapter Summary

This chapter emphasized the following general information:

Objective 1 – Define and explain the use of the linear regression tests.

- A linear regression test is used to determine the extent to which a continuous-level independent variable predicts a continuous-level dependent variable.
- A bivariate regression test is used to determine the extent to which a single independent variable predicts a single dependent variable.
- A multiple regression test is used to determine if more than one independent variable predicts a dependent variable.

Objective 2 – Identify the formula for computing the linear regression test.

- See the corresponding pages.

Objective 3 – Compute linear regression test.

- See the corresponding pages.

Objective 4 – Define and explain the use of the multiple regression test.

- A multiple regression test is used to determine if more than one independent variable predicts a dependent variable.

Objective 5 – Identify the formula for computing multiple regression tests.

- See corresponding pages.

Terms

Linear regression
Bivariate regression
Multiple regression

Chapter Review Questions

1. Determine if the following requires the use of a linear or multiple regression test:
   a. To what extent are poor academic grades and inconsistent school attendance related to the number of delinquent incidents among youth?
   b. Is prior military experience (in years) related to physical agility scores in police academies?
   c. The amount of an attorney's fee might be based on the number of charges a defendant receives.
   d. Is there a relationship between the number of prior victimization experiences, U.S. citizenship, and the amount of time it takes to identify a suspect by the authorities?
   e. To what extent are age and years of postsecondary education associated with the number of times an individual serves as a jury member in a criminal case?
   f. Is it possible that an increase in violent media content is associated with an increase in violent behavior in society?
   g. Is race and socioeconomic status associated with the number of reports associated with contaminated natural resources in a region?

When providing answers to the following questions, include the following details for each answer:

   a. **STV results in comparison to the CDV results.**
   b. **Decision related to the null hypothesis.**
   c. **The significance of the slope.**
   d. **Support (or failure of support) related to the alternative hypothesis.**
   e. **If significance is achieved, identify the nature of the relationship between the variables.**

2. A penologist believes that prison inmates who engage in cognitive-behavioral activities while incarcerated are more likely to receive parole (Henning and Frueh, 1996). More specifically, she believes that the actual number of activities an inmate is involved in is correlated with the time frame in which an inmate receives notification of their parole eligibility. Provided below are the number of programs each inmate participated in, along with the amount of time in which parole was granted. Conduct a linear regression test (at 0.05 level of risk) to determine if a significant relationship exists.

Number	Months
3	25
4	20
2	30
3	24
4	19
5	15
6	12
5	14
2	33

3. A victimologist believes that the number of past victimization experiences is associated with fear of crime (Russo and Roccato, 2010). Fear of crime is measured by using a psychological assessment scale in which scores exist between 0 and 10. More specifically, 0 represents no fear, and 10 represents the greatest level of fear. Conduct a linear regression test (at 0.01 level of risk) to determine if a significant relationship exists.

Number	Assessment
1	2
2	4
2	5
1	2
0	1
3	7
2	4
4	8
5	10

4. A gerontologist is convinced that older individuals are more likely to report crime. As revealed below, the age of each individual is identified, along with the number of times an individual called 911 to report a crime in a month. Conduct a linear regression test (at 0.05 level of risk) to determine if a significant relationship exists.

Age	Number
36	2
78	5
85	6
44	2
28	0
71	6
66	4
65	4
29	1
39	2
59	3
55	3
36	0
79	6

5. The following includes the amount of experience a police officer has along with their salary amount. Conduct a linear regression test (at 0.05 level of risk) to determine if a significant relationship exists.

Experience	Salary Amount
3	26,500
2	25,000
6	28,000
9	30,500
4	25,000
7	28,000
3	26,580
5	27,500
8	30,500
7	28,500
9	31,000
10	42,000
12	42,850
11	42,500

6. Listed below is information related to the potential value of treatment measures in response to juvenile offenses. This includes the number of months in which juveniles received family counseling and corresponding incidents of recidivism within a 3-year period. As a proponent of nonlegal options in response to juvenile offenses, you believe a correlation exists between the number of months a juvenile undergoes treatment and recidivism. Conduct a linear regression test (at 0.05 level of risk) to determine if a significant relationship exists.

Number	Recidivism
4	6
6	5
5	6
7	4
9	4
12	2
15	1
13	2
8	5
11	3
12	2
9	3
5	6
7	4

7. Research suggests that college students who major in criminal justice may hold less punitive attitudes in response to applied sanctions compared to students who are not criminal justice majors (Mackey and Courtright, 2000). Identified below are the number of criminal justice courses completed by students who identified as criminal justice majors, along with

their corresponding levels of punitiveness. The levels of punitiveness are measured based on a scale from 1 to 10. Conduct a linear regression test (at 0.05 level of risk) to determine if a significant relationship exists.

Number	Level
2	8
3	9
2	8
5	7
7	7
5	7
9	2
7	6
10	3
11	1
11	2
10	3
9	4
8	5

8. Developmental criminologists often explore the relationship between age and future behavior as a means of explaining acts of crime (Dallaire and Wilson, 2010). More specifically, they often believe that the age at which a young person engages in aggressive behavior is predictive of how many acts of crime they will engage in in the future. Identified below are the number of incidents in which a young child demonstrated aggressive behavior. It also includes a corresponding number of status offenses. Conduct a linear regression test (at 0.05 level of risk) to determine if a significant relationship exists.

Number of Incidents	Number of Offenses
3	2
7	4
5	3
4	2
7	4
9	8
11	9
12	10
8	8
7	4
5	3
7	4
6	3
9	8

Answers

1.
   a. multiple regression
   b. linear regression
   c. linear regression
   d. multiple regression
   e. multiple regression
   f. linear regression
   g. multiple regression
2. Given that the STV (–13.56) extends beyond the CDV (1.89), we reject the null hypothesis. The slope reveals a 0.05 statistical significance; thus, the test provides support that a predictive relationship does exist between the number of activities and the time frame in which notification of parole is granted. As the number of activities increases, the time frame related to parole notification decreases.
3. Given that the STV (16.43) extends beyond the CDV (2.99), we reject the null hypothesis. The slope reveals a 0.01 statistical significance; thus, the test provides support that a predictive relationship does exist between the number of past victimization experiences and fear of crime. As the number of past victimization experiences increases, fear of crime increases.
4. Given that the STV (11.12) extends beyond the CDV (1.78), we reject the null hypothesis. The slope reveals a 0.05 statistical significance; thus, the test provides support that a predictive relationship does exist between age and the number of times someone reported a crime in a month. As age increases, the number of times crime is reported increases.
5. Given that the STV (6.08) extends beyond the CDV (2.17), we reject the null hypothesis. The slope reveals a 0.05 statistical significance; thus, the test provides support that a predictive relationship does exist between experience and salary amount. As the amount of experience increases, the salary amount increases.
6. Given that the STV (–12.18) extends beyond the CDV (1.78), we reject the null hypothesis. The slope reveals a 0.05 statistical significance; thus, the test provides support that a predictive relationship does exist between the number of months a juvenile experiences treatment and engages in recidivism. As the number of months increases, recidivism decreases.
7. Given that the STV (–9.15) extends beyond the CDV (1.78), we reject the null hypothesis. The slope reveals a 0.05 statistical significance; thus, the test provides support that a predictive relationship does exist between the number of courses a criminal justice student completed and their punitiveness scale number. As the number of courses increases, levels of punitiveness decrease.
8. Given that the STV (9.52) extends beyond the CDV (1.78), we reject the null hypothesis. The slope reveals a 0.05 statistical significance; thus, the test provides support that a predictive relationship does exist between the number of incidents and the number of offenses. As the number of incidents increases, the number of offenses increases.

Bibliography

Breno, A., Ramezani, N., Guastaferro, W., Cummings, A., Murphy, A., & Taxman, F. S. (2022). What matters more in explaining drug court graduation and rearrest: Program features, individual characteristics, or some combination. *International Journal of Offender Therapy and Comparative Criminology, 67*(12) https://doi.org/10.1177/0306624X221086558

Dallaire, D. H., & Wilson, L. C. (2010). The relation of exposure to parental criminal activity, arrest, and sentencing to children's maladjustment. *Journal of Child and Family Studies, 19*(4), 404–418.

Desmarais, S. L., Simons-Rudolph, J., Brugh, C. S., Schilling, E., & Hoggan, C. (2017). The state of scientific knowledge regarding factors associated with terrorism. *Journal of Threat Assessment and Management, 4*(4), 180.

Henning, K. R., & Frueh, B. C. (1996). Cognitive-behavioral treatment of incarcerated offenders: An evaluation of the Vermont Department of Corrections' Cognitive Self-Change Program. *Criminal Justice and Behavior, 23*(4), 523–541.

Mackey, D. A., & Courtright, K. E. (2000). Assessing punitiveness among college students: A comparison of criminal justice majors with other majors. *Criminal Justice Studies, 12*(4), 423–441.

Russo, S., & Roccato, M. (2010). How long does victimization foster fear of crime? A longitudinal study. *Journal of Community Psychology, 38*(8), 960–974.

Wolff, N., Aizpurua, E., & Peng, D. (2022). Violence against incarcerated women: Predicting risk through the lens of childhood harm. *Violence Against Women, 28*(10), 2466–2492.

Chapter 14 SPSS and Workbook Questions

SPSS and the Linear Regression Test

To compute the linear regression test, consider the following:

Studies in judicial court decisions often focus on certain types of factors that influence decisions. Factors of interest may include individual (e.g., gender, mental state of offender), social (e.g., family members, coworkers), and legal (e.g., offense history, type of offense). In an effort to predict (and explain) judicial responses to certain offenses, a number of studies have suggested that certain legal decisions are made with the intent of increasing monetary fines for the purpose of deterring crime. Identified below are the number of court cases in which charges were filed, along with corresponding fine amounts.

Number of Charges	Amount of Fine	Number of Charges	Amount of Fine
1	150	4	230
1	145	4	235
1	165	4	248
1	155	4	210
1	130	4	250
2	175	5	260
2	178	5	255
2	185	5	275
2	190	5	280
2	187	5	281
3	200	6	291
3	221	6	300
3	198	6	321
3	210	6	312
3	183	6	315

You are convinced that an increase in the number of charges might predict an increase in fine amounts. Using SPSS, compute a linear regression test to determine if your hypothesis is supported.

Entry of Data—SPSS

1. Select variable view to include information associated with the variables of interest. In our example, this would include *number of charges* and *amount of fine*.
2. In the first row, include the term *charges* under the column identified as name.
3. For the remaining variable, which includes *amount*, follow the same procedure as noted above.
4. Select data view to include the scores for each variable in each corresponding column.

IMAGE 14.1

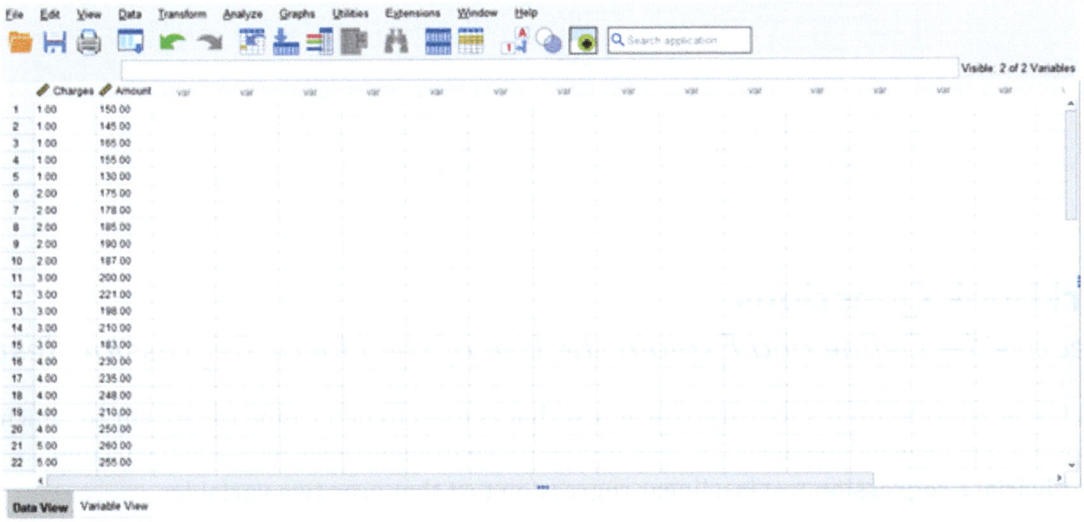

IMAGE 14.2

Analysis of Data—SPSS

1. Select analyze, select regression, and linear regression.
2. Select the variable *charges* and move it to the area identified as block 1 of 1.
3. Select the variable *amount* and move it to the area identified as a dependent variable.
4. Under the section referred to as statistics, under regression coefficient, select confidence intervals.
5. After all desired functions have been selected, select OK.

Output of Data Analysis—SPSS

The analysis of the results includes three tables of information. The first table includes the r, the r square, the adjusted r square, and the standard error of the estimate. The second table provides information that is consistent with ANOVA results. This includes the sum of squares, degrees of freedom, mean square, f-test, and level of significance ($p < 0.001$). The final table includes information regarding the coefficients. The data includes the t statistic value, along with the level of significance ($p < 0.001$) and the corresponding confidence interval. Based on your hypothesis, the results indicate a statistically significant association between the number of charges and the corresponding fine amounts.

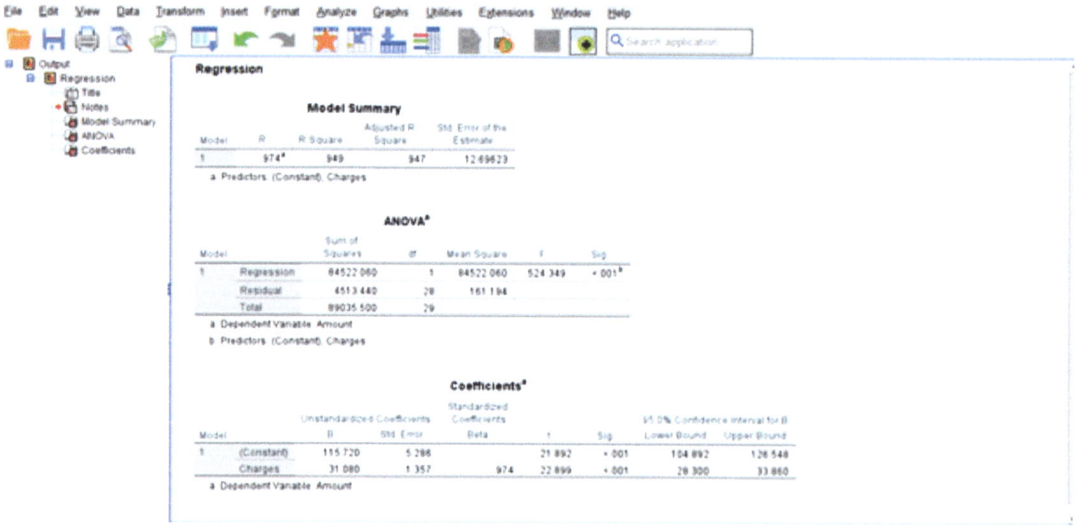

Regression

Model Summary

Model	R	R Square	Adjusted R Square	Std. Error of the Estimate
1	.974[a]	.949	.947	12.69623

a. Predictors: (Constant), Charges

ANOVA[a]

Model		Sum of Squares	df	Mean Square	F	Sig.
1	Regression	84522.060	1	84522.060	524.349	<.001[b]
	Residual	4513.440	28	161.194		
	Total	89035.500	29			

a. Dependent Variable: Amount

b. Predictors: (Constant), Charges

Coefficients[a]

Model		Unstandardized Coefficients		Standardized Coefficients			95.0% Confidence Interval for B	
		B	Std. Error	Beta	t	Sig.	Lower Bound	Upper Bound
1	(Constant)	115.720	5.286		21.892	<.001	104.892	126.548
	Charges	31.080	1.357	.974	22.899	<.001	28.300	33.860

a. Dependent Variable: Amount

IMAGE 14.3

Workbook Questions

Objective 1—Define and Explain the Use of the Linear Regression Test

- A **linear regression** test is a statistical test that is used to determine the extent to which a continuous-level independent variable predicts a continuous-level dependent variable.
- A **bivariate regression** test is a linear regression test that uses two variables.
- A **multiple regression** test is a linear regression test that uses more than one independent variable.

Corresponding Questions

1. A ________ test is used to determine the extent to which a continuous-level independent variable predicts a continuous-level dependent variable.
   a. linear regression
   b. bivariate regression
   c. multiple regression
   d. correlation

2. If a researcher is interested in whether the number of days a person is confined in solitary confinement can be used to predict the number of suicide attempts in a prison setting, the researcher would likely use a ________ test.
   a. corrective regression
   b. bivariate regression
   c. multiple regression
   d. correlation
3. A ________ test is a linear regression test that uses more than one independent variable.
   a. selective regression
   b. bivariate regression
   c. multiple regression
   d. correlation
4. A penologist believes that contact with family members plays an important role in minimizing acts of aggression and violence among inmates in confined settings (Cochran, 2012). In particular, the expert is convinced that she can predict the number of estimated reports of violence among inmates based on the number of visits an inmate receives in which they are able to communicate with family members. Furthermore, the expert also believes that the age of the inmate plays a role in the number of estimated reports of violence. This is an example of a ________ test.
   a. corrective regression
   b. bivariate regression
   c. multiple regression
   d. correlation
5. A juvenile justice expert serves as a guest speaker in a juvenile justice course at a local college. During her presentation, she questioned the students in order to gauge their opinions related to measures designed to hold youth accountable for their actions. In particular, she posed the question of whether adults should be fined if their children repeatedly engage in acts of delinquency or status offenses. Upon initially hearing the question, the students failed to respond. To that end, the guest speaker began to offer an arbitrary number of offenses, along with corresponding fine amounts. This included a trend that revealed that as the number of offenses increased, the total fine amount also increased. This led to a number of responses from students in which many expressed support. This is an example of a ________ test.
   a. selective regression
   b. bivariate regression
   c. multiple regression
   d. correlation

Answers

1. a
2. b
3. c
4. c
5. b

Objective 2—Formula for the Linear Regression Test

- See the corresponding pages in the chapter.

Objective 3— Example Problem(s) and the Linear Regression Test

- See the corresponding pages in the chapter.

When providing answers to the following questions, include the following details for each answer:

a. **STV results in comparison to the CDV results.**
b. **Decision related to the null hypothesis.**
c. **The significance of the slope.**
d. **Support (or failure of support) related to the alternative hypothesis.**

Corresponding Questions

1. Among youth and young adults, research points to various distinctions between individuals on the basis of age and levels of maturity (Tillyer and Engel, 2013). For instance, cognitive development is recognized as a process that may extend among individuals until the age of 25. To that end, a researcher believes that age can be used to predict the number of traffic citations. Based on the following, compute a linear regression test (with a risk level of 0.05) to determine if the researcher's hypothesis is valid.

Age	Number of Traffic Citations
16	31
17	28
18	28
19	24
20	17
21	14
22	12
23	12

24	10
25	9
26	9
27	10
28	8
29	6
30	5

2. Instructional information that is consistently provided to students has the capacity to influence their ideas. This is especially true in the areas of criminal and juvenile justice, where decision-making can affect the freedom of individuals who are alleged of engaging in criminal and status offenses. A common theme within justice literature is the existence of information that explores how justice systems respond to alleged offensive behavior. This often includes a philosophy of retribution, whereby punishment is often used as a means of dispensing revenge on behalf of the state. After hearing a guest speaker discuss the factors related to the use of retributive measures, a student believes that the number of previous offenses an individual has can be used to predict the number of months they will receive in terms of a prison sentence. Based on the following data, which includes criminal history and prison sentence amount, compute a linear regression test (with a risk level of 0.05) to determine if the student's hypothesis is valid.

History	Months
1	12
2	24
1	14
3	36
2	24
3	36
4	48
5	55
4	50
3	38
5	65
3	34
4	51

3. Research related to corrections show the impact of overcrowding in secure and private settings (Gunderson, 2022). People working in corrections understand the importance of management, budget, and legal consequences. Identified below is a table that includes the number of inmates housed in a detention center. The number includes the number of inmates that exceed the design limitations of housing units in the area. In addition, the table includes the number of lawsuits filed by inmates as a result of the overcrowded conditions. Based on

the following data, compute a linear regression test (with a risk level of 0.05) to determine if a statistical slope exists.

Year	Number That Exceeds Limit	Amount From Lawsuits Filed
2008	100	4,500
2009	125	12,250
2010	150	15,900
2011	125	12,300
2012	130	13,450
2013	145	14,800
2014	170	17,500
2015	165	16,005
2016	110	10,000
2017	100	5,000
2018	160	15,940
2019	175	18,000
2020	180	19,000
2021	135	13,780
2022	200	19,500

4. Studies related to delinquency prevention indicate that youth between the ages of 9 to 12 who engage in aggressive behavior (such as bullying) will likely engage in acts of more severe acts of violence (assault, robbery, etc.) as young adults (Husemann et al., 2021). Based on the data in the following table, which includes reported incidents of bullying and subsequent offense convictions among 15 individuals, compute a linear regression test (with a risk level of 0.05) to determine if the expert's hypothesis is valid.

Youth Incidents	Adult Convictions
1	1
3	2
2	1
4	3
7	5
6	4
8	5
6	4
7	8
4	4
3	2
4	4
2	1
1	0
1	0

Answers

1. Given that the STV (–6.76) extends beyond the CDV (2.13), we reject the null hypothesis. The slope reveals a 0.05 statistical significance; thus, the alternative hypothesis of the researcher is true. To that end, the results of the test provide support that a predictive relationship exists between the age of an individual and the number of traffic violations.
2. Given that the STV (21.61) extends beyond the CDV (2.20), we reject the null hypothesis. The slope reveals a 0.05 statistical significance; thus, the alternative hypothesis of the student is true. To that end, the results of the test provide support that a predictive relationship exists between the number of previous offenses an individual has and the number of months they will receive as a result of prison sentencing.
3. Given that the STV (10.22) extends beyond the CDV (2.16), the slope reveals a 0.05 statistical significance. To that end, the results of the test provide support that a predictive relationship exists between the number of inmates that exceed the housing capacity and the monetary amount of lawsuits filed.
4. Given that the STV (7.78) extends beyond the CDV (2.16), the slope reveals a 0.05 statistical significance. To that end, the results of the test provide support that a predictive relationship exists between the number of incidents of aggressive behavior and the number of subsequent convictions.

Bibliography

Cochran, J. C. (2012). The ties that bind or the ties that break: Examining the relationship between visitation and prisoner misconduct. *Journal of Criminal Justice, 40*(5), 433–440.

Gunderson, A. (2022). Why do states privatize their prisons? The unintended consequences of inmate litigation. *Perspectives on Politics, 20*(1), 187–204.

Huesmann, L. R., Dubow, E. F., Boxer, P. B., Bushman, B. J., Smith, C. S., Docherty, M. A., & O'Brien, M. J. (2021). Longitudinal predictions of young adults' weapons use and criminal behavior from their childhood exposure to violence. *Aggressive Behavior, 47*(6), 621–634.

Tillyer, R., & Engel, R. S. (2013). The impact of drivers' race, gender, and age during traffic stops: Assessing interaction terms and the social conditioning model. *Crime & Delinquency, 59*(3), 369–395.

Credits

Index

W

X

Y

Z

Printed and bound by CPI Group (UK) Ltd, Croydon, CR0 4YY
09/11/2026
14999543-0001